The Worlds of Russian Village Women

The Worlds of Russian Village Women

Tradition, Transgression, Compromise

Laura J. Olson and Svetlana Adonyeva

THE UNIVERSITY OF WISCONSIN PRESS

Publication of this volume has been made possible, in part, through support from the Eugene M. Kayden Endowment at the University of Colorado.

The University of Wisconsin Press
1930 Monroe Street, 3rd Floor
Madison, Wisconsin 53711-2059
uwpress.wisc.edu

3 Henrietta Street
London WC2E 8LU, England
eurospanbookstore.com

Printed in the United States of America

Library of Congress Cataloging-in-Publication Data

Olson, Laura J., 1962–
   The worlds of Russian village women : tradition, transgression, compromise / Laura J. Olson and Svetlana Adonyeva.
      p.   cm.
   Includes bibliographical references and index.
   ISBN 978-0-299-29034-4 (pbk. : alk. paper) — ISBN 978-0-299-29033-7 (e-book)
   1. Rural women—Russia—Social conditions. 2. Folklore—Russia. I. Adon'eva, S. B. II. Title.
   HQ1662.O47   2012
   305.40947—dc23

                                                2012016670

An earlier version of chapter 8 was first published as Svetlana Adonyeva and Laura J. Olson, "Interpreting the Past, Postulating the Future: Memorate as Plot and Script among Rural Russian Women," *Journal of Folklore Research* 48, no. 2 (2011): 133–66 (copyright © 2011, Indiana University Press, reprinted by permission of the publisher).

Contents

Illustrations

Acknowledgments

LAURA OLSON

This project could not have been completed without the financial assistance of several organizations. The National Endowment for the Humanities (NEH) awarded me a Collaborative Research Grant, administered through American Councils for International Education, which enabled me to travel and collaborate with many institutions and individuals in Russia in 2004–5, the main period of research for this book. From the International Research and Exchanges Board (IREX) I received an IARO Fellowship, which facilitated a four-month research trip to Russia in 2004. The Kennan Institute awarded me a Short Term Grant for research in Washington, DC, in 2003; Margaret Paxson of that institute gave me Svetlana Adonyeva's name and contact information, greatly influencing the outcome of this project. The European Reading Room staff at the Library of Congress was endlessly supportive and resourceful. University of Colorado–Boulder provided many types of assistance, including a research sabbatical, a grant-in-aid for equipment purchase, and two travel grants for Svetlana Adonyeva to come to Boulder for collaborative work. The book's publication was facilitated by a generous subvention from the Eugene M. Kayden Fund.

I feel a profound sense of gratitude to all the people in Russian villages who invited me into their homes for conversation, tea and treats, and allowed me to learn more about their lives. I wish to particularly thank the following individuals who, in addition to the above, gave me the gift of friendship. In Riazan' oblast: Zinaida Nikolaevna Gubareva, Valentina Aleksandrovna Chikunova, Valentina Ivanovna Aleshina, Aleksandra Matveevna Tarasova, Anastasiia Andreevna Spirina, Father Roman Ivanovich Filippov and Tamara Filippova; in Vologda oblast: Nina Aleksandrovna Kukina, Anemaiza Ivanovna Khlebosolova, Zoya Mikhailovna Khlebosolova, Angelina Dmitrievna Stulkova, Faina Vasilevna Kostriukova, Iia Vasilevna Gudkova, Tamara Vasilevna Cherepanova, Liubov Iakovlevna Pantina; in Ul'ianovsk oblast: Maria Pavlovna and Iurii Mikhailovich Postnov, Maria Ivanovna Cherviakova, Maria Dmitrievna Zaplatkina. The Golubev family, including Mikhail Ivanovich,

Anna Aleksandrovna, Valerii Mikhailovich, Liubov Golubevy, and Maria Aleksandrovna Sokolova, opened their homes and hearts to me; Valerii Mikhailovich went above and beyond the call of duty by phoning culture staff throughout the Siamzha region in Vologda oblast for me. Culture workers who were extremely helpful in guiding me to informants and providing necessary assistance with housing and transportation included Anna Iakovlevna Vasil'eva of Pigilinka, Vologda oblast; Nina Alekseevna Vostriakova in Dvinitsa, Vologda oblast; Nina Iur'evna Shaverina of Siamzha Center of Culture, Vologda oblast; and Liubov and Aleksandr Arkhipovy of Kitovo, Riazan' oblast.

The following Russian scholars were immensely helpful in guiding my research and providing access to bibliographical and archival materials: Tatiana G. Ivanova (Institute of Russian Literature of the Russian Academy of Sciences—Pushkin House), Al'bert K. Baiburin and Tatiana A. Bernshtam (Museum of Anthropology and Ethnography of the Russian Academy of Sciences), Izabella I. Shangina and Elena L. Madlevskaia (Russian Ethnographic Museum), Igor' Morozov and Natalia L. Pushkareva (Institute of Ethnology and Anthropology of the Russian Academy of Sciences), Maina P. Cherednikova and Mikhail Matlin (Ul'ianovsk State Pedagogical University), Natalia Giliarova and Elena Bogina (Moscow State Conservatory), Anatolii M. Mekhnetsov and Galina V. Lobkova (Russian Folkloric-Ethnographic Center), Anna F. Nekrylova and Viktor A. Lapin (Institute of the History of Art), Andrei Kabanov (independent scholar, folklore studio Izmailovskaia Sloboda), and Elena and Sergei Minyonok (Gorky Institute of World Literature, American Friends of Russian Folklore). Others who helped me in Russia included Anastasiia Karetnikova, a capable, wise, and adventurous fieldwork assistant; and Alena Romanova, who provided a comfortable home for me in Saint Petersburg.

Various people helped in many ways with the manuscript preparation. Andrei Stepanov and Antonina Semenova of Saint Petersburg University capably and patiently answered my questions when Svetlana Adonyeva was not available. At the University of Colorado, students who contributed their time and talents included Dmitriy Zinchenko, Anna Calvert, Karina Pulec, Yana Duday, Erica Behm, Maria Diment, Casey McCormack, and Katherine Daniel. Mikhail Matlin, Liubov Golubeva, and Galina Siarheichyk helped me with interview transcription. Chloe Kitzinger and Jordan Shedlock wrote polished and elegant "draft" translations of chapters or parts of chapters. Steve Ramos volunteered his time with a very difficult translation task. Lindsay Baillie read and provided feedback on chapters, as did students in RUSS 3701 Slavic Folk Culture: Ideals and Values in the Contemporary World during fall 2010, spring and fall 2011, and spring 2012.

Mark Leiderman and Tatiana Mikhailova helped me untangle difficult passages in transcriptions and translations and gave me comments on chapters and papers. To them and to my other colleagues at the University of Colorado I owe a great debt of gratitude for their continuous, heartfelt friendship and support. In particular, I wish to mention Rimgaila Salys, who has been an attentive, loyal, and encouraging mentor; Elizabeth Dunn, who was an advocate and sounding board; and Barbara Engel, who provided friendship, advice, and inspiration, and gave incisive comments on drafts of chapters. Other colleagues whose comments helped improve the book include Helena Goscilo, Eric Naiman, Natalie Kononenko, and Aleksey Yudin. Editors Moira Smith and Danille Elise Christensen at the *Journal of Folklore Research* helped us to clarify crucial parts of our argument. I wish to particularly thank the readers for the University of Wisconsin Press, Jeanmarie Rouhier-Willoughby and Sibelan Forrester, whose insightful comments were immensely useful. UW Press's acquisition editor Gwen Walker, editor Sheila McMahon, external copyeditor Marlyn Miller, and assistant production manager Carla Marolt all contributed their talents and visions to see the book to fruition.

My father Carl Olson, my brother Mark Olson, and my sister-in-law Karen Olson have granted ongoing moral support throughout the book's writing. My friend Elka Kepcheleva cooked our family meals for six weeks so I could finish the manuscript. My husband David Osterman has been a tireless supporter of my work and has provided concrete assistance during the production of this manuscript, including a compassionate listening ear, a critical eye, and more than his fair share of childcare. Although they don't know it yet, my daughter and son Mira and Daniel have helped me to better understand some of the issues we explore in this book, such as the desire of mothers to protect the health of their children. Stepdaughter Cybele Mayes-Osterman was an engaging playmate and role model for Mira and Daniel, allowing me to sneak away for work sessions. My mother Jean Olson helped plant in me the seeds of my deep interests in foreign cultures and folk music; her death during the writing of this book motivated me to take on roles I had not previously done, and deepened my appreciation for the memorial work accomplished by Russian village women.

Perhaps the biggest debt of all is to my coauthor, Svetlana Adonyeva, who initially guided my research in Saint Petersburg. A fount of knowledge and ideas, during my research trips in 2004–5 Svetlana was also generous with her contacts, her students, and her apartment. Later Svetlana made the trip to Colorado several times to write, and in between visits we discussed ideas by Skype and by e-mail. Throughout these years, working with Svetlana has been a profoundly enriching and inspiring experience.

Svetlana Adonyeva

First I would like to thank my interlocutors, men and women, Russian peasants. During my thirty years of field research I met many remarkable people. I cannot reproduce all of their names here, but I will name a few who were especially important for me: Tatiana Fedorovna Tochilova (Topsa, Vinogradovskii region, Arkhangel'sk oblast), Evstolia Konstantinovna Tekanova (Maeksa, Belozersk region, Vologda oblast), Taisiia Vasilevna Toporkova (Nikol'skoe, Ustiuzhenskii region, Vologda oblast), Liudmila Ivanovna and Aleksei

Alekseevich Gromovy (Anufrievo, Belozersk region, Vologda oblast), Tamara Mikhailovna Sergeeva (Parfenovo, Vashkinskii region, Vologda oblast), Anna Dmitrievna Lukicheva (Lipin Bor, Vashkinskii region, Vologda oblast), Raisa Fedorovna Moskovtseva (Goluzino, Siamzha region, Vologda oblast), Gavrila Nikolaevich and Anna Alekseevna Chikiny (Zherd', Mezen' region, Arkhangel'sk oblast), and Viktor Ivanovich Nechaev (Zherd', Mezen' region, Arkhangel'sk oblast). Meetings and conversations with these people taught me to understand not just the world of the Russian Village but also my own world. My world changed thanks to these meetings.

I am very thankful to Saint Petersburg State University, which during a situation of financial instability affecting all of Russian higher education has been able to preserve folklore research as a separate line in its budget. This has allowed us to continue the yearly folklore expeditions in which I participated at first as a student (1983–86), and then as a leader (1988–2007). Due to the fact that this work has been carried on continuously for many years, we have been able to base our research on a significant corpus of folkloric recordings made by myself and my colleagues—teachers and students of Saint Petersburg State University.

Some of the themes presented in this book arose during the process of discussion of field research. I am very grateful to those colleagues and friends who shared with me the hard work and pleasure of these field expeditions: Natalia Gerasimova, Inna Veselova, Anna Zinder, Marina Ponomareva, Maria Muratova, Marina Fedotova, Andrei Stepanov, Iulia Marinicheva, Liubov Golubeva, Ekaterina Mamaeva, Elena Perekhval'skaia, Elena Mel'nikova, Denis Veselov, Maria Ershova, and also anthropologist Margaret Paxson, Slavists Elizabeth Warner and Brian Warner, philosopher Alexander Sekatsii, and psychologist Olga Bufellakh.

I owe a debt of gratitude to the Fulbright Scholar Program, thanks to which I was able to pursue my research project "Socio-cultural Context and Communication Strategies Pertaining to Age, Status and Gender in the Russian Traditional Speech Community" at the University of California–Berkeley in 2005–6. I gained insight and inspiration from discussions of my topic at seminars at the Institute of Slavic, East European and Eurasian studies (ISEEES) and at the Department of Slavic Literatures and Languages of Stanford University. In particular, I am grateful to my American colleagues who supported me, organized these meetings, and participated in them: Yuri Slezkine, Grigory Freidin, Victoria Bonnell, Nicolas V. Riasanovsky, Eric Naiman, and Anna Musa.

I would like to express my deep appreciation to the University of Colorado at Boulder, which twice invited me to give lectures and work with my coauthor, and also to the faculty members of the Department of Germanic and Slavic Languages and Literatures. Our discussions in 2005 moved me to participate in the writing of this book.

And in conclusion I would like to thank Laura Olson as a colleague and coauthor for our collective work, which was difficult but always stimulating, and taught me a lot.

Note on Transliteration and Translation

For Russian words and names we have used the Library of Congress system of transliteration, modified to remove diacritical markings. We changed certain spellings in the main text to make reading easier for English speakers: we removed apostrophes and shortened *iia* to *ia*; in certain names, such as Adonyeva and Gorky, we used *y*. Proper (modified) Library of Congress transliteration has been preserved in citations and bibliography. Due to space considerations, we chose to provide only poetic quoted material (songs and incantations) in the Russian original along with the English translation. All other quoted material (narrative) from our field research is given in English translation only (those readers interested in original texts may refer to this book's Russian translation, which is forthcoming, or may consult the archives). Most of the material we quote is in dialect. We have made an effort to preserve lexical variants in transcriptions but have not overloaded the text with phonetic transcription.

The Worlds of Russian Village Women

Introduction

Tradition, Transgression, Compromise

Casual visitors to post-Soviet Russia encounter the subjects of this book at open-air markets and the street corners of major cities. They are *babushki*: stout middle-aged or elderly women wearing kerchiefs and selling knitted socks, crocheted rag rugs, flowers, or baskets of apples. Entering into trade with these women, the tourist often receives more than simply the proffered wares: the buyer is typically blessed, complimented, told to "eat/wear it in health." The exchange can feel like a situation of mutual honoring rather than a deal in cold, hard cash.

These *babushki* are the main permanent inhabitants of the Russian village today. They are the face of the Russian village, the backbone of the Russian household farm. In such exchanges we see their attractive open, nurturing side, but we know from history (and some may know from personal experience, too) that *babushki* can battle with astounding courage and fierceness—as in the context of *bab'i bunty* during collectivization, when women rioted to protect the economic viability of the family household. Women's protests were often more successful than men's and resulted in fewer repercussions for the participants, because officials were embarrassed to admit that they could not control disorderly women (Viola 1999, 185, 190). Russian rural women have also shown remarkable strength in the face of adversity, particularly during World War II, when they took on the tasks of feeding the country without male help (Engel 2004, 211), and after the war, when young women were drafted into logging, mining, and peat production.

The economic and cultural world of the post-Soviet Russian village is a world of adversity too, although of a different kind. It is a world very much in decline: young, talented people who grow up in villages aim to migrate to cities, a trend that began with industrialization in the 1930s. The birth rate is low; unemployment, theft, and alcoholism are such deeply entrenched parts of the village economic and cultural landscape that a recent study on the Russian village diagnosed the "profound degradation of a genetic pool" (Ioffe et al.

2006, 79, 94, 96). Cash is scarce and most households barely make ends meet; pensioners live in poverty, partly because many of them support unemployed, often alcoholic adult children on their meager pensions (Efendiev and Bolotina 2002).

Although Russia's rural population is just over a quarter of the total population, Russia is still very much a rural nation in terms of its mentality. Because urbanization happened comparatively recently, many urban Russians grew up in the village and remain in constant contact with their village-dwelling extended families, often spending summers living with their *babushka* in family village homes while helping out with agricultural family plots (Ioffe et al. 2006, 8; Vishnevsky 1998). For that reason, despite the village's disintegration, aging population, and economic and cultural problems, its culture has far-ranging and profound influence.

We hint at that influence with the first part of our title, "The Worlds of Russian Village Women." While the term "world of" in a book title commonly advertises a broad, encyclopedic view of an exotic or historical people, we mean something different by it. We mean to invoke the sense in which people create social worlds: thus, world as a social or cultural construct. The closest dictionary definition is "the sphere or scene of one's life and action" (Merriam-Webster 2003). We understand "world" as a reality constantly created by social (including communicative) practices, and we use the plural for two reasons. First, people and societies live and construct their worlds in various ways: it is difficult to accurately speak of a "Russian" world view or way of doing things. Even when we speak of regional or local practices we must always be aware that there are differences in how individuals view the world and behave. Second, every individual's worlds may be viewed as multiple, since they intersect, affect, and are affected by other worlds. The worlds of Russian rural-dwelling women encompass numerous social spaces, as they intersect with and include the worlds of their urban children and grandchildren, the world of mass media, and our own worlds, since we visited them and thus entered their social space. They and we live in a global world in which isolation is not possible (if it ever was).

In the 1920s, Edward Sapir used the term "worlds" in a similar way, in advancing his idea that social reality is constructed by language. His famous words were: "The worlds in which different societies live are distinct worlds, not merely the same world with different labels attached" (1929, 209). We value Sapir's caution against imagining that we, as cultural researchers, have access to an objective world of meanings that we share with the people we study. Our field methods and our writing have been profoundly influenced by Sapir's insight that paying attention to language—and in particular to places of communication breakdown—can help us to better understand another culture. Yet we are also aware of the danger of presenting the studied culture as more "different," more exotic and other, than it needs to be.

One way that we address this issue is by focusing our attention not only on language or culture itself, but also on the individuals we became acquainted with and the particular practices and discourses that make up their everyday lives. In addressing the subjectivity of our informants (whom we prefer to call our interlocutors), we rely to a large extent upon their oral utterances, their narratives about themselves. In addition, much of what an ethnographer "reads" when in the field is composed of nonverbal cues: gesture, intonation, facial expression, body position, actions. These can be very important in research about gender, because the ways people perform gender constitute an area of human activity that largely goes unverbalized (Sugarman 1997, 25). In analyzing subjectivity, narratives, and nonverbal behavior, we have been influenced by the work of sociologists like Erving Goffman (1959; 1967), Harold Garfinkel (1967), Alfred Schutz (1967), and Michel de Certeau (1984).

This book is in part about identity, which we define, with Charles Tilly, as the network of relationships that are significant for a person (2002, 10–11). Various types of identities are performed in this way: ethnicity, gender, locality, age, social status. Each one of these categories is not a fixed entity but is constructed through performance and within an everyday communicative context, for particular reasons. In this book, we have chosen to focus upon a few aspects of identity: location/lifestyle (rural), age status (young adulthood to old age), and gender (women).

We see gender as a performed, social identity that implies a relationship of difference and power. Here we are interested in what Sherry Ortner calls "the subtle forms of power that saturate everyday life, through experiences of time, space, and work" (2006, 128). We embrace the study of power relations initiated by Pierre Bourdieu (1977) and Michel Foucault (1978), in which people are not simply subject to the dictates of culture but exercise their agency in negotiating their relationship to culture. Foucault advocates the articulation of specific mechanisms of power used by specific groups or individuals in particular historical circumstances. "Power must be analyzed as something which circulates, or rather as something which only functions in the form of a chain. It is never localized here or there, never in anybody's hands, never appropriated as a commodity or piece of wealth. . . . [Individuals] are always in the position of simultaneously undergoing and exercising this power" (1980, 98). Certainly power is not evenly distributed, but nevertheless it is distributed. Mechanisms of power, such as life-cycle rituals—for instance, the Russian traditional wedding ritual, whose poetics emphasize the new bride's submission—are not simply one-sided situations of subjugation. There is always a way in which the mechanisms of power are utilized and transformed on the micro-level (99). Faced with structures of social control, people react in complex ways, including obedience, transgression, and compromise. It is this dynamic that we examine in this book.

The Russian rural women who are the subject of this study have rarely been framed in this manner. They have been depicted as victims of oppressive patriarchy, or celebrated either as symbols of inherent female strength or as one of the original sources of one of the world's great cultures (see, for example, Worobec 1991 and Hubbs 1988). We choose instead to see them in the context of their everyday lives, by describing how we came to know them in the context of our meetings during years of fieldwork. In depicting Russian rural women in this way, we hope to avoid the pitfall of "othering" them as exotic subjects of scholarly observation. We would like to meet them as a "you," as an interlocutor in a conversation (Buber 1970; Bakhtin 1981). We can only do this by moving from our own subjectivity to their subjectivities, minimizing the dominant position of an observer. We were participants in our conversations; we were partners in a search for mutual understanding, and for that reason one of the important tools of our research is our reflections about communicative failures.

Just as we enter into dialogue with Russian rural women, we also engage in dialogue with scholarly writings about Russian rural women and their culture. While we focus upon people (villagers) who use folklore for their own needs, other scholars focus upon the folk texts as a corpus that makes up "Russian folk tradition." In this prevailing Russian scholarly model, people are understood as carriers (*nositeli*) of tradition, as if they were flash drives (computer memory sticks, or *vneshnye nositeli*) that brought the folk tradition to scholars. We would like to illustrate this scholarly mechanism of constructing tradition, and how our own approach differs from it, with the following example. This curious example also allows us to introduce how we understand the second part of the book's title.

Tradition, Transgression, Compromise

In 2008 the Institute of Russian Literature (Pushkinskii Dom) published a CD-ROM of field recordings from the Sukhon basin of Vologda oblast. Track number 7 begins with a story about a local celebration of Maslenitsa, the Russian equivalent of Mardi Gras, and launches into the performance of a curious round-dance song sung on the holiday. The material was recorded in 1985 by folklorists Iu. Marchenko and V. Shiff (see Bragina 2008; transcription and translation ours):

> We used to celebrate Maslenitsa. It was a holiday. The last day before Great Lent. When it gets to evening, men and women bring barrels to the center of the village. The women finish their housework. The young people didn't go near. They hardly went near. The girls were afraid: the guys would throw them in the snow, so—. Well, and everyone would come, men and women. They'd burn the barrels and sing a song [each line is sung twice]:
>
> Я круг боцьки хожу, круг медовенькиё.
> Я на боцькю гляжу на медовенькюю.
> Оттыкайсё, гвоздок, наливайсё, медок.
> Напивайсё, душа, душа зятюшкина.
> Он напивсё, как бык, сам не знаёт, как быть.
> Я круг пецьки хожу, круг муравцятыё.

Я на пецькю гляжу, на муравцятую.

Открывайсё, заслон, вынимайсё, пирог.

Наедайсё, душа, душа зятюшкина.

Он наевсё, как бык, сам не знаёт, как быть.

Круг кроватки хожу, Круг тесовинькиё.

На кроватку гляжу, на тесовенькюю

На кроватке лежит душа зятюшкина

Поднимайся подол, раздувайся хохол,

Нагребайся душа, душа зятюшкина.

Он нагрёбся как бык, сам не знает, как быть.

[Around the barrel I go, around the barrel of mead
At the barrel I look, at the barrel of mead
Out you come, little nail! Out you pour, little mead!
Drink yourself drunk, my soul, soul of my son-in-law!
Drank himself like a bull, doesn't know which way is up.

Around the stove I go, around the tiled one
At the stove I look, at the tiled one
Open up, you, door! Come out, you, pie!
Eat your fill, my soul, soul of my son-in-law!
Like a bull he ate, doesn't know which way is up.

Around the bed I go, around the bed of carved wood
At the bed I look, at the bed of carved wood
On the bed lies the soul, soul of my son-in-law
Lift yourself up, you hem! Fluff yourself up, you bush!
Fork it in, my soul, soul of my son-in-law!
Forked it in like a bull, doesn't know which way is up!]

While singing the last stanza of the song, the women became momentarily confused: one sang "On the bed I lie" and the other "At the bed I look." After finishing the song, they laughed.

Here we have a song text told from the point of view of the mother-in-law, sung by a group of adult men and women who are dancing in a circle around burning barrels. Girls were not admitted to this event, while boys were present. The song tells how the mother-in-law seduces the son-in-law with mead (a sweet alcoholic drink, in Russian *medok* or *medovukha*), savory pies, and . . . sex.

We were struck by this song, with its shocking and unexplained content, and looked for other versions of it. We did not find it in publications of calendar folklore, which was somewhat strange for two reasons. First, the Sukhon basin of Vologda oblast has been well researched by folklorists for many decades. Second, most of the local population must have known the song—it was sung together by men and women, and not just privately by a few individuals but during mass community Maslenitsa celebrations, which means that it would have been hard to miss during folklore expeditions. Eventually, we did find an earlier recording of it, on an LP made in 1981 by A. Mekhnetsov and now located, with transcription, on the website "Culture of Vologda oblast."[1] However, even though the song was recorded from the same performers as the 1985 version, both the transcription of the song and the audio file leave out the last stanza of the song, regarding the bed and the sex.

One can understand why the earlier collectors chose to edit the song. First, the song contains erotic speech, which was forbidden in public discourse during the Soviet period: in fact, no erotic folklore was published during the Soviet era (Olson 2004, 133–36). Second, the song is about a forbidden sexual relationship, between a mother-in-law and son-in-law. Third, the transgression of moral norms is in no way condemned, whereas in Slavic folklore, most mentions of incest are in some way punished in the text.[2] Fourth, in a song sung together by men and women (as one of the performers described), the heroine of the song actively initiates sex by offering herself to her son-in-law.

The example serves well to introduce the major issues we address in this book. It speaks to the first word in our subtitle: tradition. Following Edward Shils, tradition in its barest sense is any cultural product that is handed down from past to present (1981, 11–12). In this example, two different traditions play a role. The folklorists followed tradition in that they censored lyrics that express desires forbidden by parts of society, even though in its full form, the song could well shine light on the essence of the Russian Maslenitsa ritual.[3]

Also thanks to tradition, women born during the Soviet era, and thus affected by the same ideology and rules as the collectors, continued to sing the song, which was formerly sung by both genders together, and was likely very old. For the folklorists who edited the piece, following conventional morality was more important than remaining faithful to the scholarly imperative of collecting accurate and complete data. For the female performers, conforming to the traditional form of the song—the ritual tradition—was more important than abiding by the moral imperative. We wondered what made these women continue to sing the song. Why was ritual tradition—or the memory of it—so important that they felt unashamed, even compelled to sing the song outside of the ritual context and for outsiders of the community? And why was it women who now sang this song, rather than a mixed chorus?

Our example shows that the transmission, interpretation, and changing of tradition involve choice. Following a rule or a tradition, as well as breaking a rule, are matters of personal responsibility, because a person makes a personal choice even when she or he acts "according to tradition" or is "following a moral imperative." Between any set of rules (social institution) and any practical act based upon those rules, there exists a gap (Volkov 1998, 168). Any person trying to decide whether to follow tradition or not, and which tradition to follow, exists within this gap. In the final analysis, a person must undergo the process that Kierkegaard called "choosing oneself": that is, determining one's own path by acknowledging one's past in relation with one's future possibilities (Kierkegaard 1971).

Transgression (the second term in our subtitle) also plays a role in our example. We understand transgression in its literal sense as crossing over the boundary of the imaginable, the allowed, or the civilized—that is, as a misdeed or "act" in Bakhtin's sense (in Russian a stepping over, *prostupok*). Here a theme fitting for a Greek tragedy is articulated publicly via the speech of folk humor. Phaedra, who fell in love with her stepson, had to die. Oedipus, who entered into a sexual relationship with his mother, had to become blind. But the mother-in-law in this Maslenitsa song, to the great pleasure of the performers, is neither punished nor judged. As the song recounts, she cares for the "soul of [her] son-in-law." Precisely this parodic "concern" causes her to offer him drink, food, and her own body. The song presents the transgression of sexual prohibitions as a form of guardianship of a young in-law. It is this contradiction that helps to create the humorous effect. But indeed, the source of the humor could be different for different listeners: men might find it funny because it might seem preposterous that a young man could enjoy sex with his mother-in-law, who is usually characterized in folklore as old and ugly;[4] women might find it funny because the mother-in-law's active seeking of a younger sexual partner rings true for them, and/or because it suggests an articulation or exaggeration of the female desire they have been socialized to control their whole lives.[5] It is hard to know, because none of the published sources contains interviews with the participants; only a fragment included after the recording (their laughter) shows for certain that the performers took the song as humorous, but not how or why.

The song is indisputably humorous, but it also represents an exaggeration of relationships that make sense when understood within the ritual context. In general, at Maslenitsa the role of all female heads of household (*bol'shukhi*) is to overfeed the family and guests. Women would prepare for months to accumulate enough milk products—sour cream, cheese, and butter—to make the feast truly an orgy of consumption. It is also important to note that Maslenitsa was related to the marriage cycle: it marked the end of the marriage season, since no weddings took place during Lent (when celebrations were forbidden) or summer (when people were too busy with agricultural work). In particular, the groom's mother-in-law had a special symbolic role to play in this holiday, since at Maslenitsa the newly married couple would return to the bride's home for their first visit in their new roles. Many songs recorded in the nineteenth century speak of the mother-in-law overfeeding her son-in-law as a symbolic welcoming of him into the family.[6] Food is often a symbolic means of facilitating social cohesion. By creating his "fat stomach," the mother-in-law helps to prepare him to produce her future grandchildren (by giving him nourishment and strength); with his prodigious prowess in overeating, the son-in-law shows his sexual prowess. That fact is underlined when, in many such songs, he returns the mother-in-law's favor by whipping her or striking her with logs, actions that have clear phallic symbolism, and also that represent the changed power relations between newly married sons and *bol'shukhi*. As our fieldwork has shown, *bol'shukhi* have indisputable power over unmarried young men, but as soon as men marry, they can challenge *bol'shukhi*, including their own mothers and mothers-in-law. The current song makes explicit what is implicit in the other songs: the sexuality of the exchange between mother- and son-in-law. Essentially, she provides him with the bride by means of which he becomes a sexually mature, viable man. Meanwhile, the song reverses the usual sexual power relations between men and women, since she initiates the act.

Parodic sex (such as sexual teasing and plays with phallic objects and cross-dressed characters) abounded within the Maslenitsa ritual, but in general eroticism within it was oriented toward the sexual activity of the older, yet still fertile, generation—their fertile power was apparently deemed more potent (in the magical sense) than that of the generation who were just starting their sexual lives (Agapkina 2002, 187–88, 197–200; Pashina et al. 2003, 691–93). In this song, a diagonal relationship is established between the older generation of one family clan (*rod*) and the younger generation of another, cementing the bond between the two family clans via erotic laughter. Transgression and the laughter that accompanies it also facilitate social cohesion. As Mikhail Bakhtin writes: "Carnival celebrated temporary liberation from the prevailing truth and from the established order; it marked the suspension of all hierarchical rank, privileges, norms and prohibitions. . . . This temporary suspension . . . created during carnival time a special type of communication, impossible in everyday life" (1984, 10).

There is a compromise (the third term in our subtitle) in this example as well. Compromise is an agreement based upon a concession, but compromise is also the result of mediation between two opposite ideas or norms. This example mediates between opposite norms: in the presence of young men (potential sons-in-law), grown men and women (potential or actual fathers- and mothers-in-law) admit the possibility of sexual interest between a mother-in-law and son-in-law. This example thus displays a kind of collision between two ideals: the moral imperative shared by members of this community, and the ritual's symbolic depiction of the meanings of the holiday. Members of the community are forced to compromise, to choose to uphold one or the other standard. Given the need to compromise, people make choices as to how to act.

Classical Russian folklore study would attribute to this song a magical ritual function, and would attribute to all participants in the ritual the same goal. The ritual would have the same meaning for all. By contrast, in our study we focus on the people themselves—their individual interests, life stories and desires—and the ways that their individual stories exist in dynamic, reciprocal interaction with social relationships and normative values.

Folklore in the Context of Lives: Plots and Scripts

Folklore is a social medium: following Alan Dundes, it is the grassroots expressive practices of any group (1965, 2). In performing folklore, a person uses preexisting, shared symbolic structures (verbal, visual, intonational, gestural, etc.) to construct his or her relationship to a group—that is, to create and re-create his or her own identity. People affect these symbolic structures when they perform folklore or rituals, since they bring with them their own interests, situate the symbols in new contexts, and interpret folklore in their own ways. Likewise, they act upon the social world in performing their relation to it. Thus, in folk culture as in other cultural phenomena, there is a dynamic interface between the personal and the social, between individual experience and shared values, between tradition and the needs of the present moment (Turner 1967, 27–30).

By attending to personal stories, we aim to bring dynamism to the study of folk culture. The previous example did not permit us to analyze the identities and worlds of the participants precisely because it involved no communication with them. The examples below show how interviews—conversations between outsiders and members of the community being studied—can yield much more than remembered folklore texts and descriptions of rituals ("information"). Interviews also shed light on the social roles, assumptions, and expectations that we and our interlocutors bring to the conversation, and the meanings and social relationships we construct during the conversation.

The dynamic context of interviews is distinguished by two parameters that develop during the dialogue: (1) social roles that are initiated, confirmed, or negated during the process of communication; and (2) an emergent metaphorical space in which the interpretations of the two interlocutors coincide. It may be that the interlocutors share much of that metaphorical space, or it may be that shared knowledge is minimal—such can often be the case when the authors of the present study, both urban dwellers, communicate with rural women. Although we understand each other on a lexical level, when we speak together about the principles that guide actions (that is, when we want to know "why" an event occurred), we must search discursively for common semantic ground and mutually acceptable communicative roles.

Thus, in telling about their own or their neighbor's past, or foretelling our (the collector's) future using moral lessons, our conversation partners *create* their own past and our mutual present and future. In this context each party in the conversation follows and transmits models of interpretation, relies on moral precepts, and performs social roles.

The following example shows how miscommunication can highlight this dynamic creation of meanings and relationships. Folklorists in the past may have assumed they were collecting information about the beliefs of their informants, but in fact field researchers have actively helped to *create* dialogues about these topics. Such a dynamic emerged, for instance, in a recent conversation with a woman born in 1922, whom we will call Anna Ivanovna S.[7] In a 2004 interview about local beliefs with two eighteen-year-old Saint Petersburg University students, she explained,

Usually the cuckoo cries "cuckoo" in the fall. But in these, in the village, the cuckoo doesn't cuckoo—rarely. We were sitting, and it came and landed. It was there, where there were two birch trees—one has fallen down. It was summer. The cuckoo came and cried "cuckoo." On the birch. [Unclear] my son died. And then it flew to the bank, to the bank, and on the bank it cuckooed again. And my nephew drowned. You see.

Simply because it cuckooed?

The cuckoo doesn't simply cuckoo. In the village. When it comes, expect some kind of unhappiness. (Vashkinskii region, Vologda oblast, 10 July 2004 [Vash 22-96])[8]

Following traditions of folklore study, this story would be classified by folklorists as a memorate (a supernatural story related in the first person) and filed with other stories about beliefs in cuckoos or other birds as omens. But we are interested in the moment of misunderstanding in this exchange. The speaker does not answer the folklorist's question about causality but disagrees with the questioner's use of *simply*. In her world, there is no such thing as "simply" when dealing with events such as death. They happen for a reason, though one cannot fully know the reason; still, an observant person can prepare for such eventualities by recognizing and interpreting appropriate signs. With her comments, the speaker assumes the social role of teacher and instructs her young hearers to stand by, ready to receive bad news: expect trouble if the cuckoo cries in the village. And although the narrated event involves death, telling this story may have a calming effect for the narrator, since the story describes a world that is predictable, organized, and devoid of accident: the death did not pass by unnoticed and unmarked by the spiritual world.[9]

Through this story, we learn that the relationship between bird cry and human death is not "simply" causative. This moment of intercultural misunderstanding is ultimately productive for scholarship: it suggests differences not only in world view, but in the strategies—communicative and mental—by which we construct our worlds.

Our conception of commonly held mental structures and strategies is influenced by Bronisław Malinowski's notion of the cultural imperative. Malinowski theorized that behavior is informed by unspoken precepts, given to us by culture, by which we are obliged to live ([1944] 2002, 99). These logical connections and expectations help us to organize and interpret our experience and to predict outcomes of new experiences. As John Searle put it, "There is a narrative shape to sequences of experiences. . . . I possess certain scenarios of expectation that enable me to cope with the people and objects in my environment." These scenarios include "how things proceed when I walk into a restaurant, or . . . getting married and raising a family. . . . La Rochefoucauld says somewhere that very few people would fall in love if they never read about it" (1995, 134–35).[10]

Such precepts are generally unspoken; they only become the subject of conversation if a person's behavior does not correspond to the general rule, or if one needs to speak of an event that goes against the usual state of affairs. For example, fieldwork is one context in which cultural imperatives come to the fore: misunderstandings arise when (to use Wittgenstein's metaphor) fieldworkers have not learned the rules by which it is customary to play ([1953] 2009). Real and anticipated misunderstandings must be negotiated using language; thus, cultural imperatives can emerge in the process of conversation.

Our study pays close attention to the temporal points of view from which people speak about themselves. As sociologist Alfred Schütz has observed, a person may speak of herself in a future-oriented way, in reference to the "project" she plans to undertake. Or someone may speak of his own past in order to interpret what has already happened. These anticipatory and reflective modes shade into one another (1962, 69–70). In what follows, we use the terms *plot* and *script* to describe, respectively, the culturally instilled ways of thinking that help people construct and describe the past, and those that interpret the present and postulate future behavior (Adon'eva 2001, 101–12).

Plots are standard formulations of past action. To make sense of the present, individuals may choose among the sets of plots that can be found in a given cultural milieu—such as in folk songs, folktales, literature, or cinema—to transform their lived experiences into knowledge, into narrative, or into autobiography. Scripts, on the other hand, are conventional projections of actions to come. Also a strategy for interpreting observed events and facts, a script allows the future to be predictable. However, any number of scripts may be applied to a single meaningful event or image, and thus the type of behavior that is encouraged by a single situation may vary. For example, a cultural imperative we have observed (in Russia and in the United States) may be phrased something like this: "As a woman, I am foremost a mother." A plot motivated by this imperative is the explanation "I left my alcoholic husband so that my child would grow up in normal conditions." The plot thus narrated involves a woman behaving so that her children's interests came before her own. A script that stems from a belief in the same underlying cultural imperative would be "I must find myself a husband who could be a worthy father for my children." In either case it does not matter whether the premise is objectively "true": acceptance of the premise shapes the way the subject understands and shapes her actions.

Of course, each individual configures her own relationship to precepts in her own way. Standard plots and scripts exist within a culture, but individuals choose and interpret them according to their own motivations. Also, common plots, scripts, and even cultural imperatives change over time, as we will attempt to show in our narrative.

An older Russian village woman illustrated how individuals link their biographies to scripts. She told us: "If the *bol'shukha* [female head] of a household is going to die, they say that the spoons clang in the cupboard." This teller interprets the unexplainable ringing of spoons as a sign that predicts the death of the mistress of the house, that is, as a script for what will happen in the future: when she hears spoons ringing, she will know her death is near. But it is also a way to compare the personal with the normative, to interpret her own past and present experience. She added: "This didn't happen in my house, see. But I heard of it." Here she suggests that she will still live awhile, since her spoons have not yet rung.

When we use someone else's plot or a common folkloric one to create our own utterance, we create our own "I." There is a tension between freedom and determination here: each script requires interpretation, so the particular way events are linked with the script will be established by the individual. Transgression against expected norms and behaviors is always possible; in fact, it is a kind of script. Nevertheless, the choice of a script determines a certain logic of unfolding events and the story's intrigue (its point).

The stories of our interlocutors transmit meaning and a way of interpreting: they teach us how to find signs and give them significance, how to see scripts in events. For example, in the story about the cuckoo recounted above, the speaker used a script in which the arrival and cry of the cuckoo function as a sign that predicts human events such as deaths, and she used a plot in which tragic events in human lives do not simply happen; rather, they unfold amidst the intervention of otherworldly forces. That is, the nephew's drowning was set in motion by otherworldly events, and the cuckoo (which is somehow in touch with that world of spirits) announced the death.

Such connections imply the existence of principles by which the world operates. It is as if the story of a personal experience is the visible part of the iceberg; the majority of it is hidden, but it is this larger part that is confirmed (and re-created) by the narrative. The invisible part of the iceberg is usually not talked about—unless, of course, it becomes the focus of metacommentary necessitated by intercultural contact, as when the folklorist asks, "Simply because it cuckooed?"

Gender as Communicative Strategy

Studying plots and scripts is one of the ways that we approach the study of gender. We attempt to ascertain the cultural imperatives and the common plots and scripts that women use in their folk narratives and practices. Personal stories give us clues about community values and the ways that individuals relate to those principles. We do not see gender as the object of description, however; rather, we describe practices and people. Gender is a means of tapping into the communicative network of relationships and meanings in the communities we study. We came to study gender through individual relationships we formed with Russian rural women. In a sense, we study women because we are women. Many of the topics we chose to discuss required private, intimate settings without a crowd present (see chapter 8 for a more precise description of these contexts). Sometimes these discussions would not have taken place had not all the participants been women. Thus, we base our study of gender upon the personal stories and the nonpersonal folkloric speech, along with the intonations, gestures, and other nonverbal behaviors of these women during our years of fieldwork. We make no claim to universality—for example, to discussing the experience of all Russian women; and we do not claim that the practices we discuss are not also sometimes performed by men. When the practices are in fact unisex—such as the telling of legends and the practice of magic—we try to sketch, in general terms, the differences we saw between men's and women's styles, strategies, and goals in these activities. But these can only be general outlines, for no gender (or other cultural) differences are absolute.

These qualifications about gender aside, we do acknowledge that gender is one of the central, structuring features of Russian rural culture today. Gendered social roles influence a person's occupation and social identity; gender permeates the organization of the material and spiritual worlds (Shchepanskaia and Shangina 2005a, 14). That state of affairs has its roots in Russian history. As Dorothy Atkinson has pointed out, during much of its history Russia's agricultural economy operated at subsistence level—physical strength was therefore of prime importance and male dominance was established on this foundation (1977, 12). Over time, patriarchy became entrenched in Russian village society; as Christine Worobec writes, in the late nineteenth century "increasing land shortage, the precariousness of subsistence agriculture, and the peasantry's burdensome obligations to family, community, and state reinforced rigid and oppressive power relations within the village," including ones based upon gender (1991, 13). Certainly many nineteenth- and early twentieth-century Russian ethnographers saw Russian peasant gender relations as oppressive. We take a neutral stand on whether gender relations were and are oppressive for women. The women we interviewed—especially those who lived under Soviet rule— rarely saw themselves as oppressed by sexual inequality. Many (especially those born in 1930–50) seemed to enjoy complaining about men, including their drunkenness and inability to take care of themselves. To these women, it was clear that if gender inequalities existed, then women were superior workers and managers, at home and outside the home. Women did tell stories of their victimization by men, but these stories were often couched in terms that emphasized the efficacy of community social networks. Individual men could commit misdeeds, even horrors, but their female victims often saw themselves as protected by their chosen spiritual practices and the social networks that enveloped them. As we show in this book, these practices and networks often belong to women precisely because they are women.

"We" and "I": The Multi-Author Approach

As coauthors, we were drawn to write this book in part by our mutual interest in gender studies. We both noticed gender as an important feature of the communicative landscape in villages. We were also drawn together by our similar approaches to fieldwork. We both had little patience with the hierarchical methods that characterize much of East European ethnography. Both of us tried to approach people as equal partners in a conversation, and we realized that in order to do this, we had to be open about who we were. Because in this book we base our observations and conclusions on our reflections about our communicative successes and failures during fieldwork, we feel the same need to approach readers as individuals. Later, in our descriptions and analyses of fieldwork, we will sometimes use "I (SA)" or "I (LO)" to indicate times when we use ourselves as examples, or draw upon our personal experience. Most of the time we will use "we "—to show that the material became "ours" in the process of discussing and writing. As coauthors, our experiences do not duplicate but instead complement each other. We came together with the wish to engage in dialogue about contemporary Russian rural women's folk culture. In this context, we see our differences in background, experience, and theoretical viewpoint as assets because this diversity enriches the analyses we present in our scholarship. So that the reader may understand our diversity, we offer separate descriptions of our backgrounds, our experience, and how we came to study gender in Russian village culture.

Laura Olson

When I began to study Russian village culture, I was a scholar of Russian studies, trained in literary analysis, with a strong interest in the cultural history and practice of folk singing in Eastern Europe (see Olson 2004, 7–12). I grew up in a cosmopolitan environment on the East Coast of the United States, where gender roles were discussed openly, feminist ideas of men's and women's equality were taken for granted among young intellectuals, and androgyny was a style practiced by many young people. By contrast with my home environment, in the Russian village the performance of gender appeared as an important organizing function of life. When I spent time there from 1995 to 2005, and walked into Russian village homes or walked down village streets, I noticed gender in how people organized themselves in space, what activities they did, how they responded to me, and how they dressed and presented themselves. Along with gender, age seemed to play a significant role in determining social relations. A few examples:

- A twenty-seven-year-old grandson, home for a visit to his grandmother, eats alone, in a separate room, and comes into the main room to sleep only when the other household members and visiting ethnographers, all women, are in bed.
- At a one-year anniversary memorial dinner for a deceased family member, elder women who conduct a religious service in the home eat first, separately from the family; the men are the last to be served.
- On the Thursday before Easter, women rake the graves at the family plot in the graveyard, and collect the leaves and garbage. Their husbands and brothers take the leaves away in baskets, and dump them in a pile just outside the graveyard.
- The Friday before Easter, a group of middle-aged women stand outside a village home, talking about dyeing eggs and making *paskha* (a sweetened ritual dish made of farmer's cheese and eggs), the price of seeds, the weather, and how burdensome

it is to live with men. The men are inside and at one point accordion music can be heard emanating from the house. Someone looks inside and reports that two husbands are sitting side by side on the couch, playing accordions. The men emerge, and one of them says: "We'll get together tonight, right here, outside." The women are amused, but rebuff the men: "What are you saying, it's a sin!" (to play music before the holiday).

As these anecdotes show, and as I learned when I consulted contemporary published materials on gender in Russian village culture, men and women possess different spheres of activity. They inhabit distinct physical spaces and perform different functions in the home economy. In many homes, the man of the house has an area curtained off from the main living space, often near the door to the outside, where he can sleep or lounge. The place to find village men during the day (weather permitting) is outdoors: men spend time in outbuildings where they keep tools and do tasks such as making or fixing gear for their household responsibilities: cutting hay and wood, plowing, seeding, transportation, and so on. The woman of the house typically has her space near the oven: here she prepares food, washes dishes, and the like (Shchepanskaia 2005, 30). Men usually do not enter this space. In household social gatherings organized by and dominated by women, men will often sit at the periphery or may come and go. A proverb summarizes this gendered division of space: "A peasant man is not a thief in the forest, not a master at home" (Kholodnaia 2005a, 377). Although he may be master of the family, his wife organizes and manages the home.

In many of the life-cycle and calendrical rituals that organize time in the village, women fulfill a leading function. They arrange the space for the ritual, prepare food, spread the word to neighbors or family, and organize help if such is needed. Elder women know the words to spells, prayers, and songs. Oftentimes women's leadership is so essential that without them, there would be no ritual. Women also conduct magic healing rituals for children and household animals. Men's sphere of activity in each of these rituals is important but peripheral: they make the coffins for the deceased, they build the house, and their magical rituals tend to be directed toward animals or other masculine activities (such as the magic of beekeepers, shepherds, or blacksmiths) (Kholodnaia 2005a, 377; Shchepanskaia 2001, 80–85).

Although sources describe men as having their own spiritual sphere of activity, when I spent time in Russian villages, I saw little evidence of men's involvement in the spiritual life of the community; in fact, men were mainly absent from the spaces I inhabited. I entered the world of the Russian village through the world of women. The village social network situated me there: as a divorced woman in her thirties and forties, I was like a daughter to many of the women I encountered when Russian ethnomusicologists and folklorists introduced me to the subjects of their studies. The village women responded to me as if I was a strangely but pleasantly naïve (because foreign) friend of their own daughters: they gave me advice about men and having babies, read my fortune, and guided me in my research process, which they saw as my own process of establishing a local social network. When I had the chance to interview married couples, often the men were more reserved than the women: they gave shorter answers and did not appear to relish talking to me the way their wives did.

My research on gender thus grew out of what and whom I knew in the particular Russian villages where I spent time, but also out of my curiosity about the differences I observed between men's and women's practices. Because I was interested in singing, the questions that preoccupied me as I researched Russian folk culture were: Why are women still actively performing this musical tradition that they say was formerly practiced by men and women together? Are women really the tradition-keepers, and was it always that way? My approach was also informed by what I saw when I accompanied or was accompanied by Russian ethnomusicologists in the field. I wondered why these scholars approached their informants as if the village women were duty-bound to preserve a tradition that the musicologists deemed valuable. I noticed that informal singing groups sang different songs when they were celebrating over food and drink than when a Russian musicologist was conducting a formal interview/recording session. This discrepancy formed the underlying impetus for archival research I did for chapter 1 of this study: I wanted to find out whether it was possible that women's folklore had been seriously misunderstood by scholars determined to use them as national memory banks—as carriers of a Great Russian national tradition. These questions also informed my choice of interview subjects—often I chose to spend time with women who were part of an informal or formal singing collective—and topics of discussion. I tried to ascertain what kinds of singing people did, when, and why; tried to participate in situations when singing would naturally occur, or to encourage singing; asked what people thought of the songs they sang; paid attention to and asked about people's life histories; and asked about and/or observed local holiday or religious traditions. In several cases I timed my visits specifically to participate in life-cycle or calendar rituals (Christmas; Easter; Trinity [Whitsunday]; Veterans' Day; parish holidays; weddings, birthdays, funerals, and forty-day and one-year memorials). Observing people doing what they do has given me a much deeper, more multi-faceted understanding than interviewing alone ever could; but interviews and conversations have helped me explore the important role played by narrative—in its many different forms—in people's lives.

Svetlana Adonyeva

I was educated at Saint Petersburg University, as a historian of Russian literature, folklorist, and literary theoretician. The method of folklore analysis I was taught was based on a structuralist typological analysis of textual variants: that is, we learned to categorize texts and account for their differences. Like all students, I went every year to collect folklore in the Russian village. It worried me greatly that what I read in libraries and heard in lectures did not match what I saw and heard in the field. The books I had read on folklore could not answer a single one of my simple questions: Why did people tell folktales? What meaning did they find there? What happens to them—and to me—when they sing? And finally, why do I sometimes feel very stupid next to an illiterate elder woman—and not want to leave her side? All these questions pushed me to look for new methodologies, to become acquainted with other disciplines (linguistics, psychology, sociology, anthropology), in order to change myself from a "collector of folklore" to a "participant-observer."

One of my early experiences in the field helped me understand the important role of transgression and compromise within the folklore tradition. In some cases tradition itself forces people to refuse the tradition; individuals must then choose whether and in what way to follow tradition's dictates. In 1988 an expedition of the Saint Petersburg Folklore department worked in the southwest Belozersk region of Vologda oblast. The tradition we saw there differed considerably from the ones we had observed in other north Russian territories, in Arkhangel'sk oblast and in east Vologda. One of the differences was that the song tradition seemed weaker here. Our interlocutors responded to our requests for this or the other song, and confirmed their knowledge of them, but did not sing. They often explained their own refusal to sing with "Oi, girls, I've had so much grief—I don't sing," or explained the refusal of another woman to sing with "She is grieving." Folklorists in the Soviet Union were trained to interpret such data about reluctance to sing as a sign that the tradition was dying out. Trying not to jump to conclusions, we did not give up, but we did suppose that this was a polite way of refusing contact with strangers, until we received a fuller explanation. Women who did not sing were those who had buried someone they were close to. The period of cessation of singing after a loss did not have a fixed length; that kind of mourning was for life. We noticed that the prohibition against singing came from "outside," through social pressure. In 1998, in the Belozersk region of Vologda oblast, a woman born in 1926 told me: "I'd sit, I'd start crying and then suddenly I'd start singing. I would look through the window, to see if anyone heard me" (Maeksa, 7 July 1998 ([Bel 17a-35]). That is, the prohibition against singing while in mourning was a social rule that women followed especially when they believed or feared they were being observed. Such a social rule had become internalized, and individuals controlled their own public singing so as not to be publically censured; but they often sang anyway, if it was therapeutic for them. For me, this example was a lesson about transgression and the powerful effect of social censure in the community.

Another episode in particular forced me to start regularly asking about gender and age roles in folklore performance. In an expedition in 1994 in the east Belozersk region of Vologda oblast, a fifty-seven-year-old woman described how they used to sing *chastushki* (short four-line lyrics that are usually sung solo in the context of a musical "conversation"). Her comments revealed that people distinguish between *chastushki* that are "appropriate" and "inappropriate" for the singer. That which is appropriate for women cannot be sung by an unmarried girl; that which is correct for a young man would be funny if sung by a man or woman, and impossible for a girl to sing. Social position, gender, and age determine the relationship of the person with his or her folklore repertoire. One can know a text and have the right to sing or speak it in public or use it in a ritual; or one can lack this right. One may also be required to sing or pronounce a text of a certain type. All changes in individual repertoire in the course of a lifetime are closely connected with one's status and the social roles that one takes on within the framework of that status. The individual folklore repertoire thus functions as one of the markers of a person's place in the social order; it also functions as a means of constructing and reconstructing his or her own world.

Structure of the Book

That this book is a product of contemporary fieldwork has to a large extent dictated its methodology and its content. Yet while we base our study upon our personal experiences with individual women, we do not confine our study to the retelling of women's stories, or structure the book according to a storytelling sequence (as does, for example, Lila Abu-Lughod in her feminist ethnography *Writing Women's Worlds*, 1993). Instead, we emphasize women's age and gender roles—essentially, the life cycle—as a lens through which we examine various aspects of women's knowledge. We examine those aspects or genres of women's folk culture that emerged in our fieldwork as productive and essential to the women we met in the field—songs, life stories, legends, practices of magic, religious rituals, life-cycle celebrations.

We begin, in chapter 1, by reexamining Russian folkloristic and ethnographic scholarship in the light of our understanding of women's knowledge. We show that scholars looked for rural informants with particular signs of individual creativity and particular relationships to tradition; in so doing, the scholars sought to increase their own public fame. Female folk performers generally fared badly in these arenas, since their folklore knowledge tended to be demonstrated in private, domestic settings, and because women had other priorities than to adhere strictly to tradition as received by a male audience. Our critique opens up space for productive rumination on the nature of women's skill and creativity.

Chapter 2 deals with the distribution of knowledge, skill, and obligations according to women's and men's life stages in village society. We show how one's age and gender status determines one's social identity, offering a limited choice of behaviors. We envision society as a network of relationships between peers ("horizontal") and between members of different age groups ("vertical"). In the first half of the twentieth century, historical and economic changes due to collectivization profoundly affected this traditional age and gender hierarchy, particularly with regard to men. In the last part of the chapter we characterize the three generations of Russian women who form the subjects of this study, looking at the major dramas that tend to figure in their life stories, their mores, and their views of tradition. Here we elucidate some of the specific ways that women transgressed against tradition or compromised with tradition.

Each of the subsequent chapters of the book elucidates one type of traditional practice that remained important in the lives of our interlocutors despite significant economic, social, and ideological changes. In particular, rituals, singing, and magic are three activities that were contested by the Soviet authorities, but that our interlocutors commonly retained. In people's lives and belief systems, rituals and music were both private and public discourses, while magic occupied a distinct private sphere that no one talked about publicly.

Chapter 3 studies the stories of courtship and marriage of Russian rural women born in different generations. We read the older stories as means of understanding how the women viewed the traditions in which they took part. In the second part of the chapter we read narratives of courtship as ways of understanding women's changing subjectivities. What kind of identities do the poetics of the courtship and wedding cycle purport to give women, and how do women construct their own life stories in relation to that tradition?

Chapters 4 and 5 examine musical practices. Chapter 4 describes the historical and personal contexts of group folk singing, and focuses upon one particular type of song that is very popular in villages today: romance songs, a genre introduced into Russian village culture in the late nineteenth century. These songs are melodramatic and patriarchal in their outlook, yet they put forward a modern view of romance as a love relationship that fulfills individual desires (rather than community needs). We liken romance songs to two other melodramatic discourses that figure importantly in our interlocutors' lives: gossip and soap operas. We argue that these melodramatic discourses serve to articulate the changing cultural paradigms of the late nineteenth to mid-twentieth centuries. In the Soviet context, to practice these ways of speaking about the deeply private constituted a kind of resistance against the obligation of civic-mindedness. In the post-Soviet period, these practices remain immensely fulfilling for rural women as they provide aesthetic pleasure and social power, express nostalgia for the culture and values of their mothers, and confirm some of the deeply held traditional values of the singers.

Chapter 5 shows how women utilize, in private, social, or official contexts, the transgressive genre of *chastushki*. In the Soviet era, *chastushki* were "domesticated" through their performance in concert settings by folk choirs; on the other hand, the public performance of certain political and erotic *chastushki* constituted a reason for arrest and imprisonment in state labor camps. Nonetheless, it was one of the most popular folk genres. People used the *chastushka* speech form to challenge or undermine the existing social hierarchy. *Chastushki* constitute ritual laughter, a genre of communication in which transgression was not only accepted but part of the "rules of the game." The ambivalent quality of this laughter is evident since, for our interlocutors, it offers a source of celebration and cultural capital on the one hand, and fear and anxiety on the other.

Chapters 6 and 7 approach magical practices from two different points of view. Chapter 6 focuses upon motherhood and how a young mother learns the skills she needs to deal with otherworldly forces that may harm her or her child. We demonstrate how, in this process, vertical relations of power between more and less experienced women are transformed into relations of mutual emotional fulfillment and trust. Chapter 7 considers magic (in particular, setting and lifting harmful spells) as a form of knowledge—and hence power—imputed to specific individuals in a rural community. While other scholars have primarily seen witchcraft as a remnant of pre-Christian belief, we examine the discourse of sorcery and the ways that it fashions social networks. We distinguish between various discourses within the village: for some, "spoiling" (performing harmful magic) is a primary archetypal narrative (plot), while for others this narrative seems to hold little appeal. A third group appears to use such narratives as a kind of social capital, in constructing a powerful reputation within the community.

Chapter 8 focuses upon women's storytelling about the supernatural world. While folklore collectors do not often hear fairy tales (fantastic stories told as entertainment) from their rural Russian interlocutors, they do hear many "believed" stories, called legends or memorates. Rather than reading such stories as evidence of exotic belief, we associate them with each individual's life story and social positioning vis-à-vis her interlocutor. Women often told us legends in the contexts of their narratives about daily lives: while teaching us how to function in their communities, or in the process of reliving their own personal feelings and experiences from the past. We argue that taking legends out of the context of a life—or indeed, of a conversation—can remove a critical element from these narratives. Legend-telling is about belief, but it is also about the choices individuals make to compromise with or transgress against tradition.

Chapter 9 deals with women's roles as memory-keepers in the post-Soviet Russian village. We describe the role of the elder female head of household in managing and directing the spiritual life of the family clan and the community. Women come to choose these mid-life to end-of-life spiritual roles due to both existential and emotional motivations. Funeral practices such as "remembering" the dead and lamenting are examples of acts that have value for elder women: as aesthetic activity, as rites of passage, as a means of developing one's inner world, and as a means of maintaining contact with the ancestors and thus fulfilling one's destiny as an elder female head of household.

Our conclusion returns to one of the fundamental questions that motivated this study: What relationships do Russian rural women have with tradition? If they see themselves as tradition keepers, is this a personal choice, a life vocation, a role handed to them by their own communities, or does motivation come from outside the community? We end our text with reflections on the nature of subjectivity and history, agency and tradition.

1

Traditions of Patriarchy and the Missing Female Voice in Russian Folklore Scholarship

We begin our study by investigating a question that absorbed us for many years as we studied Russian rural women's culture. As fieldworkers in Russian villages, we were constantly learning from the misunderstandings that arose between ourselves and rural women. We wondered how those gaps in understanding had affected the conclusions of previous generations of scholars of Russian folklore. In fact, we wondered whether earlier Russian scholars had paid any attention at all to what we thought was central, that is, the gendered organization of Russian village life.

Our research revealed, significantly, that gender figured only peripherally in Russian scholars' analyses of folk culture until the 1980s.[1] Ethnographer Tatiana Bernshtam wrote that until she published her book on prerevolutionary rural youth culture in 1988, the study of the sex and age structure of Russian society had not been taken seriously. Scholars who had addressed the subject earlier in the 1980s had, without proof, claimed that the more "developed" a society was, the less important gender became as a category (the Soviet/Marxist view); prerevolutionary scholars had noted sex and age as organizing categories in ritual, but had treated the subject as a natural outgrowth of biology and had confined themselves to description. In contrast, Bernshtam (1988, 3, 6) herself viewed sex and age categories as an essential, organizing part of the world view of village dwellers: as she put it, for villagers sex- and age-defined roles were a crucial part of the social structure.[2]

The prerevolutionary scholars Bernshtam refers to as (at best) *describing* gendered practices were ethnographers,[3] but among folklorists the degree of misunderstanding of folklore's gendered nature was more pronounced. Early scholars did not concern themselves with gender at all until they began to pay attention to their informants as people, as individuals. For nineteenth-century folklorists, "the folk" was a shapeless mass without individually identifying characteristics. For example, Aleksandr Afanas'ev, the Russian Grimm, whose collections of folktales are considered classics, recorded only *where* tales were collected, not from whom. Regional and national characteristics were of interest to these scholars, but folk texts were supposed to represent the whole people rather than just one teller (Pypin 1856, 49).[4]

The change came in the 1860s and '70s, when folklorists first sought out individual peasant performers in their search for the most talented singers and tellers among the peasantry. In so doing, they hoped to increase the quality of their collections—and perhaps partly to present an antidote to negative portrayals of peasants in journalistic accounts (Frierson 1993a, 163, 168, 173). They depicted these peasants as noble savages, village intelligentsia who preserved timeless works of invaluable national worth. In this context female performers of folktale and epic sometimes fared badly. Women's performances of those solo genres were deemed to lower the worth of those genres and either lead to or signal their ultimate demise. Meanwhile, women's preservation of other genres (lament, folk song) was lauded. The result was an incomplete picture of what women did perform and preserve, and why they chose to do so.

Thus, until the late 1980s, due to the specific agendas of folklorists, the story of women's contributions to folk tradition had not been told accurately and fully. Nineteenth- and twentieth-century Russian folk culture studies, belles lettres, journalism, and popular literature commonly depicted rural women as quintessential "sources" of tradition, and implied or stated that female villagers provided great service to the Russian people by preserving national folk "treasures." Yet at the same time, Russian scholarship asserted that men were the proper guardians of certain genres, while women's imperfect guardianship tarnished this precious cultural wealth. It seemed the women themselves were caught in between: they were given the heavy burden of representing the nation yet ultimately failed to do so. Their failure was inevitable, given that the task was to guard patriarchy's invented view of its origins. As rural women's knowledge was colonized by scholars, their own voices were rarely heard; their own knowledge was misread.

Our own experiences in Russian villages, the work of contemporary Russian ethnographers, and a critical approach informed by Western feminism allow us to propose an alternate interpretation to the question of women's contribution to folklore tradition. Below we engage in dialogue with the scholarly canon from the late nineteenth century to the mid-twentieth century, focusing on the four genres of folklore that were viewed by early collectors as central to the Russian tradition—folktale, epic, lament, and folk song. We argue that the prevailing Romantic conception of tradition as "the sayings of the fathers" (Fox 1987, 568) blinded researchers to evidence that women possessed their own, equally valuable, traditions.

We show that folklorists missed what we consider the most important information about folklore: the function it fulfilled for the people who used it. Folklorists' Romantic longing for the most ancient Ur-text meant that scholars did not investigate function; as a result, they did not value female singers and tellers as highly as males. The only genre where this gendered hierarchy did not sustain was in the lament, since laments are exclusively a women's folk genre in Russia.

Except for folk song, these four genres do not figure prominently in the rest of this book because they have not remained productive in the folk cultures of contemporary rural Russians.[5] However, with the exception of epic, each of these genres has a "successor" among contemporary folk genres. Today we collect very few magic tales (fairy tales) but many anecdotes (jokes), along with the occasional children's tale (animal tale) and everyday tale. Close relatives to the folktale that we commonly hear in today's villages are legend (told in the popular form of memorate) and personal story (see chapters 8 and 3). While memorate and personal story are among the most common folk narratives in Russian rural women's culture, they were not collected until relatively recently, in part because the words of homebound women were deemed not as interesting as the narratives of mobile men (Dégh 1995, 68). Epic has disappeared from productive life; its traces remain in Russian popular culture in the medium of film, which has updated stories to acquaint new generations with old heroes (Beumers 2011). Laments have not remained in active use for younger generations (particularly those born after World War II) but are still practiced by many elder women. The genre of spiritual song (sung in groups) may replace laments in some areas (Gladkova n.d.; see chapter 9). The folk songs that Russian musicologists and folklorist considered the most valuable were ballads, historical songs, ritual songs, and lyric songs. Today only lyric songs (in the updated forms of romances and *chastushki*) remain in active repertoires, and are sung at parties and holidays (see chapters 4 and 5).

The Folktale

In the 1860s some Russian folklorists started collecting information on their informants (sex, age, occupation, etc.); this technique began with Rybnikov's collections of epic or bylina (1861–67), and within three decades both epic and tale collectors were not only gathering information about informants but also grouping their collections by teller. They considered the individual peasant performer—and his or her repertoire and world view—the most essential organizing principle for these studies. Part of the reason for this performer-centered study was the scholars' desire to obtain the best quality performance. In the genre of folktales, Russian scholars—as well as the Grimms—determined quality by the extent to which the tales held to the principles of "ritual." In Russia this was called *skazochnaia obriadnost'* and included the word-for-word, threefold repetition of events, the formulaic introduction and conclusion, and sometimes rhyming. Scholars considered these characteristics evidence of the greatest time depth.

In these nineteenth- and early twentieth-century studies, folklorists' search for relics of ancient times led them to value male tellers more highly than females. Collectors argued that the tales were "originally" told not by amateurs, who could not have managed the verbal prowess necessary to produce the highly formulaic texts, but by wandering professional jongleurs or *skomorokhi*, who wove tales, songs, instruments, and theater into performances for rulers, boyars, and the common people.[6] In medieval and imperial Russia, wandering and professional people were not women, by definition. In a 1904 article, N. L. Brodskii emphasized this point: "The folktale, which one can hear today from any *old woman*, could only have been worked out in a certain school, and was undoubtedly in the hands of a special teller [*bakhar'*]" (61). This notion of a school and a profession a priori excludes women.

Brodskii effectively classified women as inferior informants for folktale studies because they were not the representatives of what he presumed to be the most ancient traditions. Comments by other researchers filled out this picture. The Sokolov brothers (1915, 57) argued that men were the primary keepers of the folktale tradition in the Belozersk region of Vologda province; women tellers, they wrote, were "less skilled, less experienced" than men. S. Savchenko (1914, 29–31) noted that women became *skazka* tellers "out of necessity" rather than out of skill; as grandmothers, mothers, and nurses they told tales to children, while males told stories to adults. N. Onchukov characterized tales as being largely a male activity; he highly prized magic tales told "as they were told in ancient times," with proper word-for-word repetition of events (*skazochnaia obriadnost'*). By contrast, he said that women tellers inserted into their stories realistic details about women's lives, mostly pertaining to courtship and weddings ([1908] 1998, 27, 31, 40–47). All of these collectors favored the magic tales often told by members of numerous male professions, including hunters, fishermen, woodcutters, soldiers, millers, coach drivers, craftsmen, and prisoners, in situations where people gathered at night after working together during the day. Scholars acknowledged the situations when women told tales—in the home, at young people's evening gatherings, or to children—but saw these as less essential to the maintenance of the tradition, since they believed these settings did not allow for exchanges of tales between masterful tellers.[7]

Several of these scholars produced general characterizations of women's tale-telling. In their comments, they drew heavily on existing stereotypes of women's behavior, in particular nineteenth-century Russian literary critics' assessments of women's writing. The Sokolov brothers depicted even the best women's tales as full of "sentimentality, softness [of tone], and morality"—descriptors also used to characterize women's poetry in the nineteenth century.[8] The Sokolovs said one female teller used diminutives to increase the listeners' identification with the plight of her characters; another repeated words or used tautology to increase the emotional effect of her tale ("He lamented, cried, and wept," "He sat in the chair, all black, all black already from grief"); this female teller also favored good, loyal female characters and painted male characters in "soft, feminine attributes" ([1915] 1999, 1:131). While diminutives are indeed used in female speech to children, and thus may be marked as feminine, the situation is not as clear-cut as the Sokolovs make it sound.

Diminutives of words describing household objects are used to indicate familiarity or closeness, and the example they give is of this sort. Repeated words contribute to the rhythm of the tale, not necessarily the emotional effect. For the third point, the Sokolovs did not give an example; to us the teller's descriptions of male characters seemed classically concise, such as "Once there was a rich merchant. They [sic] had a son Vaniushka" (Sokolov and Sokolov [1915] 1999, 1:192). It is difficult to fully reconstruct and assess the standards to which these folklorists held their female tellers, but clearly the paradigms of their day predisposed them to find in the tales reflections of common assumptions about women's physical weakness and softness, greater sensibility and predisposition to engage in matters of the heart (Vowles 2002, 66).

During this time the groundwork was laid for a characterization of women's tales that remained current for decades. In his 1908 *Severnye skazki* (*Northern Folktales*), Nikolai Onchukov spent a whole chapter of his introduction—eight pages—distinguishing women's folk-telling from men's. He emphasized the "realism" in women's tales: he argued that women tell tales about what they know, and therefore include descriptions of the important parts of their lives, such as weddings, births, and socializing. Onchukov admits such descriptions are accompanied by magical, fantastic events, which one has to "throw out" to see the realistic reflection of women's lives ([1908] 1998, 40–47). But by throwing out the fantastic elements, Onchukov reduces women's storytelling to mere ethnographic raw material. He focuses upon the use value of the tales to ethnographers, but is not interested in their value or function for the women themselves.[9]

For example, he singles out a tale, "Aniushka and Variushka," about two young women, one with a mother and the other without, who live two versts from each other and visit each other every day, alternating days. Onchukov assesses the tale: "If one throws out the element of the fantastic in the ending of the tale, one obtains a very realistic picture." But in the tale itself, the "ending" is the point of the whole tale, and fully colors it. In the tale Aniushka is warned three times that if she visits her friend, she will eat her, but she defends her friend, "No, we've been visiting each other for a long time, she comes to my house, I go to hers." However, Variushka does eat her friend, and Aniushka's mother arrives to find her daughter's arms and legs lying about on the porch. The villagers place iron gates around the house to imprison Variushka, she dies in her house, and the villagers burn the house. If this tale is about women's lives, we would assess it not as a realistic description of the ritual of visiting, but as a social comment on the importance of mothers (Variushka had no mother), a warning about the dangers associated with witches (see chapter 7), and a caution that girls who do not heed the warnings of their community place themselves in danger.

Three decades after Onchukov and the Sokolovs wrote, critics were still using some of the same criteria to assess tales. In a 1932 collection, Mark Azadovskii coined the term "women's tale" (*zhenskaia skazka*), that is, a tale told by women, and used this category to show how the personal characteristics of the teller reflect upon the moral side of the tale. For example, Russian tales in which a mother is disloyal often end in the death of the mother, but he noticed that his female informants softened the punishment by having the mother put in prison instead of killed (29). Like earlier collectors, Azadovskii observed in women's tales a particular "softness and gentleness of tone," and a concentration on everyday and psychological details. Of one female teller he wrote that "the plot is only a frame, a necessary hook for the everyday and psychological details" (1932, 54).

In 1969, folklorist Pomerantseva repeated some of the same phrases in her commentary on the tale-teller Anna Korol'kova, without explicitly attributing these characteristics to her gender. She wrote that although Korol'kova was a master of the traditional genre, she constantly broke the rules of the genre, tending toward the everyday and realistic. Pomerantseva saw Korol'kova's transgressions and innovations as evidence that the tradition was dying.[10] By contrast, when other critics wrote about male tellers changing the tradition, they praised such changes as productive innovation: for example, Azadovskii wrote of the male teller Egor Sorokovikov that he not only preserved the traditional fairy-tale formulaic endings and beginnings but also "creatively rework[ed] them, change[ed] them, giving them an individual coloring" (Sorokovikov et al. 1940, xxi). Such a positive valuation was rarely accorded female tellers' innovations.[11]

The argument about women's changing folktales has its roots in three assumptions: (1) that ancient folktales were told by professionals or members of a "school," (2) that rituality and tradition are found precisely in the most formulaic tales, and (3) that this formulaic quality is more highly desired than "realism." The first point rests upon Romantic notions linking tradition with education in the idea of a school. Johann Gottfried von Herder, the eighteenth-century German Idealist philosopher, wrote that "all education must spring from imitation and exercise, by means of which the model passes into the copy, and how can this be more aptly expressed than by the term tradition?" (Fox 1987, 567). As Jennifer Fox points out, in Herder's thought education does not have a progressive social role, as it does in Enlightenment thinking; instead education serves to uphold the social order, a goal that in eighteenth-century Germany, as in tsarist and medieval Russia, meant keeping women *uneducated*. For Herder, women's main social role was to provide physical nourishment for the child, not spiritual nourishment, which was given through the traditions handed down by the forefathers. Even if these Russian inheritors of Western European Romantic ideas held more progressive ideas about women's roles in society, we argue that their view of *tradition* is implicitly informed by this notion of tradition as "the sayings of the fathers," in Herder's words (Fox 1987, 568).

In fact, it is likely that if professional tellers existed, they were not the only skilled tellers of tales. Evidence collected in the twentieth century suggests that fictional oral narration was a skill many community members possessed, to varying degrees (and with differing degrees of mastery). When the most productive collecting occurred in the nineteenth and early twentieth centuries, male tale-telling regularly occurred in public space, while women's telling occurred in private, domestic space. Collectors would have needed to go out of their way in order to find female tellers. Furthermore, due to demands of modesty, many women would not have willingly told tales to strangers, particularly men (Zelenin 1914, 23–24). As Olga Kadikina (n.d., n.p.) has pointed out, in many areas even old women who were well-known tellers refused to tell folktales to researchers, saying they were "embarrassed" or "ashamed."

The norms of behavior within the community dictated the situations in which tales could be told. Middle-aged and older women and adolescent girls usually told folktales within homes (not at work or in the field, as men did), to audiences of adolescent girls or children. Often the women or girls took care of children and used tales to entertain, socialize, and/or educate them; adolescent girls used to gather for evening work parties in huts where particularly gifted storytellers lived. Evidence suggests that in many communities, women of childbearing age did not actively tell tales: they reported they were "too busy" at this age (Sokolov and Sokolov [1915] 1999, 1:190; Kadikina n.d.). Further, there is little direct evidence for grown women telling folktales to their same-age peers, as men did in work situations that required significant time spent away from home, such as fishing and logging. When women did so, it was during holiday celebrations, for entertainment.[12]

Another problem with the argument about men being the primary or "original" tale-tellers revolves around the term "professional," which could be applied to a much broader swath of tellers than just descendants of medieval *skomorokhi*. For example, older women who lacked their own homes often worked in the homes of others, doing weaving, spinning, and caretaking of children in exchange for room and board; in such cases tale-telling was often part of the skill set that made them attractive to potential employers. As Karnaukhova wrote of one teller, "She depends on tales as much as weaving."[13] Like male tellers, some women viewed themselves as tellers and were very interested in their individual reputations within the community and beyond. We know this because female tellers spoke of other female tellers within the environs, and jealously guarded their reputations vis-à-vis the other tellers: "She wanted to take 'Kostriuk' from me, but she couldn't . . . But she tells well. She knows a lot" (Ivanov 1990, 62–63; Kadikina n.d.).

The second notion at the root of this argument, that rituality and tradition are found precisely in the most formulaic tales, is problematic in that it takes an element of *some* of the tales—rituality—and determines that to be the defining feature of "folktale-ness" in general. So-called everyday tales, witty stories about soldiers, priests, jesters, wives, and beggars, were not verbally formulaic in the way that magic tales were; plot was dominant. Such tales were told by both male and female tellers.[14] Furthermore, as Karnaukhova's remarks show, animal tales that women told to children were indeed formulaic and ritualistic. The tales required mastery and commitment from a storyteller. Not all tellers took the time to perfect the genre—inferior tellers curtailed the "never-ending" repetition that is the hallmark of many of these tales. Although many tellers disdained children's tales and were surprised when Karnaukhova asked for them, some tellers, such as sixty-four-year-old P. Korennaia, a proficient teller of animal stories (whose tales had been published by her son) felt themselves to be "keepers of the tales" and saw tale-telling as "mastery" (Karnaukhova [1934] 2006, 399–400).

As we can see from the above example, the third notion, that formulaic "magic" tales are more highly prized than realistic ones or tales for children, was held not only by scholars but also by storytellers themselves, at least in the twentieth century. In both cases, if female tellers of folktales seemed like transgressors of an ancient tradition or simply as outside the tradition, this may be because both scholars and community members did not know how to properly assess or evaluate the functions of women's creative activity. If men told tales primarily to entertain themselves and others, female tellers used the folktale partly or primarily as a means of transmitting values to future generations. In fact, researchers noticed this difference but devalued the didactic uses of the folktale, associating them with everyday use and "necessity." Foucault's distinction between subjugated and subjugating types of knowledge is relevant here: "I believe that by subjugated knowledges one should understand something else, something which in a sense is altogether different, namely a whole set of knowledges that have been disqualified as inadequate to their task or insufficiently elaborated: naïve knowledges, located low down on the hierarchy, beneath the required level of cognition or scientificity" (Foucault 1980, 82).

The forms of "subjugated knowledge" that Russian village women possessed were often not available to collectors because of community taboos about whom one could tell to. In addition, community norms called for women to perform particular genres at particular stages of their lives. Pre-pubescent and adolescent girls who took care of younger siblings learned folktales. Adolescent girls also learned weddings songs, including laments, and sang them at the weddings of their peers. After marriage, young women mastered household magic (such as spells to protect the household and animals and to ensure a good harvest) and spells for protecting, healing, and calming infants and children. Later in life, they learned to lament the dead, and told tales to grandchildren and young people. With each passing stage, they did not forget the knowledge they had acquired earlier, but the "public demonstration of it was already considered improper, unacceptable, and began to be censured" by the community (Kadikina n.d.). Thus, the "subjugated knowledges" of women were often underestimated or even unexplored by folklorists who were looking for particular forms of knowledge to round out their scholarly collections.[15]

One question remains: whether women told different stories than male tellers. Bengt Holbek (1989, 42), a researcher of Nordic tales, suggests that in that tradition, since both teller and audience identify with the protagonist of the tale, men tell more tales involving male protagonists while women's repertoires contain stories featuring male and female protagonists in about equal proportion. Jack Haney (1999, 18) asserts that this is not true of the Russian material: "Even though there are relatively few Russian tales that have a feminine protagonist, these tales were usually told by men too."[16] Nonetheless, a count of the tales told by men and women in the early twentieth-century collections by Onchukov and the Sokolov brothers, and one collection from 1932–83, disproves Haney's assertion and shows that Holbek's hypothesis holds for the Russian context. Men did tell a much higher percentage of tales featuring male protagonists (male tellers told just 3 and 4 percent of tales with female protagonists in the early collections, and 25 percent in the later collection). By contrast, in Onchukov's collection, 50 percent of the tales told by women featured heroines; in the Sokolovs' it was 26 percent, and in the later collection 60 percent.[17] While we cannot speak of specific "women's" tales the way we can with epics, which are much easier to classify (see discussion below), we can conclude that women did show special interest in tales about female protagonists. Such a difference may reflect storytelling contexts and audiences: while men told tales for all-male audiences in the workplace, women told tales for groups of girls or mixed-sex audiences of young people in the context of get-togethers for young people or families. The need to tell tales that would appeal to mixed audiences may have led women to master tales featuring both male and female protagonists. Further, the storytellers' own interests and world view may have found a closer match in tales about girls and women.

Bylina

If the most ancient tradition of the folktale was seen as a masculine one, that has been even more true of the Russian bylina, the epic. The epic is associated with the formation of the nation, with national identity; the epic hero is the mythological founder of the nation. As Balashov and Novichkova (2001, 32, 37) write, "The question [that is posed in the epic], 'Who will vanquish whom?' is a matter of the birth and confirmation of the ethnos and answers the question: what will the ethnos be, that is, whose nationality will win and be confirmed in the fight?" The epic drama confirms not only nationality, but also the patriarchal social system itself, since in its depiction of the hero winning a wife, epic briefly entertains the possibility that the female family line might dominate. The female line does not: the hero inevitably wins over his bride through battle, and patriarchy is validated.

It is unsurprising, then, that the Russian bylina was seen by scholars as a male tradition. V. Bazanov and Razumova (1962, 4) expressed this underlying assumption: "Heroic bylina poetry, the poetry of masculine [*muzhestvennyi*] eloquence, originated during military campaigns and was for the most part aimed at a male audience."[18] For Russian scholars, the situation in some locations, in which women came to predominate as tellers of epics, was a sign of the decline of the tradition. Although hard facts to prove our supposition are not available, we think the existing data might be interpreted differently.

For example, it is clear that the early collectors did not seek out women as informants. They assumed that the better tellers would be men. They were men themselves, and their collecting methods brought them into contact with other men. In the 1860s, the first collector to indicate his sources, P. N. Rybnikov, used very few female informants (only three out of thirty-three, 9 percent female); his description of how he found informants shows that it would have been difficult for him to find female performers of epics even if he had searched intentionally for them. Performers became known to him when he encountered them in public places, such as inns where travelers converged—and the only travelers one met there were men. He also sought out performers who were recommended to him by those same male travelers—their friends or relatives. Occasionally these men recommended their wives or wives of their friends. One woman informant was Rybnikov's hostess where he lodged (Rybnikov [1910] 1991).

As we mentioned in our discussion of folktales, women's main activity was within the home, and their telling of tale and epic would have taken place primarily within a home setting. If collectors did not expressly ask for female tellers, they would likely have found few, due to social taboos about women performing for strangers, and due to the fact that female tellers may not have been known as such outside their immediate families. As with folktales, epics were told by men during leisure time at work activities such as fishing. Many collectors attributed the health of the tradition to the continuance of the men's fishing activities (e.g., Grigor'ev 1904, 24). However, it is likely that the masculine tradition of singing epics in public was paralleled by a feminine tradition of singing epics within the home.[19] Important in this regard is the fact that, although there are known taboos about when epics could be sung, there are no known taboos about who could sing them.[20]

Later collectors changed their collecting methods and did find more female tellers. As Aleksandr Grigor'ev recounts, he traveled in villages in 1899–1901, asking both old men and old women who in their village might know epics, and attempted to collect all the epics possible in each village. According to his own recounting, he found epic tellers of whom even locals did not know (Grigor'ev 1904, 136). In some areas he found more female than male tellers (77 percent female in the White Sea [Pomor'e] and Pinega river valley regions), and his data were borne out by the only female collector to devote her career to epics, A. M. Astakhova, who worked in the 1920s and '30s (in the same region, Astakhova's female tellers comprised 68 percent of her total). In other regions, for these same collectors, the numbers of female tellers were much smaller: from 16 percent to 26 percent (Grigor'ev 1910, 1939; Astakhova 1927, 1938, 1951).

Grigor'ev and other collectors attempted to explain this regional discrepancy by referring to the relative health of the tradition. For Grigor'ev in particular, the proliferation of female bylina singers was a sign that the tradition was dying. He contrasted the situation along the southern shore of the White Sea and the Pinega river valley, where the tradition was in decline, with the Kuloi and Mezen' river valleys (further north along the White Sea), where the tradition was still flourishing. In the latter area Grigor'ev recorded three times as many men as women. Most of the epics sung by men were the heroic type; the women sang ballads (Grigor'ev 1939). In the White Sea and Pinega areas, by contrast, women tellers were three times more numerous than men and epic telling was seen as something women did; Grigor'ev (2002–3, xiv) added that here the songs were "short, few, and poorly known." For Grigor'ev (1904, 14), the predominance of women tellers in the White Sea–Pinega areas was one of the factors that clearly showed the decline of the tradition; other factors included the shortness of the songs, the fact that most singers only knew a few, and the lack of variety in the melodies with which the texts were sung. While Astakhova did not directly attribute the decline of the epic tradition to the preponderance of female tellers, she concurred with Grigor'ev's assessment that the epic tradition was no longer truly alive in the Onega river basin (along the southernmost bay of the White Sea): epic tellers of both genders had no audience, and were laughed at by village young people. Most of the byliny that remained current in the limited repertoires of tellers were not heroic epics but bylina-novellas (Astakhova 1927, 77–103).[21] Bylina-novellas, the genre preferred by women, were linked with the decline of the tradition.

However, we interpret these data differently. We can agree with the collectors in their assessment that they found more women in one area precisely because there were fewer male tellers in that area.[22] However, we can disagree that this means that the tradition was dying. It may have simply meant that the female tradition of epic telling was more developed in one area than another due to chance factors such as the existence of good women tellers, contexts in which women's telling was desired, and the existence of texts that appealed to women. Social taboos may also have changed or been different in this area.

That certain types of texts may have appealed more to women than to men is a hypothesis that many collectors tried to develop. The early collector Rybnikov said the term *bab'i stariny*, or "women's epics," was used by one of his male informants, and he tried to fill out this picture. Other collectors noticed a similar group of epics that were beloved by women, although the epics beloved by women were not the same from area to area, and in certain areas it was difficult to identify any body of "women's epics." In general, most of the epics spoken of as appealing to female tellers have been classified by later scholars as novelistic epics or, in some cases, ballads. While heroic epics feature the battle exploits of a male hero, bylina-novellas depict a male hero's adventures, often involving love. Ballads, a more recent genre (originating in the eighteenth and nineteenth centuries), narrate tragic love affairs or family dramas and often focus upon the fate of a central female character (Kulagina 2001, 6; Bailey and Ivanova 1998, xxii).

In our examination of the novelistic epics and ballads that women singers included in their repertoires, we noticed that many of these texts feature prominent women characters who act as heroines or villainesses. One such ballad is the story of Prince Mikhailo, in which the prince's mother kills his wife, who is pregnant with his child, since Mikhailo had not asked his mother's permission to marry.[23] Why female singers may have been interested in songs with female villains and victims is the subject of another chapter of this study, on lyric song; but we may remark here that, based upon comments of women about their songs, clearly the "bad woman" holds special fascination as a transgressor of community norms.

"Ivan Godinovich," an epic identified by Rybnikov as a women's epic, is about female desire for power: Nastasia chooses the (obviously foreign, pagan) hero Koshcherishche (or Idolishche) over (the obviously Russian) Ivan when the former tells her she will become a tsaritsa if she marries him.[24] Other "women's epics" help to fill out the picture of the various kinds of agency women could evince in these texts. They include the ballad "Kniaz' Dmitrii and Domna," in which Domna kills herself by plunging knives into her breasts rather than give herself to the old and ugly Prince Dmitrii.[25] Here the heroine might be said to show agency by choosing to end her life in a brave fashion; however, a closer examination of the text shows that Domna in fact kills herself because she has been tricked into entering Dmitrii's household while he is there, thus rendering herself unfit for marriage to any other man by the community's moral standards. Since this was a real danger for Russian women in communities where this standard held sway, women tellers might have found this plot of great interest.[26]

A clearer example of female bravery is emphasized in "Stavr Godinovich," in which Stavr's very assertive wife outwits Prince Vladimir by dressing as a man and passing (with flying colors) several tests of her "masculine" skill in archery and combat.[27] A significant, very active female role is played by a stock character of epics known as a *polenitsa*, or a female warrior, who engages the male hero in battle. Stories of the *polenitsa*'s exploits are among those beloved by women tellers. Finally, other epics favored by women but not identified by collectors as "women's epics" include several with male protagonists in which wives and mothers play significant roles, either aiding their men or maintaining their men's honor.[28]

Women's preference for particular byliny suggests that a women's repertoire likely existed parallel to, but somewhat overlapping with, the men's, and that women may have sought out byliny, like they did fairy tales, that would appeal to mixed-gender audiences of young people. However, as with the folktale, scholars tended to view the women's repertoires as later phenomena that represented the decline of the tradition, and in general viewed women as inferior carriers of the epic tradition. But even if we accept the argument that a male epic tradition was in decline, that does not mean that the female tradition whose existence we are arguing for was its replacement or the cause of its decline.

Despite the argument about women's participation in general, certain female bylina singers were singled out by scholars as significant exceptions to the rule. These female singers, whose repertoires were broader, were hailed as worthy carriers of Russia's national folk tradition.[29] For example, in 1915 and 1916 folklorist and performer Olga Ozarovskaia brought seventy-two-year-old epic singer Maria Krivopolenova (one of the informants from whom Grigor'ev had collected in 1900) from her home on the Pinega river in Arkhangel'sk province to give concerts in Moscow, Petrograd, and several provincial capitals (Novichkova 2000, 15–16). Writers and scholars such as music critic V. G. Karatygin made much of the "grandmother" (babushka, as Ozarovskaia called her), who "gives off an aura of ancient culture" and of the "patriarchal way of life" (Karatygin 1927, 230–31; Novichkova 2000, 17). Krivopolenova was viewed as a traditional teller who passed on what she had learned without inserting her own changes in style or content (Alekseev and Popov 1937, 87).

By contrast, another such female epic teller, Marfa Kriukova, a sixty-year-old (born 1876) from the Onega River in Arkhangel'sk province, was hailed by scholars as a "creator" who both preserved and updated the tradition. While in earlier periods scholars viewed changing the tradition as contributing to its decline, politics changed that assessment during the 1930s.[30] During the Stalin era, journalists, writers, and scholars made use of Kriukova's skill at creating new epics to produce a new "Soviet" epic that provided legitimacy to the regime. Kriukova was a considerable phenomenon in the 1930s: she performed for students, workers, and writers in Moscow, Arkhangel'sk, the Caucasus, Georgia, and Azerbaijan, and her epics were featured on national radio. In 1937, on her first trip outside of her home region, the newspaper *Pravda* arranged escorted tours of all the cultural sights in Moscow; her 1938 trip to the Caucasus showed her Stalin's homeland. Both trips were meant to encourage her to create new bylinas, which she called *noviny*; she created new epics on contemporary themes such as Lenin, Stalin, and the achievements of the Soviet Union. She was made a member of the Writers' Union in 1938, and received a pension of 150 rubles—a very large sum for a villager (Astakhova 1939, 176–77; Lipets 1939, 3, 5; Alekseev and Popov 1937, 84).

The phenomenon of folk singers being brought to the city to perform raises the question of whether their skill was manipulated by the managers and impresarios who wished to appeal to the public's desire for a symbol of the nation's ancient past. Certainly Kriukova's skill was shaped by the entourage of journalists, tour guides, and scholars who worked with her. While scholars may have preferred male epic tellers to women, in the popular sphere it was women—like Kriukova and Krivopolenova—who became iconic guardians of the country's folklore wealth. This may in part have been because female performers could (and did) sing and tell various genres of folkloric texts: lullabies, lyric songs, ritual songs, dance songs, ballads, folktales, proverbs, and laments, in addition to epics. Both in the late nineteenth century and in the 1930s, the popular image of the Russian babushka appeared to function as a powerful balm for city people. In the next section we examine this phenomenon in more detail using an example that reflects more directly upon the question of gender, since it takes place within the women's genre of the lament.

Lament

While scholars viewed folktale and epic as originally male genres, lament was a different story altogether. Evidence collected in the nineteenth century suggests that laments were, at that time, exclusively a women's folk genre in Russia. Earlier evidence is more uncertain: literature of the tenth to thirteenth centuries attributes laments to women, men, or sometimes to "people" in general, which has given scholars reason to think that both men and women performed laments in ancient Russia (Chistov 1960, 15–16; see also Konenenko 1994). Additional evidence to support this idea is the fact that other neighboring cultures do have male laments (Georgians, Ossetians, Ukrainians, Serbians), and that within the corpus of recorded Russian laments, several sections are told from a masculine point of view, a masculine "I" (Ul'ianov 1914, 241–42; Chistov 1960, 16; Chistov 1988, 79; Kononenko 1994; Chistov 1997, 480).

   Since scholars have seen lament as an exclusively female genre in Russia, they have used this genre in particular as a place to wax poetic about women's role as "folk poetesses" and "folk priests-custodians of the legends and precepts of the fatherland," in particular with regard to laments about the death of sons and fathers, and laments for army recruits (Ul'ianov 1914, 241). Natalie Kononenko (1994, 25) notes that scholarly collections of laments often include more laments for the passing of men than for women.[31] However, scholarly emphasis on women's funeral laments for men does not mean that women did not ritually lament the passing of their mothers, sisters, and daughters. Our field evidence suggests that in fact women do and did create poetic laments to mark the passing of female relatives, and there is no reason to suggest that the situation was different in the past. If scholars and performers emphasized the lamenting of men, it was more likely because the loss of men was seen within patriarchy as more important and more closely related to the survival of the nation.[32] The importance to the community of the loss of a man was also shown in the length of the mourning period, which was shorter for widowers than for widows (Madlevskaia 2005, 30).

   Within the Russian patriarchal system, women have indeed functioned as spiritual guardians. They are in charge of the correct performance of important life-cycle events, and the funeral and memorial rituals are an important part of their knowledge (see chapter 9; also Prokop'eva 2005, 637–38). In this context, the fact that only women perform laments, a poetic genre that fulfills a central function within the funeral and memorial rituals, is not surprising. Men have an important part to play within the ritual: they make the coffin. But as a rule, they are silent during the actual rituals (Adon'eva 2004, 196, 199). Women, on the other hand, play one of two different roles within the funeral ritual. Their "initiation" comes the first time they must lament, that is, when they lose a loved one, typically a child or husband. At this time with their laments they express their grief but also, it is believed, "properly" send off the loved one to the other world, the world of death. After that initiation, women repeatedly perform laments within memorial rituals that occur at certain intervals after the death, and within calendar rituals devoted to the memory of ancestors. Once women have been initiated, they have a choice: they may continue to lament only for their own family members, or they may become skilled lamenters, in which case they take on the role not of initiate but of initiator for other women undergoing the initiation (Adon'eva 2004, 220–22, 227, 231, 234).

These experienced, initiated lamenters, known for their skill, were the types who were called upon by folklorists to give examples of their work when the genre was first "discovered" by scholars in the 1860s.[33] Folklorists saw the lament as poetry—similar to folktale or epic—rather than as a primarily ritual form. But because of its integral place within ritual, the lament has a significantly different character than those genres. When it is taken outside of a ritual context and performed as poetry, for a folklore collector, it becomes unnatural (Likhachev 1987, 522–29). Nonetheless, the character of the texts dictated by these experienced lamenters lent itself to being interpreted as art, because in the mouths of experienced lamenters, not only grief is expressed. These women possess both "the gift of a distinct kind of vision, and a particular social status—earned and ratified by society— that gives them the right to speak about others' moral duty" (Adon'eva 2004, 233). Their work has been linked with epic: indeed, in many cases their poetry has phrases and passages in common with bylinas (Adon'eva 2004, 233; Kononenko 1994, 28).

Irina Fedosova was the most famous Russian lamenter of the late nineteenth century. Her laments, collected between the 1860s and '80s, and performed for the Russian public in the 1890s, contain examples of a kind of socially conscious poetry that castigates villains and elevates heroes of the peasant community to which she belonged. Her story helps us illustrate the ways in which this genre, and women's knowledge in general, was perceived—and misperceived—by scholars, journalists, and the general public.

As we saw in the section on epic, starting in the 1890s folklorists conceived the idea of showing folk performers themselves to city audiences. The second such performer to be brought to Moscow and Petersburg from the Russian North was Irina Fedosova, seventy-five years old at the time. She was received with enthusiasm by urban audiences. To showcase these peasant performers, folklorists and classical musicians created folkloric evenings, "ethnographic concerts," for the entertainment and edification of the public. They also arranged concerts in scholarly societies, schools, and private houses, and took out advertisements in Saint Petersburg and Moscow newspapers offering these performers for hire for private concerts (Chistov 1988, 49; Smirnov 1996). Folklorists thereby hoped to make some money and also to increase their cultural capital. Their forays into arts management took them to such unlikely venues as the 1896 All-Russian Exhibition of Industry and Art in Nizhnii Novgorod, where Fedosova performed.

A peasant woman from the Russian North—near Lake Onega, in Karelia—Fedosova was the subject of much attention from folklorists and intellectuals from the 1870s on, and from the Russian public in the 1890s. She was first "discovered" by Elpidifor Barsov, a teacher of psychology and logic at a seminary in Petrozavodsk. He significantly advanced his career when he handwrote her laments from her dictation in the late 1860s, and published them in three volumes from 1872 to 1885. Her impresario for the 1895–96 Moscow and Petersburg concert tour and the Nizhnii Novgorod exhibition was a different man, Pavel Bogdanov, a teacher at the Petrozavodsk Women's Gymnasium, who also apparently dreamed of making his career with Fedosova's help. Bogdanov played the role of emcee at many of Fedosova's appearances, including the one in Nizhnii Novgorod. Maksim Gorky, who wrote a series of sixty articles on the All-Russian Exhibition for a liberal paper, the *Odessa News* (*Odesskie novosti*), characterized Fedosova as a breath of fresh air compared to her pedantic emcee: she was bright, lively, full of humor and intelligence. It seemed unbelievable that she was, as the impresario told the audience, ninety-eight years old—in reality she was seventy-five.

At the concerts Fedosova sang epics, ballads, and wedding and lyric songs, but she was best known for her laments (the advertisements for her concerts called her a lamenter, *voplenitsa*), and this was the high point of the concert for Gorky. To Gorky and others concerned with critiquing the culture of tsarist Russia, Fedosova represented the true Russia, untouched by pseudo-folklore, pseudo-art, or the spirits of decadence and bureaucratism. In Gorky's description of the public's reaction to her concert, the audience first feels overwhelmed, then "bursts out into thunderous applause," and finally begins to cry, succumbing "to the originality of her soul-grabbing laments"—it is so "unlike everything they listen to day after day, year after year" in their cafés and bars. Due to its deep connection with "antiquity," Fedosova's lament touched even an "audience desiring light entertainment": "One could hear some kind of general sigh. This is truly the people's poetry, a groan created by the people, our 100-million-strong masses" (Gor'kii 1953b, 232–33; 1953a, 189.).

To Gorky, Fedosova was not just symbolic of authenticity and Russianness; she embodied those qualities, brought them to life for an audience who lacked them. Gorky's words illustrate the irony in such pronouncements: although her poetry belonged to the "people," it was not familiar to the Russian audience. "The people," to whom Fedosova belonged, was an exotic Other for these cityfolk. Furthermore, Fedosova was clearly being framed in this way in order to make a point about those cityfolk. Fedosova had been framed in multiple ways by various men: first by Barsov, then by Bogdanov, both of whom wanted to make careers from her art, and finally by Gorky, who wanted her to exemplify his ideal of the *narod*, the people.

Why did Russia want to hear laments? Clearly at century's end, during a period of steady industrial growth, famine, and poverty, continuous reaction and counterreaction, and ten years before the first Russian Revolution (Riasanovsky 1993, 396, 431), Fedosova served as a lightning rod for the country's anguish. Her expression of sorrow offered a release of emotion, and melodramatic emotion at that. For Gorky, and for many others like him, her songs of Russia's ill treatment of the peasant seemed to imply a call for significant change. For others, she captured the grief of personal loss. As Kirill Chistov (1988, 287), a leading scholar on Fedosova, comments: for Nikolai Nekrasov and others, Fedosova "was interesting not for her individuality but, on the contrary, for her typicality, the precision with which she conveyed the conditions of peasant life." What they did not realize was that even among peasants Fedosova was not typical: she was, indeed, an experienced, gifted lamenter. There existed others like her, but certainly not more than one or two in any given community.

One defining characteristic of the genre is that laments are improvised. For Gorky, and perhaps for other listeners, this gave the performance an aura of freshness and authenticity. It also probably allowed the performance to affect the audience emotionally more than arranged and constructed folk performances did. Yet Fedosova's laments were both improvised and constructed. Chistov argues that in performance she had to make up for the fact that the lament was taken out of its ritual context. In fact, community norms made it taboo for anyone to sing funeral laments outside of a funeral. The reason for this is that funeral laments have a specific function within the ritual: they aid the dead person to cross over to the other world. Thus, Fedosova preserved a certain distance from the actual situation of lament, even while she tried to counterbalance this distance within her laments by acting roles, performing situations she had seen, heard of, or imagined, or even piecing together sections of text from various points of view, making each single text polyphonic (Chistov 1997, 479; see also Kremleva 2004, 672–74). In compensation for the distance from the "real thing," she may have either intentionally or unconsciously used available techniques to increase the emotional impact of her laments. She made folklore into art (Chistov 1997, 464).

Folklorists did not always recognize the degree to which Fedosova was creating while lamenting. Barsov, who "discovered" Fedosova in 1867 and made his career from this discovery, thought there existed particular traditional laments, with standard texts, for particular family relations: thus, when he spent two years writing down her laments, he would ask her to tell a generic "Lament of a widow for her husband," "Lament of a daughter for her father," "Lament of a daughter for her mother," and so on. He thought she was *remembering*, not creating (Chistov 1997, 479). Fedosova gave Barsov what he wanted, but in several cases it was clear that she had particular people and particular situations in mind when constructing these improvisations for him. The degree of their misunderstanding became clear when, at a concert at the Polytechnical Museum in Moscow in 1896, he asked her "to sing some of her laments that he had recorded." She answered, "But I don't remember those dead people any more. I can't lament anything about them," and proceeded to make up new improvisations on the same themes (Chistov 1997, 480).

The horizons of folklorist and performer differed considerably. The metaphorical space of their shared knowledge was very small—indeed, this is what frequently happens when urban folklorists communicate with rural women about their lives. Barsov not only missed the essential improvisational nature of the laments but also argued that Fedosova was a "professional" lamenter, when in reality funeral laments were never done for pay. His argument reflected scholars' commonly held preference in late nineteenth-century folklore studies for professional folk performance.

Finally, he and others misunderstood her age. Bogdanov introduced her as ninety-eight when she was seventy-five. At the time of Barsov's intensive collection of Fedosova's laments, she was probably thirty-six years old; he put her age at around fifty, and his description of her further emphasized her advanced age: "extremely ugly, short, gray, and lame, but with great spiritual strength and a highly poetic nature." She became an embodiment of the grotesque and even the sublime for these men: supremely ugly, lame, and ancient, but also inspiring awe. The exact date of her birth is not known, since female peasants had no reason to know their birth years (unlike men, who had to know them due to military service). Rural women's age can be estimated based upon their own accounts of how long they spent in each life stage, and that is how the account of her birth in 1831 was calculated by later scholars (Chistov 1988, 23–25). Clearly, both Barsov and Bogdanov viewed Fedosova in a way that was consistent with their preconceptions about peasant women being grandmotherly. As Olga Kadikina (n.d.) points out, the important role of the old woman in the fairy tale—as witch, evil-doer, or donor—surely played a role in the perception of an old woman as someone who "knows"; that is, she possesses knowledge of folklore, magic, and ritual.

Fedosova's case calls to mind Foucault's distinction between subjugated and subjugating types of knowledge. Like many Russian peasant women approached by collectors in the nineteenth century, Fedosova initially declined to tell her laments to Barsov due to community taboos, and when she finally relented, she set her own conditions for the collection. As Barsov reported, her words to him were: "What do you want from me? I don't know anything and can't fathom anything; what laments are you talking about?" When Barsov's landlord, whom she knew, assured her Barsov was not going to harm her, she admitted that "there was no one who could best her in singing, as God was her witness; if she sang at a wedding the old people would dance, if she lamented at a funeral the very stones would cry. Her voice was so free and gentle" (Barsov 1997c, 253–54; 1997a, 263–64). During the two years that Barsov visited her daily to write down her laments, she set her own conditions for the recordings, based upon the folk-Christian calendar and her household duties.

As Barsov told it, although she appeared to participate willingly in the work, Fedosova still wondered what the purpose was, and worried that something bad could come from it. In the middle of their work she would complain to him, "Don't send me, for Christ's sake, to an unknown, far-off land, don't lock me in a bolted prison, don't take me away from my birth-land!" After such outbursts Barsov would reassure Fedosova and, as he put it, "reestablish her trust" in him. His career depended upon her participation: after his publication of several articles based upon her laments, Barsov received the attention of the most well-known philologists in Petersburg and Moscow, and was invited to work in a Moscow museum, significantly advancing his career (Barsov 1997a, 265; Chistov 1997, 406–7).

Fedosova's initial reluctance to perform laments outside of their ritual context indicates a concern on her part about transgression of community norms; her expressed fears about being taken away to a "far-off land" indicate that she knew her position vis-à-vis the folklore collectors was not an empowered one. The language of her protest was precisely that of the lament, which emphasizes the powerless position of the living in relationship to the all-powerful, personified, supernatural Death.[34] However, although with Barsov she rhetorically emphasized her lack of power, Fedosova did benefit from her association with folklorists, and knew it. She dictated a somewhat satirical *eksprompt* (impromptu) to this effect while living in the home of O. Agreneva-Slavianskii, another folklorist who based a three-volume collection on Fedosova's knowledge: "I eat and drink / And don't bow to anyone. / I eat till I'm full / And drink my fill. / I don't poke my nose in anyone's business / And don't lift a finger." As we interpret this little text, after a lifetime of living in poverty and being taken advantage of by others, Fedosova had the sense of being justifiably taken care of (Chistov 1988, 45–46, 48). Later, based upon her fame and her earnings from her tours in the mid-1890s, Fedosova showed that "not lifting a finger" was not her ultimate goal: unselfishly, she reclaimed family land that had been rented out, married off her nephew, gave money to her village to build a school, and helped to reclaim the community's logging rights in a forest on the east side of Lake Onega (Chistov 1988, 48–54). In so doing, she fully exercised her agency despite the demands and limitations placed upon her by patriarchy.

Fedosova was a woman with extraordinary skill and a strong will. Her autobiography, which she dictated to Barsov, tells us something about the experiences that may have made her this way. As a young woman, she chose marriage to a widower, thereby skipping the years of subjugation to other women that a young bride was usually obliged to go through. She jumped directly from being a young girl to being a female head of household (*bol'shukha*), the second most powerful position in a peasant family.

To the folklorists who wrote or read about her or the public who saw her in the late 1890s, Fedosova had become a poster child for tradition and nation. Collector, impresario, and journalist viewed her as an ancient teller of remembered texts, a kind of Russian Homer, both exotic and one's own. But she was not conveying ancient tales passed down by generations; she was creating texts in which she employed art, tradition, and powers of self-expression in equal measure. Fedosova's case provides us with yet another example of ways in which the subjugated knowledges of women were viewed through the distorting lens of folklorists. In spotlighting the lament, the folklorists were searching for their own idealized notion of a Russian traditional folkloric performance genre; to them, this "authentic" genre would be worthy of communicating an essential part of the great Russian national culture.

Folk Song

For prerevolutionary scholars, women were inferior tale- and epic-tellers because they stayed close to the hearth; the exchange of tales and epics, which could be accomplished only in public situations where tellers from various families or regions participated, was considered important to the mastery of the tradition. Scholars said the opposite regarding women's participation in singing. Evgeniia Lineva in 1904, Zinaida Eval'd in 1928, and Iurii Kruglov in 1979 commented that women were more likely to retain old music-making styles since they rarely ventured out of the narrow circle of home and family, while men traveled to cities and other villages for employment and army service (Lineva 1904, 32; Eval'd 1928, 177; Kruglov 1979, 20).

Unlike the collectors of tales, late nineteenth- and early twentieth-century song collectors did not remark upon the gender of their informants. This was partly due to the fact that in Russia there was very little solo singing; most folk singing was done by community groups, often of mixed gender. Starting in the late nineteenth century, however, collectors did make lists of their informants, and we can learn from these what genres of songs were sung by which genders. A count of the informants for Fedor Istomin's collections in Arkhangel'sk and Olonets provinces (in the far north) in 1886 and in Vologda, Viatka, and Kostroma provinces (northeast of Moscow) in 1893 shows that both men and women sang spiritual songs (*dukhovnye stikhi*) and round-dance songs (*khorovodnye pesni*); other genres tended to be performed by either men or women, but the data could vary by area. For example, in the Vologda-Viatka-Kostroma area, groups of men dominated in the singing of drawn-out (*protiazhnye*) songs about love, family problems, and soldiers' and prisoners' lives, whereas in the more northerly Arkhangel'sk-Olonets area, the drawn-out love and family songs were sung mostly by women. In all the studied areas, women dominated in the singing of laments and wedding songs, while men dominated in the singing of Christmas songs (Istomin and Diutsh 1899; Istomin and Liapunov 1899).

These data show what ethnographic studies also tell us: that women were the leaders of both wedding and funeral rituals, and a significant portion of their repertoire was linked to these two events. While ethnographic accounts show that groups of girls were important conductors of spring and summer rituals, when round-dance songs were sung, young men also sang such songs or had their own songs (six out of twenty-one such songs were sung by groups of men, and ten out of twenty-one by mixed groups in the Vologda-Viatka-Kostroma area).

Later, during the Soviet period, collectors began to try to observe folk songs in context, to comment upon the gender of the singers, and in general to apply ethnographic methods to their collection.[35] Scholars identified several folk song genres as primarily or exclusively women's genres: *chastushki* (witty sung limericks) (Pomerantseva and Mints 1959), wedding songs (Eval'd 1928), songs for certain calendar holidays (e.g., Knatts 1928), and lyric songs about defiant wives' and daughters' complaints, such as songs about choosing, tricking, or killing a husband (Rozanov 1940; Rubtsov 1958).

The common perception in all these twentieth-century studies of folk song genres was that women were better preservers than men. Thus, women's limited geographical exposure was considered inconducive to masterful storytelling and epic singing, while it was named as the reason for women's high status as exemplary preservers of folk song. A gendered hierarchy of folklore genres is at work here: precisely the most valued genres of Russian folklore were said to be better preserved by men. Not by coincidence, these are solo, not communal, performance genres in which a single teller can make his mark and express his creativity, just as within prevailing notions of literary authorship. That is, folklorists modeled their understanding of oral literature upon their notions of written literature. That was clear within Herder's discourse, which constantly linked written authorial creation with the oral artistic traditions of the nation. Our understanding of creativity will have to be rewritten if we are to properly understand women's contributions to Russian folklore.

2

Age and Gender Status and Identity

Structure and History

In anthropology the concepts of age and gender are usually used in describing traditional societies in which they serve as defining factors of social hierarchy. In fact, all societies (those with which we are familiar, at any rate) use age and gender as markers of social status; there may be varying degrees of differentiation between groups marked by age and gender (age-gender groups), and age-gender groups may perform various functions and have various responsibilities in society. In this chapter, we first describe the particular system of age- and gender-related statuses in the Russian village of the late nineteenth to early twentieth century, and indicate changes in that system that occurred in the Soviet period. In the second part of the chapter, we describe and examine the ways women of different generations viewed their own functions and responsibilities at various life stages.

In describing these practices, we wish to avoid some of the limitations of earlier approaches. Many scholars, Russian, English, and American, have viewed Russian society through the lens of liberal feminism, and reached the conclusion that the patriarchal structure of the Russian family was detrimental to women's freedom. We wish to avoid such evaluative judgments here: they seem to us one-sided. They postulate women as victims rather than as actors negotiating within a system that imposes its constraints on all members. Along with Pierre Bourdieu, we recognize that all family structures arise due to economic conditions. Not just women, but every individual is constrained when he or she is born into a given social system. While every individual's experience is unique and unrepeatable, it is a variation on that of the group (1990, 60).

Bourdieu theorizes a system of conditioning that he calls habitus. In the introduction we described cultural imperatives: habits of thinking, evaluating, and acting in a certain way. The habitus is an accumulation of such inclinations, and also their realization in life. Habitus exists in each individual as a pattern of perception, thinking, and activities that allows for the active presence of past experience. It guarantees that the behavior of individuals is similar and consistent over time. Habitus is a product of history, and as such, reproduces both individual and collective practices. Consequently, it also renders history according to patterns generated by history (Bourdieu 1990, 53–54).

For Bourdieu, social structure dictates how people act, but not automatically or rigidly: "Through the habitus, the structure of which it is the product governs practice, not along the paths of a mechanical determinism, but within the constraints and limits initially set on its inventions" (Bourdieu 1990, 55). The habitus regulates practice by setting limits upon the information that is available to individuals: "the habitus tends to favor experiences likely to reinforce it" (61). Transmission of the habitus occurs early in life, through various means. For example, one's parents might prescribe a certain program for one's life. On the one hand, this prescription is presented as a cultural imperative that, translated into linguistic terminology, is verbalized in hypothetical (counterfactual) terms. In the intro-duction we called this type of speech a "script." On the other hand, there are also stories about the realization of such programmatic prescriptions, which are situated entirely in the past (which we have called "plots"). Such stories tell not only about the realization of these imperatives, for example, the preservation of tradition, but also give examples of vio-lations and transgressions—which may be offered or received either as cautionary tales ("not for the likes of us"; "here's what happens if one doesn't follow the norm") or as potential counters to tradition ("here is another option"). In this schema, choices for girls, boys, women, and men are limited by what the habitus offers them. Real life, of course, exists in the zone of present action, and implies a certain degree of freedom.

The constraint implied by the habitus may be seen in concentrated form at the junc-tures of life-cycle rituals. Such rituals contain symbolic texts and actions that are aimed at molding and guiding a person's psychological development. For example, in the Russian traditional wedding, a girl laments her marriage publicly, in an improvised yet traditional form. She does this as a matter of course: to lament is to reach the life-stage when one laments. Unlike previous commentators, we do not take the lament as an expression of the bride's sadness at leaving the parental home, and therefore as a confirmation that her position as a married woman is one of victimization.[1] Instead, we view the lament as part of a rite of passage. This rite of passage contains texts—including private, secret texts— that express for the bride a whole range of emotions: sadness and happiness, fear and exu-berance, regret and determination. As we show below and in chapter 3, public laments are varied, and may have the bride perform the duty of honoring her parents as well as show-ing loyalty and subservience to her new family. Showing subservience in the context of a ritual does not necessarily imply feeling or being subservient. In fact, as Humphrey and Laidlaw have argued, rituals are framed discourse in which one temporarily gives up agency in order to perform the ritualized act: "you both are and are not the author of your acts" (1994, 99). In a ritual context, you do have a certain agency in that you may bring a personal interpretation or reaction to the acts (102, 265).

As we interpret the wedding lament, the structure of the wedding itself is designed to allow the bride to feel that she is entering a new social role by symbolically marking (i.e. lamenting) the death of the former identity. In ritual, the neophyte's identity is representatively changed when he or she is passively led and re-clothed, and enters into the new identity symbolically (Adon'eva 1998a, 26–28; 1998b, 63–85; 1999; 2004). Thus, laments and other ritual texts are ways that a bride is brought into her new role. To what degree and in what ways that inculcation is or is not "successful" depends upon each individual situation, and is difficult for researchers to discover. The evidence we possess and use in this chapter is contained in stories and remembrances of texts, which are influenced by all the factors that dictate how memory is constructed as well as by the present conversational situation. Regardless of these caveats, such stories are valuable both to our interlocutors and to us.

The value of stories to the teller is linked to the process of identity construction. In Jungian and post-Jungian psychology, the internal development of an individual is a movement toward self-discovery, which involves experiencing crises (Erikson 1959; Sheehy 1976). An age-related crisis can occur when there is a conflict between the strategies of behavior judged as "legitimate" for one's age group—learned through education, language, everyday life, and everyday practices—and one's internal needs (Maslow 1970). We can see this best in examples where the person's age status changes externally or circumstantially. Society appraises him or her as belonging to a certain age group, but the person's internal feeling suggests he or she has not changed, such as a new mother who wonders why her old, childless friends relate differently to her, or an old woman who dresses "like a teenager" because she still feels young. A person grows out of his habituated behavior as a child grows out of his old clothing. The drama of this situation lies in the fact that it is just as difficult to shed those clothes as it would be to shed one's skin: this age-related crisis is psychologically experienced as a loss of one's identity. Thus, we should understand identity not as a status, but as a process. Rites of passage may aid in this process because they offer ways of learning a new identity. They symbolically remove the trappings of the old identity and show a person that they are no longer who they were.

Telling stories aids in working through age-related crises. A person gains his or her identity through life experience and through discursive thoughts and utterances; however, identity can also be lost, for example, when one must deal with socially imposed roles that do not seem to "fit" anymore. One way of dealing with these crises is to narrate one's experience: in the process of narration, the events acquire a plot, and the narrator acquires his or her identity. We can see this in several of the interviews quoted below: in talking to us, the interlocutors relive their experiences. By assigning names to what they have done, they make firm breaks with an old identity and consciously embrace a new role. This process can continue even in old age, even after having told a story many times.

This, then, is the subject matter of this chapter: the plots that women use to tell about themselves, and the practices of bringing these plots to life. We will try to describe what is strictly individual for every woman, but is also borrowed from common knowledge. Moreover we will try to show that their use of common knowledge—which includes folklore— is a means of creating a unique personal history, which, in turn, either supports tradition or introduces some new relations into it—thus, in the final result, influencing the habitus of the group as a whole.

What we intend to do here involves representing the personal life of the Russian rural woman both diachronically, that is, in historical terms, in relation to tradition and innovation, and synchronically, in relation to social relationships and identity. We begin with a description of the age and gender system of the Russian village before collectivization. In this first section we describe changes to this system that occurred in the Soviet period, during and after collectivization. In the second part of the chapter we focus upon the specific worlds of different Soviet generations. In this chapter (and throughout the book), we rely on data collected between 1983 and 2009 in the northern and central areas of Russia from women born before 1951. Of course, these interviews are comprised of stories remembered from the women's (or their mothers') youth, and represent autobiographical memory, not "facts" per se. However, what we present here is not history, but a subjective view of history gleaned from our interviewees and from our experiences with them. In our own fieldwork we have tried to consider how norms and customs are expressed in discourse (in interviews) as well as how those same social phenomena are expressed in practical life—that is, in interactions between ourselves and our interlocutors in the village. For this reason some of the conclusions we reach below differ from those provided by other researchers. As much as possible, we compared and checked what our interlocutors told us with existing information about Russian rural culture from two other types of sources: (1) data collected by other folklore collectors from the late nineteenth century to the end of the 1920s, and (2) Soviet-era historical data from primary and secondary sources.

Age and Gender Status in the Twentieth-Century Russian Village

In spoken Russian there are words that designate different age classes for men and women. These words not only indicate physical age but also imply an entire set of rules, perceptions, and relations, that is, scripts for behavior. For men these include:

- *paren'* (pl. *parni*): boy, from birth to marriage[2]
- *muzhik* (pl. *muzhiki*): married man, from marriage until he becomes a *khoziain*
- *khoziain, bol'shak, sam* (pl. *khoziaeva, bol'shaki*): master, from the moment he gains the status of master of his home and farm due to the death of the old *khoziain* or allocation of separate households, until he becomes a *starik* or until death

• *starik* (pl. *stariki*): old man, from the time that a *khoziain* is too weak to manage the farm, until death (Adon'eva 2009; Levkievskaia 2001, 106–14).

The normal life of a villager, the fulfillment of his years, was defined by successively occupying these status stages.

 Of course, within these delineations there were other sub-categories. For example, although a boy was referred to as a *paren'* from birth, there were small rituals—such as first haircut, first pair of pants, and so on, that marked various stages within this age category; we do not delineate these here. There are also possible deviations from these age statuses. For example, there was the status called *bobyl'*, an older man living alone, who for some reason did not have a family and children, such as a retired soldier. This status was economically and socially damaging: plots of land were allocated according to the number of men in a family. The absence of land and family indicated a low status for the *bobyl'* among *muzhiki* and *khoziaeva*. Therefore *bobyli* always had some other occupation, such as weaving baskets or nets, owning a small business, or producing handicrafts. A *bobyl'* did not work on the land because it would not be enough to feed him. Knowledge of crafts, but also of fortune-telling, was a source of compensation for *bobyli*.

 In Soviet times the status and term *bobyl'* no longer had economic connotations. It was merely a term used to describe an old man who lived alone:

> There used to be a *kel'ia* [cell, hut] here. An old lonely man, a *bobyl'*, lived here. He did not have a family. I don't know where he, grandfather Vasia, [unclear] came from. We all used to run to him. And he would tell us stories, and talk at length about all kinds of things. He'd gab and gab, and we'd sit with our mouths open. And there he would guard the church. During the winter like this past one, there was a huge road that led to Pokrovskoe. During bad weather, as I remember, he would go up to the bell tower, and would show people where the road was—ring the bells so that one could hear where the wagons should go. Grandfather Vasia lived there while the church remained open. But when the church was closed, he was taken to a home for the handicapped. (Woman born in 1929, Bosovo, Vologda oblast, 25 July 2002 [Vash 17])

Like *bobyl'*, the term *starik* also ceased to have economic meaning during the Soviet period; it referred more to age than to specific household functions. We came to this conclusion because in the ethnographic materials of the twentieth century, we have not found any data showing a *bol'shak* transferring the *bol'shina* (i.e., the role or institution of being in charge of a household) to a younger man. This can be explained by the degeneration of the institution of the male *bol'shina* in the Soviet period, which we will discuss later. Materials from the end of the nineteenth century, however, mention that a *bol'shak* could transfer the *bol'shina* when he became physically unable to perform the functions of the *bol'shak* (Firsov and Kiseleva 1993, 181–82).

Women's age classifications (scripts) were as follows:

- *devka/devushka* (pl. *devki, devushki*): girl, from birth to marriage
- *molodka/moloditsa* (pl. *molodki, moloditsy*): young bride, from marriage to birth of her first child or her first daughter
- *baba* (pl. *baby*): a married woman, but not the mistress of the household
- *bol'shukha, khoziaika, sama* (pl. *bol''shukhi, khoziaiki*): mistress of the household (Adon'eva 1998a)
- *starukha* (pl. *starukhi*): old woman, from physical infirmity till death.

A woman became a *bol'shukha* either when she married into the *bol'shina* (i.e., she married a widow or man whose mother had died and who had no married older brothers, or a man who was already a *bol'shak* for other reasons), or when her mother-in-law died, or when her mother-in-law decided to pass on the *bol'shina* to one of her daughters-in-law because she had become physically unable to continue her duties. At that point the father-in-law remains a *bol'shak*, but the wife of the oldest son becomes the *bol'shukha*.

The word *starukha*, like *starik*, was more frequently used to define age than status. A husband-*bol'shak* could call his wife-*bol'shukha* a *starukha*, without meaning she had relinquished her *bol'shukha* role. But the term could also be used as a status marker: a woman herself, who is deciding to pass the *bol'shina* to a younger woman, could consider herself a *starukha*.

This kind of usage has been a cause of confusion for folklorists and their interviewees:

> *Does your daughter also weave?*
> Yes, she does. I passed everything to my daughter. This year I'll be seventy years old. I've become an old *starukha*.
> *But you look so wonderful!*
> If I'm wonderful it's all because of grandpa [my husband]. We've lived together [happily] forty-five years. (Woman born in 1938, Azapol'e, Arkhangel'sk oblast, 7 July 2008 [Mez 1-122])

The woman used the word *starukha* to explain why she gave "everything" (i.e., the *bol'shina*) to her daughter, but the folklorist thinks that she is lamenting her physical age, and proceeds to pay her a compliment.

The status of the *bol'shukha* is described in detail in the unnumbered card file of the Pskov Oblast Dictionary (*Pskovskii oblastnoi slovar'* 1950–70).[3] The remarks of interviewees, in the form of scripts and plots removed from the context of the interviews in this archive, show that the idea of a female *bol'shina* was common in the Soviet countryside during the second half of the twentieth century:

> "While she is still alive, the *bol'shukha* is the son's mother. But after her the son's wife will care for the home."
>
> "Once the mother-in-law dies, then she [daughter-in-law] will take over the *bol'shina* immediately after."
>
> "During my first year I became a *bol'shukha*, a complete *khoziaika*. My mother-in-law died, and I became a *bol'shukha*."

Being placed in any age status suggests that one is embedded in a particular network of horizontal and vertical relationships with other members of society. Horizontal relation-ships are those between peers; vertical relationships are those among members of different age groups. In one's new status, one is governed by specific rules with regard to material property and specific obligations.

Horizontal Relations: *Parni*

Horizontal relations between people belonging to an age group were relations of both agreement and competition. At stake during competition was "honor." The task of the boys was to gain "male honor," which involved the number of amorous relations he had or appeared to have, the daring attitude he displayed in relating to *devushki*, and the bravery he exhibited in fights (Kholodnaia 2005b, 2005c, 2005d; Adon'eva 2010). *Parni* (plural of *paren'*) would engage in group or individual fistfights for prestige—that is, for "honor" (*chest'*) and "glory" (*slava*). Prestige was defined by bravery and valor in personal behav-ior, as well as group prowess in the fights called *shatiia na shatiiu*, or tribe against tribe. The *ataman* was the leader of his *vataga* (group of *parni* from one village), and he was the undisputed favorite among the *devushki* (girls). Fights were somewhat ritualized in that they were preceded by exchanges of *chastushki* (short ditties) among *parni* groups. Fights functioned and still function as a regular element of male behavior during calendar holiday celebrations in villages:

> Поиграй повеселяе
> Хулиганского еще,
> Мой товарищ хулиганского
> Играет хорошо.
>
> Ты, товарищ, не ударишь,
> А ударишь—не убьешь,
> Если я тебя ударю,
> Через пять минут помрешь.

[Play the songs, the hooligans'
Chastushki one more time!
I've got a friend who plays the hooligans'
Chastushki really fine.

You, my friend, won't even hit me,
But if you do, you sure won't kill me,
But if I hit you just one time,
You'll be dead in five minute's time.]

(Woman born in 1933, Nikol'skaia, Vashkinskii region, Vologda oblast, 8 July 2000
[Vash 8-1])

Parni fought together against groups from other villages and also competed among themselves for status. The status of the *paren'* is defined not only by his behavior but also by specific property relations. Any earnings, though rare since *parni* generally worked for the family, would be invested only into his *sprava*. A *sprava* included clothes (hat, boots, etc.), means of traveling (horse, bicycle), weapons, and objects for personal use, such as pocket watches and so on. These objects constituted the symbolic capital of the *paren'*. Any decision about the *sprava*—acquiring a new object or trading something no longer needed—could be made only by the father-*bol'shak*. The father who "kept" his sons "well" was the one whom fellow villagers respected.

Thus, the main behavioral features of a *paren'* were audacity, risk, the transformation of obtained resources into symbolic capital, and numerous love encounters. What is also important is the lack of personal responsibility in everything apart from one's own body, which could be injured in fights. Village society and the authorities considered the *bol'shak* responsible for his *parni*. The groups that judged the *paren'* were his own *vataga* (group of *parni*) and the *devki*. But the *muzhiki* (men) of the village also judged him in the arena of labor: from an early age *parni* participated in general male labor, such as haymaking, care of horses (including pasturing), and fishing. The older men's opinion was for them exceptionally important.

Horizontal Relations: *Devushki*

Like *parni*, *devushki* were also evaluated in terms of honor (*chest'*) and glory (*slava*) (or reputation). The creation of a reputation was a social task that both boys and girls needed to perform during their adolescence and young adulthood, since "glory" was that which they would take with them from this age status to the next one, the status of an adult. The task of the girls was to preserve their honor before marriage. For a girl, honor was synonymous with virginity, but was also judged by the community based upon her behavior. If a girl was seen meeting secretly with a boy, or associating with married men, she was harshly judged by the community. As one woman born in 1953 told us she had been taught by her mother, this reputation was impossible to "wash off," and remained with a woman for life (Tsenogora, Leshukhonsk region, Arkhangel'sk oblast, 13 July 2010 [DAu10-108_Arch-Lesh]). Stories of the fates of such girls were told to us by many rural elder women: they were called "ruined girls," were excluded from community activities, were harshly punished and even beaten or killed by their fathers, might not marry, and might be forced to leave the community. Whether they managed to marry or not, they were said to be subject to humiliating maltreatment (name-calling, rape) by husbands and other men: women told us that no one would protect them, because of their reputation. Such stories provided an important socialization function for girls, who learned to control their behavior due to fear of the far-reaching consequences (Borisova 2011). Girls were expected to socialize in groups with boys of their own age at evening work-parties in homes in the winter (called *besedy* or *posidelki*), and outdoors in the summer (*gulianiia*). In these socially accepted ("public") contexts girls and boys could develop special friendships, and it was considered appropriate for girls and boys to express physical affection or, in some villages, to sleep next to each other after a party with a group of peers (Shangina 2005, 181).

The *slava* (glory) of a girl was based upon how well-off the family was, as well as her intelligence and healthy body. Potential suitors and their families also wanted to see her ability to work, sing, dance, and behave with dignity in social situations. The older standard of social behavior for girls required them to speak moderately, to show respect to elders, to wait to be chosen at dances, and so on. A newer desirable characteristic of girls for some families was the girls' readiness to answer quickly and wittily to any comment or *chastushka* (sung limerick), or, as observed in the Russian North in the late 1920s, to walk together with a friend without being first asked by a boy during spring outdoor festivals (Knatts 1928, 198). Such girls were called *boikie* (self-assured, lively), *khodovye* ("walking, going"), or *boevye* ("fighting") (Mamaeva 2010; see also chapters 3 and 4). These newer standards of behavior were not accepted universally and all at once, but gradually, and at varying times in different geographical locations throughout Russia. However, for all generations, for girls to not participate in social gatherings was judged negatively. Girls were expected to show off not only themselves as potential marriage partners but also their family's honor and reputation.

The honor and glory of the *rod* (clan, family) were to a large extent reflected in a girl's behavior and dress. At her birth, a girl's mother and grandmother gave her a suitcase or trunk with fabric or clothing and decorations they had woven or prepared. The girl herself added to this collection throughout her childhood: starting at about age eight, she would weave belts, embroider, and sew (Balashov and Marchenko 1985; Kolpakova 1928). When she was ready for the initiation to the "big *beseda*"—the young people's parties for which older girls "rented" a local house (in exchange for food or fuel)—she would begin to wear a special headdress, which showed she was entering the courtship period. This headdress, which was either prepared for her or was passed down from one of her elder relatives, was called a *poviazka* (from *viazat'*, to tie), *kokoshnik* (from *kokosh'*, hen), *krasota* (beauty), or "flowers." The big round-dances that took place outdoors in summer were a kind of marketplace where the *rod* could gain prestige and symbolic capital through the behavior and dress of their "bride." The family invested significantly in her dress: for example, during the three days of a parish holiday, the girls in the Pinega region of Arkhangel'sk oblast would change their outfits two times each day. The elder women would stand at the side and evaluate who was best dressed and sang the best (Bernshtam 1992; Morozov and Sleptsova 2004, 353; Kalashnikova 1999, 36; Knatts 1928, 190).

Thus, unlike a boy's, a girl's reputation depended to a large extent upon the efforts of the elder female members of her *rod*. However, especially in the generations born during and after the late 1920s, a girl could create her own reputation by being witty, lively, and brave. Throughout the generations discussed in this book (born in 1899–1950), however, a girl's honor was valued: that was the expected script for girls' behavior. A girl guarded her own honor, but in the final analysis her parents answered for her honor. This can be seen clearly in an example from nineteenth-century materials (cited by Dmitrii Zelenin) that we also heard about from elder women during our fieldwork in 2009–10. In a tradition in Arkhangel'sk oblast, if a young husband let the guests know that the bride was not a virgin (which he did symbolically), her parents were publicly shamed by having a horse's yoke put on them (Zelenin 1991, 337). In other villages the family of the groom would serve "white" liquor (vodka) to the parents of the bride if she was not a virgin, and "red" (wine) if she was (Morozov et al. 1997, 337).

Vertical Relations: Obedience before and after Marriage

In general, young people who were not yet married obeyed not only their parents but also those of their parents' age. This form of vertical relationship was preserved in the forms of address that young people used for members of the village: they addressed older men and women of higher status as *diadia* (uncle) and *tetia* (aunt). The vertical relations changed when a *paren'* and *devushka* got married. Having become a young wife, a bride (*molodka*) ceased to be socially subordinate to her own parents. Instead, she obeyed her husband's family: her husband and her new in-laws. Thus, the connection between parents and married daughters became horizontal. Mutual help, advice, visits, and celebratory hostings were offered on both sides, but not obedience. After she entered marriage, a woman submitted to her new family, and in turn, her husband and his parents took on the responsibility for the well-being of their wife and daughter-in-law.

Male obedience was structured differently. Prior to marriage, *parni* maintained obedience to their own mother-*bol'shukha* and to other *bol'shukhi*, whom they addressed as *tetki* (aunties). A man ceased to obey this class of mothers after he got married. This change took a ritual form during a part of the Russian marriage rite, the "bride's trial," on the second day of the wedding. The ritual is connected to the act of showing the signs of a girl's virginity, but it can also include an assessment of her domestic abilities. The ritual verification of the woman's domestic abilities and her introduction to her new domestic obligations were completed on the first morning that her husband spent at home, on the second day of the wedding. The *bol'shukha* and the household *baby* threw trash, such as old things, hay, sand, or money, onto the floor; the mother-in-law then presented a broom to the bride, and she had to sweep it up. If the new wife did not sweep the floor clean, they would say to her: "The bride can't even sweep, she sweeps and it's still dirty" (Adon'eva and Bazhkova 1998, 204–12). The stories that we recorded in the Belozersk area villages (in Vologda oblast) about these trials were accompanied by mournful accounts by storytellers about how psychologically difficult it was. A trial could go on for as long as it was necessary, and friends of the mother-in-law would gather to watch, such that the young woman would be surrounded by older, strange (if she was from a different village) women, relatives of the husband, and neighbors. She had no right to resist what was going on. Only her young husband could end the trial. As for discussing the question of virginity, it was he who decided what information to bring out to the public. For example, in Arkhangel'sk oblast villages, the morning after the first night of marriage, a fried egg was served to the young husband. If he began to eat it from the edge, then it meant that his wife was "pure." But if he ate the egg from the middle, it meant that she had lost her virginity prior to marriage.

Thus the second day of the wedding was also a day of trial for the young husband: it was the first time in his life that he could publicly rebuff his own mother and women of her age (*tetki*), by defending his wife against them. He could also refuse to rebuff his mother, and instead give his wife over to them, so that they could take matters into their own hands. But in doing this, he would be showing that he had not succeeded in completing the initiation of becoming a man.

> *People told us that on the second day the groom was asked: "Did you break the ice, or did you trample dirt* [led lomal, ili griaz' toptal]*?"*
>
> Aha! Yes, they would ask, but after all the groom didn't want to laugh at his own wife.
>
> *And what does that mean? That is, did you break the ice or trample dirt?*
>
> "Trampled dirt" meant that she was not "honest" [*chestnaia*, a virgin], but "broke ice" meant that she was.
>
> *And what was his response?*
>
> What'd he say? He'd say, "It's none of your business, none of your business. I got married, and I'll live." That's all.
>
> *And what if she was a virgin?*

I don't know what he'd say if she was. He wouldn't disgrace her in any case. He got married, so he'll go on living. (Woman born in 1928, Mar'inskaia, Siamzha region, Vologda oblast, 22 July 2005 [Siam 1-117])

A mother's power over her son ended when he married, but the sons had to remain obedient to their father, the *bol'shak*, until he transferred the *bol'shina* to one of them, or the extended family home was partitioned and a son or sons received (or built) their own home.

A word is in order here about obedience in the culture of Russian peasants in the late nineteenth to early twentieth centuries. Occasionally it has been claimed by culturologists that Russian peasants, as a group, were passive, even masochistic (e.g., Rancour-Laferriere 1995). We see it somewhat differently. We agree with Boris Mironov, who argues that this was a society characterized by a highly interactive style, in which socialization of children occurred through informal means, within the family: oral tradition and observation of living examples and rituals were the most important ways that young people learned what was expected of them. Due to this kind of socialization, the high illiteracy rate, and the influence of the village commune (*obshchina*), young people were dependent upon their parents and tended to be oriented toward tradition. Within the community, informal social control of a negative sort included gossip, remarks made to the person's face, sarcastic nicknames, or disdainful treatment. Very serious breaches of common morality could lead to exclusion from the commune or even physical punishment resulting in death. In general it was impossible for a peasant to survive if he found himself in conflict with the commune (Mironov 1985, 444–50). The high level of mutual interdependence of individuals and families required for survival meant that incentives and opportunities for radical opposition to tradition were few.

The social task of a young married man was to contest with other *muzhiki* for recognition in order eventually to be accepted into the *skhod*. A *skhod* was the collective governing organ of the village, consisting of *bol'shaki*. It is important to understand the nature of the psychological relationships inside this group. Having reached the age status of *bol'shaki*, the men who had grown up together as *parni* of the same *vataga* remained as *parni* to one another. They were united by a common past full of festivities, fights, and army conscription. They learned responsibility and decision-making from the elder men, their fathers. In men's company, in places or situations associated with men—fishing, working in artels, doing construction, bathing in the *bania* (bathhouse), and engaging in festivities that involved the production and consumption of beer—the young men obtained experience that would be essential when they became household leaders and members of the *skhod*. Fathers devoted much time to raising sons: they took them on fishing and hunting trips for many days at a time, where apart from obtaining specific skills, young men also learned much from listening to the conversations of the older men.

Collectivization and the Decline of Age-Group Socialization for Men

Before the Soviet period, the household heads (*bol'shaki*) were responsible for every-thing—the behavior of members of the family as well as their material well-being—in the eyes of government authorities and the *obshchina* (peasant commune). The *bol'shak* was considered to be the hereditary owner of the house, garden plot, and household goods (the fields were owned in common by all members of the village commune) (Atkinson 1983, 3). The household—the home, the yard, land, weapons, animals, transportation, machinery—and also "personnel"—the family, close relatives, and sometimes hired work-ers—prospered and subsisted because of the *bol'shak*'s skillful management.

Relations between men of different generations changed considerably with the arrival of Soviet power. The Soviet authorities dismantled the male age hierarchy. The "strong" *bol'shaki*, who were experienced and successful landowners (or as they were called by the Soviets, *kulaki* and *seredniaki*), were to be liquidated as a class (Danilov et al. 1999). The state defined kulaks not so much by economics but by culture: in effect, the state "kulakized" the countryside by identifying anyone who resisted collectivization (and the peasants did evince a strong degree of unity in their resistance) as counterrevolutionary and a kulak (Viola 1996, 24). Those defined by the local powers as kulaks were shamed and evicted from their homes, sometimes taken away in the dead of night, often left without any property at all, and sent to remote regions of the country. More than a mil-lion families (around five to six million people) were dekulakized; the heads of household were often executed or imprisoned, while their families were exiled. The Party sought to blame counterrevolutionary attitudes on male peasants in particular, while women who resisted collectivization were pronounced by those in power as victims of the kulak (Viola 1996, 27–33).

As a result of this transformation of the countryside, by the beginning of the 1930s the institution of the *obshchina/skhod* was completely destroyed. As the managing organiza-tion of the agricultural commune, the *skhod* (and in the 1920s the commune), which used to consist of male heads of household, was replaced by the kolkhoz system of manage-ment, which controlled collectivized farms, and by an agricultural committee, or *sel'skii sovet*, which had territorial jurisdiction over villages (see Chernenko 1967, Golembo et al. 1949; Pesikin et al. 1982, Ivnitskii 1972; Korzhikhina 1986; Viola 1996, 40). Before col-lectivization, the people in charge in villages (the members of the *sel'sovety*) were often non-Party members (Viola 1987, 224). The cadres who carried out collectivization, however, were militant party members and Civil War veterans; their crude, heavy-handed, top-down style of leadership during the years of collectivization had a profound effect on the culture of the village in the years to come (Viola 1987, 78, 128, 217). The experience of these new leaders during the Civil War and in their training as Communists had shaped their mentality and methods. In their collectivization work, they utilized the mandatory assistance of village leaders, those designated as poor peasants, landless laborers, and others

(Viola 2005, 231). However, in many cases the peasants resisted collectivization through direct attacks on local authorities (including murder and arson), and indirectly through riots, getting rid of their property, fleeing the village, and butchering farm animals and consuming, selling, or preserving the meat.

Although statistics do not exist on the household composition of the village officials of the late 1920s and early 1930s, anecdotal evidence from our informants tells us that those who carried out collectivization were not successful *bol'shaki* and had not fulfilled the usual life sequence of male peasants. Rather than devoting themselves to farming and household management, as *parni* they had left for the Civil War or to work in the city; rather than having the interests of their own multi-generational households at heart, they fulfilled the interests of the Soviet power.[4]

As many of our informants saw it, the revolution in the Russian countryside was a conflict between male generations, and there is some evidence that this was in fact the case. Setting young against old was a priority of the regime, as can be seen in the different treatment of heads of household and families: while *bol'shaki* were shot or put in prison, families were exiled and could later return. Families of young men who were Civil War soldiers or worked in industry were supposed to be left untouched. There were cases of kulak sons who were not exiled due to their involvement in factory or Party activism; sometimes such young men advocated for the "rehabilitation" of their fathers (Hindus 1988, 255–56; Viola 1996, 82, 87). Other young people were the agents of collectivization, and worked against their families. Thus, for example, in 1930 a letter from a Red Army soldier named Voronov received wide attention (*Krasnyi voin* [*Red Warrior*], 13 February and 14 May 1930). In answer to his father's announcement that "they are taking away the last grain, not reckoning with a Red Army family," Voronov wrote: "Although you're my father [*bat'ka*], I didn't believe a word of your kulak songs. I am glad that I gave you a good lesson. Sell the grain and take the *izlishki* [extra] to town—that is my final word" (Churkin 2006). *Izlishki* was the part of the grain that the peasants were responsible to give to the Soviet government; from the point of view of the peasants, this amounted to a forced tax. In dealing with his father, the son takes the point of view of the city and the Soviet government.

In general there was conflict between generations: the young were more likely to embrace the new order, while their elders were less likely to do so. It was the Communist Youth League (Komsomol)—composed of young people from seventeen to twenty-one years old—who engaged in heavy-handed antireligious propaganda campaigns aimed at profoundly changing the culture of the village (Viola 1996, 50). These youth groups often made decisions about dekulakization and the conversion of churches to secular uses (such as clubs). For example, "During the process of dekulakization, the Borisogleb Komsomols liquidated several households that hired day laborers because the daughters of the householders [*khoziaeva*] married kulak sons" (Lindner and Nikulin 2004, 83–89). That is, Komsomol members decided which of the "householders" (i.e., *khoziaeva*, *bol'shaki*) to destroy. In another case women rioted when the Komsomol decided to transform the local church into a school (Viola 1996, 196). In one case the home of a Komsomol member was set afire by "kulak types" after he had denounced them. Before they set fire to his house, the men went around complaining that some *mal'chishka* (young boy) had taken over the reins of the village and was disenfranchising the successful peasant (Viola 1996, 123)

Many parents disapproved of the ways that the Komsomol taught their children to be independent and to flout authority. Some blamed a rise in "hooliganism" (troublemaking) on the Communists. In general observers of village culture noted a decline in morality—measured by a rise in promiscuity, venereal disease, prostitution, and hooliganism among the youth in the village in this era (Viola 1996, 51).

Collectivization eliminated the peasant family household as society's main unit of production, although the household remained a strong source of identity for villagers (Viola 1987, 178). Together with this, collectivization also destroyed the system of rites of passage, which allowed for boys to gradually assume greater and greater responsibility during their lifetime—including the army farewell celebration, wedding, acceptance into a male artel (such as fishing work-groups), trips with the father to the market to sell goods or animals, entry into the *skhod*, and acquisition of the *bol'shina*. In particular, the destruction of the artel and of local mills and markets that were intrinsic to male peasant culture had profound effects upon village culture, as villagers now had to receive many goods and services from the center, making them more dependent upon the state (Viola 1996, 41).

As a result of these changes, we argue, age-group socialization for men born in Soviet times continued only through the stage of *muzhik*. The rites of passage that still remained for men included the *vataga*, army/war, and marriage. It was these models of behavior belonging to the *paren'* that were effectively passed on by Soviet generations, with the result that many grown males exhibit strong value orientations toward collectivism, responsibility toward one's group, risk, and aggression (see Il'in 2010; Kon 2002; Morozov 2001, 2004, 2007). In the Soviet period, social institutions for age socialization failed at the stage of acquiring the *bol'shina*: men went to the front and perished in war, they went to help develop industry or build the infrastructure of the growing USSR, they helped to develop "virgin lands" on USSR territory, served in the military, they did time in labor camps and prisons, and so forth. The evaluator of a man's worth shifted from the elder men of the village community to the central Soviet power and its representatives. The only means by which men could move upward socially was to climb the party ladder, from the Pioneers to the Komsomol and the Party. The structure of these relationships took the form of "male societies"—similar to *vatagi*, where the value of the collective superseded the value of one's own family.

In any case, in the new USSR property (measured as livestock and other farming necessities), household farms, and personal accountability for them no longer existed. There was only the "unlimited" property of the government, different levels of access to it, and various levels of accountability for this common property, now called "people's assets" (*narodnoe dobro*).

The failure of the male institutions for age socialization was particularly apparent in the postwar generations. The crisis of middle age in rural traditional culture had formerly been resolved by the change in social status: a man became a *bol'shak*. Tradition compensated for the behavioral limitations that accompanied each of the age stages with a corresponding increase in status: even while forfeiting a piece of one's freedom (due to increasing responsibility), a person could make gains in power and authority. The social institutions that supported men's transition from one age status to another were for the most part destroyed by the end of the twentieth century in rural Russia.

The Traditional Socialization of Girls and Women

The traditional system of age roles for women changed in the Soviet period, but it developed in a different manner from that among men. In this section we first describe the organization of women's age and gender status prior to the 1930s, and subsequently look at the changes in the Soviet period.

Women's age and gender status was marked by external indicators—clothes, hairstyle. From ages five to six, children of both sexes were dressed identically in "long" shirts. After the age of five, girls wore dresses, and boys wore trousers. The first "holiday" attire for a girl was made when she was turning fifteen, and at that time she also received her own first real pair of shoes. These clothes would be worn for the first visit to church; subsequently, they were worn on holidays. Married women and *devki* covered their heads with shawls for everyday attire, but if they wore festive head decorations like ribbons, headdresses, and other ornaments as part of their holiday dress, the crowns of their heads could be left uncovered. Prior to marriage girls wore their hair in a single braid, whereas married women wore their hair in a bun or a haircomb. Unmarried women continued to wear their hair in a single braid. These *starye devy* (old maids) were called *sivokosye* (blue braids) (Adon'eva and Bazhkova 1998, 208).

Girls received training in women's work from an early age. From the age of seven they could work as nannies to care for young children. Between the ages of ten and twelve, girls went to work in the fields with their parents: they cut grass, raked, and stacked hay. At this age they learned to cook, but the *bol'shukha* did the main cooking and made the fire in the oven. Girls were only allowed to help her, not take over the task themselves. They were taught to spin from ages five to seven. At first they were given poorer quality fibers, fit for a rougher yarn. Later they were given flax, and finally, from ages ten to fifteen, they spun the finest flax fibers, yielding a finer yarn or thread. The elder women of the house, the mother and grandmother, taught them to spin. Starting at age thirteen to fifteen their mother taught them to weave (*snovat'*). Often their weaving skills took on an independent character only after they moved into their husband's home. There the loom was under the watchful eye of the mother-in-law who could re-teach the bride how to weave.

In Vologda oblast we were told about the rite of the "the first thread." When a girl was taught how to spin, the first ball spun from the roughest linen fibers was thrown into the oven—this was generally done by the grandmother. The girl had to sit on the snow with a "bare behind" until the ball burned completely. The thinner and better the thread, the faster it burned, and the less time she had to sit. They either repeated this ritual until the girl learned to spin, or completed it once, after which it was considered that the girl could spin.

When the time came to get married, as a rule a girl could already embroider, weave, cook, and perform other domestic chores. However, at her husband's home after the wedding, her responsibilities were limited and dictated by her mother-in-law. This subordination of the daughter-in-law was acted out in the ritual described above, in which the new bride had to sweep up something after arriving in the groom's home after the wedding. Other aspects of the wedding ritual could also teach the bride to be ready to fulfill the demands of the mother-in-law. In one ritual described to us in the Belozersk region of Vologda oblast, the bride was "taught" a lament by her older female relatives during the ritual of engagement, when the groom's family comes for the bride's family's public agreement. The elder woman or women would start the line, while the bride would follow with her lamenting voice, singing "alongside" the other(s). This lament, sung by a woman born in 1907, described the behavior required of the bride and helped to emotionally prepare for her new, subservient role:

Как лихая-то свекровушка,
По утру да станет тихонько,
По утру станет ранехонько
Она ходит да всё настукивает
Как говорит, да вся нарыкивает:
Ты вставай-ка, сноха заспяшша,
Ты вставай-ка, да задремяшша!
Дак во чистом-то польице,
Во широком во раздольице,
Во лугах ли да пастухи пасут,
Во лугах ли да косцы косцят,
На горушках да пахари пашут.
Уж и я-то, да сиротиночка,
Я раным, да встала ранешенько,
Я умылась да небелёшенько,
Как уже я вышла-то в чисто польюшко,

Посмотрела, да сиротиночка,
Во все четыре да сторонушки:
Во полях ли да пастухов нет,
Во лугах ли да косцов нет,
На горушках пахарей нет.

[How that bold mother-in-law
Gets up quietly in the morning,
Gets up very early,
She moves about and bangs about
As she speaks, she roars:
"Get up now, my oversleeping daughter-in-law,
Get up now, oversleepy one!
Out in the clear field,
In the broad one, the valley,
In the meadows shepherds tend to their flocks,
In the meadows the grass-cutters cut the grass,
In the hills men plow the fields."
And I, a little orphan,
I got up, yes got up early,
I washed up, and brightened my face,
And as I walked out on the clear field,
I, an orphan, looked,
In all four directions:
In the fields no one is tending to the flock,
And in the meadows no one is cutting the grass,
And on the hills no one is plowing.

(Zakhar'ino, Kirillovskii region, Vologda oblast, July 1993 [Kir 2-13]).

This lament, which the bride would sing to her mother, symbolically describes what the bride's experience will be like in the new household: at home, with her parents, she was allowed to sleep in, and this was a symbol of her status as a beloved one; by contrast, in this song, in the home of the mother-in-law, she is awakened so early that no other people are to be seen yet in the fields. Furthermore, the mother-in-law tricks her by telling her that it is late and she has overslept. The song emotionally prepares the bride for feelings of loneliness and betrayal that she may experience in future; it also tells her mother that the bride will miss her. Other, magical tactics were also used to influence the new relations. Daughters and granddaughters were taught the following private text, which helped them gain a sense of emotional control:

There used to be a fashion: when you'd drive away from the ceremony, you
shouldn't converse with your groom—if you spoke first, he'd be in charge. My
grandmother taught me this. She goes up to the threshold [i.e., the bride after the
ceremony goes up to the threshold of the groom's home], and says [to herself]:
"I step on the threshold, and step over my father-in-law, I walk over another
threshold—my father- and mother-in-law. Three thresholds, and on the final
one—"my brother- and sister-in-law, I step over everyone." (Woman born in
1903, Savino, Belozersk region, Vologda oblast, July 1996 [Bel 2-43])

This text uses the language of incantations to make manifest that which the bride
desires. It shows that the combination of desire, actions, and words can influence the
spiritual world when pronounced at this liminal time and place: the bride's first step over
the threshold of the groom's house after the wedding ceremony. By pronouncing that she
"steps over" various family members, the bride claims power over them.

Another ritual at this liminal moment invoked the spiritual world to accomplish the
acceptance of the bride into the family of the groom. In the same Belozersk region of Vologda
oblast, in the morning of the second day of the wedding, the mother-in-law would take her
daughter-in-law to the yard to "overfeed" the animals: the mother-in-law would throw her
own shawl over the shoulders of the daughter-in-law in order to disguise her for the cattle
(since cattle are believed not to accept strangers), and the two women would both go out to
the yard. Her daughter-in-law had to have prepared a gift in advance, which she had baked
in the home of her own parents. Usually this would be a *kolob* (a bun made out of unleavened
dough). In the presence of the mother-in-law, the bride would break the *kolob* into pieces,
and feed it to all the animals. With this ritual the bride and her origins were symbolically
accepted by the animals as a new member of the household (Adon'eva 1998a, 231–49).

While the mother-in-law headed the *bol'shina*, she did all the boiling, baking, and cooking, and looked after the small children. The *molodka* went to work in the field and washed
linen and clothing—as the proverb states: "a mother-in-law at the table, a bride in the yard."
When the mother-in-law was in the house, "don't touch a thing, just work" (woman born in
1936, Azapol'e, Mezen' region, Arkhangel'sk oblast, 8 July 2010 [Mez 1-123]). She directed
all the housework; as long as she was able, she did not let anyone else light the stove or cook,
but when she could no longer cook and heat the oven, she herself relinquished her duties,
and the *molodka* or *baba* then took her place. When the *bol'shukha* no longer possessed the
strength to perform the household work, the *bol'shina* was passed on. In Vologda oblast,
this custom was usually done on *Pokrov* (the festival of the Protection of the Mother of
God) on the fourteenth of October—the day when winter traditionally began and the *izba*
(hut or cottage) was heated for the first time. The mother-in-law and her daughter-in-
law baked a *rybnik* (a pie containing a whole fish; *rybnik* was an important component of
wedding and memorial feasts). Older and younger woman kneaded the dough together,

with four hands, by which action the mother-in-law gave her daughter-in-law the right to cook the food. The bride then became a *bol'shukha*, and the mother-in-law "will just sit down when the food is served" rather than serving (Adon'eva and Bazhkova 1998, 207–8).

A significant sphere of women's traditional knowledge and duties was transferred only when a woman attained a specific age status. After women gave birth to children, they could participate in burial ceremonies, lament at funerals, and become involved in ritual activities related to commemorating parents. As a rule, *znakharki* (healers), lamenters, and matchmakers were older women, that is, either *bol'shukhi* or *starukhi*.

Women who did not fit into the regular categories of age status found other roles for themselves, and did possess some of this knowledge. A woman who did not marry was known as a *staraia deva*; as one woman told us, if they had not married by age twenty-five to thirty or so, women rarely succeeded in finding husbands (woman born in 1928, Siamzha region, Vologda oblast, 27 August 2006 [Siam 1-6]). Such women were less likely than other women to take on roles related to childbirth, although they did often care for children. Nevertheless, the following interview shows that there were exceptions to this general rule. In it, a woman born in 1938 tells us about her much older sister-in-law, born in 1914, who had never married but was "like a mother" to her; the sister-in-law helped her give birth and care for the children: she knew how to wash children in the oven—in this area of Russia, the ovens were built large for washing.

> *Why did it happen [that she didn't marry]?*
> Because of the war, she had to care for her younger brother and sister . . .
> *They didn't have parents?*
> Their father died early of a heart attack, and their mother lost both her legs, so she [the elder daughter] . . . didn't marry. She didn't marry a widower, her father didn't let her, he said, don't marry a widower. . . .
> *Why couldn't she marry a widower?*
> He came from a different village . . . He came to live with a widow here, he had a son, and apparently their father didn't like him, . . . he said you'd do better to go out and lie on the road, than to marry a widower. (Zakharovskaia, Siamzha region, Vologda oblast, 13 August 2006 [Siam D-Txt 1-62])

The story of any *staraia deva* is a story of compromise: in this case, although the unwritten rule allowed only mothers to learn the magical skills needed to care for children, this woman probably learned such skills early in life, as her mother was disabled and could not do many of the tasks needed to care for her younger children.

In general, knowledge of magic was passed on according to changes in age status. As a rule, *devushki* were not informed about magical activities. A married woman who had not given birth to children—a *molodka*—would have been taught how to care for a child, but would not have access to healing magic or knowledge relating to birth. Only *bol'shukhi* and *starukhi* knew the whole repertoire of healing magic (see chapter 7). Usually only those who had already had their own children and were post-menopausal could play the role of *povitukha*—midwife. The *povitukha* needed to be an experienced woman and one whose reproductivity was no longer an issue, since her ceremonial task during birthing was essentially to receive the soul from the world of the dead and arrange its proper reception in the world of the living. Because of this, the birth was covered with a shroud of secrecy: for six weeks after the birth, the *povitukha* would live with the new mother or, at any rate, would take on the responsibility for her care and the care of the infant. Only she could visit them until the end of the six weeks.

The following interview with a woman born in 1924 shows quite clearly the hierarchy of women's age statuses as it relates to childbirth and motherhood.

I myself gave birth alone. If I tell you you're going to laugh about the way that I gave birth. I gave birth to my oldest one in the cattle shed. You know, the place where you'll find cattle, in the cattle shed, you know. The floor was covered over [with cloth or hay], everything was clean . . . I came home, we ate supper, and I climbed onto the oven [to sleep]. And suddenly my belly felt like it was being torn. I hopped off the oven, grabbed the sheet, and went to the shed. I think: "Should I do it 'in the wind' [outside]?" I don't know—it was my first, so—!

I got to the shed, spread out the sheet, and got on my knees, and gave birth. My little girl was singing [crying softly]. But my *muzhik* [husband] wasn't sleeping; [before the birth,] I [had] said to him: "Don't go to sleep, I don't know what might happen to me." I assumed that my time had come [to give birth]. [Afterward,] he led me to the hut, and I put the baby in the hem of my chemise, folded the chemise over her, and we went over there, up the stairs, and entered the hut [the umbilical cord was still attached]. "What should we do?—he said—we don't understand anything." The *babka* was asleep there, my mother-in-law, she was still young, she was only fifty-two years old. I said: "Go get grandma." She lived nearby, she was pretty old. I said: "She helps with birthing, so run over there." He ran over quickly, and beat on her window. "I'm coming, I'm coming!" She came, and cut the umbilical cord, and did everything how it's supposed to be done. She gave me a piece of bread to eat, sliced off a chunk of bread—they used to bake big round loaves—she cut off a chunk, salted it, and said: "Eat up. Bite it three times." I bit it three times, chewed it, and the placenta came right out.

She knew, she knew a lot. It was obvious that she had gone over to the oven, and probably smoothed things out [cast a spell]. I ate this bread, and I had no pain, nothing at all, as if I hadn't even given birth. The baby was three [kilos] 800 [grams] [eight pounds, four ounces].

Did she wash the baby right away?

No, she wrapped her up . . . and said: "We need to heat up some water." Back then there was no gas, nothing at all, so she said, "This evening we'll wash the baby, but not right now." She said, "Let her keep warm on the oven."[5] And that's all. The *babka*—my mother-in-law—got up, heated up the oven, placed a few logs in, and warmed [the baby] up a bit. When she [the grandmother] came from lunch, she herself climbed onto the oven and washed him. After all, back then, we washed up in the oven.

Everyone washed up in the oven, because there was no *bania*. It used to be you'd steam up there using birch branches, and all illnesses went away, people never got sick.

When they built a new oven, they built them according to the saying: "Build it high enough so that your head can't reach it." When you sat in the oven, your head shouldn't touch the top, that's how tall the ovens were.

That's how I gave birth. (Pirogovo, Siamzha region, Vologda oblast, 9 July 2005)

From this story it is clear that the mother-in-law does not volunteer to assist in birthing because she is "young," fifty-two years old. Instead, they summon a woman who is older and more knowledgeable. As a rule, *starukhi* who could assist in birthing (*povitukhi*) were well known in the village. One woman explained: "Usually it's an old woman; young women don't know how to do it. They didn't pass the knowledge to the young ones. Only when a woman has grown old and is approaching death will she pass on the knowledge to her daughter or daughter-in-law. They didn't pass it to those outside the family, only along the family line." A woman who assisted in birthing would also cast a spell on the child to prevent hernia. "They would say an incantation against hernia over the child in the bathhouse. The mother would hold him, and the grandmother would cast the spell" (woman born in 1926, Nadkovo, Belozersk region, Vologda oblast, 19 July 1994 [Bel 10-10]; Adon'eva and Bazhkova 1998, 209).

Elder women (*starukhi*) played other important roles in the village. The young people of a village would gather at *besedy* at the home of a woman who lived alone, such as a widow or single old woman. They would rent out her hut for Yuletide, paying her in firewood and food. One of the activities during this season was fortune-telling. The old woman played an important role: she blessed the bowl that was used in divinations, and conducted the divination. Young people placed their rings in a bowl covered with a cloth; as everyone sang a fortune-telling song that recounted a series of different fates (marriage to different kinds of husbands, wealth or poverty, etc.), the old woman would shake the bowl and pull out one ring at a time (while not looking); it was believed that the owner of the ring would receive the fate that was being sung while her ring was pulled out. Here the old woman performed the role of a mediator between the other world and this world; she could play this role precisely because her age meant closeness to the other world (Madlevskaia n.d.) and probably also because of her presumed lack of need for a fortune related to reproduction or wealth. Thus, *starukhi* made sure customs and rituals were observed; they facilitated and organized the activities of the younger generation, and in this way passed on tradition. Frequently our female interlocutors in the village referenced their own grandmothers ("I heard this from grandma"), or village *starukhi* who knew "how it should be."

An important role played by *starukhi* both in the past and present is conducting funeral rituals. To them falls the responsibility of taking care of the physical remains, since according to widely held belief, anyone who may still bear children should not touch a dead body. Like *starukhi*, *bol'shukhi* also memorialize the dead, but they do not become actively involved in conducting memorial or funeral rituals until they have experienced a significant loss (see chapter 9).

In some areas, the change in status from *bol'shukha* to *starukha* was marked by visible signs: women sewed for themselves a special headdress: a hat from fine fabric that covered the entirety of the head, worn under a scarf. In general the traditional costume of elder women was darker in color and had less ornamentation than the costume of younger women (Prokop'eva 2005, 636).

In village culture the relationships among the *bol'shukhi* were substantially different from the relationships among men. They were those of rivals, as the following proverb illustrates: "All axes work together, but the rakes work separately."[6] This proverb describes the different relationships among *bol'shaki* and among *bol'shukhi* in the village. Raking up the mown hay was women's work, so the rakes here stand for women. The proverb suggests that *bol'shukhi* did not have a community of equals like the men did in the form of the assembly. Instead, *bol'shukhi* were evaluated or appraised by their *rod*. But *rod* for a married woman was not her own family, but rather the family she entered when she married. If she got divorced, or her husband died, a peasant woman would be unlikely to return to her parents' home, according to our interlocutors.[7] This rule, which seems so strange to urban dwellers, survived for a very long time: rural women born in the 1930s to '50s told us that after marriage no return to the parental home was possible. However, in their stories about their lives, some women told us that they did return to the parental home (see chapter 3); these were apparently viewed as exceptions to the rule.

The *bol'shukha*'s role was vital to the maintenance of the peasant homestead. Yet, in comparison to other age statuses, whose characteristics have attracted the attention of ethnographers and folklorists, the institution of the women's *bol'shina* in the Russian village has not been well documented. Because of their centrality to peasant society and because their function has not been thoroughly described in scholarly literature, we will devote a good deal of attention below to analysis of the institution of the female *bol'shina* and describe how this theme unfolded in our research on gender relations. In a sense, *bol'shukhi* are the heroines of our book, since they were the people we most often interviewed and spent time with in Russian villages.

The *Bol'shukha*

A significant part of the farmstead's care—the garden, animals, homemade utensils, clothes, and everything related to the production, preparation, and storing of food—was under the *bol'shukha*'s control. All women of the family, children, and unmarried men submitted to her authority. The *bol'shukhi* oversaw the behavior of all members of the rural community and the formation of social opinion, as well as its public expression. The house, animals, and children (her own and her grandchildren) were all under the care of the *bol'shukha*. The *bol'shak* evaluated the *bol'shukha*'s caretaking skills. His criteria for evaluating her work included the health of the family and animals, since it was assumed that she should be able to ward off or prevent evil spells from "envious neighbors." Her success was also reflected in peaceful relations between members of the family, rational organization of the family's everyday life, appropriate distribution of resources, and the state of their clothing. Her responsibilities included organizing all family rituals—both calendar holidays, during which family visited, and life-cycle rituals: funeral wakes, weddings, and sending off sons to the army. The *bol'shukha* remained a significant category of social status throughout the period we investigated (women born before 1951) but, as we explain below, the *bol'shukha*'s authority began to be questioned by generations born after 1930.

   In our fieldwork, the question of the *bol'shina* as a status emerged out of insufficient understanding.[8] In 1995 we stayed in one of the friendly rural homes in the Belozersk region in Vologda oblast. We brought food with us, hoping that it would please our hosts. I (SA) then went to the kitchen and stood by the oven in order to cook something tasty from the food we had brought. My action, for some reason, amused our hosts, a fifty-five-year-old couple. The wife, Liudmila Ivanovna, sat down, looked at me slyly, and said nothing. The husband then immediately started to call me by my patronymic—"Borisovna." Behind their gaiety one could sense embarrassment. My blunder was explained to me a day later. We spoke with Liudmila Ivanovna about her relationship with her mother-in-law. Not mentioning yesterday's incident, she mildly explained to me that standing by the oven and cooking can only be done by the woman of the house. Daughters, and daughters-in-law—that is, young women—could wash dishes and assist, but could not direct the process. I quickly understood the mistake I had made: only wishing to help and please, I had violated the system of seniority, and as a result, they no longer understood how to relate to me. Having thought that I was laying claim to the position of the *bol'shukha*—that is, equal to their status—Liudmila Ivanovna's husband quickly expressed his agreement by calling me by my patronymic without my first name, the same way that one addresses a *bol'shukha*.

Having stumbled into this role by accident, I started to pay attention to how men and women talk about relations of seniority in the home. It was particularly interesting to learn how relationships are formed between the mother-in-law and her daughter-in-law. In the urban areas of Russia these relations are customarily considered problematic. But listening to stories of village women, I became convinced that these relationships take on a different form in the village. The position of head of the family belongs to the mother-in-law, and to our interviewees (those of the first and second generations, born between 1899 and 1929—see below) her position was undeniable.

> We were taught to weave by women who [know how to] *snovat'* [set up the loom]. The young ones don't have the ability, but when they get married, their mothers-in-law or mothers will show them. They are taught how to *snovat'* [after they get married]. But if a mother-in-law is young, then she herself will weave [and not teach the daughter-in-law yet]. The daughter-in-law will start weaving when her mother-in-law gets older. Back then old folks [*stariki*] were respected—they were the householders [*khoziaeva*]. If a mother-in-law couldn't do it, only then would she teach the children. The mother-in-law lights the oven and rocks the children in their cradles; meanwhile, the young ones work. (Woman born in 1926, Nadkovo, Belozersk region, Vologda oblast, 13 July 1994 [Bel 18-290])

This woman depicts to us a standard script: the young bride would be taught to weave after the wedding, at the mother-in-law's discretion. The mother or mother-in-law was the only one who knew how to bring the loom into working condition. "Children" (younger women) took on the work of the older women only when the mother-in-law could not do it herself. "The *stariki* were respected" suggests it was up to the older women—the *bol'shukhi* (note again the confusing use of the word *stariki*, here meaning the elder *bol'shak* and *bol'shukha*)—to make the decision to pass on their duties. They were the authority.

I (SA) first heard about the ritual of passing on the *bol'shina*—which was mentioned above in connection with baking a pie with fish—in Vologda oblast in 1994, when an old village woman explained to me how bread was to be baked. This was physically demanding work, because the sixteen-kilogram (thirty-five-pound) piece of dough had to be kneaded repeatedly in the *dezha*, a large wooden trough. When the hostess felt that she did not have the strength to do the work, she gave the task, as well as all the other duties of the *bol'shukha*, to a younger woman, her daughter-in-law. This often happened during *Pokrov*—that is, a particular time was set aside for it: during the night without any witnesses. The *khoziaika* finished the dough, and then kneaded it together with the successor—with four hands. The woman explained that before this day the daughter-in-law could help, for example, in preparing the filling for pies, but she never kneaded the dough itself. Clearly, she had learned by watching the process, and at the time of transfer could perform the kneading together with her mother-in-law, and then later by herself. Thus, we learned that the passing down of female authority in the house was regulated by ritual: the transfer of authority was carried out according to mutual consent.

This was one of several actions that the *bol'shukhi* did not demonstrate to the world but conducted privately. Such private activities included taking care of the dead by commemorating *roditeli*, the ancestors, which is done only by *bol'shukhi* and *starukhi*. Typically, a woman would take a leading role in such activities only after her own personal experience of the death of a close relative (Adon'eva 2004); we discuss this in more detail in chapter 9. Another of the private tasks done by the *bol'shukha* is the job of preparing the clothing for the dead (see chapter 9). Care of the dead is central to the role of the *bol'shukha* because it places her as the authority in charge of the family's relations with the family's ancestors and the other world—a source of social, moral, and spiritual power.

The *bol'shukha*'s power is emphasized by another aspect of her household functions: feeding the family. The fact that the *bol'shukha* is in charge of food preparation, of bread-baking, and of care of the cow suggests her central role in sustaining the family's well-being. In the Russian peasant household prior to collectivization, the *bol'shak* was a provider of material well-being in that he made crucial decisions about farming and controlled access to amassed property (e.g., money from sale of household produce). His tasks included sowing and plowing, harvesting, care and maintenance of tools and the horse, cutting trees, hunting, fishing, chopping firewood, and fetching water. While many of his tasks occurred outside the homestead, the *bol'shukha*'s were centered upon the home. Besides cooking and lighting and tending the oven's fire, her farming tasks included tending to the other animals (cows, sheep, goats, poultry), planting and maintaining the kitchen garden, and helping with weeding and reaping of potatoes, grain, and hay (Bridger 1987, 6). Like the *bol'shak*, the *bol'shukha* was also a provider—more directly in that she handled and delivered the food to the family members. In fact, when sociologists studied women's contribution to the maintenance of the household in the 1920s, they discovered that rural women spent six times longer on domestic labor than did men (Bridger 1987, 11).

These divisions of labor remained after collectivization, with the significant change that each adult family member now had a specialized job within an industrialized collective farm, and the household no longer functioned as the main unit of economic production. Nonetheless, the Soviet rural household retained its kitchen garden, small land plots for family use, and the right to own small numbers of domestic animals, enough to feed the household (this economy was called, in official parlance, the "Personal Subsidiary Farm" [*Lichnoe Podsobnoe Khoziaistvo*, LPKh]). This was an economic necessity since the labor-day (*trudoden'*) in-kind compensation system did not provide enough to feed the family.[9] While men devoted significant energy and time to their work on the collective farm, women often devoted much of their energy to the LPKh and worked fewer hours in the kolkhoz (Bridger 1987, 14). This state of affairs continued in the post-Soviet period as well, as women became de facto heads of household farmsteads (Denisova 2003, 183, 224).

The Cow as Symbol of *Bol'shukha* Status

In their devotion of time and energy to the LPKh, women maintained the significance of the family farm—both as a needed supplement to the pay from the kolkhoz, and as an important symbol of their identity as farmers continuing the activities taught to them by their ancestors. They did this despite the state's strong message—taught in propaganda, through the educational system, and at the workplace—that as Soviet citizens their primary duty was as workers for the national economy. In fact, the whole country's economy was dependent upon women's labor in the household barns and plots, because it was due to them that the families were able to survive on the low pay from the kolkhoz. The kolkhoz production could then be used to feed the urban population and could be exported to provide the government with much-needed capital (Bridger 1987, 13).

This context helps us to understand one of the characteristics of *bol'shukhi*: they attributed great importance to their cows. In my field research in Vologda oblast, starting in the 1990s, I (SA) began to suspect that the cow was more than simply an animal that gave milk, and thus a central source of sustenance for the peasant family. In the following section, I tell several interwoven stories about my fieldwork, showing how I came to understand that the cow actually stood for the *bol'shukha* status for these women in Vologda oblast.

When I was recording some statistics at one of the village administration offices in the Vashkinskii region, I spoke with a woman who worked there as an accountant. This beautiful forty-year-old was mother to a seven-year-old boy, and was married to the local head of the village administration. It was her husband's second marriage, which was hotly discussed and censured by the villagers. But we did not talk about these circumstances of village life with her. Instead, she complained that she was bewildered by the fact that her husband had made her get a cow even though they made a good living, and always had money for milk and meat. In order to understand her confusion, it is necessary to explain what it means to "keep a cow." For a woman this entails waking up at four or five every morning, and staying close to home because the cow has to be milked regularly, and she is the only person in the home able to do so. Also, in order to keep a cow a family must make hay, and hay mowing is an extremely hot and laborious job; the mowers go out to the fields at dawn and return at night. In other words, having a cow changes the life of a woman as well as the lifestyle of her children. My interviewee's confusion was connected with the fact that keeping a cow did not correspond to any practical need. Why did a husband who was well-off and occupied a rather high status in the region make his second wife, a beautiful woman from the city, take care of a cow? I began to look for answers, while listening more attentively to stories about cows. That is, by listening to the repeated plots of narratives, I endeavored to uncover the underlying cultural imperative and script regarding cows.

From our sources we learned that a woman who knew how to tell fairy tales lived in the neighboring village. The woman moved about the village with such speed that it took several hours for us to find her: when we got to each place where we were told to go, she had already disappeared. After running around the village and surrounding fields several times, we finally caught up with her at home. Liubov Ignateva came out to talk with us on the *zavalinka* (ledge surrounding the house). Seventy-nine years old, she had four grown children and several grandchildren. Her unmarried son in his forties lived with her. She had a daughter who worked as a milkmaid and lived with her husband in the same village. Liubov Ignateva's youngest daughter was a teacher, who came to visit during the summer with her son, and also kept a home in the vicinity. When we came to this daughter, she told us she had bought this home in order to spend the summer near her mother. Living with Liubov Ignateva was a five- or six-year-old boy—a relative from the local regional center whom she "snatched" to "plump him up"—he had been "badly malnourished in the city." All the younger branches of her family tree were there with her, alive and healthy and with successors, with the exception of her unmarried son. She appeared proud of them. It turned out that the reason she was wandering about the village was because her cow and calf did not return after grazing the previous night, and she was out looking for them.

Why would an old woman living in the company of her children who have their own farm and animals, and who love and take care of her, take upon herself the difficult task of keeping a cow? Was her keeping of a cow related to her continuing function as a mother—to her own unmarried son and to her adopted boy? Clearly, from a practical standpoint, the cow helped her continue to feed and thus to mother these "sons." Why, at seventy-nine, was playing the role of mother still important to Liubov Ignateva? When she spoke about the cow—at that time others had come to listen: the son-in-law, the young boy relative, and one of her daughters—her eyes had a cheerful and meaningful sparkle: "So what, I'm seventy-nine, and I do keep a cow."

Liubov Ignateva told us one fairy tale the following day, but during that summer we did not get to meet with her again. When we came the next summer, we learned that her unmarried son had died. Because she was mourning his death, I decided not to bother her. But we did meet up with her in the village, and we talked a little bit. She said that after her son's death, she was going to slaughter the cow and to give up keeping cows. But then she decided to take on one more calf. I realized that conversation about cows was not only about cows. It was also a conversation about a woman's worth: her maternal quality, maturity, caretaking ability, ability to feed others, and independence. Keeping a cow was a script that fulfilled the cultural imperative that a woman is responsible for feeding her family. It seemed that the cow stood as an alter ego for these women, as a "feeding mother" who constantly gave of herself. With her stories about her cow, Liubov Ignateva was implying the plot that, despite expectations to the contrary, she had not refused the role of the *bol'shukha* even when she remained alone at home.

This helps explain the story of the woman married to the head of the communal farm. This husband made his wife feed a cow so that she could earn her status as a *bol'shukha* among the other *bol'shukhi* of the village. Living without a cow would have meant keeping the status of *molodka*, and consequently, discrediting her own husband's status as a *khoziain-bol'shak*. In the village, a *bol'shak* cannot have a wife-*molodka*. It is not so much her age that is important, but her conduct.

Let us return to the story of the cows. I was interested in the role that magic played in the ritual introduction of new animals to the yard. I asked Elizaveta Mikhailovna about it. She was born in 1921, and one of the residents of the same location:

> *How were new cows introduced?*
> We lead them up to the yard, we lead them into the yard, and [you take] the footprints that it [makes] . . . "Go home, this is now your home. Live peacefully." And you throw its footprint toward it.
> For example, my mother-in-law and I bought a cow. She took it into the yard, and said to me: "Ton'ka, fling the footprints!"
> There you have it, girls. Since I got married in Yakunino I've had three cows in my time. (Parfenovo, Vashkinskii region, Vologda oblast, 19 July 2001 [Vash 20-259])

Elizaveta Mikhailovna had counted out her age in cows. She no longer kept cows; she spent winters in Saint Petersburg with her daughter. Hers was the standard, expected script: to give up the *bol'shina* when one remains alone. Her story also has another plot: that, at least for many women of the first two twentieth-century generations (born before 1930), skills used in the *bol'shina*—such as the proper care of cows—were taught not by women's own mothers but by their mothers-in-law, that is, through a relationship by marriage.

In another village two years earlier, I went with one of the female villagers to a pasture. I went to her home by prior arrangement—we were told that people invite her to come and "feed" the deceased—in other words, to perform a funeral ceremony for them. But soon afterward she hurried off to care for her calves, and I went with her. And suddenly she remarked: "This'll be the last year I keep a cow!" She looked at me strangely, as if this was a test, and with interest she was waiting to see how I would react. We were obviously not talking about the cow, but about something else, but I did not know what. Nonetheless I asked why. My question disappointed her—it was not the correct reaction. She was dissatisfied with me, she lost all interest in me, and refused to have further conversations.

The essence of this became clear to me later when, having spent three weeks conversing with villagers, I learned that this sixty-seven-year-old woman lived with a lover, "a roommate," who was twenty-five years younger than she, and whom she had "seduced" away from his young wife. The decision not to keep a cow is essentially to acknowledge one's old age, to rid oneself of the burden of the *bol'shina*, and to switch to the age class of *starukha*. In addition, it affirms the end of one's sexual life. Refusing to keep a cow is not only an economic act but is also symbolic. For this woman to acknowledge herself as a *starukha* by refusing to keep a cow, while she had a young lover, would be nonsense. This woman was testing my knowledge of her concrete situation and general "female" competency by declaring her refusal to keep a cow. I did not pass the test. I did not know what she meant. My assumption that there was something else behind these discussions about cows emerged after these sorts of communicative failures. These failures were not always as problematic as the one described above; but when I failed to understand the emotional thrust of stories about a last cow or the difficulty of maintaining one, in a certain sense I was unsuccessful in my communication with my interviewee. One of the village women with whom I met every summer over the course of ten years returned to this theme repeatedly. She was gradually preparing to live without a cow. In the beginning she talked only about the necessity of letting it go, but the next summer when I came, I discovered that the cow was alive, and that it had a calf. The talk returned again to her regret about the necessity of declining a cow. After several years she did stop keeping cows. When she talked about this, Liudmila Ivanovna cried.

In Vologda villages, it seems that the *khoziaika* had to keep a cow in order to show that she was still in charge, and was still a provider for her family. The position of the man as a *bol'shak* was unambiguously the position of *khoziain*. In the twentieth century, *bol'shaki* did not transfer the *bol'shina* to a younger man; they remained in their posts until the end of their days. But women did pass the *bol'shina* to their daughters-in-law when they no longer possessed the strength to care for the home. We argue that in Vologda oblast, having a cow and taking care of it is a major defining characteristic of the female *bol'shina*. And the cow itself—a mother who provides for all—becomes a metaphor for this status, and accordingly for the woman who has that status.

However, it would be incorrect to think that keeping a cow is a function of the *bol'shukha* generally, and that it is a widespread phenomenon. It is true for Vologda oblast villages, but in Pskov oblast villages, the poker (used to tend the fire in the oven) was her wand of power, and served as a metaphor for the *bol'shukha* status (we give an example in the second section, below). In Arkhangel'sk region the position of the *bol'shukha* was symbolized as a special place in the house, the *zakut* or *kut*, the corner behind the oven. Only she could go there and no one else, until the time when she led her successor to that place. All of these various symbols of the *bol'shina* have to do with food production and with the domestic duties that have been woman's sphere for centuries.

We can explain the fact that in different locations the status of *bol'shukha* is symbolized by various things in the following way. Things close to people—animals, plants, means of transportation, work tools, living space—are surrounded by a dense network of repeated practical actions, which connect the person, space, and thing in a single operative whole (habitus). These practices are demanded of us by society—that is, a *bol'shukha must* keep a cow, just as in many American cities a well-off family *must* have a certain kind of house. Objects and places of daily life are maintained in a field of practices performed by that thing's *khoziain*—its owner, guardian, patron, and so forth. These things structure the use of time in the life of a *khoziain*, and they require a specific amount of his or her life-force. Regarding the cow in particular, we can say along with Bourdieu that the choice to own something, undoubtedly, is a costly choice. It is not free insofar as society demands from its members those practices that characterize that person's place in that society. "Property appropriates its owner, embodying itself in the form of a structure generating practices perfectly conforming with its logic and its demands" (Bourdieu 1990, 57).

The *Bol'shukha* during the Soviet Period

Let us now summarize the different responsibilities of the members of the community according to the standard scripts, and clarify the specific role of the *bol'shukha* and its changes during the Soviet period. Prior to collectivization, the *bol'shak* took care of family and social welfare. He was part of the *skhod*, and the *skhod* judged him. The assembly was responsible to the authorities for the collection of taxes, the distribution of land, and sending the young men off for military service. The well-being of the community depended upon the sensible and competent behavior of the householders. The *paren'* was responsible for himself, and if he was an *ataman* (leader), then he was responsible for his *vataga*. In the eyes of her parents, a *devushka* was responsible for her (and the family's) honor and reputation. In the eyes of his father and society, a *muzhik* was responsible for himself and his wife. A *molodka* was the center of the husband's family's attention, since they had chosen her and had great expectations for her as a potential worker and mother. The *baby* (young mothers) were responsible for working in the field with the men, looking after their children, and helping the *bol'shukha* in the home. Both the *molodki* and *baby* were judged by their husbands, the *bol'shak*, and (most of all) the *bol'shukha*. But unlike any of these, the *bol'shukha* was accountable to only one person: her *bol'shak*.

In the Soviet period, with the gradual disintegration of the status of male householders, the institution of the *bol'shukha* gathered strength in the 1940s and '50s. In addition to her traditional responsibilities, the *bol'shukha* took on social responsibility to the state for the family and thus took over one of the traditional jobs of the head of the household (*bol'shak*). This happened for a few reasons. As we saw above, the woman's sphere was the maintenance of the household with its plots and domestic animals, and it was to the state's advantage to allow this to continue. According to the state, the household was no longer an economic unit of production, although in reality it performed an important economic function. This function of women—in essence to feed the farmers who fed the country—was never officially acknowledged by the state.

Furthermore, during the Soviet period men's and women's spheres of activity became more and more separated. Due to men's migration away from the village, women predominated in the agricultural sector starting in the 1930s and continuing throughout the twentieth century, but they worked in the lowest-paid and lowest-status agricultural jobs. In order to stop the flow of men away from the collective farms, farm heads tried to favor men for positions in management or mechanized agriculture. As a result, men earned more and spent more time on their work on the state farms than did women (Denisova 2003, 84, 173). This situation led to an even greater separation of the areas of activity of rural men and women than had traditionally been the case, with women being involved with the homestead in addition to their work for the state farm, and men primarily working outside the home, for the state (see also Gal and Kligman 2000, 54).

Gendered state propaganda and policies were also factors in shifting roles during the Soviet period. In the 1930s the state had encouraged both men and women to join the industrialized work force (including the "industrialization"/collectivization of agriculture). That pressure for women to join the workforce and enter public life did not change, but starting in 1936 the Stalinist state also engaged in a pronatalist campaign that encouraged women to devote themselves to motherhood. One of the policy changes was a ban on abortions except for those to save a woman's life or health (Engel 2004, 178). The view of motherhood as the central goal of all females permeated the discourse surrounding womanhood in all official contexts, such as in hospitals, clinics, and schools (Rivkin-Fish 2005, 102–3). Precisely at this juncture, the word "holiness" actively entered the official discourse of Soviet motherhood (Iushkova 1937, 28). The understanding of motherhood as holy was not traditional—peasant women had always been both farm workers and mothers, and, as we show in chapter 6, although rural dwellers viewed motherhood as a rite of passage and as necessary to support the family's continued economic survival, they did not see it as an exalted or exclusive position.

From the state's point of view, every woman was responsible for becoming a mother and every mother held the responsibility for the home and children. This was further emphasized in the family code of 1944, which both protected marriage by making divorce more difficult to obtain and shielded men from responsibility for out-of-wedlock offspring (the law made it impossible for the child of an unwed mother to use the father's name or claim an inheritance). As Liubov Denisova writes, "All of these 'favourable' policies implied and stipulated that aside from money, fathers had no role in childcare and the position of women was codified as that of its main providers" (Denisova and Mukhina 2010, 75). The cultural imperative of women as sanctified mothers was bolstered the same year when the state introduced "motherhood medals," modeled after military medals, given to women (including single mothers) who bore five or more children (Engel 2004, 223, 225). Notions of women as de facto mothers and mothers as the main parental caretakers, the larger numbers of single mothers, and the greater division of spheres of activity between farming women and men resulted in a situation in which the *bol'shukha*'s status included many of the responsibilities that in traditional society had belonged to the *bol'shak*. These included socializing both male and female children, being responsible for them before the state, making sure the household was properly run, and handling the household purse strings. To be sure, in the eyes of the state men were still in charge, and women were expected to cater to their men (Dunham 1990, 216). In the rural household, men still performed some of the traditional functions of *bol'shaki*: discipline of children and the more difficult physical labor needed to maintain the family plots, such as plowing. However, the state had "usurped 'head of household' as a masculine image and produced very few alternative pictures of masculinity" (Gal and Kligman 2000, 54).

The cult of motherhood, together with women's increased desire to exercise personal will (which we describe in chapter 3), were likely the background to the conflict between young married women and their mothers-in-law that we noticed in the stories of women who reached adulthood in the 1960s and '70s. The elder and younger wives were both mothers, thus they had the same status in the eyes of the state. Each had the same responsibilities toward children, husband, and household. They were two mistresses in one house, which might be described, using the Russian proverb, as "two she-bears in one den." As the proverb suggests, they cannot live together. This was a sharp divergence from the earlier cultural script, according to which the newlywed woman was initiated into the workings of the household by her mother-in-law and acquired from her most of the required skills. Many of the women of the third generation (born in 1930–50) sought to live separately from the husband's parents' family. We explore this conflict further in the section on the third generation, below.

The relationship between the *bol'shukha* and her son also changed during the Soviet period. The traditional wedding was a ritual that, among other things, changed the relationship of subordination of son to mother. After the wedding their relationship became one of equals and both submitted to the father. However, in the Soviet period, fathers, who had disappeared, or who had transferred their authority to the sphere of the state economy, were sidelined from the family hierarchy. The absence of a strong father meant that during the Soviet period the relationship between mother and son remained "vertical" after the son's marriage. The married son was not equal to the mother, as he would be in a typical nineteenth-century family; instead, he was subordinate not to his father but to his mother, who was often the only person in charge of the household.[10] This type of relationship encouraged a man to act like a bachelor.

The Soviet village man continued to behave like a *paren'* to the end of his days, while the Soviet woman—once she had become a mother—quickly turned into a *bol'shukha*. Indeed, one prevailing stereotype of the Soviet man was as a "big child": "disorganized, needy, dependent, vulnerable, demanding to be taken care of and sheltered, to be humoured as he occasionally acted out with aggression, alcoholism, womanizing, or absenteeism" (Gal and Kligman 2000, 54). If he was too childish, she was too responsible. This brought women a sense of "gratification, moral superiority, and power in the household from their centrality and apparent indespensability"; but also "a sense of victimization and perennial guilt at their never being able to do enough of anything, especially mothering" (Gal and Kligman 2000, 53).

What we have traced thus far in this chapter is a static description of the hierarchical system of age and gender classes of the Russian village. We have also drawn the general outlines of the changes occurring in the Soviet period. It goes without saying that such a description is conditional and that there are substantial differences in local means of symbolizing statuses or transitional rituals. What the various local systems have in common is the presence of age and gender classes as structures that organize the social hierarchy in the Russian village, define the distribution of economic and social functions and power among the various age and gender-related social categories, and offer life scripts to men and women. Our next section refines this general picture by differentiating the practices, world views, mores, and values of each subsequent generation of Soviet women.

Three Generations of Soviet Rural Women

Our main informants for this study were women who belonged to different Soviet generations. Chronologically these generations can be defined only approximately: those born in 1899–1916 (before the October Revolution); 1917–29 (from the Revolution through the beginning of total collectivization of the village); and 1930–50 (women who came into their youth during the postwar years, and into their period of social activity—their working life—during the last three decades of the Soviet Union). In conversing with women, we always felt emotional differences in the generations due to the significant differences in the plots of their stories, and the resulting differences in cultural imperatives and scripts. In terms of general features, our periodization coincides roughly with the schema presented by David L. Ransel in his monograph on rural mothers in Russia and Tataria (2000, 4–7).

The First Generation: 1899–1916

The first and oldest generation of our informants were women born at the end of the nineteenth century and the beginning of the twentieth century, between 1899 and 1916 (for Ransel this generation ended with 1912—that is, those born before World War I). These women were born into "large" peasant families. In other words they were raised by grandmothers who stayed at home and headed the *bol'shina*, while family members of the middle and youngest generation worked outside the home. At the head of the family was the *ded*—the father of the father, whom everyone in the house was expected to obey. These women received a traditional upbringing and education: they went to "small" and "large" *besedy*, learned to spin from the grandmothers, and underwent the initiation ceremonies

First, second, and third generations: mother (born early 1900s) flanked by two sons (born 1920s), their wives, and children in Riazan' oblast, 1956. (COURTESY OF G. FAMILY ARCHIVE)

of the first skein of flax and first menstrual period. They took part in parish celebrations, were baptized as infants, fasted with their family, and went with their parents to church to receive communion at holidays. Their childhood took place in the village *obshchina*, still untouched by Soviet power. Many of them were married off according to old customs: that is, by agreement of the boy's and girl's parents and with the help of matchmakers. It was from this generation of women that we recorded folklore genres belonging to the wedding cycle, wedding laments, and the description of the entire process of the wedding ceremony (see chapter 3). At the beginning of collectivization—the end of the 1920s— these women had already married or were just about to marry. Their children were born in the 1920s at home without any medical help, and they were watched by grandmothers and grandfathers, who educated them.

During collectivization, many of the successful *bol'shaki*—that is, forty- to seventy-year-old farmers who had large families—were officially treated as kulaks. These were the fathers and fathers-in-law of these women. Their husbands, who had gotten back on their feet and become the heads of families after the devastation of collectivization, were taken to the front during World War II; so too were their grown or growing sons. These women took up the *bol'shina* during World War II. These were mothers and mothers-in-law of the following (second) Soviet generation. The upbringing they received entailed maintaining obedience to elders and to their husbands. However, their life experience, shaped by the upheaval of the 1930s–'40s—collectivization, the back-breaking labor of the war years, and the postwar famine—often produced critical attitudes toward the Soviet authorities. In secret, many regarded the authorities chosen by the Soviets as fools, and kept away from them; in general they also preserved the rules and foundations that they were taught in childhood, in quiet defiance of Soviet programs for social change. In the new economy these women did not tend to play leading roles (they were not often forewomen, for example); and they did not keep medals or diplomas from the Soviet government, like their daughters did. If they had negative ideas about Soviet policies, they tended to keep these secret from their daughters, so that their daughters would succeed in the new society.

As David Ransel noted, these women were devoted to religious rules, and accustomed to hard labor since they had grown up working together with their family on land that was not yet collectivized. They were used to giving and receiving support and help; in other words, they maintained the norms of the pre-Soviet peasant *obshchina* (Ransel 2000, 6). During this period of radical transformation of the very basis of their existence (1920s and '30s) and the privations of war (1940s), each woman had to decide on her own how to survive and make sure that her children also survived. Any decisions regarding difficult situations with the authorities were made without support from those outside the family, since in the 1930s public expression of opinion that went against Soviet ideology could bring great misfortune to families.

The demographic catastrophes of the Soviet era—the purges of the 1930s, which annihilated most of the active and capable peasant males of the first Soviet period, and the war, which destroyed a large part of the male rural population of second Soviet generation—determined the special fate of these "older" women. It was they who, with their back-breaking labor, kept the Soviet village alive in the 1940s and '50s, and they who preserved the cultural legacy of the village—old songs, stories, and rituals—by using tradition to its fullest extent, not as an aesthetic cultural artifact (not through the prism of nostalgia), but as a world view and a set of life skills and strategies. They taught their daughters and daughters-in-law these rituals and their specific relationship to the surrounding natural world. From what we observed and what they told us, it seems they did this very delicately, and only when the younger generation sought them out for help or advice: they did not lecture, but strove to help, and the younger ones watched and learned or did not learn (below we detail mostly what they did learn; laments are an example of what they did not; see chapter 9).

For example, in 1998 in Vologda oblast a woman born in 1926—that is, of the second generation—began her monologue with a story about how to look after a cow, how to perform the ceremony for the first grazing of the cattle in the summer pastures, and how to perform the ritual for moving animals into a new cattle shed. She explained that one had to ask for permission from the *domovoi* (house-spirit) in the cattle shed and the house. She talked about how she was taught by her mother-in-law, and then about what she was and was not taught by her mother:

> One has to make a circle around the cattle on Egorii [Saint George's day]. You hang the icon of Saint Egorii over the gate. Then you walk clockwise around the animal, and you sprinkle holy water. And on Great Thursday before Easter, we would cut part of the tail of the cow. You throw it in the cattle shed, into the manure. Our mother-in-law would help when the animal got sick. When the cow had mastitis, she'd utter some words. She'd pass her own hair over the udder—her hair was long. She understood everything about cattle. I was taught that when one moves to a new place, a new home, one must ask the *khoziain*. It is necessary to bow at all four sides, all four corners of the cattle shed.
>
> *Khoziain, khoziaika*, little children!
> Here is your child.
> Give it to drink and eat, and take good care of it.
>
> Beginning clockwise, one must ask for permission from the *khoziain* to enter the home. You invite the priest to say a prayer over water to sanctify it.
>   My mama used to correct us, when she was dying, she'd say "*Matushka* [mother; here, term of endearment for children], don't believe in omens—ask God, believe in God, and in no one else." She'd go to lament the dead for other families, and would baptize newly-born children. She had the ability to heal hernias [with incantations], and to heal arms, to put a dislocated arm back in place. She'd recite charms against hernias, but I didn't memorize the words. Mama taught us incantations, when something aches, or hurts, in order to take away the pain. I listened in, and I memorized everything. When I hurt myself, I say an incantation for myself, but I never tell people what mama said:
>   "*Pokrov*, Holy Virgin Mother, take off your imperishable garment, erase from the Lord's slave Evstolia all woe, illness, pain, aches. Forever and ever, Amen."
>   Mama says: I don't believe in sorcery. And I never wish evil upon anyone. I only do [magic for] good. When she died, our house was full of people [coming to pay their respects]. (Maeksa, Belozersk region, Vologda oblast, 18 July 1998 [Bel 20-1])

Although she denied belief in "omens" and "sorcery," the mother of our interviewee possessed specific skills that it is customary to call magical. Asking the priest to complete a prayer in the new home, addressing the spirit of the house with a request to let them occupy the new residence, the prayer-incantation to the Virgin mother, and spells against hernias (a magical means of healing) made up the general set of skills possessed by women of the first Soviet generation—the mothers and mothers-in-law of our interviewees. The beliefs they expressed formed part of a religion we will call folk Christianity, that is, what earlier culturologists termed "dual belief" (*dvoeverie*) (see chapter 7 and Levin 1993). These rules were based upon a dialogic relationship between the world of the living and the world of the dead (the spirit world): "Everything had its *khoziain*: the stone, tree, forest, field; with everything, one had to know how to come to an agreement" (woman born in 1918, Georgievskoe, Belozersk region, Vologda oblast, recorded 1988 [Bel 18-301]). These kinds of beliefs, knowledge, and abilities were never spoken about publicly: older women told them to younger ones privately, in person, and only when the younger one had a real reason to know something. In a similar way, only privately and only in answer to our direct questions did they share with us their ideas and skills.

During the 1930s–'80s, the only opportunity for these women to display publicly something from the "old life" was to participate in folk choruses. This activity—encouraged by the Soviet government—was important to village women, mostly because it allowed them not to hide, to be open, if only in relation to a particular part of one's biography. On stage with the choir they sang folk songs in which they could express and relive strictly personal emotional experiences through lyrics that everyone knew (see chapter 4).

The Second Generation: 1917–29

The second generation comprises women born during the Soviet era; they were brought up in the early years of Soviet rule, and were "Soviet" by upbringing. Unlike their mothers, they were not baptized, or were baptized secretly or later than usual. They were often not religious or returned to religion only later in life. These women, on the one hand, received definite traditional knowledge about life: they were told fairy tales and sung lullabies. They heard their mothers sing laments as their mothers sent their fathers and brothers to war, and many of this generation learned how to do this themselves. Their mothers-in-law used domestic magic to heal animals and children; they watched and learned this also. On the other hand, they were educated in Soviet schools. Their life stories centered around work, war, famine, heroism, and need. If we were able to speak more closely with them and to switch registers, to get away from the usual complaints about life, they supplemented their tales of woe with stories of a happy prewar youth with young people's parties (*besedy*) and love intrigues. From a woman born in 1922: "Our youth was poor, but somehow life was filled with exuberance. We lived happily. The youth [enjoyed themselves] in the clubs. I told you before, a long long long time ago they used to put on concerts and scenes [*postanovki*]. The old folks. But now . . ." (Pin'shino, Vashkinskii region, Vologda oblast, 12 July 2004 [Vash 26-127]).

Many women of this generation married as a *samokhodka*—which literally means "one who goes by herself," without the help of matchmakers, and by her own choosing—

Second generation: two sisters (G. family, left) pose with three sisters from the family into which the younger G. sister has married, late 1940s. (COURTESY OF G. FAMILY ARCHIVE)

or sometimes, as in the case recounted here by a woman born in 1923, due to the boy's convincing:

> *Did they come to ask for your hand?* [*referring to traditional practice in which representatives of the young man's family would come to the girl's parents to ask for her hand*]
>
> No, I went as a *samokhodka*. The situation is like that now here. Take me for example. I was approached at the first party [of the season], and he persuaded me, told me where he'd take me, where he'd haul me, and where I should go. And so I got married and lived my life. I gave birth to four children, and have four grandchildren—six, and four great-grandchildren. (Mys, Vashkinskii region, Vologda oblast, 13 July 2001 [Vash 8-2])

In the belief structure of this generation we see the remarkable combination of Soviet ideology, which was displayed in their relations with the government and particularly in their striving for social recognition, and magical practices in private family and village life. For example, in the Siamzha area of Vologda oblast, a woman born in 1922 who enjoyed great authority in the village as a *znakharka* (healer), and had healed both people and animals, also talked about herself as an exemplary kolkhoz worker (*peredovik* and *udarnik*). In general women of the second and third Soviet generations depend on public opinion and governmental approbation. Both generations lovingly preserve all "declarations of respect," awards or souvenirs received as prizes for achievements in work and study—such as printed diplomas with seals, or engraved pens, samovars, or tea sets.

At the same time, we did not often find women of the second generation expressing doubts about the beliefs and norms of the pre-Soviet village. When they talked about the absence of fully fledged traditional weddings in their biographies, they characterized this lack as a violation of rules that occurred as a consequence of economic problems such as poverty and hunger. To them, the rule was still to have a wedding. Thus, a woman born in 1923 answered in a proverb or rhyme—that is, a formulated, mythological plot—my (SA) question about whether or not she had a wedding:

> He returned from war, and I married him.
> *Did you have a wedding?*
> "A dog led a dog and put it to bed" [*Sobaka sobaku vela i spat' poklala*]. I got married as a *samokhodka*. During those years, what kind of wedding could we have? We ate moss.
> *Did you ask your parents for permission?*
> Of course! How did I get married? [I'll tell you.] We came from Shubach from the festival. We had dated [*guliali*] for many years. I got married, came to my mother-in-law's to live, and she received me well. I was poor, he was poor. His right arm wouldn't unbend when he returned from the war. I addressed her informally, with "*ty*" [the informal "you" pronoun]. When the children grew up, we bought a small house. Then my husband "traded his harrow for a large mansion."
> *So he died?*
> Completely young. I gave birth to four in the cattle shed with the animals. I had no time.
> *But the afterbirth, the umbilical cord?*
> Mama [mother-in-law] lived with me. I'd give birth in the cattle shed, and I'd bring it in. Mama would be making *bliny*. "Mama! Take the child."—"Oh my lord! Bless the child, Nad'ka." She'd throw it on the oven. There was a quilt there. Only three days would pass and then back to work. (Timino, Vashkinskii region, Vologda oblast, 17 July 2001 [Vash 10-00])

This story provides a good example of the ways in which women's life stories imply rehearsed narratives (plots) that conform to ready scripts—in this case, the script of the *samokhodka*. As the last part of the above story shows, this woman, a new widow, relied on her mother-in-law to help her. Raised by pre-Soviet grandmothers, rural women of this second generation preserved the intra-family hierarchy of obedience: they obeyed their mothers-in-law whether their relations were friendly or strained. Her final comment—that she went back to work three days after the birth—was something we heard often from rural mothers. On the kolkhoz farms, there was little tolerance for women missing work due to caring for a child. This practice contrasted significantly with the pre-Soviet tradition that kept a woman out of public sight for forty days after the birth in order to keep her and the child safe from the evil eye (Baranov 2005d, 536).

The experience of postwar widowhood affected this generation. They married at the end of the 1930s and '40s. Their husbands left for the front and perished. By the end of the war more than half the women of this generation had become widows. In the Arkhangel'sk region we were told how widows gathered at festivals separately from family pairs. They had their own problems and interests.

Не ругай меня, мамаша,
Что я шоферу дала,
Ты сама же говорила,
Нужно вывезти дрова.

[Don't curse at me, mom,
That I "put out" for the [kolkhoz's] driver,
You yourself said
We have to [get someone to] bring [home] firewood.]

This *chastushka*, which we recorded many times, resonated with the postwar situation in which there were few able-bodied *muzhiki* in the village. These men held positions of authority—chairmen or brigade leaders—and they had machinery at their disposal. Whether they helped widows or not, and under what conditions they helped them, depended upon their desire and influence.

The living situation and social roles of women of the second and the subsequent generations changed from the traditional norm. Due to the village to city migration trend that has been in effect since at least the 1960s, the children of the second generation of women (and subsequent generations) often move far away from home for work and visit on holidays and during the summer; those that stay in the village often move into separate houses within the village. Thus, when women of the second generation became *bol'shukhi*, often there was no one to pass the *bol'shina* to. More often, since the 1960s, a couple with grown children is left alone in a village home, sometimes until death. The mistress and master of the village home remain nominally the *bol'shukha* and *bol'shak* as long as they are able to maintain the home. Often the husband dies first, leaving the woman as *bol'shukha*—but she is also a *starukha*. That is, as well as being a householder, she fulfills the main functions of a *starukha* in the village, such as being responsible for the maintenance of *poriadok*, or correct order in rituals, particularly death rituals.

Several practical solutions enable these elder single female heads of household to remain in their village homes until death. In some areas it is common for a widowed woman to move to the urban home (apartment) of a grown child during the winter, when life in the village is most difficult. She returns in the spring in time to plant some vegetables in her garden. Other ways that widowed *starukhi* maintain their homes even when they are physically weaker include keeping a goat instead of a cow (goats need less food and are easier to milk); hiring local men to help with heavy household chores such as repairs, plowing, and preparing firewood (payment may be made in the form of trade, for example the man works for a meal or for homemade or store-bought liquor); having their children visit often; having a grown but unmarried son or daughter live with them; and looking after each other.

For example, when I (LO) visited the village of Krasnoe in Riazan' oblast in 2004–5, an eighty-year-old widow, Valentina Sergeevna G. (born in 1925), whose sight was nearly gone,

"Baba Nastia," Anastasia Spirina (b. 1918), with one of her goats, Lenino, Riazan' oblast, 2005. (PHOTO BY LAURA J. OLSON)

received daily visits from her next-door neighbor, also a widowed *starukha-bol'shukha*, who was four or five years younger. The neighbor bought bread and other staples for her. Despite needing help to keep her household going, Valentina behaved like a *bol'shukha* with younger people: while I stayed with Valentina she insisted upon cooking for me at least some of the time, and upon my eating what she had cooked. She likewise cooked for her grandson who came to visit for Easter. She also kept a goat, although to do so was obviously a physical hardship for her. But her behavior at a memorial service for her deceased daughter emphasized her role as *starukha* in that she organized and directed the entire process. She gave to others chores related to food and house care, but kept for herself chores related to the proper carrying out of the ritual.[11]

The Third Generation: 1930–50

The third generation of rural women was born between 1930 and 1950. Their youth was spent during the 1950s and '60s. The beginning of female intergenerational conflict emerged in this group. As we pointed out in the previous section, many young people of this generation moved away from the village; those who did stay in the village often tried to establish their own homes as soon as possible (usually the obstacles were financial). Women told us that while living with the husband's parents, they often came into conflict with the mother-in-law. For example, a woman born in 1938 spoke of a conflict with her mother-in-law that ended in her victory. She took control of the *bol'shina* without waiting

Third generation: two seventeen-year-old girls, Ul'ianovsk oblast, 1956. (COURTESY OF ELIZAROV FAMILY ARCHIVE)

for her mother-in-law to transfer it willingly. Her story was prompted by her commentary on the *chastushka* that she sang us:

Меня худо одевали,
Из худого дому я.
Сероглазый из хорошего
Ругали за меня.

[They dressed me badly,
I'm from a bad home.
And a gray-eyed boy from a good home
Got in trouble over me.]

Did this happen to you?

Yes, it happened, for example, in my life. They did not love me. I wasn't loved. Why the hell [*kakoi leshii*] wasn't I loved, you tell me: I neither drank nor smoked, and I knew how to do everything. I could dance, sing, and do everything. I was cheerful, I gave birth to good girls, I don't know, not monsters, and I myself am not a monster, but my *babka* [mother-in-law] didn't love me, didn't love the fact that I was from a poor family. But if I'd been from a rich family—who the hell [*leshii*] knows what she needed. Or maybe it was that generation, like it used to be—they wanted to be obeyed. I lived [with her], I was afraid, I didn't take power right away, only later, when she said that "I wouldn't trade flowers for your *vybliadki* [offspring of a slut]. What the f—! [*Ni khera ukha!*] We lived three years, after three years of living together, I still hadn't given birth, and she calls me a *vybliadok*. And I had one in my stomach, it was our third year living together, and she called me a *vybliadok*. I waited for my husband to come home from work, and when he came, I cried and cried to him. But the insult stayed with me, and I stopped calling her mother. I used to call her mother. And then—what kind of mother is she to me, if she said that to me. And then I got sick. It was due to nerves. They took me to the city, and at the hospital we chatted with the *baby* [other female patients] about life. And then Valentin came to see how I was doing, and he brought both of them [daughters]. And the women in the ward saw that Valentin had come to visit. I went back to the ward in the evening, and the women said to me: "Who's dearer to you? Your mother-in-law or those two little girls? So look: you'll lie here awhile, get better, then you yourself seize control. Stop eating crumbs from your mother-in-law's hands, and worrying and thinking about all this."

So then that winter my mother-in-law went to visit her daughter in Velikii Ustiug. We took care of the house. She came back, and we had freshly baked *pirogi* [meat-filled rolls]. And she sits at the table, refusing to eat my *pirogi*. She disdained them. And I made very delicious pies, you know, and she wouldn't eat them. Or maybe she was doing it out of pride; she was a very proud woman. So. And it was eating me. Damn! [*Blin!*] She wouldn't eat. It was then that everything turned around for me. I'm not stupid, so I said to her: "You'll eat them! Like them or don't like them, whether I make bad or good *pirogi*!" And I said: "That's enough now!" From now on you'll eat my pies all the time: bad ones—you'll eat them, and good ones—you'll eat them too." I said to her: "Enough. You've controlled this house for many years, and now," I said, "you'll eat what I make." And that's all. I took the *bol'shina* from her. That's all. I started to bake, and light the oven myself. What, am I supposed to die because of my mother-in-law? (Krasnovo, Kirillov region, Vologda oblast, 19 July 2003 [Kir 26-3])

This story thematizes storytelling: in it, the young wife tells her story to women at the hospital and learns from them what she should do. As in other speakers' stories, the main elements of the narrative are contained in a folkloric text that the storyteller cites, emphasizing the mythological nature of this plot. The domestic hearth literally became a place of struggle for power between the older and younger generation, between mothers-in-law and daughters-in-law. Everything that organized this work—oven, kitchenware—became stable metaphors of female leadership—the *bol'shina*. If in the above story the key theme is *pirogi*—or, to be more exact, the question who will bake them, and who will eat them, in the following example, the symbol of power is the poker, used to spread out the coals in the oven. In the Pskov dialect, it is called a *kliuka*: "Niushka's mother got sick, and the daughter-in-law became the *bol'shukha*. When she got better, the daughter-in-law did not give the *kliuka* back. Instead she told her mother-in-law to take the bucket, and give the cows some water" (*Pskovskii oblastnoi slovar'* 1950–70, 1957).

Both examples show that daughters-in-law took the place of mothers-in-law at the oven. In other words, the daughters-in-law took the leading position in the home for a while when the mother-in-law was away, and upon her return refused to relinquish the position they had taken. As a result of such conflicts, it was common for women of the third and subsequent generations to tell us that they had learned important life skills (such as healing magic) from their own mothers rather than their mothers-in-law, as had previously been the norm.

Many women of this generation were children of the war years and of the immediate postwar years; they were orphans (in Russian, defined as a child lacking one or both parents) and also children born out of wedlock to widows of soldiers. From childhood they acquired puritanical views regarding sexuality from their own mothers as well as others, such as *tetki* and neighbors. In the following example, the woman, born in 1950, reporting to us about the illegitimate children in her generation, does not tell us whether she herself has a father; and she contradicts herself about the morals of these illegitimate children:

What if it's an illegitimate child?

That is the most interesting thing—it used to happen before us and happened after us, but in my generation—not a single one. We were very honest [*chestnye*] as *devki*. Not a single one [gave birth out of wedlock]! Somehow they drilled it into our heads, that this was shameful!

Shameful? And what about the previous generations?

There were [girls who gave birth out of wedlock], then. But it's like this, girls: in our village it goes by family tradition; whatever family it started in, would continue like that. I won't point any fingers.

And they called them vybliadki [*children of whores*]?

Yes.

And how did they relate to this? Once the child had grown . . .

A *vybliadok* is a *vybliadok*. The nickname was always there. And then after the war, do you know how many *vybliadki* there were?

After the war?

Yes, of course. People became widows at twenty and twenty-two, so what do you want? Of course, they gave birth to a lot of kids. In 1949, 1947, and 1948—do you know how many?

These were their birth years?

Yes, yes. Before 1950. All those women were very young. I, for example, don't judge anyone for the fact that they gave birth to a child. And by the way it was all from two *muzhiki* in the entire village. All the kids looked alike. And now they still look like each other. (Davydovskoe, Siamzha region, Vologda oblast, 13 July 2005 [Siam 26-50])

It is clear that it was not the children themselves who called children born out of wedlock *vybliadki*. They learned this from adults. Again, the notion of *vybliadok* formed part of a mythological plot. It was not a script because, by definition, the *vybliadok* identity refers to a woman's birth, something that happened in the past; it was not a path that women chose, but something that happened to them. This plot allowed people, like the storyteller, to make sense of their own life story in relation to others. Of course, this plot was a judgment from outside the family: married couples and "honest" widows did the judging. It is evident from this conversation that for those of this generation the fear of being publicly accused of wantonness and of being belittled was, as the female storyteller put it, "drilled into their heads." Both *vybliadki* and those who teased their peers experienced such fear. Such cruel judgment of extramarital affairs in the postwar years had particular motivations. The postwar demographic crisis, which emerged after the death of a significant part of the male population, was offset by children born out of wedlock. Female competition for men was very high. Those widows who abstained from having extramarital affairs talked about those who did not. In the Mezen' region of Arkhangel'sk oblast we were told that a woman's refusal to marry a man with whom she had borne a child was considered no less a sin than adultery. The publicly discussed sin here was refusing a "male resource."

Another story is worth considering in this regard: a woman born in 1935 told us that her younger sisters were different from her. We were interested and asked what she meant by that. She called her sisters "*vybliadki*" and explained that she herself was born in wedlock. After her father had died at the front, her mother gave birth to two daughters by the chairman of the kolkhoz immediately after war; using his authority, he forced her to be his lover. When the chairman became a widower, he offered to marry her mother, but her mother refused. Because of her mother's refusal, the entire village talked about her. The woman acknowledged the circumstances of the birth of her two sisters as shameful, and this shame never subsided. To this very day she considered herself "different" from her sisters.

Women of this generation attended Soviet schools, heard Soviet songs, and watched Soviet films. They used state hospitals but nonetheless made use of traditional magical practices. In the following example, a woman born in 1950 talks about an incantation she used when her child was crying from fright:

> First is the incantation. This is for frights. In order to heal a child, when it's afraid.
> So: "Jesus Christ himself was flying in the clouds. He brought three bows, three
> wooden arrows, and thirty-three metal arrows. Come to us, Jesus Christ, to your
> divine slave X [insert name of patient]. Jesus Christ, shoot all evil eyes, evil glances,
> and fears. Amen, amen, amen. That's how the incantation goes.
> *This is from your mother?*
> Yes, it is. (Kimzha, Mezen' region, Arkhangel'sk oblast, 7 July 2007 [Mez 20-63])

Domestic magic in particular seems to be the most essential of all the traditional skills of motherhood, as we discuss in detail in chapter 6. Note, however, that this woman learned her skills from her own mother, not her mother-in law, as was typical of previous generations. Women of this generation also know songs sung at the table; usually these are romances and ballads. However, almost none of these women have the ability to sing laments (see chapter 9).

Like women of the second generation, these women hope for government acknowledgement of their accomplishments. Unlike the previous generation, women of the third generation celebrated their weddings with rituals. The wedding reentered everyday life in the 1960s and '70s, but it resembled a generic celebration more than a rite of passage. These events were devoid of features that characterized traditional wedding rituals, such as seeking permission from one's parents and the bride's lament prior to marriage. Thus, women of the third generation grew up thoroughly "Soviet" in many regards but still maintained private rituals and practices that linked them with earlier generations.

These, then, are the heroines of our study. We have broached here many of the topics that we will examine in more detail later on: romances and weddings, life stories, singing, motherhood, relationship to the other world, and death. Each of these aspects of the worlds of our interlocutors represents a locus for engagement with tradition. Women did not simply accept transmission of tradition passively. Rather, each woman and each generation incorporated that which tradition offered it; each used tradition in its own way—violating, rejecting, or adapting tradition to the forms of life that were produced by history.

3

Subjectivity and the Relational Self in Russian Village Women's Stories of Courtship and Marriage

In the traditional understanding of the contours of a woman's and man's life story, marriage is the summit. It permits the continuation of the *rod* (clan), which is essential for the survival and health of the community and the abundance of crops (Paxson 2005). In addition, prior to collectivization, marriage had important economic functions for the family and community. A man's family gained a worker (the bride); the woman's family lost a worker but also lost responsibility for her. In a woman's life span, the wedding was the moment when the cultural imperative to unite with a mate in order to bear successors was first fully expressed. Ethnographers have shown the special importance of marriage for women in the traditional belief system by pointing to the past existence of some local Russian traditions in which there was a separate funeral ritual for women who died before marriage. This ritual incorporated elements of the wedding in order to "finish out" her life story: the dead was dressed in wedding clothes, and in some areas her family members would sing laments referring to her as a "white swan," the symbol of the bride in weddings songs (Baranov 2005a, 75–76).

The Russian traditional wedding is a complex ritual rich in symbolism, and for this reason it has been studied closely by Russian ethnographers. In this chapter we do not synthesize or repeat this work (see Matossian 1968, Worobec 1991, and Rouhier-Willoughby 2008 for descriptions of the traditional wedding ritual). Instead, we approach accounts of courtship and of the weddings of Russian rural women born in different generations as means of understanding women's subjectivity. We investigate the ways that women are culturally positioned as female through the poetics of the courtship and wedding cycle, and how they configure their own life stories in relation to that tradition, as well as to cultural plots of romance and of Soviet womanhood.

We understand subjectivity to be consciousness of self in relation to community expectations and norms. Subjectivity has been the subject of much discussion by feminist theorists, particularly poststructuralist feminists, starting in the 1970s and '80s (Row-botham 1973; Kristeva 1980; Cixous and Clement [1975] 1986; de Lauretis 1987). Along with these theorists, we embrace the notion that the subject is not unitary, rational, and disembodied (as per the liberal notion of the self; Frazer and Lacey 1993, 45) but rather is embodied and constructs itself in multiple, sometimes opposing ways, through interplay with other subjects and discourses. This pluralistic model of the self describes both men's and women's subjectivities; but there is a difference between accepted understandings of selfhood for men and women. Because the group identity of Western white men is dominant, it is invisible; it is possible for men to perpetuate the illusion that they exist as autonomous individuals without being tied to a group. As Susan Stanford Friedman writes: "A white man has the luxury of forgetting his skin color and sex. He can think of himself as an 'individual.' Women and minorities, reminded at every turn in the great cul-tural hall of mirrors of their sex or color, have no such luxury" (1998, 75–76). Women thus have a double consciousness of both existing and being looked at as *woman*.

Without the illusion that they are separate, women possess greater access to a relational identity. This is doubly true for women belonging to non-dominant and indigenous cul-tures: often the cultural norms of such groups reject ways of speaking about the self as separate and teleological. Native American women, for example, tend to see themselves as inherently situated in a community of kinship relations and interactions with the earth and cosmos (Sweet Wong 1998, 169). This model of affiliated or relational subjectivity is particularly applicable to the cultural position of Russian village women.

In the analysis of women's stories that follows, we highlight the embeddedness of women's subjectivity within a web of social relations. The signs of such a relational iden-tity include emphasis on maintaining or enhancing kinship relations, giving and accepting gifts, relying on others, allowing others to decide or lead, and seeking external approval, advice, or support. We choose to avoid judging these ways of constructing selfhood as backward or detrimental to women, because we think they serve the important function of establishing oneself in relation to community or family. In contrast, ways in which women construct themselves as self-conscious individuals include self-expression, agency, inten-tionality, desire, self-consciousness, and self-reliance. These are the foundations of West-ern liberal selfhood, and it is customary to assume that women living in patriarchal rural cultures do not possess these means of constructing the self. But we find the traces of this kind of selfhood even within the Russian rural tradition. We argue that it is important to examine both of these ways of constructing selfhood, because for women (and probably for men too) one does not exist without the other.

Another dimension of our investigation below is the ways that the narratives of women's experience are constructed in relation to plots and scripts—discourses offered by society. This is not a simple matter: these discursive systems may be numerous and conflicting. We isolate three broad sources that inform the narratives of our subjects:

values and norms from rural culture, city culture, and official Soviet culture. Expectations associated with rural culture were communicated in rituals (the courtship and wedding rituals), songs (lyric songs, ballads), traditional narratives (fairy tales, legends), gossip (stories about others' lives and behavior), life stories (autobiographical stories of elders), and other traditional verbal pronouncements, such as proverbs. The culture of the city began to influence Russian rural culture in the late nineteenth and early twentieth centuries; it was accessed through peasant outmigration or seasonal factory work, and might also have reached village women through songs (a link we discuss in more detail in the next chapter). The entirely new discourses of Soviet culture made their way into the village starting in the 1920s. The official culture of Soviet ideology was transmitted via the schools, the Party and other official organizations, the media, and the basic Soviet social unit—the collective (Kharkhordin 1999).

We begin below with an analysis of courtship and wedding rituals as told to us by women of the first generation (born between 1899 and 1916). This first section serves the dual purpose of providing context for the personal stories that follow, and also allowing us to see the ways in which women's narratives about their local traditions give glimpses of women's subjectivity. Even such a patriarchal institution as the traditional wedding, we argue, leaves room for—and indeed, may require—a bride's active initiative. In the second section we show how women's stories of their own weddings borrow elements from rural tradition in creating their relational identities, while also constructing a self-conscious identity. Here is it not so much the case that women born later necessarily possess a greater sense of self, as one might expect—but that in the later periods (particularly 1940s–'60s), the choices and desires expressed by young women are heeded by those close to them. Thus their active selfhood is encouraged and supported from the outside as well as existing as an inner voice. In the third and final section of the chapter, we look at possible reasons for the social changes we observed; in particular, we trace self-assertiveness to the influx of city culture at the end of the nineteenth century and to Soviet education practices, which, while they aimed to increase collectivism, may have had the opposite effect.

Courtship and Wedding Rituals in the 1920s

The first generation, women born in the early twentieth century, recount the traditional courtship and wedding rituals of the 1920s–'30s. The methodology of fieldwork affected how we approached this generation. Between approximately 1983 and 2002, when most of the interviews with this generation were conducted, Russian scholars did not generally record life stories or personal stories of courtship. The researchers at Saint Petersburg State University tended to ask directed questions about specific aspects of the wedding and courtship rituals, and to classify the answers according to ethnographic subject matter, following accepted practice. Neither tapes nor transcripts of entire interviews were kept, as a rule (with some exceptions). Olson began to record personal life and courtship stories in 2004; Saint Petersburg State University kept transcripts of entire interviews starting in 2006. At this time few women born during the first part of the twentieth century were living and able to be interviewed. Nevertheless, there is much usable information in the interviews done in the late twentieth century. Some of the women did talk about their own weddings, and women who addressed their remarks to the wedding tradition in general said much that helps us to understand women's self-construction in relation to ritual, family, and community.

Women who married in the 1920s described to us courtship rituals very similar to ones practiced in the nineteenth century (Worobec 1991, 128–30). The basic script for traditional marriage prior to the 1861 emancipation of the serfs proposed that a bride be chosen by the parents of the groom. Toward the end of the nineteenth century, particularly in areas that had more outmigration and contact with urban environments, courtship rituals and the accompanying songs began to emphasize the notions of romantic love and free choice. Economic factors played a large role: young men who earned wages outside the household in factories or trades were more likely to assert themselves in opposition to the wills of their fathers. Nonetheless, parental control, guidance, or influence in the choice of a spouse remained a reality throughout the post-emancipation period (Worobec 1991, 135). Our sources show that it remained important to some well into the twentieth century as well.

Marriage was nearly universal partly due to economic reasons, as Barbara Engel has shown: under the system of land allotment used before collectivization, peasant men received their full allotment of land only when they married, so it was to the household's advantage for him to marry. Due to the interdependence of individual, household, and community, it was to everyone's advantage for a suitable bride to be found—one who would enhance the household of the groom through her moral character and her work abilities (1990, 697–98).

Such was the situation described by our informants born in the early twentieth century as well. Through courtship rituals, a bride could be chosen by the young man or by his mother and female relatives, or through their direct influence upon him. Mothers and aunts of young men scrutinized carefully both the girls in their community and girls who came to visit during holidays, looking for girls who were well groomed and likely to be good workers.

Girls and their mothers did their part to ensure they received good matches. Girls used divination rituals to discover their "fate": it was commonly believed that there was one man with whom they were fated to be, and that this was controlled by otherworldly forces that could be known through magical means during Yuletide. Girls met boys locally at young people's evening parties, or mothers of girls of marriageable age sent their daughters to stay with relatives in other villages when those villages were having holiday celebrations such as the parish holiday (each parish had its own yearly holiday, usually the day for which the church was named) and spring holidays. During such holidays in Arkhangel'sk province, local and visiting girls would gather twice a day to dance the *khorovod*, a circle dance in which girls walk, holding hands, while singing a song. In this dance the girls effectively ranked their eligibility: those from the best and richest families had the right to stand in the front of the line; at the very front of the line, before the rich girls, danced the young brides, *moloditsy*, who had married the previous season (see also Frank 1992, 717). Villagers and visitors would stand at the sides and watch. Future mothers-in-law looked for daughters-in-law: they scrutinized their clothes, and how the girls sang and walked.

The very act of wearing "holiday clothes" signaled that a girl was ready for marriage. For each *khorovod* the girls would try to dress in a different outfit. In this context, richness of ornamentation of their clothes signaled to others their family's economic well-being—and hence, some commentators have pointed out, the work values of the family (Saf'ianova 1989, 98). As we pointed out in the previous chapter, in Arkhangel'sk, Vologda, and other northern provinces, the girls showed with the restraint in their behavior and dancing style their modesty and "honor." In terms of the society's values, girls were supposed to be— and to show themselves to be—good workers, from a rich family, from a good *rod*, modest, pretty, and not "fast" (*guliashchaia*). For later generations, the list of desirable qualities included self-assertiveness (*boikaia*). By contrast, the social code dictated that boys show themselves as possessing skill (in dancing or playing instruments), as being brave, as gang-leaders (*ataman*), and good fighters. With their dancing style, which they performed separately from the girls, boys showed off their individuality and improvisational skill (Morozov 2006, 93–96). These dances, then, provided a setting in which young people performed gender and social status.

When a groom and his family had chosen a bride, they set about to obtain the agreement of the parents of the bride. The agreement began with the engagement (*svatovstvo*). The parents of the groom, or a female relative of the groom (*svakha*)—that is, people of the same age status as the parents of the girl—came to the home of the bride. These matchmakers (*svaty*) tried to make their way to the home of the girl unseen by neighbors, since if they were refused the reputation of the boy would suffer, and also because they were afraid someone could ruin the match with the evil eye. When they entered the home, they stood by the door and used metaphoric language to state their purpose: "You have something for sale, we have come to buy it" (*vot u vas est' tovar', a my prishli pokupateli*). The metaphorical expression both protected the desired outcome from potential harm from the evil eye and also emphasized the material basis of the exchange. If the girl was at home, and if she agreed to the match, she would come out at once. By her actions, her parents could tell her opinion about the proposal.

Thus, all the participants used territorial language to indicate their intentions: the matchmakers entered the home but waited to be invited further; the girl showed her willingness by coming forward as if to meet the matchmakers. If the parents of the future bride agreed, they invited the matchmakers to drink tea and agreed about the types of presents the bride would give to the family of the groom.

In general the wedding ritual marks two different transitions, each centered around the bride. It symbolizes the horizontal movement of families toward one another, and the vertical movement of the bride from the role of daughter (*devka*) to the role of wife (*baba*) (Levinton 1977; Baiburin 1993; Bikmetova 2009). The horizontal plane involves the creation of new social bonds, contributing to social cohesion in the community and between communities. In this plane, the bride plays a socially circumscribed role in which her actions are predetermined by tradition and community expectations. The vertical plane focuses more on the bride's individual growth. Here tradition again determines her actions, but there is more room for the bride's agency and choice and expression of personal emotions. The poetics of the ritual imply the bride's loss of freedom as a girl, but also her loss of responsibility for guarding her maidenhood—thus, a new kind of freedom and power, and the beginning of her achievement of her life's goals (the cultural imperative to bear children).

While both of these transitions are centered upon the bride, the horizontal plane is the one most concerned with family and community. In this aspect of the ritual, the bride herself, as she moves to a new home, acts as a symbol of community ties: she creates a new *svoi* group (a group of people who consider themselves closely socially connected) and contributes to her new *rod*. This is accomplished through the symbolic softening of the boundaries between the two families via copious visits of representatives of one family to the other during the wedding period. The vertical plane, on the other hand, enacts the bride's own passage through symbolic actions, songs, and objects. Much of the poetry sung by the bride and her girlfriends during the events at the bride's own house (prior to the movement to the groom's house) reflects upon the bride's own journey.

But the wedding itself is a community affair, as becomes clear in that very poetry, and in the final analysis, the wedding is neither a personal nor a religious event (as it is commonly seen in the West), but an event of clans and community. It is in the eyes of the community, not so much in the eyes of God or another higher authority (after the Revolution, this authority was the Soviet government), that the couple are married (Bikmetova 2009). This fact has been noted by many commentators: while the traditional wedding is composed of two parts, the *venchanie* (church service) and the *svad'ba* (celebration), it is clearly the *svad'ba* that is the essential event (Pushkareva and Levin 1997, 94; Kononenko 2007, 51–53).

The horizontal transition of the bride and the changing shape of the community—the ways that the concept of *svoi* can be enlarged and reconstructed through marriage—are emphasized by the part of the rite that follows next after the engagement: the girl's family visits the groom's home. Especially if the groom was from another village, the girl's family would take this opportunity to scrutinize the property of the groom, so that they could be sure that the match was one of economic equals. This part of the ritual showed clearly that the match was an economic one between households rather than a personal love affair of young sweethearts.

Following this, the betrothal—the cementing of an agreement between the two families—took place. Only after the betrothal was finished and thus the joining of the two families was secured did the wedding celebration shift its focus to the vertical journey of the bride as she rises in status. During the *devichnik* (a party at the bride's house the evening before the wedding ceremony) and many of the rituals accompanying the *svad'ba*, the bride could ritually experience the death of her former identity and her rebirth in her new roles of wife, sexual being, future bearer of heirs, household laborer, and deferential daughter-in-law.

In the section that follows, we show how women of the first generation spoke about their own and others' weddings. We quote and analyze the description of one woman, Natalia Pavlovna R., born in 1901, of Staroe Selo in the Belozersk region of Vologda oblast (7 July 1996 [Bel 1-22]). We modified her story a bit, rearranging sections to present them in the order of the events (transitions between rearranged sections are indicated by ellipses). Natalia Pavlovna's story begins with the betrothal, which is called by various names in various regions of the Russian North, emphasizing the element of agreement through talking or drinking: *sgovor* (agreement), *propoi*, *propivan'e* (drinking agreement), *prosvatan'e* (conclusion of matchmaking agreement). The groom, with his parents and close relatives, would come to the home of the bride:

> And they would do a *propivan'e*: When the groom would come with his family, they'd lay the table and drink vodka. And they'd brew beer, many barrels. They'd eat a meal, and then dance. If they didn't have their own musician, they'd invite one with an accordion. They'd dance, and then drink tea. . . . They would light candles and pray to God. Then it was already law. And if the bride wanted to marry another, now she wouldn't dare—she'd be afraid of God. And after the tea the groom's family would go home, and the bride would start lamenting. Then they'd go to the church and tell the priest that such-and-such a girl, let's say Natalia, is getting married to Ivan. And the sexton, after the mass, would announce that they are getting married . . .
>
> The bride would sit at the home of her parents, prepare the gifts for the wedding: to her father-in-law a shirt—and make sure it had an embroidered hem—to the groom a shirt, and to the rest of the relatives, an embroidered towel. If the groom had a large family, then the bride would be left with nothing, she'd give everything as a gift. They embroidered the towels for the icon corner [*bozhnitsa*] for the wedding very richly, and they'd tie those to the horse's yoke when riding to the church. In the evening [before the wedding day] . . . for the *devichnik* the girl would

visit her relatives in the village. She'd dress in a nice dress, braid her hair (no matter what kind of hair she had—still, she had to braid it), and put flowers (called *krasota*) on her head. She'd go around to her relatives in the village, and they [the female relatives and the bride] would lament. If she didn't know how, then they'd get a woman lamenter, and the bride would throw a shawl over her head and raise her voice together with them. . . .

At night [i.e., later that same night] they'd heat up the bathhouse and lead the bride to the bathhouse. There they'd put on a Russian sarafan and a chemise, and flowers on her head. And she'd go about the house lamenting. Everyone had their own lament. She'd be thanking everyone. And in the morning, before the morning, about 3 a.m., they'd take off her flowers—it was called a *krasna krasota* [beautiful beauty], that meant her freedom as a girl [*volia devich'ia*]. Her brother or someone younger would sneak up and take off her flowers, and then she'd cry even more. They'd comb out her hair, make a married woman's headdress: a *kika* [a headscarf tied over the hair and knotted on top of the head so that the two ends form "horns"], and they'd cover her face and her hair with a scarf with *kist'i* [fringes]. Before the wedding the bride wore funereal white or black. If the bride's mother or father was dead, she'd go to the cemetery [i.e., an elder woman in her family or a godmother would take her to the cemetery the day before the wedding] to lament that she had no one to bless her. In the morning the bride would get up and lament again, until the groom came. Then everyone would sit at the table, and she would sit down, too, in the clothing in which she would be married [*venchat'sia*—to be married at the church]. And her girlfriends would again sing songs to her. When the young people left for the church from the bride's home, an older woman (a relative of the bride) would sweep the road [ahead of them] with a birch broom, and when they came to the groom's house, that woman would again sweep the road. While they were being married in the church, [someone from the bride's family] would take the bride's dowry to the groom's home. [People from the groom's family] would meet them there, grasp the trunks with mitts [mitts were used by both parties to show that the trunks were heavily laden], and set them in the anteroom.

After the church ceremony, they'd go to the groom's house in a "train." As the young couple walked into the groom's home, they'd shower them with grain. They'd eat, dance, and they'd lead the young couple to bed. In a separate room they'd have made a bed with the bedding that the bride had prepared [pillows, quilts, mattress], and the best man [witness] would lead them to sleep. When they filled up the mattress with straw, the bride would put money into the mattress for the person who filled it up. The groom would lie on the mattress, and the bride would ask him, "Ivan, the bedding is mine, but the will [*volia*] is yours, will you let me in?" And she'd lie next to him, and the best man would whip the groom with his stick and say, "Who are you sleeping with, Ivan?" And he had to answer, "with Natalia." And then he'd whip the bride too, and ask "Who are you sleeping with, Natalia?" And she had to answer, "with Ivan," and if she didn't love him and she didn't want to say his name, the best man would whip her so it hurt more, so that she'd say it. He'd get her to, and then the young couple would lie there awhile and then would go back to the table again for tea, and the bride would then invite the groom's family to drink a glass of beer and she'd give them their presents.

This normative account—a script—is similar to many of the descriptions we received from the oldest generation of our interlocutors when we asked them to talk about the wedding ritual. Natalia Pavlovna is describing the wedding of the 1920s based on the general contours of the weddings she participated in, probably as a girlfriend, and possibly her own wedding as well. In her account, she emphasizes the aspects of the ritual that were imperative for the bride to accomplish: after the betrothal she wouldn't dare change her mind about the marriage; the shirt for the father-in-law had to have an embroidered hem; no matter what kind of hair she had, she had to find a way to braid it; if she did not know how to lament, she had to raise her voice with other women; if she did not have parents to bless her she had to lament that fact at their grave; even if she did not want to marry the groom, she had to say the groom's name when the best man was hitting her with his stick. The way Natalia tells this account gives us some hints about how she, her cohort, and the community at large viewed the process. She keeps implying the possibility that a girl undergoing the ritual did not want to marry or did not feel suited to the process. We cannot know if that was true for her, but clearly it was true for some women at the time. Perhaps few were perfectly suited to the wedding ritual, but everyone had to undergo it, or live the unenviable life of an old maid. These were compromises that individuals made. The ritual itself accommodated all kinds of real women's personal differences and psychological uncertainty through its own predictable logic; this is seen in Natalia's emphasis on what had to occur. One senses that, for this teller and perhaps for many of this generation, the inexorable wedding ritual was a fact of life that they did not question. Indeed, as Humphrey and Laidlaw write, "In adopting the ritual stance one accepts . . . that . . . one will not be the author of one's acts" (1994, 98). This giving up of one's ordinary sense of freedom and intentionality defines the fundamental nature of ritual (Humphrey and Laidlaw 1994, 97, 99). Neither wholly pleasant nor wholly unpleasant, neither good nor bad, it just was. As a phenomenon of social life, tradition requires individuals to compromise.

The wedding ritual likely fulfilled an important function for the bride's psychological development, as we pointed out in chapter 2. A rite of passage aims to transform the initiate's way of thinking, her picture of the world. According to Victor Turner (1969, 95, 170–71), in any coming of age ritual this function is fulfilled by the liminal phase, in which the person undergoing the ritual is passive, humble, obedient, and accepts arbitrary punishment without complaint. The person must be abased before he or she can rise to a new social position with more power and responsibility; such an experience allows him or her to make a clean break with the former identity and acquire humility, so that she or he will behave with compassion in future when dealing with others who are subordinate. From this point of view, the parts of the wedding in which the bride is passive or debased may provide an experience (of suffering, humiliation, etc.) that allows to her feel the cessation of her former identity.

While performance of a ritual requires temporarily setting aside one's personal intentionality and freedom, the ritual texts themselves sometimes ascribe agency to the bride's acts. This can be seen in a story about her wedding from Maria Iakovlevna, born in 1912. She first describes times when she performed the role of "girlfriend" for other brides, and then her own *devichnik*:

Before the *devichnik* the bride dressed me: she put flowers on my hair, and braided a ribbon into my hair . . . So [for my own *devichnik*] I was in the anteroom, and mama was in the kitchen. I came out and addressed my first lament to mama:

Да государыня, добра матушка,
Посмотри на меня, пожалуйста!
Коли ловко да снарядилася?
Хорошо ли сподобилася?
Мне пристало ли платье цветное,
По голове ли цветы лазоревые?

[My mistress, my good mother,
Look at me, please!
Have I dressed myself skillfully?
Can I be considered worthy?
Does the colorful dress look well on me,
And the sky-blue flowers on my head?]

   Then again:

Вот сама я знаю да сама ведаю,
Догадалась красна девица
Платье цветное да не заношено,
Лицо белое да не запачкано,
Руса косонька да недорощена.

[Here I myself know and I myself see,
The beautiful girl has guessed:

My colorful dress is as yet unworn,
My white face is not smudged,
My blond braid is not grown out [i.e., I'm still young to be married].]

Everyone joined in, and then my girlfriends started the song "A white swan."

Then the next day, [a bride] would give away her *krasota*. I gave it to my male cousin: he came up to me and took my flowers, and took them off my head. I got up and went to him and began to lament, and everyone started crying. And then I went to the anteroom and sang to my cousin as soon as I got up from the floor:

Соколочек да братец милый!
Вы, соседи, да вы, соседушки,
Все соседи да малы детушки,
Разойдитеся вы, пожалуйста,
Вы мне дайте да путь-дороженьку,
Вы мне дайте во очи видети
Соколочка да братца милого

[My dear brother, my little falcon!
You neighbors, oh you, neighbors,
All you neighbors and your little children,
Move aside, please,
Give me a path, a road,
Let me see with my own eyes
My little falcon, my dear brother!]

Then the people would part—there were a lot of people there, from all the villages around. I went up to my cousin, and there [beside him] was sitting my sister's husband, my *dever*. I went up and fell on the feet of my cousin:

Соколочек да братец миленький,
Благослови-ка да Боже-Господа,
Меня в путь-то да во дороженьку,
Во широкую да во проезжую,
На чужую-то дальнюю сторону,
Ко чужому-то да чуженин-чуженцу

[My dear brother, my little falcon!
Please, Lord God, Bless
Me on my way, on my road,

On the wide and passable one
Toward the foreign, faraway place
Toward the foreign foreignness.]

(Orlovo, Belozersk region, Vologda oblast, 7 July 1996 [Bel 1-29])

In her laments, Maria Iakovlevna recounts the ways that the ritual asks a young woman
to acknowledge the patriarchal family structure. A bride must give deference to her male
sibling (here, a cousin) as she prepares to leave and to accept a new sort of brother. But
she does it by claiming her newly elevated status vis-à-vis the neighbors with their "little
children," whom she commands to let her through on her own path. The very mention of
her transition as a "road" suggests intentionality, although tradition has dictated these
images. The established poetic images capture the sense in which this is a personal transition in which no one can aid her (short of blessing her): she must rely on her own internal
resources as she departs on that "wide and passable" road to the unknown.

In this context, the clothing she wears symbolizes her new status, her new life. In her
lament, Maria Iakovlevna asks her mother whether she is well dressed. Such language
expresses deference to her mother's opinion—in effect asking, "Am I dressed well enough
so as not to cast shame on our family?"—emphasizing the bride's relatedness rather than
her individuality. But she also answers her own question, affirming that she has done well:
"Here I myself know and I myself see," showing the ability to do and choose for herself.
What she sees, though, seems to contradict the self-assuredness of these lines. In poetic
formulas common to wedding and funeral laments, she describes her dress as new and her
braid as short, indicating that she is not ready to be married: perhaps no one is ever fully
ready for the break with a past identity implied by a rite of passage.

Thus, we argue, these traditional words make reference to both the relational and the
individual self; they express and perform both obedience and self-reliance. Similarly, the
woman's performance of these laments is itself both active and passive. Young women
do not "compose" these texts, but neither do they just repeat what elders dictate. Women
often told us that they themselves chose what to sing, but when we asked them to show us
how it was done, they said that an old woman was usually present and they sang "after
her"—that is, with her, following her lead. Even if young women generally followed what
older women sang for them, we presume some brides produced what amounted to "their
own" texts: influenced by the texts they had heard, but not copying them word for word.[1]
In those cases when women lamented solo, there was likely room for them to choose traditional words that suited their own situations, and probably to change the laments
slightly, omitting some images and incorporating other traditional formulae.

Relatedness and individuation, constraint and freedom are important leitmotifs of the
wedding poetry itself. This is particularly true with the bride's symbolic action of saying

farewell to her *volia vol'naia* (willful will) and her *krasna krasota* (beautiful beauty). While the two images carry different semantic loads, they are often used together and may, in the final analysis, represent the same thing—the bride's maidenhood, her honor and worth as a girl. In essence they represent her *devka* persona, which is now being shed, honored, and mourned.

But this is a complex sort of mourning, as we see when we look at examples. They suggest that it is not unequivocally the case that the girl was better off or even more free when she was a girl. Ironically, *volia*—freedom or will—can imply responsibility, as it does in the following example (told by Maria Mikhailovna, born in 1913), where it is related to the notion of honor:

> They would usually set the wedding party for Sunday, and the bride would do the *devichnik* on Saturday. In the morning her godmother would heat up the *bania* and would lead the bride to wash; when they walked to the *bania*, the godmother would sweep the ground ahead of her with a broom, and on the way back, too. At the *devichnik* the lamenter would sit in the corner, and girlfriends on both sides of the bride. The closest one would sit on the right side. The bride sits in the first place by the doors. Her hair is in a bun, and she has a garland on her head, and flowers in the bun. When the *devichnik* ends, she gives the flower to her closest friend and says, "You take my *volia vol'naia* [willful will]. My *volia* has not been ridiculed, my *volia* has not been besmirched." In the evening the groom comes and brings her a present on a tray, and stays at the bride's house to have fun, they party all night, and in the morning he goes back on a horse. (Antushevo, Belozersk region, Vologda oblast, July 1994 [Bel 1-32])

If one must keep one's *volia* pure, as in this example, what kind of freedom is it? Levinton (1977) sees it more generally as the symbol of that which the girl loses in marriage: her virginity, and the social position of a girl. We would add that the social position of a girl was not characterized by unqualified freedom, but involved the difficult social responsibility of keeping her reputation and her honor intact, as Maria Mikhailovna implies here. Indeed, the now-betrothed bride—no longer a girl who has to watch after her reputation—is free to party all night with her husband-to-be. The purpose of keeping her honor intact was the maintenance of patriarchy: under that system, women are constrained to be loyal to one man (through the institution of marriage) so that paternity may be established. Thus, here "will" is not simply the individual ability to do what one wants, but it encompasses the tension between a girl's freedom—say, her will to choose a partner—and a girl's responsibility to behave in such a way that he will ask for her hand—that is, to uphold the values of patriarchy. In Russian village society the unmarried woman appears as the self-policing subject of the Foucauldian panopticon: she must control her own desire in order to fulfill the roles set out for her in patriarchy (Foucault 1979). However, as Oleg Kharkhordin has argued, the Russian model of mutual surveillance is the reverse of the panopticon, since it involves "a single person being surveilled by all," that is, by the collective (1999, 114). Marriage is neither the onset nor the cessation of freedom. Rather, the moment of marriage implies the bride's movement from one patriarchal institution of control (her birth family) to the next (her in-laws' family).

In marrying, then, the girl has neither increased nor decreased her power, but she has initiated her rise up the power ladder toward the top rung, the *bol'shukha* position, where women are maximally empowered and also maximally responsible. As we pointed out in chapter 2, rites of passage compensate for the increase in responsibility by offering an increase in status. To be sure, the bride enters her new family in a disempowered position. She must heed the will of all adult members of the family; as we showed in chapter 2, only her husband can intervene with his mother and sisters for her. Yet she is also the pride of her new family and raises to senior rank among her girlfriends. The position of a *molodka* is an envied and cherished one, as shown in numerous traditions: in many spring rituals on *Semik* (the seventh Thursday after Easter) and *Troitsa* (Pentecost, or the Day of the Holy Trinity), *molodki* conduct rituals together with *devushki*. In Arkhangel'sk *molodki* occupy a favored position (at the head of the line) in girls' dances; in weddings, *molodki* play leading roles in the *devichnik* ritual. As Inna Veselova and Galina Kabakova have argued, just as an "honest" *devushka* brings *slava* (glory) to her parents, so a *molodka* brings fertile, productive energy to her new *rod* (Veselova 2006; Kabakova 2001).

At the moment of her marriage, the girl undergoes a separation from her peer group that is necessary for her to eventually rise to fully potent female adulthood. The bride separates from her girlfriends as she symbolically gives them her prized possessions, *volia* and *krasota*. In one village, before she is led away to the *venets* (church ceremony), the bride sings to her friends a song containing the words "Take my *krasna krasota* / And my *vol'naia volia*," and they answer, "We will take your *krasna krasota*."

> Then . . . the girls sing that, and she breaks a spoon with her fist, she wraps a tablecloth around it and throws it to her girlfriends. . . . You have to break a wooden spoon with your fist.
> *What is the* krasota?
> *Krasna krasota?* It's your beauty, your youth, youth. You see. I give you my *krasna krasota* and *volia vol'naia*. I give it all to my girlfriends. Take it. Like that."
> (Woman born in 1913, Glushkovo, Belozersk region, Vologda oblast [Bel 1-19])

The spoon represents her family of origin: it was given to her by her parents, and she ate from one bowl at home with her family, thus partaking of a general *dolia* (fate, lot, share). The breaking of the spoon suggests the irrevocability of that which is occurring, and the bequeathing of that spoon to the girlfriends implies a final farewell that can be likened to the preparations for death. This ritual act indicates that the girlfriends metaphorically constitute a collective unit such that the qualities possessed by one can be transferred to the others. Indeed, in regional traditions throughout Russia, the symbol of *krasota/volia* is either bequeathed to the girlfriends, or a drama is played out in which the groom attempts to buy or steal, and then destroy, the symbolic object.[2] N. Zorin points out that the groom's actions toward these objects suggest that they are a symbol of the bride's belonging to the group of unmarried girls. She cannot marry as long as she is connected to and identifies with this group (2004, 118–19).

The bride's connection with a group of girls in a similar social position suggests that the vertical aspect of the ritual is about her exit from this group and her individuation with regard to the group. The poetry emphasizes this, as a repeated refrain in the songs sung by the girlfriends to the bride shows:

Отставала лебедушка
От стаду лебединого, от стаду лебединого.

Приставала лебедушка, приставала лебедушка,
Ко серым ко чужим гусям, ко серым ко чужим гусям.

[The swan departed
From the flock of swans, from the flock of swans

The swan joined, the swan joined
The gray unfamiliar geese, the gray unfamiliar geese.]

(Woman born in 1918, Karl Libknekht village, Belozersk region, Vologda oblast)

Such poetry, which depicts the bride's leaving one flock and joining another flock, raises the question of the bride's individual identity as opposed to her relational identity. We suggest that the marriage ceremony may mark the first time in a girl's life when she leaves an identity behind: up until now, she may have seen herself only in relational terms, judged from the outside by her parents and peers. Now that identity is given away, and she is subsequently given a new script to follow (by the elder women in the groom's family). The fact that she can shed an identity suggests that such identity is conditional, not an essential part of her. Perhaps marriage is the first moment when a girl must find what is left when she sheds her socially dictated persona.

As she sheds this persona, she honors it: it is gone, but it was worthy; it was even wonderful. This is the essential impulse behind the rituals involving the *krasota* and *volia*. We see this impulse taken to its apex in the following poetic text, a lament performed by

Anastasia Mikhailovna P., born in 1906 (from Lavrov, Belozersk region, Vologda oblast). This lament explores metaphorically the tension we have seen between freedom and responsibility in girlhood and marriage:

On the morning of the wedding, the bride tells her girlfriends what she dreamed the night before:

Ой, вы, миленькие подруженьки,
Ой, как задушевны да белы лебеди,
Ой, мине ночесь-то темна ноченька,
Ой, как не спаласи да не дремаласи,
Ой, как много снов да мне наснилоси,
Ой, много виденья да наказалоси.
Ой, как посреди-то да ночки темные,
Ой, как приходила да воля вольная,
Ой, как у окошка да постучалоси,
Ой, как у ворот-то поколотиласи,
Ой, как зашла в избу боеючи,
Ой, как говорила опасаючи,
Ой, как ко кроваточке подходила,
Ой, как за головушку подержала,
Ой, как русу косонъку поправила.
Ой, моя-то сказала да воля вольная:
Ой, пущай-ко а поспит да красна девица,
Ой, да пусть поспит-то да поволюется,
Пока у своих-то родных родителей.
Ой, теперь пошла да воля вольная,
Ой, как из избы-то пошла во двери,
Ой, из дверей-то пошла на улицу.
Ой, как улицей-то пошла девицею,
Ой, как по горам-то да пошла заюшкой,
Ой, как по подгорью да горностаюшкой,
Ой, как по лугам-то пошла лисицею,
Ой, как по лесам-то пошла куницею,
Ой, как по белым озерам белой лебедъю,
Ой, как синим морем да серой утицей.
Ой, как синее морюшко всколыбалоси.
Ой, как серая утица захлебаласи.
Ой, тут воля с неволюшкой повстречаласи.

Ой, как ты откуда да идешь, волюшка?

Ой, от душечки-то да красной девицы.

Ой, как ты же куда-то пошла, неволюшка?

Ой, как к душечке-то да красной девице.

Ой, девочъя жисть мине кончается.

[Oh you, dear girlfriends,

Oh, how dear are the white swans

Oh, last night, dark night

Oh, how I tossed and turned

Oh, how many dreams I dreamed

Oh, many visions appeared to me

Oh, how during the dark night

Oh, how *volia vol'naia* came to me

Oh, and tapped at the window

Oh, and banged at the gate

Oh, and came into the hut afraid [of being seen/heard]

Oh, and spoke secretly,

Oh, and came up to the bed,

Oh, and held my head [as if blessing her]

Oh, and she fixed my blond braid.

Oh, let the beautiful maiden sleep

Oh, let her sleep and use her *volia*

While she's at her born parents'.

Oh, now *volia vol'naia* went out

Oh, went out by the door of the hut

Oh, and from the door went to the street.

Oh, as a girl she went by the street,

Oh, as a rabbit she went by mountains,

Oh, as an ermine she went by hills,

Oh, as a fox she went by meadows,

Oh, as a marten she went by forests,

Oh, as a white swan she went by white lakes,

Oh, as a gray duck she went by blue sea.

Oh, the blue sea surged,

Oh, the gray duck gulped.

Oh, and here *volia* met *nevolia* [unwill].

Oh, whence do you come, *volia*?

Oh, from the dear beautiful maiden.

Oh, where are you going, *nevolia?*
Oh, to the dear beautiful maiden.
Oh, my life as a girl is ending.
Oh, my life as a *baba* is calling me.]

While in real life unconstrained female desire or a hypothetical girl's will would be a threat to patriarchy, in the poetic language of women's laments such unfettered freedom is an important trope. Anastasia Mikhailovna here tells a fantasy of girlhood freedom as the freedom of wild animals. As in epics and fairy tales, the character *volia vol'naia* is a shapeshifter, who can change from girl to ermine to duck as she goes over different terrains. Here *volia* not only means freedom but also performs her freedom through such traveling and shape-changing. Only when the sea surges and the duck gulps water does the freedom end: the very medium that carried the duck and symbolized freedom (the sea) now chokes the duck and makes it stop swimming. Girlhood itself contains the seeds of its own demise: to be a girl is to be destined to marry. The beauty and the freedom of the "dear beautiful maiden" have but one purpose, in this world view: to become a *baba*, a childbearing woman. Despite the necessity of marriage, and of the end of *volia*, the girl who enters into this life transition spends ample energy and power re-creating the complex image of *volia* in her laments. With this poetic honoring of her girlhood, she imaginatively sends herself off to the land of the *baba*.

She also spends her creative energy in physical ways during this time. She has been creating her dowry under her mother's tutelage for some time (since age eight or so); now she must embroider the shirts and the towels that will be given to the members of the groom's family. As Mary B. Kelly has shown, the production of these pieces involves skills akin to learning a language—the symbolic language of shapes and forms. In addition, the young embroiderer assimilates a manual craft (the skill to produce and work with fine thread), and engages in highly creative work. In order to serve a sacred ritual function, the cloths must be both traditional and original; girls produce them not by slavishly copying the examples of their forebears but by trying out new combinations based upon those examples (1996, 161–66). The basic purpose of the towels was to address the spirits of the bride's family's ancestors, to ask for their help and protection (Zorin 2004, 122). These towels and shirts then serve as public record of the bride's skill and creativity, as a woman born in 1910 related: "At the wedding, [in the groom's home] they'd hang the towels for everyone to see, they'd hang them on the wall, to show that she had a big dowry—on nails: towels and tablecloths she'd woven" (Kostino, Belozersk region, Vologda oblast, July 1996, [Bel 1-26]). The fact that the towels were hung in the home of the groom suggests further that they may have served as a kind of sacrifice to the ancestors of the groom's *rod* (clan), and also that by predisposing those ancestors toward the new member of the family, the towels may have had a protective function for the new bride (Zorin 2004, 121).

The public nature of this display also took the following form, as described by a woman born in 1903:

> If the [groom's] family was big, you had to give a lot of gifts, so that everyone, you know, was not insulted, so that [they'd say]: "What a bride! She gave gifts to everyone!" And they'd give them at the *svad'ba*. Either the godmother or a close aunt. Everyone would be sitting at their tables, helping themselves to food and drink. And then they'd bring out those boxes with the presents. So the godmother would start performing, saying, "Dear guests, our bride wasn't wandering about the forest, she wasn't busy stripping bast, but she was getting gifts ready! Here you go, matchmaker dear, the bride gives this to you!" She'd take them all out, and whoever was sitting there would get something, she'd give to all, and would stand on a chair all that time: there were lots of people, and she'd yell from her chair. (Savino, Belozersk region, Vologda oblast, July 1996 [Bel 1-52])

The bride's gifts not only showed off her skill and willingness to work hard; they served as tangible symbols of the social cohesion created through the wedding. The performance of the godmother makes both of these functions clear. Since the towels were created under the mother's tutelage and also inherited by the daughter through the maternal line, they served not only as a sign of the bride's own identity but also of her maternal family identity; they kept that meaning throughout the life of the woman (Zorin 2004, 122). That the bride does not present the fruits of her labor herself suggests that her role is that of the novice here: those undergoing age rituals typically must be passive, and are represented by others acting in their stead (Turner 1969, 95). While this moment in the ritual shows off the bride's skill, which might be viewed as an active embracing of the recognition she is due (something like a one-woman art exhibit), in fact the honor of her mother's family is also being exhibited and judged. The dowry and gifts are clearly the culmination of years of preparation and not only of her own efforts but those of her mother, sisters, and other female relatives.

All of the poetry and much of the material symbolism of the courtship and wedding rituals may be read in terms of a complex dichotomy: the bride is both active and passive, both creatively inspired and required to perform, both pursuing her own journey with a certain degree of intentionality and serving the community by performing a representation of the group to which she belongs.

Personal Stories

The previous section tended to address general questions about the wedding ritual, rather than telling personal stories of the participants. Personal stories often do not give the ethnographic detail that is desired from an "informant" when an ethnographer is trying to reconstruct a ritual that can no longer be viewed in real life. In fact, as will become clear in the sections below, when asked to tell about their marriages, most women omitted details about their weddings but included copious details about their engagements. For some women this is a reflection of what was interesting or flattering for them—the choice of a life partner, the time when a beloved man showed his serious interest. Their stories took the form of a romance plot. For those whose marriages were not particularly success-ful, the stories might not be flattering but could still be interesting or entertaining to listen-ers, and might therefore raise the status of the storyteller in the community. These stories often conformed to other plots, familiar from folk texts and literature, which included the stock characters of villains and villainesses.

Even if personal stories omit ethnographic detail, they give us the speaker's attitude toward the events that she is recounting, or at least, an attitude remembered, desired, and performed that day in the particular relational and discursive situation of the interview or conversation. Some of the stories quoted below were offered without any prompt-ing; others were a response to an initial question, such as "Tell me/us how you met your husband," "Tell me/us how you got married," "Tell me/us about your wedding," but in general, these were narratives in which the narrator was invested, not reports designed simply to fulfill the needs of the ethnographer (Polanyi 1985, 13).

These stories were products of interaction; they were not monologues. After asking our initial question, we made follow-up questions to facilitate our understanding of the story, and we expressed our reactions to what we were told (e.g., surprise, compassion, laughter) in order to encourage storytelling. This process "blends together the conscious-ness of the investigator and the subject, perhaps to the point where it is not possible to disentangle them" (Frank 1979, 85).

While these qualifications about personal stories as conversations are true of the inter-views we introduce below, in fact we begin our investigation with a different kind of nar-rative: an extended memoir dictated to folklorists and told from the first person. This source is one of the few existing memoirs of a peasant woman born in the first genera-tion (or just one year before it). Agrafena Glinkina, born in 1898 in a village in Smolensk oblast, was a noted folk singer whom ethnographers and musicologists interviewed and recorded many times in the 1950s and '60s. She knew more than three hundred songs, and sang very musically, with beautiful ornamentation and great feeling.[3] Despite her "one grade" of primary school, she wrote her memoir in the 1950s, which was then typed by Russian literature specialists, and finally published in 2007. She died in 1971 (Shchurov 2007, 3–4). A central event of her memoir tells of her wedding against her will to a man twenty-one years her senior, a distant relation whom her parents wished her to marry. Her account intersperses her feelings—of physical and emotional sickness, of wishing for her own death or the death of the groom—with descriptions of the various parts of the wedding ritual.

Her tale underlines our earlier point, that the ritual was designed to accommodate all possible variables, including a bride undergoing the ritual against her wishes. In several instances Glinkina describes how those who guided the ritual (young brides at the *devichnik*, the priest at the *venchanie*) responded when she did not participate or acted inappropriately: after commenting on her inappropriate behavior and seeing that she did not stop the behavior, they simply ignored her and continued on with the ritual. The bride's assertive self-expressions (at home she said, "If you like him so much, marry him yourselves!" and at the church ceremony she said, "I do not agree" to the marriage) were not taken seriously: one relative called them "caprices" and another said that she would cry for a while and then accept it; the groom, too, was of this mind, and so he made no attempt to smooth things over with her. Other behaviors she used to signal her disapproval were telling her sister she would commit suicide, crying too much at the *devichnik* (instead of lamenting appropriately), walking on the opposite side of the street as her groom on the way to register the marriage, and sitting on the opposite side of the carriage as her groom after the wedding. Nonetheless, she went along with the flow of the wedding: it happened by its own logic, as if without her. Her transgressions did not affect the inexorable force of ritual tradition. After a day of marriage, she ran away to her sister's house, and eventually back to her parents', where, after much difficulty, she obtained a divorce (Glinkina 2007, 70–79).

Glinkina's memoir shows that the wedding ritual was first and foremost designed to suit the needs of the community, and only secondarily to suit the needs of the bride. Through the contrast of her behavior—extreme passivity and resistance—with the stories of other women, we can see more clearly, as if in relief, their agency and initiative. Without the bride's initiative, the wedding proceeded, but it did not proceed "properly"—the participants kept stopping the progression to ask what was wrong. Glinkina's behavior was an exception, and was noticed as such; in the majority of cases, the bride assented to the wedding. Not many behaved with such flagrant contempt, as the surprised reactions of the participants showed. We have here an interesting case of a very self-assertive heroine who nonetheless submits to patriarchal power and to the wedding's logic. This tells us that young women's self-assertiveness and self-knowledge—and ability to express it—are not the provenance solely of later generations. Yet Glinkina's case shows that these qualities were clearly an anomaly in the early twentieth century: those around her did not value those qualities in a young woman.

In contrast with Glinkina's tale, the stories told by women born in the 1920s and '30s (whose marriages occurred during the 1940s and '50s) show that individual choice—not only of which partner to marry, but when, where, and how to marry—was becoming increasingly more common. These women often contrast their own self-assertiveness to the notions of fate and compulsion that were such an integral part of the traditional wedding as described by the previous generation. The importance of family approval and community cohesion still form central themes against which women judge their actions, but they acknowledge individual choice and desire as inherently valuable. Nonetheless, it is important to acknowledge the differences we found among the stories. These stories differ from one another but do not fall into neat generational divisions. In general we can say that women born later or having greater contact with city culture were more likely to phrase their stories in terms of self-interest as opposed to relational subjectivity. However, affiliation never disappeared; in fact, it might be viewed as the foundation of agency. We can place the stories on a continuum ranging from more to less affiliated and more to less self-focused, while recognizing that almost all these stories contain elements of both.

The narrative of Aglaia Paramonovna D., born in 1918 in a village on a river in the Leshukonsk region of Arkhangel'sk oblast, presents a self based primarily upon affiliation, with little consciousness of personal desire. Her story seems to hark back to the previous generation in its emphasis on obedience, acceptance, and passivity; but due to the upheaval of the time in which she lived, her story is very different from the narratives of the traditional weddings we examined earlier. Those who told us about the traditional wedding displayed confidence that there was a set order to things, that they were surrounded by those who knew the order, and that they were supported in going through the ritual. Their memories of their weddings showed that agency was important to them: they sang poetic laments, gave away their symbolic maidenhood, and gave carefully wrought presents to their new family members—all traditional acts that we read as showing skill and agency. Aglaia's narrative is different in that it emphasized the subject's lack of choice, lack of support, and lack of agency. Her wedding took place in the early thirties, just after her village's collectivization. The traditional order was shattered and a new order had not yet been built.

When we first met her, Aglaia told the story of her marriage and wedding disjointedly, in a matter-of-fact tone. A few days later she admitted that she was ashamed to talk about her marriage, especially when her sons were present. She shooed her sons out and gave more details the second time; but the core description of the wedding itself remained the same, almost word for word. Her first story concentrated on extraneous facts, such as the work that she and her future husband did at the time, the physical structure of her parents' house, the date of the foundation of the kolkhoz, and the kind of entertainment in which young people engaged. When asked by the interviewer, "Did you want to marry him?" Aglaia answered, "I probably got used to him. Probably got used to him." She omitted her own feelings about her husband, who was an exile, probably a former kulak who was released from prison and sent to the North. As she later explained, he showed up in her village looking for building and carpentry work, and Aglaia's father hired him. Then the kolkhoz chairman sent Aglaia together with her future husband, Aleksei, and other men to a logging camp where they worked together for some time. When they returned, he asked her parents for her hand.

She described her agreement to the marriage as follows: her sister came into the room to ask if she was willing to marry him. She said nothing, but her sister understood and went out to tell her parents.

> *So she understood right away that you agreed?*
> Yes, yes.
> *Meaning you liked him, you had worked with him?*
> Yes-yes-yes, yes-yes-yes-yes, yes.
> *Was he a good guy?*
> Not bad, not bad: he didn't scare [me], didn't give me any frights, didn't beat me. There weren't any, no bruises. There was nothing like that. So we lived like that. (Interview with Iulia Marinicheva, 11 July 2009)

Aglaia's story emphasizes her own passivity vis-à-vis the wills of others: as she repeats several times, her future husband told her father, "If you give her to me, I'll take her; if you won't give her, I'll take her." She describes the wedding itself in similar terms: "A woman came in, combed out my hair, braided my braids, they dressed me, they sat me and Alesha at a table, and across from us the chairman of the kolkhoz." What Aglaia portrays is part of the traditional wedding: a girl's single braid would be unbraided, signifying the fact that she was losing her attribution as an unmarried girl, and then her hair would be re-braided into the two braids worn by married women. According to ritual theory, the bride is supposed to be passive during this liminal period. She is led, her tresses are combed, the table is set, and she and her man are put at the table. But something is missing here. Aglaia does not tell who braided her hair; when pressed, she remembers the girl's name, and identifies her as "a neighbor," not a girlfriend. What happens is utterly strange to her:

> How did they all appear at our house, the chairman, the chairman's mother, and that one, how did I call her? Ustinia!
> *Filippovna.*
> Yes, yes, Ustinia Filippovna. How did they appear, how did they get there?

The traditional wedding, with its predictable course of events, and the bride's conscious knowledge and preparation does not provide context to understand Aglaia's utter bewilderment.

In Aglaia's narrative the territorial significance of the wedding, the marriage of two families to increase *svoi* and to intermingle two *rody*, is missing: the wedding, such as it is, takes place in the bride's family's house, but the house is transformed into public, official Soviet space by the presence of the kolkhoz chairman and his mother. There can be no exchange between families because the groom is without a family; the kolkhoz chairman has come with him instead of a father. The young couple will live in the bride's house, so her parents, who have three daughters and no sons, acquire a worker, which is to their advantage. Nevertheless, the parents' actions underline the transgressive nature of what is occurring: because her husband was an exile, her parents and sisters did not sit in the same room as the bride and groom. "The table is set. No one came—not my father, nor mother, nor sister, nor girlfriends. I married such a man. An old one, an exile."

While her wedding is missing the relational aspects that we found so crucial in the descriptions of the earlier weddings, Aglaia's story makes clear that such relations are important to her. Their absence is noted and remarked upon. Her shame at telling her story suggests that her values dictated a different outcome, but history—the influx of exiles into the North, collectivization, the role of the kolkhoz chairman in the private lives of citizens—imposed a departure from tradition. Despite her shame and the painful memories of her wedding, Aglaia does not make her tale melodramatic: she speaks neither of her misfortune nor victimhood. Later, when speaking of a death in the family, she asserts, "I lived a good life, why should I cry?"

Aglaia's story, and indeed her whole interview, gives little sense of entitlement. Aglaia tells the story as if she has no desires. Perhaps her desire, her passion (for what, we do not know) is so deeply hidden that even now, in her eighties, she cannot speak of it. Her subjectivity harks back to older models. In a comment about someone else's life choices, she exhibits her belief that individuals do not control their fate: she remembers a story about a young man who was forced by his parents to marry a certain girl, not the girl he wanted. "That's how it was! The father, the father and mother commanded. That's how it was. [*Sighs*]" (18 July 2009). In connection with that memory, she remembers and performs a song that she used to hear the married women sing, about a young wife forced to marry an old man. In it, the young wife runs away from him, gets herself dressed and made up, and goes to the *beseda*. He finds her there and beats her: "He beats my body as much as he wants. / Oh, I submitted to the old man, / Bowed to his right foot, / I won't do that anymore, / I'll kiss you, my dear."[4] The song recalls her comment that "he didn't scare [me], . . . didn't beat me. There were . . . no bruises."

Aglaia's stories are infused with her memories of family power relations and traditions that belonged to the generation of her mother. Yet she already lived in a different world. Her elder sister had a traditional Russian wedding, but she herself did not—there were no songs, no girlfriends (only the neighbor who combed out her hair), no traditional toasts, no dances. Her memory of her marriage emphasizes her passivity as a young bride, unable to speak, unable to act, without a sense of individual will. Now, in her old age, Aglaia is not a passive person: she actively offers her own composed poems, traditional songs, *chastushki*, and life stories to visitors. She generally lets herself be led by the interviewer, yet she has opinions and intentions, and at times she makes these clear. The interview is more copiously sprinkled with traditional texts than many, and most of these texts she performs

without prompting, just as they come into her head. Yet she is modest, and tends to denigrate her own singing, reciting, and tale-telling before doing it: "You probably don't want
that, but . . ."

Aglaia's interview suggests that in the culture of Russian rural dwellers, as in many cultures, awareness of oneself as an individual with desires distinct from those of one's parents or peers is acquired with age. In the culture of our rural interlocutors, the change may
be connected with the turn toward spirituality that would occur after a woman became a
bol'shukha and acquired the responsibility of maintaining connection with the ancestors.
At this age, women spoke of their actions toward the ancestors as due to their conscious
choice, arising from the sense that they alone knew (perhaps intuitively) how to best care for
the *rod*. Their lives then culminated in this most important act, as we recount in chapter 9.

Aglaia's storytelling differs from that of many of our other informants of the second and
third generations, who threw themselves into discussions of love matters with pleasure.
Whether they were recounting memories of "winning" a boy or leaving a bad husband,
most of these women had a clear sense of their own desires, ability to choose, and success
in love. With Aglaia's story, we are reminded of the geographical isolation of her community, in the northernmost region of Arkhangel'sk oblast. The area is sparsely populated,
with a poor transportation network. Settlements are located along rivers, and most land
forested. Aglaia grew up in a community whose values support the survival of the group
rather than the self-fulfillment of the individual. In societies like these, autobiography—in
the sense of a consciously constructed narrative of the individual's life—is in a sense "not
possible," as Georges Gusdorf suggests. "Community life unfolds like a great drama, with
its climactic moments originally fixed by the gods being repeated from age to age. Each
man [*sic*] thus appears as the possessor of a role, already performed by the ancestors and
to be performed again by descendants" (Gusdorf 1980, 30). Feminist theorists of autobiography have since corrected Gusdorf's theory: it is not that autobiography *per se* is not
possible; rather, what is impossible is autobiography in the sense of a story about a hero, a
"gatherer of men, of lands, of power, maker of kingdoms or of empires, inventor of laws
and of wisdom" (Gusdorf 1980, 31). Women's autobiography is different.

Aglaia's is a story about "group consciousness" that comes to us through other con-
sciousnesses (Friedman 1998, 76). For Aglaia has not produced an autobiography; it is
only in the course of multiple long, intense conversations with a curious, caring, open-
minded, and dedicated young folklorist (Iulia Marinicheva of Saint Petersburg State University) that Aglaia's story has been delivered to us. In fact, the same could be said of many
of our interviews; but in Aglaia's case it is doubly true because of her reticence.

The courtship story of Anna Pavlovna P., born the same year as Aglaia (1918) in Riazan'
oblast, is quite different. The self presented here is balanced between group- and self-
orientation. Anna's story acknowledges her active choice but also recognizes that acting

on one's own desires might not be acceptable in the community. Anna has a romantic relationship with one boy, while a different boy, Fedor, is seeing her girlfriend. But Anna notices that Fedor is "always around" her, and indeed at Maslenitsa, on the way home from the club, Fedor makes a proposal to her. She tells him to wait until spring, which displeases him: he says "strike while the iron is hot." When I (LO) asked why she wanted to wait until spring, she explains that she was most concerned not to insult her girlfriend. The drama of the story revolves around the question of the heroine's choice between loyalty to her friend or to Fedor. To describe this situation, Anna quotes a *chastushka*: "'My girlfriend and I were good friends / I would tell her everything / And that girlfriend / Became a competitor'—there's such a *pribas'ka* (*chastushka*). And I was somehow uncomfortable with her." Anna's actions here suggest that in the 1930s, community norms dictated that Anna put her friend's needs above her own: as she puts it, if she were to accept the boy's proposal, "Then she [my friend] would say, she's such-and-such, she doesn't help out, she [cares only about] herself." Nevertheless, as our analysis of the traditional wedding shows, the bride must separate from her group of girlfriends in order to mature. In the end, Anna Pavlovna emphasizes that she "won" the groom: "But anyway I won. I beat everyone. My friendship with him continued." As Anna herself points out, the plot of the story is like that of many romantic songs regarding female rivals. The self described here is as conscious of her own self-interest and agency as she is aware of the needs of others (Krasnoe, Kasimov region, Riazan' oblast, 2 May 2005).

In the second and third generations, stories of brides "winning" their grooms are many. Like Anna Pavlovna, Ksenia Alekseevna Ch., born in 1925 in Vologda oblast, told her story as one of victory over another woman. Unlike Anna, however, Ksenia betrayed no remorse or care for the other woman, and painted herself as shamelessly self-advancing. Ksenia told this story when we first came to her home, before I (LO) turned on my tape recorder; my only record of it is the notes I took in my notebook. It seemed that Ksenia was greeting us and introducing herself with this story. Ksenia's story performs agency and asserts the cultural plot of feminine boldness: she says that as an unmarried girl she was *boevaia* (feisty) in that she danced with boys. Subsequently, just after the war, she "married" a married man, a lieutenant in the army, by stealing him (*otbila*, literally "beat him away") from the woman he had married seven years earlier. The story is a bit unclear in my (LO's) notes, but it seems that for some reason the other woman had returned to live with her own mother during the war (thus, she was absent when the "stealing" took place). Ksenia and her husband lived forty years in an unregistered marriage. The plot in Ksenia's story that likens female competition to warfare is common for the period: we see it in *chastushki*, for example, in the following song exchange between two friends from the Siamzha region of Vologda oblast, Zoia Venediktovna K., born in 1932, and Evdokia Timofeevna Kh., born in 1933 (the friends sing alternating four-line ditties):

Ой подружка дорогая
Как не стыдно говорить
Наживи себе милого
И к тебе будёт ходить

Ой подруга дорогая
А нажить-то наживу
Да у тебя хорошей дролечка
Возьму да отобью

Ой подружка дорогая
Кудры русые не вей
У меня у бойкой девушки
Попробуй перебей

А я девчонка боевая
На подмошки ахала
Да береги подруга друга
Отбивать приехала

Бивай моя подруга
Отбивать тебе идёт
Но запомни дорогая
И за мной не пропадёт

[Oh, my dear girlfriend
How are you not ashamed?
Get yourself a boyfriend
And he'll come to see you.

Oh, my dear girlfriend
Why should I get one?
You have a nice boyfriend,
I'll just "beat him away."

Oh, my dear girlfriend
Don't fan your blond curls
Just try to "beat away" the guy
From this bold girl.

I'm a fighting girl
I helped myself by pretending to faint

So watch your guy, girlfriend
I've come to "beat him away."

Go ahead and "beat," my girlfriend
"To beat him away" suits you.
But remember, dear
I'll return the favor!]

(19 October 2004)

Perhaps surprisingly, the theme of competition with other girls in stories and songs of the second and third generation did not mean that girls had abandoned the code of girls' honor. The women from Pigilinka who sang the above *chastushki* said that as girls they lived by a code of behavior for courtship that did not allow boys to enter the home of the girl, nor girls to go alone with a boy just after meeting him. However, the *chastushki* quoted above do show a departure from the passivity of earlier generations. In contrast to lyric songs collected earlier, these *chastushki* are remarkable because of the playful, ironic, active mode of each heroine (in part this is due to the demands of the genre; see chapter 5). The plot of stealing a man uses a military term—*otbivat'*, formerly used to describe Cossacks or epic heroes stealing horses from enemies. Stealing implies intention and disdain for the interests of others. To be sure, songs about female competitors existed earlier—the concept of competing for a man is not new. But earlier lyric songs spoke of the heroine as victim of the actions of an evil, untrue man and evil, female competitor—connotations that are absent here.[5]

Like the *chastushki*, Ksenia's story does imply the relatively new social acceptability of "stealing," but what is remarkable here is Ksenia's rejection of traditional morals: to live with a married man without a wedding, and to talk about it without shame, suggests a radical departure from the system of girls' honor under which their parents lived. Ksenia positions herself as a radically self-assertive person, but does not mention her act as an act of transgression (she does not describe or present herself as a "bad girl" or a girl who suffered from her reputation). On the contrary, she describes her position as justified, because the man did not love his wife. In fact, Ksenia's act has a certain consonance with tradition. Marriage to a married man is a fairly common motif in Russian folklore: we see it in folktales, for example in "The Feather of Finist the Bright Falcon," in which the heroine must quest for her man, and finds him already married to a baker's daughter; after three trials she successfully takes him from the baker's daughter and marries him. No explanation is given of how she can marry him when he is already married, and indeed few readers question this, since it is clear that he was fated to be with the heroine. In her own story, however, Ksenia does not use the language of folklore—for example, she does not use the word *suzhenyi* (fated groom) to describe her husband. Nonetheless, the concept of a traditional morality—what one might call a "natural" morality, following Marie-Luise von Franz (1995)—that predates the Christian notion of marriage may underlie Ksenia's story.

A historical explanation is also possible. Contributing to Ksenia's choice to live in an unregistered marriage is the time when it took place: just after the war, men were viewed as a scarce resource and it was common for women to live with men out of wedlock— although it was also censured, as we discussed in chapter 2. Furthermore, Ksenia's story of her unconventional marriage followed her narration of a different story of unconventionality, reversal of fortune, and opposition to authority: Ksenia's family was dekulakized in the 1930s. Her family owned a mill and an inn for travelers; her father and other family members held important lay roles in church (her father read prayers and was a singer in the church choir). Her father refused to join the kolkhoz (although her brother did), was sent to Siberia, and "disappeared without a trace." During the post-Soviet period, when rehabilitation was offered to victims of political repression by the Russian government, her family sued but they received nothing. Collectivization wreaked havoc not only with possessions, farms, and families but also with values and relationships with authority. Perhaps Ksenia's rebellious self-conception was formed during these times.

If Ksenia's story contained little reference to traditional morals, that was not true of the story of her contemporary, Valentina Sergeevna G., born in 1925. Valentina's long, multi-part story exemplifies well the tensions between a modern and a premodern sensibility that we commonly see in women of this bridge generation. As in the other stories, there is a rival, but not a female one—rather, Valentina is wooed by two men. She tells this five-part story about the time just preceding her courtship and marriage, when she was studying to be a nurse practitioner (*fel'dsher*) and living with her mother and other students.

1. Story of how Valentina and her mother had a problem with the stove in their house and moved into the home of the extended family of her future husband, Ivan. Valentina's boyfriend at the time, Volodia, was in jail for stealing honey, so the grandmother in the family where they were staying teased her that if Volodia was there he would move them out! That is, he was in danger of losing her since there was another eligible young man around.

2. Story of how she dreamed her fate when she was in the third year of study to be a nurse practitioner. She, her mother, three male students, and one female student (Dasha) were living with an older woman, Babka Katia. She and Dasha asked Babka Katia to tell their fortunes, and they gathered all the necessary objects for the fortune-telling. Meanwhile the boys teased the girls: "Hasn't anyone come out to you yet? Hasn't anyone come yet? It'll soon be twelve o'clock, maybe someone came? Maybe you have seen someone?" Valentina told Dasha, "Let's go to bed." Valentina dreamed of Ivan (whom she eventually married), but told Babka the next morning: "I will never get married. He's older than me, and besides

he has been going to *posidelki* [girls' work and courtship parties]." She added, "I already got an assignment, I will go far away, to the Iaroslavl' region, and there I'll marry." Babka answered, "No, my dear, that is your *suzhenyi* [your betrothed]. You will go away, and will come back from there. You'll come back." Valentina answered, "But they won't let me." Babka Katia: "They'll let you. You yourself will leave."

3. Story of Valentina's move to the Iaroslavl' region with her girlfriend Sashka. Valentina "did not like it there, there was cattle right in the hut where I lived, straw on the floor, they had cows." Also, the regional health center where she was to work was located in a house whose floors and furniture were black with dirt. So when she was asked for her documents, Valentina said she would bring them the next day. She had decided to leave: she gave the food she had brought to Sashka to lighten her suitcase and took the train to Tuma. From there she walked home, a trip of two days. When she returned, her mother had received a letter from the authorities, and was worried that Valentina would be brought to court for breaking her contract. But Valentina reasoned this would only be a problem "if I had worked, if I had run away from work." Meanwhile her friend Dasha had gotten a job as a nurse locally, and one of her bosses was Dasha's father-in-law; this man knew Valentina's stepfather, and came to Valentina's home to invite her to come work for them, which she did.

4. Story of Valentina's dream about her future husband. "I worked here, and I was going home from work, and I go right to their house. Into the house. His mother: 'Oi, girl, sit down at the table,' and she brought a cup of soup, rich soup, and I sat there at the table, I said: 'No, I'm going home.' . . . I went to their door, 'I'm going home.' I sat down again, and 'No, you sit, sit,' but I put the spoon down and went again [to the door]. 'Wait, wait, girl,' I sat down again, and stayed there. I thought, probably that's it. . . . I stayed."

5. Story of how Valentina and her three girlfriends attended a party at her betrothed's house when he came home from the war. His mother and father planned that when he returned they would kill a calf. "We were barefoot, it was Saturday. We were outside. And San'ka Fox said, and San'ka Timosha, 'They are singing there. Under the window, on the bench, there are lots of them. Let's go look at the *zhenikh* [groom, eligible bachelor]!' The girls crept over in their bare feet and Ivan's father said, "'Look, Ivan Vasil'evich, the *nevesty* [brides, marriage-eligible girls] are here! Will you sing songs with us?' They: 'We will!' We loved to sing songs." On the way back home, the girls fell into the swamp and scratched up their knees. Valentina got into bed, but her mother called her out, and Valentina saw that her knees were all bloody. She cleaned them with iodine. Soon her girlfriends appeared; they also needed to be cleaned up. Her mother asked, "What did you climb into? . . . I heard

you singing songs. But why are your legs, your knees all bloody?" (Krasnoe, Riazan' oblast, 27 April 2005)

During an earlier visit, Valentina had explained how the actual engagement took place (we will call this part 6):

6. Two weeks after she returned from Iaroslavl', Valentina started to work locally. She was wanted for work in a different village, but her boss wanted to keep her on, so he lied and said that she needed to stay locally, since she was getting married in January. He told her that when the authorities in the other place asked her, she should tell the same lie: that she was marrying. She didn't sleep all night before she had to go to the other village and tell the lie. She was afraid that people from her village would find out, and she still wanted to "play awhile"—to not be married. The false news was spread by a local woman who happened to be present when Valentina told the lie, and Ivan's aunt found out. The aunt told him, "You're going to lose your bride. She'll be stolen out from under you." So one night, the young people were at *posidelki* and they were all sleeping on the benches. Early in the morning, Ivan asked Valentina if she was getting married. She said no, she still wanted to "play a little." He said, "Get up and get dressed." She said, "Vania, I'm on duty, I'd like to lie here a little more." "Get up, get up, get dressed." She got up and they went out. Ivan said, "We're going to your house." "What for?" "We're going to talk about the wedding." "Oi! I'm afraid!" "Why are you afraid? I'm not afraid. I'll go ahead and you go behind me. I'm not going to give you away to anybody." When they got to Valentina's house, Ivan told Valentina's mother, "We are going to come to you today." "Why?" "To agree about the wedding." Valentina said she was silent: "I was so afraid . . . And when they came, Mother, Father, and Ivan [sat at the table], and I sat to the side. He said, 'She'd get along with anyone. She has a mild character. She's good. I'm not going to give her away to anyone.'" They married 20 January (Krasnoe, Riazan' oblast, 4 December 2004).

Valentina's story clearly shows the tension between a modern and a traditional sensibility. It engages with the theme of fate that was such an integral part of women's understanding of the marriage process. Yet the storyteller negotiates her relationship to fate: while she asks the fortune-teller to help her see her fate, she does not initially *accept* the fate that she dreams about. To the young Valentina, work and career are more important than a husband. Furthermore, she has already received a work assignment and sees this as a more important directive than the one offered by the prophetic dream. At this point in the story (section 3) it seems that her allegiance to the Soviet authorities takes precedence over tradition. Clearly, she negotiates her relationship to the fortune-telling itself (in section 2): although she and her girlfriend ask Babka Katia for help in performing the ritual, the boys' satirical comments lead Valentina to end the ritual.

It should be noted that the tradition recounted here does not see fortune-telling as the passive reception of a vision from a gifted seer or from objects, but instead enables the subject herself to see her future (in dreams). Thus, fortune-telling, like dreams, may be seen as the revelation of deep-seated unconscious desires. In this context, Valentina's rejection of her own vision (by saying, "I won't get married") constitutes a serious distrust of tradition and negation of her own desire. But the third section of the story shows that Valentina's allegiance is ultimately not to the Soviet government but to herself. Rather than obediently accepting the work directive, Valentina makes her own choice based upon her own value of cleanliness and her sense of her self-worth, and in so doing faces the possible censure of her mother and the authorities.

She escapes such consequences, and her familial and personal connections allow her to establish her career near to home. Valentina's recounting of how she got a job through connections—that is, strictly speaking, through *blat* (calling in favors)—betrays no effort to hide what she did: rather, Valentina shows herself to have the social competence to achieve her career needs with the help of her social network. As Alena Ledeneva has shown, *blat* was ubiquitous in the Soviet Union, not only in urban settings but also in the countryside; *blat* exchanges were viewed as reciprocity, and the networks they built "served to certify a social community"—that is, to increase social cohesion (1998, 134–35). Valentina's is a tale of a relational self that also emphasizes self-reliance and even resistance: the subject knows her own mind and speaks it, even when her choices conflict with the demands of society and authorities.

While the heroine exercises her own agency throughout the story, there are many traditional elements. Territorial symbolism figures significantly within the fourth, fifth, and sixth sections. The bride's dream of entering her future in-laws' house and deciding to stay may be read as prophetic (and was probably recounted because it seemed prophetic to Valentina). Her story of visiting the future in-laws' house and singing there with girlfriends shows the important roles played by the female cohort: without her group of girlfriends, she could not have had these adventures, since girls socialized as groups in order to protect their honor. Her remark that she "would like to play for a while" gives us insight into the concept of *volia*; for Valentina, the process of courtship is not a heavy task but pleasurable. During my (LO) interviews with her I heard numerous, repeated stories of boyfriends she spurned; these attest that courtship was flattering and strengthened her sense of self-worth. Nonetheless, she quickly allowed Ivan to take over when she realized he was proposing marriage. In this section of the story (5), she changes her self-depiction from an active, self-confident young woman with an important job to a frightened and passive child who must be led. Perhaps the most significant traditional element of this story is the storyteller's insistence that her groom was her "fate." In fact, the point of the first five sections, which were told in succession, is that despite her resisting that fate, her two dreams and the interpretation of the elder woman made the ending clear from the outset. It could end

Evdokia Timofeevna Kh. (b. 1932) and her husband (b. 1940) on the day of his conscription into the Red Army, Vologda oblast, 1960. (COURTESY OF KH. FAMILY ARCHIVE)

no other way than with her happy marriage to Ivan. Thus, ultimately Valentina situates her story within the standard cultural plot of wedding ritual tradition. The selfhood she constructs through her story is balanced between tradition and modernity, between other- and self-focus.

The story of her two marriages told by Evdokia Timofeevna Kh., born in 1932 in Vologda oblast, contains few traditional elements, and although the self described is deeply affiliated, the manner of telling strongly emphasizes self-focus and self-reliance. In essence, this is a story of resistance that depicts the heroine as not accepting a subordinate role toward her man. Evdokia's first marriage to "Vasia" ended after three months; she separated from him and later married a man eight years her junior, who came to live with her and her parents. During the story Evdokia gives several explanations for the first marriage's failure: Vasia's expectations and values differed from those of his bride (he expected her and her family to wait on him in a formal fashion); he beat her "for no reason"; and a supposed jealous ex-girlfriend of his who was pregnant with his child arranged to have a magical spell put on Evdokia so that she would start hating him. Evdokia's story has much in common with melodramatic plots that women would be familiar with in romance songs (see chapter 4). In accordance with the typical plots of such songs, Evdokia would seem to play the role of victim: the evil-doers are both a villainess (the "other woman") and a villain (the groom himself). However, Evdokia does not fully play the victim. She depicts herself as a strong person with an excellent support network (her parents, sister's family, and even his own mother and aunt), who has no need to put up with humiliation. In her story, her ability to express herself strongly in opposition to her husband is foregrounded:

> And I'm no worse and no better, Laura. I say to him, "You're stupid." I say, "You're stupid." [...]
> I wasn't going to play up to him. [...]
> And he up and says, "Wait, I have to talk to you!" I say, "What's to say?" [...]
> My father says, "She won't go . . . She won't be going with you anymore." I say, "I'm not going with you anymore." He: "How is that you won't be going, what will I say at home?" And I say, "Say whatever you want."

Evdokia depicts herself as negotiating her relationship to community opinion. She asserts that she does not care about either his or her own reputation: she emphasizes this when she states that she married Vasia despite women's warnings that he was not a good person. She exercises her agency throughout the story, first in choosing Vasia and then in choosing to reject him. She exemplifies the type of the "fighting woman" that we saw in the *chastushki* quoted above (indeed, she was one of the singers of those *chastushki*). Yet the story is formulated at least partly in terms of a melodramatic plot: her rejection of him is overdetermined, explained not only by the fact that he criticized her and her family and beat her, but also by magic (that is, the intercession of higher powers) and love intrigue.

Evdokia's story emphasizes that self- and other-focus are not opposite poles on a continuum, but rather are inextricably linked. Evdokia's ability to care for herself comes from her support network: her parents and sister. This is a particular kind of other-focus, very different from what we saw in earlier models: she does not speak of what she does for others or of her fear of others' judgment, but rather of how she is helped by them. The strong words that she says to Vasia in the story are repeated *after* similar words of her father's, and it is through consultation with her parents that she decides to leave Vasia. Reports of other women of this generation showed that this kind of support was rare; more often, women who were unhappy in their marriages did not return home. The reason for the family's reacceptance of Evdokia in their home may have to do with the personality and views of her father, or the fact that she was the youngest of two girls: as she quotes her father, "We don't have anyone else [at home]; don't go back, to hell with him." For her parents, to have Evdokia at home was not an undue burden; indeed, as it turned out, she later brought a male worker to the family, which must have lightened the financial burden on her parents.

Evdokia's story is remarkable in its coherence and flow, suggesting it has been told many times. Indeed, Evdokia herself told the story to us twice (on two successive visits), and emphasized slightly different aspects each time. The story is also remarkable in its thematization of self-expression. An essential part of the story is the storyteller's repeated quoting of the remarks she made to Vasia, suggesting the heroine of her memories speaks her desires clearly and forcefully.

Indeed, many of these second- and third-generation women are masterful storytellers who clearly enjoy narrating their experiences. Several of the stories emphasize their heroines' acts of self-expression as critical moves at key moments of their stories: for example, more than one told a perspective suitor to "wait." Women quote themselves directly (attributing to themselves particular, well-chosen words), and often repeat the critical phrases that helped to cement their long-ago life-changing decisions. The heroines of these life stories emphasize their ability to speak in *opposition* to the demands of others. Perhaps unsurprisingly, in narrating their young adulthood they find the definition of their selfhood in what amounts to a kind of rebellion. Desire itself—the expression of that which one wants, as opposed to that which one does not want—as it turns out, is more difficult to speak of. The narrators we examined here largely omit or use other means to configure their desire. Valentina is the one exception: she speaks of it obliquely, in terms of fortune-telling, fate, and dreams, as well as directly: "to play for a while."

We have said that the combined relational and individual selfhood constructed by the majority of the life stories of the second and third generations is already present in the stories of wedding tradition, in an embryonic form. Yet the rebellion, agency, and self-expression—and the *acceptance* of these actions and words by the families and community surrounding these women—are notable differences between these later stories and the first generation. These appear to be relatively new elements that allow for greater individual delineation of self, because that self is supported in its explorations of desire and independence. In the final section of this chapter, we suggest some reasons for the change.

The Cultivation of Agency and the Personal

We have already suggested some reasons why women may have shown increased agency and self-consciousness in the Soviet period. With Ksenia's story, we connected her rebellion vis-à-vis community morals with wartime deprivation and her family's earlier dekulakization. In essence, we supposed that the experience of dekulakization could have affected citizens' trust of authority and willingness to accede blindly to public opinion, morals, and convention. In effect, by singling out individuals to repress, the Soviet government may have contributed to the growth of individualism. Kharkhordin describes something similar: he argues that the Soviet collective gave birth to a new kind of individual subjectivity that was born out of the need to dissimulate. Soviet individuals in effect split off a part of themselves that was to remain inaccessible to all but the most trusted insiders (1999, 357). Of course, we cannot know if that was the case in this instance.

We also traced girls' self-interest and willingness to compete openly with other girls for a man's affections to songs (*chastushki*) bearing similar self-conceptions. Indeed, as

Stephen Frank has argued, and as we will later show, the *chastushka* genre itself changed village culture by giving young people expanded means of expressing personal opinion and satire publicly (1992, 723). Thus, it was not that competition did not happen in earlier periods but that *chastushki* provided a means for the unabashed public expression of the emotions provoked by difficult social situations.

A deeper underlying reason for the change may include exposure to city culture. However, it is not the case that rural tradition had never changed previously, nor that exposure to industrialized, urbanized culture toward the end of the nineteenth century fractured and destroyed village life while cultivating self-interest and competition, as the clichéd view would have it. As Frank has persuasively argued, village youth accepted parts of city culture and retained elements of tradition that suited them, consciously carving out a culture that served their needs. In the post-Emancipation period, there was evidence of young people's growing self-assertiveness in villages, which contemporaries attributed to city influence that reached the village through outmigration (seasonal or permanent work in cities). The change could be viewed in increased youth control of their winter evening parties, the new "fashions, dances, songs, games, attitudes, and ideas"—sometimes overtly romantic or erotic ones—brought back by young male outworkers, and the young people's insistence on their own choice of marriage partner (Frank 1992, 712–17). Indeed, many villagers themselves felt outmigration changed men and women: they became more bold, independent, outspoken, and less willing to submit to authorities; women's sexuality, they felt, became dangerously free of patriarchal control. Other villagers, for whom patriarchal control was oppressive, found the city a source of opportunity and freedom (Engel 1993, 458–59).

Education played a large role: the Soviet government began an intense program of education focusing upon rural children and rural women in the 1920s and '30s. As Evgeny Dobrenko has argued, starting in the 1930s the Soviet educational system engaged in a style of teaching specifically designed to inculcate values, including aesthetic values and images of the New Soviet Person. This educational approach, called "nurturing" (*vospitatel'nyi*), was both broader (encompassing more areas of knowledge) and also more normative (it tended to inculcate the same standards in each individual) than a content-based (*obrazovatel'nyi*) approach (Dobrenko 1997, 147). With this approach, even rural women who received only four grades of education (our second generation, those who entered school in the 1920s and early 1930s) potentially acquired a heavy dose of ideological reconditioning. The effectiveness often depended upon teachers, support given by the kolkhoz chairman, the parents' ability to afford shoes and clothes, and so on (Fitzpatrick 1996, 226–27). Those who received the seven-grade compulsory education starting in 1939–40 (thus, our third-generation informants born in 1932 and later) would likely have been very familiar with Socialist patterns and ideas from school reading.[6] The education heavily influenced not just what children read but also how they interpreted what they read. In particular, one of the important aesthetic characteristics of the main literary style, Socialist Realism, was the "positive hero," whom authorities hoped young people would model themselves after. The ultimate goal was the "development of the Soviet person" (Dobrenko 1997, 147, 284–93). In particular, women's acceptance of new ideas about womanhood was spurred by narratives about positive Soviet heroines, which were ubiquitous in Soviet media and literature (Chatterjee 2002, 140). These forms of propaganda familiarized rural women with new ideas about men's and women's equality within the family and in the workplace, and about women's right to choose livelihood and husband.

Soviet pupils were actively encouraged to weaken or break ties with family and tradition, which may have contributed to their acquisition of an enhanced consciousness of self and individual desire in relation to community norms and expectations. In particular, schools and extracurricular programs cultivated in children a spirit of voluntarism, activism, and initiative. Programs that assisted in changing the attitudes of young people toward tradition were the antireligious campaign, the literacy campaign, organized cultural activities (such as public readings, plays, and holiday celebrations), and the campaigns for improved hygiene, sanitation, and health care (Partlett 2004; Hoffmann 2003). These campaigns were successful insofar as the peasants themselves chose to modernize. For example, the war against religion (involving direct propaganda by Komsomol members) did not meet with adult women's broad approval due to the aggressive manner in which it was conducted, and also due to women's deeply seated beliefs (Gaditskaia and Skorik 2009, 301–3; Tirado 1996, 353, 359); however, it was more successful with the younger generation. Most significant was the program of "eradication of illiteracy," called by its Soviet acronym *likbez*. *Likbez* was effective in changing women's consciousness because it was popular among the women themselves—particularly young rural women, who saw education as a means to greater opportunity.

William Partlett argues that the hygiene campaign—which connected bodily hygiene and domestic order with triumph over disease—was "crucial in transferring a modern sense of agency to children," because it fostered belief in the efficacy of science. In essence it taught children that the way they treated their environment mattered in practical, life-and-death terms. Children were encouraged to bring the knowledge they had acquired in school home to their parents, which fostered a sense of individual initiative and purpose (Partlett 2004, 884; Hoffmann 2003, 16–18). Of course, hygiene impacted primarily the sphere of responsibility of women.

To be sure, collectivism was the desired end goal of all of this activism and initiative. Holiday celebrations—Soviet rituals, created to replace or transform traditional rituals—were important technique for fostering a spirit of collective based upon new ideals (Partlett 2004, 885). As Kharkhordin has argued, the collective (*kollektiv*) was at the core of the identity formation of the new Soviet person. The Soviet collective took as its method of control mutual surveillance, in which "the group is entrusted with the task of controlling itself."

The Russian rural community had used this method for centuries, but the Soviet model added one essential ingredient: a higher cause, that is, the inculcation of moral perfection in order to build a utopian society (Kharkhordin 1999, 110). The subjectivity implied by this model was a self always morally judged by the collective, always seeking self-development and self-perfection, especially through hero identification. Self-fashioning became a goal achievable through these means (1999, 357–58).

Thus, there was some contradiction in Soviet selfhood: the construction of a collective self was desired, but the means to achieve collectivism implied cultivating agency and self-fashioning, which are at the foundations of individualism. As David Hoffmann has written, the Soviet government "espoused an illiberal subjectivity that sought to enlighten and transform individuals even as it opposed individualism" (2003, 16–17). The contradiction was not felt as such by our interlocutors. The Soviet collective was a comfortable concept for peasants, who anyway were used to self-policing (Kharkhordin 1999, 129–30). Village conceptions of selfhood had been moving in the direction of increasing self-assertion for some time, so by the Soviet period it was not new for elders to be complaining that young people were too eager to flout community values. Gradually, some of the new behaviors were accepted by the older generation; by the time our informants of the third generation were marrying, after World War II, self-assertion and self-expression were common enough that they were not looked at as anomalies, and Soviet propaganda ensured that there were plenty of forceful female models for young women to follow. As for elements of tradition, clearly the second and third generations retained many aspects of the culture of their mothers, while embracing new values that suited their self-interests. In particular, singing— both traditional songs and newly composed ditties—and magic—using the powers of the other world in spells and fortune-telling—stand out as spheres of activity that were not eradicated, much as the Soviet authorities would have liked to accomplish this. In people's lives and belief systems, magic occupied that split-off private sphere that no one talked about publicly; the same was not true for music. Our next two chapters show that women's traditional singing was and is a practice that spans the public and private spheres, offering a publicly acceptable way for women to express a world of private emotions and individual responses to socially dictated roles.

4

The Pleasure, Power, and Nostalgia of Melodrama

Twentieth-Century Singing Traditions and Women's Identity Construction

Group singing is one way that Russian rural women construct identities, both public and private. On the one hand, folk singing is a public activity that has been encouraged by the state and its various organs, both during the Soviet period and after. It is a way for women to participate in the discourse of the world beyond their village. On the other hand, in their singing at home, at parties with friends, or in their handwritten notebooks, many rural women have chosen individual repertoires that have important personal significance for them. These songs may have their origins in the Soviet period or in the nineteenth century; they may be mass songs played by state radio in the 1950s and '60s, or songs that only locals know. Women's choices of songs are not made by the criteria folklorists use to categorize their songs; they choose songs based upon the principles of individual and group memory and personal pleasure.

As we will show in this chapter, the repertoires chosen by village women are composed largely of romance songs that represent a world view they apparently no longer subscribe to—that of melodrama, a cultural mode that supports a highly patriarchal order. With overwrought emotion, the songs portray hapless female victims whose honor is cruelly taken by villains, or villainesses who are untrue to their men. In the older (nineteenth-century) songs, often a final "moral" explicitly decodes the recounted events as a caution to young girls; sometimes the older songs end in suicide (of the wronged girl) or murder (the man kills the untrue woman), which also sends a strong cautionary message. Many of the newer songs in this vein take on the point of view of the wronged woman, and she often complains that, due to shame, she is unable to express her desires.

These songs reflect the changing cultural norms of the late nineteenth to mid-twentieth centuries. As Anthony Giddens has argued, the concept of romantic love, which came into being in the late eighteenth century, "reflected the aspirations of women in a society becoming much more individualized, but still subject to the rule of patriarchy" (Giddens and Pierson 1998, 140). In this context, melodramatic romantic plots draw both from the new culture of modernity and from the world of patriarchal tradition. Insofar as the songs project a new script—an ideal of male and female intimacy, with the "promise of emotional equality"—they are modern; insofar as they perpetuate the "ethos of seduction and abandonment" and the division between virtuous and fallen women, they represent a world view characteristic of village tradition (Giddens and Pierson 1998, 140–41).

As we saw in the previous chapter, our interlocutors of the second and third generations did not tend to describe themselves as victims of patriarchy. Rather, the heroines of their personal stories expressed their own desires, chose their own spouses and life work, and "won" their men. Thus, certain aspects of these melodramatic songs did not express their own plots and habitus. But even though our interlocutors had moved beyond the traditional plot of marriage, which was based upon ritual and a community-dictated moral code that upheld duty and the economic survival of family, they still lived within and participated in the maintenance of a patriarchy, with its attendant traditions, expectations for women and men, and moral codes. As we will show below, it is precisely this mix of patriarchal morality and a modern view of romance that the songs express. We see expression of this traditional-modern duality in two of the daily practices of our interlocutors: verbal gossip and television soap-opera watching. Taken together, these manifestations of melodrama suggest that the melodramatic mode expresses central aspects of the subjectivities, value systems, and collective memories of rural women born before 1950.

In the Soviet context, in which civic-mindedness was encouraged and the personal sphere was anathema to the project of building Socialism, to choose to sing about the world of private feelings constituted a kind of resistance. Louise McReynolds and Joan Neuberger have demonstrated why melodrama was popular in the Soviet context: "As an alternative to the old intelligentsia's valorization of reason, propriety, and public and political commitment, melodrama offered its audiences a world of feeling, sensation, and private moral dilemmas." But it also "explored the social issues that preoccupied its audiences and offered models of behavior for changing times" (McReynolds and Neuberger 2002, 3). It seems clear that villagers choose songs partly based upon some of the same criteria that draw them to soap operas in their daily serial-watching rituals: access to a world of feeling; the pleasure of identification with victims and judgment of villains; and a gateway to discourse about important social issues that concern women, such as societal expectations, their treatment by men, and questions of female agency.

We link the attraction of melodrama with pleasure, power, and nostalgia. We begin below with an analysis of the place, meaning, and function of songs and singing in the lives of women born during the first half of the twentieth century. We show that the singing of romance songs, most often done in groups, affords village women aesthetic pleasure and social power, and allows them to express nostalgia for the culture and values of their mothers and/or their own youth. These song texts, of literary origin, belong to the literary

genre of melodrama. We suggest that the songs are pleasurable to our interlocutors because they allow singers to identify with the predicaments of the heroines and experience
moral superiority when judging others, including villainesses. The songs confirm some of
the deeply held traditional values of the singers, specifically women's honor, responsibilities toward the *rod*, and fate.

In the songs, a villainess's characteristics tend to be painted in broad brushstrokes;
the villainess character is far more developed in television soap operas, which our interlocutors watch daily. These melodramatic television serials give the viewer vicarious pleasures—of identification with the villainess's rebellion and her hedonism (which we call the
"daughter" position), as well as judgment (the "mother" position). Rather than nostalgia
for the values of the mother's generation, their soap-opera watching offers a glimpse of
the clash between tradition and modernity that is characteristic of the generational conflicts between twentieth-century mothers and daughters. We explore that relationship from
another point of view in the final section of the chapter, in which we show how women use
melodrama to speak about the behavior of others in the verbal mode of gossip.

Pleasure, Power, and Nostalgia in Women's Singing

Songs are complex combinations of stories and music that stimulate cognitive, aesthetic, and
emotional reactions in hearers and listeners. They are part of social and ideological practice and help to construct identities. Several aspects of group singing strongly supported
women's values and social identities: this was an activity that created and maintained *svoi*-
groups (groups of people who consider themselves *svoi*, one's own) and performed social
cohesion by publicly presenting texts and melodies that everyone knew and that evoked
strong memories from performers and audience. When we visited women of all three generations in Russian villages, they offered us both stories and songs, as if to show that these
were ways for them to tell about themselves. Their songs often accompanied their stories:
even if we did not ask for songs, they often inserted them into their narratives to illustrate
a point or show the truth or commonness of what they were telling, just as one cites a
proverb. When they saw that we were interested in their songs, they would take out handwritten songbooks to jog their memories and offer us more material. Often we took pleasure in the aesthetic beauty of their singing, sang with them on the repeated lines, and tried
to arrange meetings of several women so that they could show us how they sang in groups.
For many women, although the texts of songs were important, singing in groups was one
of the main pleasures associated with singing. Group singing also had specific meaning for
each individual: for some, it was a source of self-worth and identity. To paraphrase a few of
the comments we heard regularly: "I sing," "I sing a certain part," "I was invited to sing
at such-and-such an event," "I sang better/more than others." For others, the mention of
singing was connected with feelings of past inadequacy ("I was not chosen to sing") or rifts
in the fabric of the *svoi*-group ("They took so-and-so instead of me"). For a few women,

singing was not a large part of the stories of their youth, but among women of the first and second generations these were in the minority.

Both the texts and the contexts of songs and singing were important for our interlocutors. Both could be symbolic, could represent memory, and could have a practical function (communication). We became aware that for some women, songs functioned as tangible markers or "handles" that allowed them to access memories of community events or personal milestones, and as symbols of something they valued. Very few women kept narrative diaries, but many kept notebooks of song texts they wished to remember. In this sense, the notebooks did constitute a sort of diary. When introducing a song to us, women often remembered whom they had learned it from and when they had sung it. When asked, some explained what they liked about the song and what it meant to them (mostly these comments referred to the song's text, not its musical fabric). Often, however, they simply wished to share the song, as if it were self-explanatory. And in a sense, songs are self-explanatory: to listen to or sing a song is to have a joint experience with the other hearers and singers.

The history of women's involvement in singing tells us something about the reasons for the continued importance of this activity for them. In prerevolutionary Russian village culture, group singing was a means of tapping into otherworldly and social power. In ritual contexts, singing was believed to bring about a magical result, such as an increase in a harvest or the fertility of a bride; on the social plane, it contributed to a strong sense of group cohesion (*svoi*) (Propp [1961] 1993, 3; Lineva 1904, vol. 1). Most Russian singing was polyphonic (heterophonic): a type of choral singing in which each member improvises his or her own part, independently of the other melodies. In ritual singing, the text was often most important, and the melodies imitated the intonations of speech and served the function of conveying the text; by contrast, in lyric singing, especially in the "drawn-out" or *protiazhnaia* song, the melody was as important as the words in conveying the song's feeling. Melodies had their own musical structure, independent of the words; a single syllable might be sung with a whole melodic phrase (Zemtsovskii 1964, 6, 41). It was an elaborate art, which a person learned gradually through listening, imitating, and being included in family and community music-making.

In some Slavic cultures, singing is strongly associated with women, while instrumental music is associated with men (e.g., Bulgaria, see Rice 1994). This is true to some extent in Russian culture, but it does not comprise a general rule. Before the demographic changes of the twentieth century, Russian village singing was traditionally performed by both sexes. Nevertheless, several genres of Russian song were strongly associated with female singers in many geographical regions: wedding songs, spring and summer round-dance songs, and lyric songs about love and family. When girls and women sang together in groups separately from men, they did so either because men were not present (e.g., women were working together), or because the women had an important ritual function to fulfill. For example, girls and women played important roles in spring and summer calendar rituals, whereas men fulfilled significant roles in the caroling rituals (and their corresponding songs) belonging to the winter and early spring, such as Christmas (in some regions men conducted the ritual called *koliadovanie*) and Easter (those who went from house to house as *volochebniki* were men).[1] In addition, there existed men's lyric, non-ritual songs associated with male occupations: army life, wandering, robbery, or prison.

Several twentieth-century events contributed to an increased separation and difference between men's and women's singing: during World War I (1914–18), the Civil War (1918–21), and World War II (1941–45) young male soldiers learned new songs and sang together with their regiments for the purpose of passing the time, maintaining spirits, or keeping step. At the same time, especially during the earlier two wars, young women who stayed at home in villages retained local styles and continued to celebrate traditional agricultural holidays. Men returned from war with new repertoire and singing styles that were more "national," while the women's tended to be more "local" (Kruglov 1979, 20). It was also true that the male population declined enormously as a result of these wars and due to outmigration (Meyer 1991, 208–24). With fewer men, village women were forced to sing in groups of women or by themselves. Meanwhile, instrumental music, which had always been associated more with men than with women (with some local exceptions) remained largely the provenance of men.[2]

Both before and after the Revolution, informal choruses composed of men and women, or men or women only—as the occasion arose—existed in almost all villages. These were formed spontaneously when people worked together or were based upon the members living near one another. Courtship was a time of life when these ensembles formed among same-age and same-gender peers: up until the mid-twentieth century, girls would sing while doing handiwork for their dowries at evening parties; boys would visit the girls at these work parties, and would sing along and/or sing their own songs. While the traditional wedding was still practiced, same-age girlfriends formed groups that performed important ritual roles during each other's wedding rituals, including singing.[3] Although these situations ceased to be performed, the social relations remained throughout life: when, in the late twentieth and early twenty-first centuries we asked elder women whom they would sing with, they often named two or three girlfriends and refused to sing with others, because they had not sung together in their youth.

During the Soviet period, handmade dowries and traditional weddings fell out of favor, calendar holiday observances became official celebrations of agricultural and economic progress, and villages were encouraged to form official singing groups. The cultural administration of the region or village organized such holidays and choruses. Official choruses rehearsed and performed in the public space of the village *klub*, were directed (especially after the war) by trained cultural workers, and generally sang approved song repertoire from sheet music or from special magazines for cultural workers. Much of this published music was composed; any folk material in these published materials was arranged for three vocal parts, and there was no folk material of local character (Zemtsovskii 1965, 82–83). Such official choruses did not use local costumes or homemade instruments but purchased identical factory-made, stylized costumes and mass-produced instruments out of the sponsoring kolkhoz or town cultural budget ("Eshche raz o narodnykh instrumentakh," 1965). The result varied in quality from village to village, but in general it was an imitation of the professional folk choirs and orchestras. Since musical performance could not be professionally done at the village level, the musical quality was sometimes quite poor, and the aesthetics were that of kitsch (Zemtsovskii 1965, 84, 86; Olson 2004, 48). Nonetheless, women (especially of the second and third generations) willingly participated, and were proud of the awards they garnered, such as samovars or tea sets. For Soviet citizens, approval from the state was a means to achieve public honor. For its part, through the conferral of honors the state showed its power to discern the "good" from the "bad." As judge of merit it replaced the role previously played by the community (by peers) in conferring honor (Brooks 2001, 125–27).

While Soviet policy dictated one sort of folk culture, individuals negotiated their relationship with this music (see also Olson 2004, 49–50). Some refused to sing Soviet music, and not all official groups sang it: for example, in Krasnoe in Riazan' oblast, a longtime leader of the village choir after World War II supported the singing of traditional songs, such as songs that belonged to weddings and to calendar holidays. Thanks to her support, the official chorus kept traditional music in its repertoire even while other village choruses were developing (or had developed) a Soviet repertoire. As a result, musicologists visited Krasnoe in the 1970s–'90s in order to record and study a closely knit ensemble with a pre-revolutionary repertoire. In other villages, the repertoires of choruses were mixed: some incorporated songs of a national character or from the Soviet era, as well as *chastushki* and traditional songs.

Official and informal choruses coexisted. As part of their negotiated relationship to official culture, our informants recounted many ways in which their non-official singing continued to be important for them throughout the Soviet era. Village dwellers sang music of their own or group choice spontaneously in contexts such as working alone at home or in the field, waiting for transport to a work site, in a bus or tractor on the way to a work site, while staying overnight at a work site, outdoors at spring and summer festivals, or at home with family and friends during a holiday feast, birthday party, or wedding. From their accounts, the official and informal, public and private contexts were fluid and contiguous, even overlapping: official singing groups gathered together and sang in informal contexts, and at official holidays official groups would perform to an assembled audience, but before or afterward, at the peripheries, loosely knit groups would entertain themselves

Holiday on a village hilltop: "Day of Songs," mid-June, Pot'ma, Ul'ianovsk oblast, early 1950s.
(COURTESY OF ELIZAROV FAMILY ARCHIVE)

with song (on the overlapping of public and private in Socialist space, see Gal and Kligman 2000, 51).

The careful manner in which membership in casual choruses was handled was testament to the social power and aesthetic pleasure the members received through their participation. Members apparently determined the group's membership according to aesthetic principles, age and gender, and/or personality. In the 1950s Soviet musicologist Anna Rudneva recounted how one spontaneously formed chorus in Voronezh oblast excluded a young woman who wanted to join, even though she knew all the songs and had a good voice: members said "she doesn't fit with us, she doesn't sing, she 'breaks' the song, she sings roughly [*grubo*]" (Rudneva 1994, 200). An elderly woman in Krasnoe, Riazan' oblast, told me (LO) in 2005 that as a young woman she had wanted to sing with the neighborhood group but was excluded because one singer in particular was jealous of her skill. When one spends time with a well-established (in Russian, *spetyi*—well-sung-together) singing group, one appreciates the complex balance of interpersonal relations—involving both mutual support and rivalry—and aesthetic principles that holds it together. In order for a group to exist, there must be at least one strong leader who can shape the song aesthetically: such a leader will typically start the song, will determine its pitch, vocal timbre, and tempo, and influence its ornamentation. Experienced singers sing independently, varying the melodic line each time, connecting each variation with the text of the song; yet each singer must constantly be thinking of the ensemble and the polyphonic sound they are producing, or else his or her voice may dominate, which is not desirable in most regional styles (Rudneva 1994, 203, 213). Evgeniia Lineva, a musicologist and folk revivalist from the late nineteenth century, described this tension between the individual and the group principle in the philosophy of such choruses in the following way:

> A folk choir . . . consists of singers who pour out into the improvisation *their own* feeling, who each strive to display their own personality, but at the same time care about the beauty of the whole performance. Even the best folk singers do not like to sing alone. "You can't sing alone," I often heard, "it's better in an artel." This expression "to sing in an artel" is very characteristic of the folk style of singing. In a singing artel every member is both a performer and a composer. . . . If the ideal of a disciplined chorus is *the submission of the whole to the personality of the conductor*, then a folk chorus represents, on the other hand, *the free merging of many personalities into one whole*. . . . A folk chorus sings not "like one person," but like many people, inspired by their common feeling of love for the song, pouring out into it their grief and joy. (Lineva 1904, 1:xxix)

Although the language of this quote sounds somewhat romanticizing, it corresponds to my (LO's) field experiences with informal choruses in the 1990s and the first years of the twenty-first century. Singers often commented directly upon the aesthetic values they wished to produce with their music. In the Krasnoe ensemble, the singers said of a well-sung song that it *naladilas'* (was smoothed out), that all voices *rovno shli* (went along evenly) and said of a poor performance that the singers were *v raznabrod* (in confusion, wandering in different directions). When I asked what they thought of while singing, one woman said "*ia podbiraiu*" (I choose) what to sing (i.e., what pitches to sing): she "matched" (*ladiu*) with others while they "matched" with her. Singers also said they think about the content of the song.[4] This notion of individual aesthetic choice is important: the group and tradition dictate a general group sound into which individuals must fit themselves, while the individual performs her freedom via her aesthetic creation within the framework of these constraints. In singing groups the individual and group principles are always in negotiation with each other.

The choruses studied by Lineva and by Rudneva were often mixed-gender, but when I (LO) came to study the folk chorus in the mid-1990s, it was already largely a female phenomenon. Only among Cossacks and some Old Believer groups (e.g., the Semeiskie of the Transbaikal region) was men's singing on a par with women's.[5] The reason for the feminization of the folk chorus has to do with the feminization of the Russian village in general. Besides the wars that decimated the male population of Russia in the early to mid-twentieth century, Russian men's life expectancy has been significantly lower than that of women. Further, outmigration, starting with collectivization in the 1930s, was overwhelmingly male (Denisova 2003, 173–74; Gaditskaia and Skorik 2009, 299). A lack of men forced women to sing in all-female groups. Such feminization of the musical culture of the village did nothing to increase its perceived value. Soviet propaganda, including posters from the 1920s and films from the 1920s through '40s, contributed to the impression of rural women as backward.[6]

Thus, while women-only singing groups were traditional—related to the courtship, wedding, and spring-summer ritual cycle—in the twentieth century, they also came about for historical and ideological reasons that were disadvantageous to women. When we observed these informal groups it was clear to us that they performed more than a musical function for their participants. They were carefully constructed social groups with their own complex and changing internal hierarchies, their own standards for membership, and their own folk culture. The women in such ensembles had been together for so many years that they often seemed to treat each other as the equivalent of siblings or relatives. They bickered over perceived power roles, such as the right to sing a special part, or the right to dictate the text. Each ensemble had its own informal and formal repertoire: its members knew many songs in common, and sang them together at birthday celebrations, weddings, the ritual of seeing soldiers off to war, calendar holidays, and funerals and memorial feasts. A visiting ethnographer, too, was cause for a celebration, and, as at

The chorus of Tsenogora village, Arkhangel'sk oblast, performs *khorovod* for visiting ethnographers, 2010. (PHOTO BY SVETLANA ADONYEVA)

birthdays, the women would gather for a traditional Russian *zastol'e* (group celebration at table with food and drink) at one of the member's houses. If these feasts included men or adult children, then the women often sang a different repertoire that the men and younger generations also knew; but they also sang their own repertoire, temporarily excluding the men and younger women.[7]

Although the state had provided resources and trained professionals to guide village folk singing since the 1930s, in the 1980s new emphasis was placed upon the preservation of ancient local traditions. Culture workers encouraged informal village choirs to become official performing groups and to present ethnographic material from their own mothers and grandmothers on stage. Given a venue to perform in public, the informal groups acquired a new reason to gather. The members were conscious of their hobby as something that marked them as special members of the community. When we visited in the 1990s and the early years of the twenty-first century, many of the aging members of these relatively new groups—women of the second and third generations—bragged about their many performances and awards from the local authorities. As in the Soviet period, these official singing groups were sources of power for these local women, who gained a public voice and recognition from authorities regionally, and social importance locally.

The members were conscious of the fact that this was an all-women activity, and one that older members of society or men viewed with ambivalence. Their stories emphasized their intention to rehearse and perform despite all odds. We see in these stories a strong exhibition of women's agency. Members spoke of having to secure the (reluctant) acquiescence of their husbands or mothers-in-law in order to attend rehearsals, celebrations, and concerts. Aleksandra Pavlovna A., born in 1941, described how in the 1960s her mother-in-law would complain when someone would call for her (she was in her twenties at the time) to come to rehearsal in the evening. "You're away all day [at work], and you're away in the evening, too!" So Aleksandra would bring her mother over to sit with her mother-in-law while she rehearsed or performed (Krasnoe, Riazan' oblast, 5 May 2005). Zoia Venediktovna K., a strong-willed, funny, and spirited woman in her seventies (born in 1932), used a *chastushka* to tell us about her involvement in their village chorus:

Я старушка боевая
Заняла позицию
Дед скотину обрежат
А я на репетицию.[8]

[I am a fighting old woman
I've taken up my arms [lit.: assumed my position]
Let my old man feed the cows
I'm off to rehearsal now!]

Zoia's song expresses a sentiment we heard often from women who sang in group settings; they characterized that activity as oppositional, and stated their dedication to continuing it. To pronounce that the husband would do the women's duty (taking care of the domestic animals) while the woman takes a militant and thus manly stand by participating in public life, emasculates him while elevating her status in society. The speaker here constructs her agency by borrowing metaphors of the self (I'm a fighter [*ia—boevaia*]) traditionally associated with masculinity.

In stating that going to rehearsal is associated with the oppositional stance of being *boevaia*, Zoia's *chastushka* engages with age-old debates regarding the propriety of women's performance on stage. In effect, her word underlines the transgressive nature that public singing on stage had, and still has for some Russian rural women. In the eighteenth and nineteenth centuries, Russian women's appearance on stage was deemed incompatible with demands that she be modest and restrained. For the most part, only women of lower-class origin appeared on stage. It was assumed that women who appeared on stage thereby made themselves sexually available (Rosslyn 2003, 260). In the twentieth century, as more women made careers on stage, these associations disappeared for the urban public, but for all the generations of rural women we survey here (those born before 1951), codes of women's behavior remained rooted in the performance of modesty.[9] Or perhaps it is more accurate to say that such codes remained a recognizable reference point in the discourse of these women—women of the second and third generations certainly violated these codes in their behavior during their lives but always referred back to the behavioral codes of their mothers or grandmothers.

Ages and Generations of Singers

Due to the government's attitude toward singing during the Soviet period, there is, in general, a difference between the experiences of women of the different generations. Women of the first and second generations grew up participating in the group singing traditions of their mothers. They sang traditional songs at holidays and on work breaks. The main difference between the repertoires of the first and second generation is that the second generation lost many ritual songs (wedding and calendar holiday) and incorporated more Soviet-era songs—romances and songs from mass media—in their personal repertoires. It was women of the second generation who experienced the influence of Soviet official culture, which encouraged them to leave behind the older songs and to sing the music distributed by the government's cultural workers and played on the radio. These women lamented to us that during their youth, their singing of old songs was not appreciated by culture workers and local young people, sometimes even their own children. They were taken as "drunk or a dummy" if they sang old folksongs (Olson 2004, 179). Younger people would ask about their singing style, "Why are you yelling?," which suggested that the youths of that time (the third generation) were reacting to the difference between the

loud, open voice used in Russian local singing styles and the rich, smooth sound of urban
singers or the refined, sweet sound cultivated by the Soviet folk chorus.

By the time women of the third generation became young adults in the late 1940s
through about 1970, their decision-making was more accepted than it was in their mothers'
or grandmothers' generation. In some ways they were heavily influenced by city culture
(and modernity in general), and kept or rejected elements of their mothers' culture as it
suited them. These general tendencies were reflected in their aesthetic choices: they often
chose *chastushka*-singing over work-songs, and they might dance the waltz, quadrille, and
foxtrot instead of round-dances. However, they were thoroughly familiar with the culture
of their mother's generation: some had active and others passive knowledge of it. Such
differences depended heavily upon the local culture. In some villages, young women of
the third generation—particularly those born in the 1930s—would sing older lyric songs
such as dance songs, romances, or game-playing songs, while in other locations they only
wanted to sing *chastushki*. After marriage, while raising their children, many women of
the third generation told us they did not have time for singing, other than participating in
group singing at community holidays or during work breaks (i.e., at the work site). The
demands of the kolkhoz work with its fixed shifts and labor-day (*trudoden'*) compensation
scale meant that women were always struggling to maintain all of their responsibilities. Only
when their children were grown, many told us, did they begin to take seriously the traditional singing they had heard and participated in as children or young people—longer,
more complicated, or slower lyric songs (called drawn-out songs), longer romances, and
religious songs. These were the songs they associated with the generation of their parents
or grandparents—and thus their attraction to such songs was born of nostalgia.

This was the story of Lidia Pankratovna P., born in 1939, who belonged to a singing
group called "Golden Age" (*Zolotoi vozrast*) in a village in the Siamzha region of Vologda
oblast when we met her in 2004. She told us that the repertoire sung by "Golden Age"
belonged to the generation of her mother. Her generation did not engage in traditional
games and dances with texts about agricultural work (such as cabbage and linen) or sing
ballads and romances about unrequited love or prison life, as did her mother's generation. Instead, they danced the waltz and polka and sang *chastushki*. However, when asked
in 1992 to join a group that would serve as a "source" (*kladez'*, wellspring) for the ancient
wisdom of the foremothers, Lidia readily agreed. She described the process of remembering the music from her youth:

> You understand, I somehow want . . . to remember all this ancient stuff, all
> that our mothers, grandmothers—my mother sang all the time. She'd be doing
> something, and she'd be singing, singing, singing . . . When I was an adolescent,
> I didn't pay attention to these songs. And now they are all coming to my mind.
> Can you imagine? . . .

And you didn't sing them earlier?

No!!!... I didn't sing anything—she'd sing, and I wouldn't even notice, I'd walk past, all of that I just listened to in passing. And now they're all coming to my mind, these songs. You understand, word for word, even.... You know, I still have a good, you know, memory, memory of childhood I mean, all that happened then. We were little. We were five years old, and it all got recorded [in my mind], at that time, it all got stuck in there..., and [when I tried to access it] it kept going, going, going. As if from a recording tape, everything kept going, going, going, and I started to remember it all, but [all those years] it was all unwanted, no one remembered it, all that childhood memory.... (Nikulinskaia, Siamzha region, Vologda oblast, 20 October 2004)

For Lidia Pankratovna, her mother's songs were symbolic of her mother's generation and the former lifestyle associated with it. In her comments, she shows her own nostalgia for that lost world. Her desire to perform her mother's songs may have been influenced by a cultural leader in the village, a younger woman, Anastasia Ivanovna N., who directed a local children's folk ensemble. Anastasia used Lidia and others in "Golden Age" as teachers for the children's ensemble. However, Anastasia's and Lidia's nostalgias were quite different: Anastasia's conformed to what Svetlana Boym has called restorative nostalgia, with its utopian, whitewashing impulse, while Lidia's was the nostalgia of "individual and cultural memory," which Boym calls reflective nostalgia (2001, 49). While Anastasia idealized the past "as a value for the present" and wanted Lidia to tell only about the traditions of her mother's generation, Lidia herself told us about the real-life contexts of the songs, suggesting her concern for "historical and individual time" or memory (49). In fact, while Lidia was telling us about how her family (which owned a horse-changing station and a store) was dekulakized and collectivized (an event she apparently knew about from family stories), Anastasia interrupted her and said, "Tell about the cheerful things, too! Parties, handiwork, dances..."

Despite this Pollyannaish influence, for Lidia the songs remained, as she said, "about all of life"—that is, about the life she experienced in her youth. For example, after she sang us a song from her mother's generation about linen production, she described in detail her own work with linen, a process that took some minutes to explain due to the exacting and complex nature of the work. She described her own role in this process, which was her first job after school: "I was the leader of a work cell/gang [*zven'evoi*], I collected it and managed the whole process, from the beginning of the sowing to the end. And we turned it in to the government, both linen fibers and flax stems we turned in." Lidia's discourse shows her Soviet understanding of work: the hierarchical, organized, factory-like nature of the labor process and the proper recipient of the final product: the government. Yet she also understands the song from her mother's generation because she did process linen by hand.

Her world was already quite different from the social milieu to which the song belonged, the world of girls' work parties. Thus, later she participated in the reconstruction of the past conducted by the post-Communist cultural authorities of her village (personified by Anastasia), but she recognized the difference between this reconstructed past and the blemished reality of her own past. As Boym theorizes, those who experience reflective nostalgia are conscious precisely of the "sense of distance" between now and then, between the reconstruction and the memory; it is this awareness that "drives them to tell their own story" (2001, 50).

If women of the third generation could appreciate the dance and work songs of their mothers due to their own contextualized experience, this was doubly true of romance songs. Romance songs, sometimes called "cruel romances," are popular with middle-aged and older women of all generations. Lidia Pankratovna sang us several romances from her mother's repertoire, indicating, "This was mother's favorite song," "Here's another my mother loved." These are not dance songs or songs associated with particular calendar or life-cycle rituals but songs that can be sung anytime and anywhere, are known by many, and are best suited to the all-purpose ritual *zastol'e*. One key to the songs' survival and success into the twenty-first century may lie in their association with the kind of ritual that has also survived—the *zastol'e*, which is conducted without fail at birthdays, weddings, and calendar holidays. In the context of these rituals, the songs help the participants express and create togetherness and emotional peaks.

The songs and their manner of singing are ideal for table celebrations because of their slow tempo (they are not to be danced to) and sometimes complex melodic structure and polyphonic texture (in some local traditions). This kind of music-making is best done when people have a lot of time and the ability to sit close to one another, concentrate on the singing, and enjoy the sonic environment created. Even if the songs are not sung polyphonically—polyphonic singing is a difficult skill that, in many communities, has not survived to the present—these songs are always sung in harmony, with at least two vocal parts, which contributes to the richness of the sound and the group character of the singing. The aesthetic of these songs demands a group: if one person starts a romance song alone, others invariably join in.

Thus, a complex history contributed to the current situation in which groups of middle-aged and older village women sing, both on and off stage, the repertoires of their youth or of their mothers' generation. In part, romance songs have remained popular because of the group settings in which they are sung, with all the social pleasure and power that entails. Not all women belong to such groups—in each village today probably a minority of women do—but the groups function as the "face of the village," representing it at public holiday celebrations, and giving the participants rare opportunities for travel, public acclaim, awards, and social capital. But additionally and importantly, for many village women born before 1950, romance songs are valuable because they are connected both with the traditional value system of the prewar village and with the modern script of romance and personal happiness. The next section looks at this question in detail.

Romance Songs as Melodrama

Romances entered the Russian rural folk-singing tradition in the nineteenth century through literary sources—usually poems by eighteenth- and nineteenth-century authors, or popular songs that originated in cities. They became a mass phenomenon through cheap printings in the late nineteenth and early twentieth centuries—in fact, people of all social groups enjoyed such songs (Adon'eva and Gerasimova 1996, 339–40). In the rural sphere they were spread orally and were "folklorized"—that is, people changed the texts and created their own ways of singing them. Russian folklorists call them "romances," "cruel romances," or "contemporary ballads."

Romances are lyric songs: the poems they are based upon borrow techniques from the traditional peasant lyric, so that romances often have the same or a similar form. Typically both traditional peasant lyrics and romances begin with a description of nature (for city romances this may be a city park or a ballroom), and follow with a monologue or dialogue (Lazutin 1965, 36). The point of traditional lyrics is to illustrate the emotional state of the speaker(s); romances may do the same but inject an element of tragedy, either by describing a tragedy at the end of the song or by hinting that one is forthcoming.

Romances deal with themes of rupture or transgression: in them, societal rules and expectations are broken. Their plots describe unrequited or unfulfilled love, unfaithfulness of a man, adultery, marriage without love, and elopement. When the theme of the song is female desire, often the desired man is inappropriate in some way: he is married or a ladies' man; thus, female desire is thwarted, its realization always put off. If the songs speak of happy love (some of the songs are of an "elegiac" character; see Zubova 1984), this is depicted as now past or threatened; faithful love is contrasted with adultery or is faced with societal disapproval, for example, due to the heroine's inappropriate social class. When fate is mentioned in a song, it is invoked as an explanation for unhappiness, and sometimes becomes a justification for suicide or other means of self-destruction.

In the twentieth and early twenty-first centuries, romances have continued to be beloved by middle-aged and older Russians. Adon'eva and Gerasimova call them the "most popular songs being sung today in the countryside" (1996, 340). Rural women's repertoires and manner of singing the songs differ from those of urban dwellers and men. In Oleg Nikolaev's (n.d.) study of the songs as an essential component of the typical urban Russian *zastol'e*, he argues that themes of wild nature, the road, wandering, fate, death, Cossack freedom (*volia*), and loneliness abound in the urban singing style, and that Russians typically do not finish these songs—they do not know all the words. According to our observations, this is true only of mixed-gender company. Rural women know, and sing in mixed company, the songs often begun at urban parties—like "By the Wild Baikal

Steppes" ("Po dikim step'iam Zabaikal'ia"), "Wanderer" ("Brodiaga"), "Oi, The Frost, The Frost" ("Oi moroz, moroz"), and "The Brave Khaz-Bulat" ("Khaz-Bulat udaloi")— but they characterize these as "men's songs," since the texts represent a masculine point of view. The songs our interlocutors choose to sing in all-female groups tend to represent a woman's point of view or feature a female protagonist. Furthermore, village women do tend to know many verses to the songs they sing (enough to complete the narrative), they often sing slightly different words than canonical versions, and they sing them with some of the features of their local musical style (such as a precentor [*zapevala*] and single vocal descant). Thus, we argue, despite the national level of recognition of some of these songs, in a sense they belong to the local folk culture of our interlocutors. Women choose such songs due to the nostalgia and personal pleasure they evoke.

Among the older cruel romances in rural women's contemporary repertoires are songs such as "A Young Cossack Walks along the Don River" ("Po Donu guliaet kazak molo-doi"), based upon an 1835 poem by poet Dmitri Oznobishin, about a girl who falls from a bridge on her way to be married to a Cossack; "If I Had Golden Mountains" ("Kogda b' imel zlatye gory"), about a girl whose lover convinces her to elope to a foreign country and then cheats on her; and "On the Silver River" ("Na serebrianoi reke"), in which a young man finds his lover in a church, getting married to another; she defends herself, saying the new groom is rich and she is in love with him. We also include in this category songs composed in the twentieth century with similar romance plots. Some of these newer songs would not be called folklore by many Russian folklorists, but we include as folklore any songs that are sung in a spontaneous way by our interlocutors. Among the Soviet-era romances they favored were "As You Were" ("Kakim ty byl") from the 1949 film *Kubanskie Kazaki*, about a girl who is in love with a troublesome, wandering man; "How Many Golden Lights" ("Ognei tak mnogo zolotykh") from the 1957 film *Delo bylo v Penkove*, about a girl in love with a married man; and "I Drank Myself Drunk" ("Napilas' ia ia p'iana"), which expresses the point of view of a young wife whose husband is cheating on her.[10] These songs were not composed for folk choruses; instead, in the case of the first two songs, they formed part of popular culture that then became folklorized without the intervention of the Soviet organs in charge of culture. They are not Soviet songs per se but rather Soviet-era songs.

The roles played by the female characters in the songs fall into a few general categories: most commonly, the main female character plays the role of hapless victim; less often, the song asserts her strength (often, attributing it to her love). If there is a villain, it is often male, but sometimes a villainess—the girl's or the man's mother, or the "other woman"— causes the heroine's grief. The song may end with the villain's regret, when he or she sees the grief and loss that she or he has caused. The male villain's remorse thus provides a context in which the female victim's loss is seen as redemptive. When a song depicts a female villainess, the result is invariably destructive: in nineteenth-century imaginative works, the victim is the only socially accepted position for women within the victim-victimizer dyad (Matich 1983). Songs with female villains (in Russian called the "evil-doer-ess" [*zlodeika*]) often take the point of view of the man in decrying her harmful acts.

The plots of these earlier romances and Soviet-era songs reflect the clash of modernity and tradition, and express women's and men's fears about the resulting social ruptures. The songs show how patriarchy, with its control of women's sexuality, is threatened by women's desires for self-fulfillment. In the older songs within this category, this threat is put to rest and balance is restored; in newer songs, emotional self-fulfillment in relationship is a goal not easily cast aside by heroines.

The songs' themes and symbolic language imply this mix of traditional and modern viewpoints. The traditional belief in a higher power to which one might appeal for redress or justice appears in a few of the songs, but most adhere to a modern secular world view that suggests humans are powerless before the ravages of misfortune; as Adon'eva and Gerasimova put it, in these songs "the animosity of the world . . . is uncontrollable and, as a result, inescapable." Some of the songs do attribute misfortune to the ravages of fate, but most emphasize the randomness of misfortune: events happen "suddenly," and the only action one can take is to avoid similar situations (Adon'eva and Gerasimova 1996, 346–47). The point of view of the songs straddles cruel fate and cruel chance, poetic justice and randomness. This hybrid traditional-modern world view makes the songs antithetical to the official Soviet viewpoint, which emphasized rational action taken to further a common goal.

The reason for the songs' world view may be traced to the urban, literary, and upper-class origins of the poems from which many of the songs were derived, and the changing social conditions (e.g., class upheaval at the end of the nineteenth century) that they describe. But these are folklorized texts, and the folk culture of any group dispenses with that which does not interest it. Obviously, the phenomenon of melodramatic romance songs made its way into rural culture—and stayed—for a reason.

One important way in which these songs might be said to speak to rural women's concerns is through their narration of a conflict between the individual and society. The transgressions and ruptures in these songs occur because of a divergence between the heroine's personal desires for love, sex, or freedom, and her need to live up to the life scripts dictated by her society. That is, she must maintain her virginity before marriage and be faithful and obedient to husband and parents. In return, she receives their protection, but her agency is curtailed. To be sure, earlier peasant lyric songs also often depicted conflict between individual and societal norms. For example, many women's songs described the heroine's unhappiness at being forced to marry against her will or her complaints about her husband. Romances continue this complaining mode but are different in their depictions of the (often dire) consequences of lack of fulfillment of the traditional woman's life script. In other words, they imagine the possibility that the heroine chooses other life paths—including suicide.

The heroines in these songs employ a few strategies in response to the clash of personal and societal fulfillment: most commonly, they address it through means that either work against or bypass women's agency: self-negation (suicide), withdrawal, some form of silence, or appeal to a higher power. Other strategies involve a degree of agency: symbolic communication (e.g., through song), transgression, and work. With the first type of strategy, subjectivity is lacking; in the second, it is sought. Clearly, based upon our conclusions in the previous chapter, the songs do not represent the particular subjectivities and strategies of our interlocutors, the singers of the songs. Nonetheless, many of these songs represent the struggles and feelings that women of all generations experienced when they had to decide how to negotiate with society's dictates.

We find it helpful to situate these songs alongside the literary genre of melodrama. Melodrama is, of course, a form of drama, but in recent years scholars have argued for its wider application. The works of Peter Brooks, as well as of film scholars John Mercer and Martin Shingler, suggest that "a melodramatic sensibility can manifest itself across a range of texts and genres" (Mercer and Shingler 2004, 95). Melodrama becomes a viable mode whenever social and psychological stability is threatened by economic or political upheaval. In these works, order is restored, and ethical norms reaffirmed, with the "confrontation and expulsion of the villain" (Brooks 1995, 15, 204). Linda Williams, a scholar of melodrama in American film, writes: "What counts in melodrama is the feeling of righteousness, achieved through the sufferings of the innocent" (1998, 61).

In particular, female victims are a staple of melodrama: their suffering is the crime against virtue that is the central action of melodrama. Melodrama calls upon prevailing societal stereotypes about femininity itself, which in the late nineteenth and early twentieth century saw women as silent, obedient, modest, devoted to a single man, and self-sacrificing (Holmgren 2002, 80–81, 84–85; Gledhill 1987, 30). As Leon Metayer writes, nineteenth-century melodrama tends to "make an example of the heroine," to enforce lessons of "fidelity and submission to the male" (1996; see also Holmgren 2002, 88). Thus melodrama is a conservative mode that reconfirms the ethical norms of patriarchy via the drama of female suffering. While the song romances in the repertoires of Russian village women do not each express this drama of villain and victim fully, taken as a group they operate within this melodramatic mode. Many of the songs are complicit with the norms of patriarchy, in that they applaud female victimhood as a mode that exalts the woman morally and permits the man's redemption. Not all the songs operate this way, however. Some, especially the more recent songs, express an emerging female subjectivity that is inconsistent with the victimhood model.

Since not all the songs express complicity with patriarchy, we found it useful in analyzing the songs to speak of a range of points of view or strategies, following the work of Ann Kaplan on the mother figure in American melodrama. Kaplan argues that we may discern distinct points of view in melodramatic texts: they may express *complicity* with the norms of patriarchy by featuring female characters who are disempowered and whose desire for a man proceeds from their own lack of subjectivity; or the texts may *resist* patriarchy's demands, offering a glimpse, however small or metaphorical, into a female subjectivity that generates its own desire. Complicit texts—those in which melodramatic elements predominate—represent the female character as a function of male desire, and seem primarily to address a male audience. Even if they are narrated by a female narrator, they present the female standpoint from an uncritical patriarchal point of view. Essentially, they illustrate male fantasies, or take the point of view of the "mother" who protects the interests of patriarchy. Meanwhile, resisting texts are more closely allied with feminist realism than with melodrama. Resisting texts speak from the position of the woman and about her own experiences of pleasure and oppression. Female desire or fantasy is assumed to exist, even if its expression is thwarted (Kaplan 1992, 69–70, 74). These texts take the point of view of a "daughter" who questions patriarchy's effects upon women as individuals.

Complicit Texts

About two thirds of the songs we studied are complicit: they depict women as victims of men's carelessness, self-interest, or cruelty, and many do so in such a way as to emphasize women's lack of agency. Several present the tragic plot as a cautionary tale to young women and to young men. For example, a woman born in 1918 in Riazan' oblast recounted to us a song she loved, "By the Muromsk Road" ("Po Muromskoi dorozhke"). In this song a woman's betrothed leaves—the song does not say for what, but since he promises to return and marry her in spring, it is understood that he must have left by the Muromsk Road for the city, for work. The song's speaker dreams that he breaks his vow and marries another, and indeed he returns in spring with his new beautiful wife. When he sees the speaker, he lowers his eyes because he realizes that he has "killed her heart." This song belongs to the classic melodrama mode: the heroine, a virtuous woman, is unjustly wronged by a male villain, and the text uses symbolism (the three pines) and the language of gesture (lowering the eyes) and emotions (the woman's tears) for its effect on the listener. Folkloric tradition is present in the song in the form of the prophetic dream; but the song describes the entry of modernity into village culture, via the lure of opportunity in the money-based economy. The thrust of the song is to reassert the values of tradition: the last two stanzas affirm that the victim's tears have an effect even upon the villain, since he feels remorse at what he has done:

Я у ворот стояла,
Когда он проезжал,
Меня в толпе народа
Он взглядом отыскал.

Увидев мои слезы,
Глаза он опустил.
И понял, что навеки
Мне сердце погубил.

[I stood by the gate
When he drove by
And he sought me
With his glance in the crowd

Seeing my tears,
He lowered his eyes
And understood that
He'd killed my heart forever.]

In other complicit texts featuring female victims, the woman enters the global world of modernity, leaving behind the local community. Such a girl is at fault despite her victimization by a man. For example, in the song "Oh, Sailor, Sailor, Sailor" ("Akh moriak, moriak, moriak") a girl becomes involved with a sailor, who takes her away despite her mother's advice:

"Ах, моряк, моряк, моряк,
Аленькие губки,
Ты возьми меня с собой,
Я во рваной юбке."

"Если хочешь, прокачу,
Ты садись со мною,
Я на юбку шелку дам,
Будь моей женою."

"Ох, пойду-ка я спрошу
Матери совета;
И тогда поеду я
Плавать вокруг света."

Не послушалась она
Матери совета,
И поехала она
Плавать вокруг света.

Через года полтора
Дочь идет уныло,
На руках она несет
От матроса сына.

"Ты прими же, мать, прими,
Семья небольшая!
Будет внучек звать тебя:
'Бабенька родная.'"—

"Вот ступай, дочка, ступай,
С кем совет имела.
Ты свою родную мать
Слушать не хотела."—

"Уж пойдем, сынок, пойдем,
Здесь нас не примают.
Сине море глубоко—
Там нас ожидают."

Она к морю подошла,
Море колыхнулось;
Крепко сына обняла,
В море утонула.

Как по синему по морю
Труп ее несется,
А моряк на корабле
Едет и смеется.

Вот вам, девушки, наказ,
Как в ребят влюбляться;
А еще вот вам наказ,
Как с моряками знаться.

["Oh, Sailor, sailor, sailor
[You with] red lips,
Take me with you,
I'm in a ripped skirt."

"If you want, I'll take you with me
Sit with me

I'll give you silk for a new skirt
Be my wife."

"Oh, I'll go and ask
My mother's advice;
And then I'll go with you
Around the world by ship."

She didn't listen to
Her mother's advice
And went
Around the world by ship.

In a year and a half
The daughter returns crestfallen,
In her arms she carries
The sailor's son.

"Mother, take him, take him,
Our family isn't big!
Your grandson will call you
'Grandma dear.'"

"Dear daughter, go, go
With the one with whom you held counsel.
You didn't want to listen to
Your own dear mother.

"Let's go, my son, let's go,
We're not wanted here.
The blue sea is deep—
We're expected there."

She walked up to the sea,
The sea surged;
She held her son tightly
And drowned in the sea.

Her corpse floats on the
Deep blue sea,
And the sailor on the ship
Sails and laughs.

There's a lesson for you, girls,
How to fall in love with guys;
And there's another lesson for you,
How to associate with sailors.]

In this conflict between traditional values and modern possibilities, patriarchal tradition wins. The last stanza explicitly confirms the song's moral stance: the sailor is not blamed for his dissolute life, nor is the mother blamed for not taking in her daughter and grandson; only the daughter herself can be blamed for leaving behind her honor, the protection of her family, and her community. The suicide by drowning of the wronged woman is a common plot in such songs, as in legends about girls who committed suicide after becoming pregnant out of wedlock—thus, this motif has deep roots in folklore (Vinogradova 1986, 92; Ivanits 1989, 76). According to this cultural plot, a girl's shame is properly resolved via self-destruction. While this song depicts the daughter's independence and agency (in her intentional disobedience of her mother), its point of view is that of a judging mother whose ultimate loyalty is to patriarchy. This song depicts the destruction of female agency as the appropriate ending of this script, making this a highly complicit text.

Of course, even if the text is complicit with the norms of patriarchy, that does not mean that singers and listeners necessarily agree with that message. For example, when singing or listening, individuals may have lamented or objected to the events described.[11] When our interlocutors of the second and third generations sing songs like this today, they appreciate them with the distance of reflective nostalgia but not necessarily ironic distance. They do not typically laugh at these songs; more often than not, if asked about the song they paraphrase it and say "this happened" or "such events did happen." When asked, sometimes they say that what the songs recount is "bad" or "sad," but singing such songs never dampens the group's mood. The comments of Lidia Pankratovna were typical: "It's about everyday life [zhiteiskaia]"; "It's about all of life. About all of life." When we asked Lidia and others what they meant by this, their answers suggested that the feelings expressed in the songs were similar to those that they had experienced in their own lives: sadness, loneliness, desire, love.

The songs may express deeply felt emotions for singers and listeners, but ironically many of the complicit melodramatic songs depict the female protagonist's inability to express herself and her feelings. Female lack of self-expression runs the gamut in these songs, from muteness to symbolic expression. The songs told from a male point of view tend to lack any female speech. An example is "The Soldiers Rode Home" ("Ekhali soldaty"), which the singers in Krasnoe, Riazan' oblast, used to sing on Conscripts' Day (when new conscripts were taken to the army) and on Veterans' Day. In this song the wife is guilty of infidelity; only the mother-in-law speaks in the wife's defense, before the cuckolded husband cuts the wife's head off. Such punishment reflects a melodramatic world view that is complicit with patriarchy: in the plot recounted here, which we see in Russian epics as well as in ballads and romances, women's infidelity merits death because it threatens patriarchy's very foundation.[12] With its silent and guilty female character, "The Soldiers Rode Home" is typical of older romances:

Ехали солдаты со службы домой,
На плечах погоны, на грудях—кресты.
Едут по дороге, родитель стоит.
—Здорово, папаша!
—Здорово, сынок!
—Расскажи, папаша, про семью мою.
—Семья, слава богу, прибавилася,
Жена молодая сына родила.
Сын отцу ни слова, сел он на коня,
Подъезжает к дому, стоит мать с женой.
Мать держит ребёнка, жена во слезах.
Мать сына просила:
—Прости, сын, жену . . .
—Тебя, мать, прощаю, жену никогда.
Заблестала шашка во правой руке,
Слетела головка с неверной жены.
—Ой боже, ты мой боже, что я натворил:
Жену я зарезал, сам себя сгубил.
Маленька-малютку в приют отдадил,
А коня вороного с седлом отдадил.

[Soldiers rode home from service,
Epaulets on their shoulders, on their chests—crosses.
They ride along the road; a parent stands there.
—Hello, father!
—Hello, son!
—Tell me, father, about my family.
—The family, thank God, has an addition,
Your young wife bore a son.
The son said not a word to the father, sat on the horse,
Rode up to the house, there stands the mother with the wife.
The mother is holding the child, the wife is in tears.
The mother pleads to the son:
—Forgive your wife, son . . .

—You, mother, I forgive; my wife—never.
The saber shone in his right hand,
Off went the head of the unfaithful wife.
—Oh God, my God, what have I done:
I slaughtered my wife, damned myself.
Surrendered the little baby to an orphanage,
And the raven-colored horse, surrendered with the saddle.]

One important concept in many of these complicit songs is fate (*sud'ba*) or lot (*dolia*). This implies the traditional view that at birth, each person is meted out a share of the communal good. One cannot change or affect one's lot; it is predetermined from above (Levkievskaia 1999, 114). Along with this, God appears as a figure to whom women appeal to improve their own lot, as well as for justice, and protection for loved ones. For example, the heroine in the song "I Was Born" ("Urodilas' ia") was born beautiful, but because she is poor she stands little chance of getting married—a plot that belongs to the traditional, economy-centered view of marriage. She addresses this problem by seeking help from God:

Уродилася я, эх девушкой красивой.

Эх, я красива да бедна, да плохо одета,
Никто замуж не берёт девушку за это.

Пойду с горя в монастырь помолюся,
Пред иконою святой я слезой зальюся.

Не пошлёт ли мне господь той доли счастливой,
Не полюбит ли меня молодец красивый.

Все подруженьки мои гуляют с мужьями,
А я, горька сирота—с чужими людьми.

Как у пташки есть гнездо, у волчицы—дети,
А у меня, у сироты—никого на свете.

I was born, oh, a beautiful girl.

Oh, I am beautiful but poor, so badly dressed,
Nobody marries a girl like that.

I'll go with my sorrow to a monastery to pray,
Before the holy icon I will spill my tears.

Won't the Lord sent me a happy lot,
Won't a handsome young man fall in love with me?

All my friends are walking with their husbands,
But me, a bitter orphan—with strangers.

Like the bird has a nest, a wolf has pups,
But for me, for an orphan—there is nobody in the world.

A version of this song was performed by the female villain in the 1953 film *Wedding with a Dowry* (*Svad'ba s pridanym*): there, the song functioned as an emblem for the backward, superstitious, kulak peasant. This negative figure is personified in the film by a character who speaks in dialect, wears a knitted wool scarf on her head, tells fortunes with cards, and sells berries at the market—a figure with whom rural elder women all over Russia must have been able to identify.

Despite the song's negative associations in a canonical Soviet film, it has continued to be popular with retirement-age rural dwellers. The official chorus in Ermolovo, Riazan' oblast, performed it in casual fashion at a celebratory gathering with a visiting ethnomusicologist from Moscow and a group of American adults (1995). The group of six women and two men sang it in their local style, with a *zapevala*; when the chorus enters, most of the voices sing the lower, "bass" part (the man sang this an octave below) and just one singer performs the more highly ornamented upper, *podgolosok* part. After the song was over the eldest female singer (eighty years old at the time), who had sung the lead line and the upper *podgolosok*, echoed the last line of the song, referring to herself: "I, an orphan, don't have anyone in the world." The male accordion player answered, "And you don't need anyone." Taken aback, she asked, "What?" He told her: "It's too late." Two of the women took up her defense: they asserted that it was better to have a companion in the house in order to have someone to talk with.

Clearly, the song's text had immediate personal resonances for female members of the group. For the women of this generation, who lived through World War II, the song raised real-life issues of loneliness and abandonment: many lost all their male family members. While Modleski (1982) has argued that Western women's practice of watching daily televised soap operas provides a "collective fantasy" of community for those who "have had too much solitude," we can say that for Russian village women, songs (as well as televised soap operas) provide a real basis upon which to construct community. In this case, the participants' commentary suggests that for them, the experience the song recounts is very much gendered. This complicit song reiterates the common plot of the female subject's lack of agency, not only in the arena of courtship but also in life in general: happiness is determined not by personal actions but by such circumstances as the economic well-being of her family.

The women singers participate in a verbal strategy of solidarity and community, banding together in support of their fellow singer, articulating her position in response to the man's implied criticism. The women's performance of interconnectedness reflects a fact of village life in Russia: individuals need each other to survive. This reality resulted in cultural traditions such as the peasant commune (*obshchina*) and the belief system we describe in several chapters of this book (chapters 7, 8, and 9), and also in women's informal rituals such as what Collette Schulman terms "women's conversations" (*bab'i razgovory*) and the "institution of friendship" (*institut druzhby*) (1977, 381). The particular circumstance of "orphanhood" mentioned in this conversation has its own life script: in the household-based economy before collectivization, widows were economically and socially disempowered, since it was difficult for a woman alone to manage a household (Engel 2004, 56). Some of the economic problems of widows were ameliorated starting in 1964 with the extension of state pension benefits to rural retirees. Women-headed households were very common: nationally they were almost 30 percent of the total number of households in 1959 (Lapidus 1978, 169). Widows often suffered from a lack of physical and economic support, and loneliness and/or the need for interconnectedness was a common topic in conversations of widows.

Resisting Texts

While such complicit songs were popular, about one-third of the songs in the repertoires of our informants of the second and third generations hint at strategies of female resistance to socially constructed power relations. These songs offer glimpses of an alternative to the melodrama model. A popular song, likely of twentieth-century origin, "Am I Guilty?" ("Vinovata li ia"), offers a much more ambivalent interpretation of women's guilt and women's silence than the complicit songs. In this song, which the Krasnoe women sang in 2005 at the seventieth birthday party of one of their members, the heroine has become intimate with a young man before marriage. She regrets this not because of her loss of honor, but instead because of betrayal by her lover, who "said [she] would be his":

Виновата ли я, виновата ли я,
Виновата ли я, что люблю?
Виновата ли я, что мой голос дрожал,
Когда пела я песню ему.
Виновата ли я, что мой голос дрожал,
Когда пела я песню ему.

Целовал миловал, целовал миловал,
Говорил, что я буду его.
А я верила все и как роза цвела,
Потому что любила его.
А я верила все и как роза цвела,
Потому что любила его.

Ой, ты, мама, моя, ой, ты, мама, моя,
Отпусти ты меня погулять,
Ночью звезды горят, ночью ласки дарят,
Ночью все о любви говорят.
Ночью звезды горят, ночью ласки дарят,
Ночью все о любви говорят.

Виновата во всем, виновата во всем,
Еще хочешь себя оправдать.
Ах, зачем же, зачем, в эту лунную ночь
Позволяла себя целовать?
Ах, зачем же, зачем, в эту лунную ночь
Позволяла себя целовать?
(Repeat first stanza)

[Am I guilty, am I guilty,
Am I guilty for loving?
Am I guilty that my voice wavered
When I sang him a song?
Am I guilty that my voice wavered
When I sang him a song?

He kissed and loved me, kissed and loved,
He said I would be his.
And I believed it all and bloomed like a rose,
Because I loved him.
And I believed it all and bloomed like a rose,
Because I loved him.

Oh you, mama of mine, oh you, mama of mine,
Let me go out
Stars shine at night, and kisses are given at night,
At night everyone speaks about love.
Stars shine at night, and kisses are given at night,
At night everyone speaks about love.

[You're] guilty of all, guilty of all,
And here you are trying to justify yourself.
Oh why then, oh why did I allow myself
To kiss on that moonlit night?
Oh why then, oh why did I allow myself
To kiss on that moonlit night?
(Repeat first stanza)]

To value love over honor, as she does here, is inherently a modern stance. The refrain in the first stanza (also repeated as the last stanza) suggests that feminine love, unexpressed verbally to her lover but so deeply felt that it is obvious to observers, is beyond reproach: "Am I guilty for loving? Am I guilty that my voice wavered when I sang him a song?" In a plot characteristic of modern views of love, the heroine's defense against the charge of lapsed morals is her deeply felt emotion, her love. This world of feeling is then juxtaposed to—and deemed superior to—the traditional world of community expectations.[13]

The third and fourth stanzas eloquently capture this tension between female feeling and patriarchy's demands that women control or repress their desire. In these stanzas the song speaks of the conflict with societal norms from a position of female subjectivity. The third stanza accomplishes this in a dialogue with the heroine's mother, while the first two lines of the fourth stanza describe either the mother's verbal castigation of the daughter or the daughter's internalization of the mother's voice and her repentance. This is a "daughter's" song in which the daughter has assimilated some of the mother's point of view. "Am I Guilty" thus supplies an eloquent justification of women's self-fulfillment, at the same time as it gives voice to the norms that repress her desire. And of course, in many of these later songs there is an irony in the eloquence with which the heroines of these songs assert their inability to express themselves. This kind of double-voiced expression illustrates women's negotiated position vis-à-vis patriarchal social norms.

A very popular song nationally, also likely of twentieth-century origin, "I Drank Myself Drunk," at first glance seems like a resisting text, and indeed it may be interpreted as such by the many women who enjoy crooning it at *zastol'e* celebrations.

Напилася я пьяна, не дойду я до дому
Довела меня тропка дальняя
До вишневого сада
Довела меня тропка дальняя
До вишневого сада

Там кукушка кукует мое сердце волнует
Ты скажи-ка мне расскажи-ка мне
Где мой милый ночует
Ты скажи-ка мне расскажи-ка мне
Где мой милый ночует

Если он при дороге, помоги ему Боже!
Если с любушкой на постелюшке
Накажи его Боже!
Если с любушкой на постелюшке
Накажи его Боже!

Чем же я не такая чем чужая другая
Я хорошая я пригожая только доля такая
Я хорошая я пригожая только доля такая

Если б раньше я знала что так замужем плохо
Расплела бы я русу косоньку
Да сидела бы дома
Расплела бы я русу косоньку
Да сидела бы дома

[I drank myself drunk, won't make it home
A path led me far
Into the cherry orchard
A path led me far
Into the cherry orchard

There the cuckoo is cuckooing, vexing my heart
You tell me, tell me, [cuckoo],
Where my dear one is spending the night
You tell me, tell me, [cuckoo],
Where my dear one is spending the night

If he's on the road, God help him!
If he's in bed with a lover,
God punish him!
If he's in bed with a lover,
God punish him!

How am I not suitable, how am I different?
I'm nice looking, I'm fine looking, but this is my lot.
I'm nice looking, I'm fine looking, but this is my lot.

If I'd known that being married is so bad,
I'd have unbraided my blonde braid
And sat home
I'd have unbraided my blonde braid
And sat home.]

Based upon my (LO's) experiences, singing this song in a group of women—while drinking—provides an occasion for women's bonding in female solidarity versus an imagined or remembered male oppressor. This song directly expresses women's anger through the heroine's purposeful transgression: the female narrator gets drunk to drown her sorrow at her husband's infidelity.[14] The heroine's power of firm speech is striking here: she curses him, albeit indirectly (and drunkenly). In this sense the song recalls a large category of traditional lyric songs that baldly state a wife's disappointment with her husband.[15]

However, other aspects of the song suggest the heroine's passivity and the traditional script of managing relationships through appeals to the spiritual world. The expression of her anger is mediated by a higher power: "Punish him, God." She asks a cuckoo bird (whose behavior is traditionally thought to predict misfortune) to tell where her husband is tonight, and complains of her lot (*dolia*) since she is as attractive as other women. In a fashion that recalls and imitates traditional village lyric songs, her complaint is framed not against this particular man but against "marriage": "If only I had known that marriage was so bad, I'd have unbraided my blonde braid and sat at home."[16] Here her description of an alternative lifestyle for herself suggests a somewhat unhappy substitute for married life but the only one possible in Russian prerevolutionary society—to sit at home in one's parents' house.[17] While this song presents feminine subjectivity in feminist-realist style by expressing a woman's anger and resistance to marriage, it asserts that there is no exit, no solution to the woman's dilemma within the bounds of patriarchy. She must either stay home alone or tolerate her husband's infidelity. The only balm left for her is to drown her sorrows in drink. The song overtly resists patriarchy, but the heroine's resistance is partly framed in melodramatic and traditional terms. In other resisting texts we see similar negotiations between traditional and modern, complicit and resisting: like many folkloric texts, these songs are products of conflicting viewpoints, and individuals may interpret the texts in widely varying ways or be drawn to them for a variety of reasons.[18]

The Lure of the Soap-Opera Villainess

Romance songs are stories of transgression and rupture—whether that is configured in relatively uncomplicated ways (as in complicit texts) or in highly contradictory terms (as in resisting ones). When the acts of transgression belong to a woman, then the plots of the songs are driven by a villainess. Typically, the destructive acts of these female characters are motivated by jealousy of another woman's happiness, and the plots are examples of divine justice: a woman who does wrong is often "punished" when misfortune befalls her.

In the worlds of our interlocutors, the villainess features prominently in yet another melodramatic genre that fills their leisure time: the televised, serial "soap opera." Villainesses of contemporary soap operas are complex characters who perform a wider range of female behaviors than do villainesses of either nineteenth- or twentieth-century folk songs. We observed complex reactions to villainesses when our conversation partners watched American, Russian, and Latin American soap operas, such as *Santa Barbara* (USA, 1984–93; shown in Russia 1992–2002), *Clone* (Brazil, 2001–2, shown in Russia 2005–8), and *Karmelita 1 and 2* (Russia, 2005, 2009). Here the role of the transgressive woman is developed: women do not simply fall in love with other men; they sleep with men for financial gain, trick their men, cheat and lie to both men and women. As Tania Modleski puts it, the soap opera villainess "continually works to make the most out of events which render other characters totally helpless" (1982, 97). Villainesses are central to the plots of these soap operas, and from our observations, their complex expressions of self-focus are key to the popularity of these characters.

Modleski explains the attraction of soap opera villainesses: they express women's hidden anger. Soap operas direct the spectator's intense and multilayered hostility toward this character, "the one woman who repeatedly tries to gain control over feminine powerlessness"; in so doing, these texts "further insure against the possibility of women's becoming more self-assertive" (1982, 33). That is, the manipulative actions the villainess undertakes "to turn her powerlessness to her own advantage are always thwarted just when victory is most assured." Female spectators, Modleski surmises, despise "the villainess as the negative image" of their ideal selves, but also enjoy watching her act out their secret desires (1982, 94–97). In this sense, she is an embodiment of their "feminine anger," what Dorothy Dinnerstein (1976, 236) calls women's "split-off fury," the underside of the feminine woman's capacity for empathy. But ultimately, the soap opera text is constructed in such a way as to encourage spectators' hatred of this character, and viewers end up cheering on precisely the forces that conspire against the realization of their hidden desires for agency or revenge.

While as fieldworkers we were not privy to hidden anger and hostility, we did observe that the villainesses of soap operas were the subject of much attention. Women seemed to derive pleasure from censuring these characters. In Krasnoe, a group of women I (LO) had interviewed during several previous years about their singing got together regularly (nightly) to view soap operas. I was surprised when they announced that one of their birthdays would be celebrated at table at the same time as the *kina* (dialectal pl. of "movie") start; and indeed, the television was turned off only when the serials were over (it was on for roughly two hours, from 5:30 to 7:30 p.m.—and at this time they proceeded to sing romances until 10 p.m.). During the group watching of *Clone*, the women traded comments about the actions of the characters. There was one man present, but he excused himself from the room during the shows. At one point, with a slight smile on her face and her eyes on the television screen, the birthday woman began to chant repeatedly in a low voice, drawing out the stressed vowel, "*Con* artist, what a *con* artist!" ("Aferiiiiistka, aferiiiiistka kakaia!"). She was referring to a female character who had tricked several men in order to acquire an apartment. It seemed that there was a certain pleasure for the viewers in the extreme badness and remorselessness of this character—as well as the pleasure in judging her.

The women's comments about the characters and the group nature of their viewing— and indeed, its ritual regularity, to the point that it not only serves to pass the time but also constitutes one of the foci of important celebrations—suggest that the serials have taken deep root in their culture. The language they use to talk about these shows has specific content pertaining to their own lives. We observed a similar type of sympathetic commentary when these women were listening to each other's stories: for example, while one woman was telling how she was beset by local witches, another crooned, "The bastards. The *bastards*!" ("Vot svoloch'. Vot *svoloch'*!").

Viewing and talking about the narratives constitutes a ritual action that helps to maintain friendships and a sense of community. Within this context, clearly, the bad woman's role in the melodramatic text is not simply the moral one of showing what women should not do. Rather, through their comments on villainesses village women can define an identity, perform agency, and reinforce community cohesion. If in a group setting I label a character as a "con artist," I proclaim not only that I am not a swindler but also that my community rejects such behavior. We shape our world by defining its boundaries: the Other—here, the bad woman, the one who destroys the community—is as important to our self-concept as are role models we want to or are encouraged to emulate. But by imagining such behavior along with the shocking televised program, one can also participate in the fantasy of the forbidden.

On this additional level we may see the bad woman as, potentially, a rebellious woman who purposely thwarts accepted roles. She offers the possibility for women to imagine female freedom and a particular kind of self-centered, pleasure-seeking agency, both of which may seem inaccessible in traditional social networks and within the Soviet value system. A similar tension between judgment and identification, pleasure and horror may be seen in gossip, a folkloric speech genre that echoes many of the functions of romance songs and soap operas.

Gossip: The Speech of Melodrama

The melodramatic imagination was heavily active in gossip, which was sprinkled throughout nearly every conversation with our interlocutors. We define gossip as the practice of telling unverified (often unverifiable) stories, most often about the personal lives or reputations of others.[19] Many gossip stories were tales of women's victimization. Like classic melodrama, they often took a point of view complicit with the norms of patriarchy. As with the song about the sailor who corrupted a young woman, often such gossip was intended as a cautionary tale and a judgment that should influence behavior. Traditional social norms—women's honor and respect for family ties and hierarchical relations—were reinforced through such tales. A few examples: during our conversation, Lidia Pankratovna, the member of the singing group "Golden Age" (born in 1939), supplemented her performances of songs with stories of others' lives. She said her daughter had chosen a bad, drunken husband who beat her; she lived with him for ten years, until he almost drowned her, and then he was put into prison. She only left him when they put him in jail. Lidia Pankratovna hadn't wanted her daughter to marry him but did not forbid her from doing so; however she did warn her not to come crying to her later. After the daughter had left the husband, Lidia Pankratovna said, she told her: "If only you had listened to me, you would have found such grooms! You'd have gone so far in life." In a similar tale of women's victimization, Evdokia Timofeevna Kh., whose life story we analyzed in chapter 3 (born in 1932), told us about the marriage of her first husband's sister—who, she emphasized, was literate, unlike herself. Despite being better educated, this woman was an alcoholic and was beaten by her husband.

Both of these stories emphasized that the woman's flaws of lack of self-control and respect for family caused her misfortune; in each case, although the man was the villain, he was not faulted by the speakers as much as was the woman. Both of these speakers took the "mother's" or *bol'shukha*'s point of view in judging other women's choices. Such stories peppered almost all conversations we had with rural women. We understood that the stories were not necessarily meant as specific cautions for our own lives but that in general they constituted a discourse that allowed women in positions of relative social power to "lay down the law" and express the morals of the community.

A story of violence against a woman came from Evdokia Timofeevna and her friends Zoia Venediktovna K. and Nina Vasilevna S. (all born in the early 1930s); the event happened in their youth. A young man felt spurned when his girlfriend's mother did not allow her to marry him, because she was going to go study (apparently the girl agreed with her mother, although this point was left unclear); he stabbed her after an Ivanov (Saint John's) Day celebration in a different village, but he used a short knife and she did not die right away; he took her back to their own village, got a razor and slit her throat, then shot himself. Apparently, the young couple were to be entombed together, but one member of the storytelling group asserted that they were not after all: the mother wouldn't allow it. The two endings show the legendary nature of this story. We interpret these alternate endings as offering two different judgments of the events: if the two had been buried together, it would have meant that their love was true and that the mother had interfered unjustly. But if the mother's will to keep the two separated won out in the end, that suggested the primacy of a mother's moral judgment.

In direct reference to mothers' judgments, Lidia Pankratovna told us two stories meant to show that going against a mother's curse could have bad results. Her husband's sister got pregnant out of wedlock, and their mother was so mad she cursed the daughter: "May you be cursed!" ("Bud' ty prokliata!"). "And she [the daughter] was not able to have a child: she lost three, perhaps because her pelvis was too narrow. Only the fourth lived, and that one was premature, born through Caesarean section. That's what a mother's curse is." Another woman who was cursed by her mother ended up with an illness such that "everything hurts." Lidia Pankratovna capped her performance with an admonition to a young female student folklorist: "Keep it in mind for the future." She meant: make sure you do not go against your parents.

Like the plots of melodramatic songs, such stories provide a storehouse of plots about women's fateful mistakes or victimization, meant as cautionary tales. As in the songs, here patriarchal tradition answers modernity: young women who assert themselves against the advice or dictates of elders meet with bad ends. In the story of the murder-suicide, not even following the mother's advice can save the girl from the possessive wrath of the young man, perhaps because the mother was advising the girl to study (to pursue independence) and not to marry. Here the young man asserts his power over all females. Young women who tell the story—as we imagine Evdokia, Zoia, and Nina might have done in their youth, since the story dated from their youth—might be expressing their fears that similar fates would wait for recalcitrant girls.

In all of the stories described above an important role was played by the mother, who acted as a controlling force or moral compass in her daughter's life. Note that in these stories, set in the Soviet period, the father does not appear as an authority figure: perhaps because fathers were absent or disempowered, or perhaps because mothers told the stories. At any rate, the plot that women who went against their mother's advice ended up unhappy seems to suggest the primacy of mothers as moral judges in the community. These tales were also apparently meant for entertainment, to increase social cohesion, and to enhance the status of the storyteller. The speakers' own life stories, however, were very different: almost none of the women we interviewed emphasized the melodramatic aspects of their own stories. The reason, we suppose, lies in the fact that the only available subject position within melodrama is the victim. The other available point of view, the villainess, is not generally a viable subject position for autobiography (Spender 1980, 121).

Conclusion

We find it remarkable that the lure of melodrama was powerful for generations of women who may have emulated the much-feted Soviet heroines. These role models overfulfilled norms in work, took on work traditionally reserved for men, and still excelled in producing new workers for the state (Chatterjee 2002, 158). In this context, melodrama constituted an alternative discourse. We have identified a few reasons why melodramatic discourse may be attractive to rural women: first and foremost, it belongs to the private realm of emotions and personal life, a sphere that was all but neglected in Soviet culture. Second, the drama of these texts revolves around the clash between the personal and the extrapersonal, that is, between the desires of young women and the traditional moral code of patriarchy. Melodrama's attraction is enhanced by elder women's nostalgia for this patriarchal world, but nostalgia alone would not be enough to maintain it as a productive discourse in women's lives. We think that whether their own lives participate in such drama or not, women respond to this central narrative because it reconfirms the traditional values and beliefs they grew up with (women's honor, women's responsibility to elders and to the *rod*, and fate), and also because it allows them to identify with female victims and villains who resist patriarchy's demands. Even today, the drama of resistance is still actual, still enacted on a daily basis, as their gossip stories show. Through such texts women tacitly enact both stances of judgment (a maternal point of view) and identification (a daughter's position).

Melodrama provides a key to the aesthetic and moral world of Russian village women. As in women's stories of the supernatural (discussed in chapter 8), stories in the melodramatic mode tell of the construction of personal relationships and the fabric of the family. Whether juxtaposed to the other world or to the public world of work and government, this world of the family is so central to the value systems of Russian rural women that their subjectivities are based upon it, as we argued in chapter 3. The personal sphere of our interlocutors is a world defined predominantly by relationship, and only secondarily by individual acts and intentions. To be sure, singular acts were important to our interlocutors, as their life stories showed, but those acts arose out of the support network provided by the family. Our next chapter explores further how a subjectivity can be constructed as both enmeshed and singular, in the context of a different musical discourse, the solo genre of the *chastushka*.

5

Transgression as Communicative Act

Rural Women's Chastushki

If the melodramatic mode in singing, gossip, and television-watching expressed women's relationship to community and addressed the clash of tradition and modernity, the singing genre of *chastushki* allowed rural women to be actors in dramas or comedies of their own creation. These individually composed ditties comprised a speech genre in which people could express publicly what was otherwise taboo. This medium for intentional transgression helped to increase individual social status or social honor, gave women a voice within and beyond the village, and contributed to community cohesion.

Stephen Frank has argued that the entrance of the *chastushka* into village culture in the late nineteenth century helped to change the way young people expressed themselves: these short, satirical songs were critical of serfdom, agricultural work, government authorities, or parental authority; mocked the local priest or deacon; or made uncritical reference to drunkenness and brawls (Frank 1992, 723–24). Whereas previously the folklore genres of mummery and folk theater allowed for public satire through physical comedy, the *chastushka* gave greater access to a verbal satirical, critical, or rebellious voice.

The *chastushka* continued to perform this satirical/critical function in the Soviet and post-Soviet periods. Since *chastushki* are so easily composed, memorized, borrowed, and modified, they can be used by individuals to refer to any matter that the author wishes to bring into the public arena. Each short text is two, four, or six lines of rhymed trochaic trimeter or tetrameter, and is sung or declaimed by an individual or small group, to accordion or balalaika accompaniment. Any opinions that an individual expresses in *chastushki* automatically become public utterances since *chastushki* are borrowed by other singers and become public currency. Taboo subjects are de rigueur, and can include opinions that should not be stated publicly according to laws, rules of public conduct, or social etiquette (such as political critique or social secrets); or views that should not be stated because of conventional age and gender restrictions on addressor and addressee.

Since *chastushki* erase social hierarchies and fly in the face of social conventions, they are often accompanied by laughter. This is usually an open, ambivalent, playful kind of laughter that may be best described as carnival laughter (Bakhtin 1984, 11–12). Nonetheless, *chastushka* texts and the laughter accompanying them have a subversive element, since they defy social rules rather than transmitting or upholding them.

In Russian culture scholars have identified *chastushki* as primarily a women's genre, although men also participate in it. Since women and young people were lowest in the social hierarchy of the village, a communicative tool whose purpose was specifically to permit open expression of personal desires and opinions must have been especially welcome to them. In many world cultures, women are excluded from public satirical discourse because to laugh at someone implies superiority and a challenge to social reality, whereas women are often viewed as helpmates whose main role is to reproduce (to create, not to destroy reality) (Apte 1985, 69; Walker 1988, 98). However, women in many cultures do commonly participate in carnival humor.

This chapter discusses three types of *chastushki*: those that have to do with everyday life; erotic *chastushki*, many of which use the Russian cursing language *mat*; and those that enter the public discourse of politics. The first two types bring private matters into the public sphere. If a *chastushka* is accepted and repeated by the community, the expressed opinion becomes associated with common opinion, thus no longer belonging to private, individual speech. Because *chastushki* become associated with the group, they can create, annul, reshape, or reconfirm *svoi*-groups. Thus, *chastushki* help to formulate an individual's relationship to a social group.

Chastushki about politics can also help shape an individual's relation to a *svoi*-group. But here an individual is speaking about his or her relationship to events and policies that originated outside the community. That is, even if his or her speech is directed at an audience of peers, he or she is (often ironically) referencing the national sphere. These *chastushki* enter into dialogue with the official discourse of government.

During the Soviet period, political *chastushki* frequently were misinterpreted by the authorities. Officials saw *chastushki* as direct, personal speech—not indirect, anonymous speech, as they were seen from within the community. During the Soviet period, if information about illicit political (satirical) *chastushka*-singing was reported to the authorities or if officials witnessed such performances, they often arrested the singer.

In the glasnost and the post-Soviet periods, people were no longer arrested for *chastushki*-singing. During this time, we studied women's participation in the production and performance of political *chastushki*. Women's involvement in the singing of political *chastushki* is remarkable since politics is generally seen as a man's topic. We argue that when women enter the arena of political discourse through the medium of these songs, they may be intentionally communicating their social judgments to a broader public audience—an audience linked with the nation, rather than women's immediate social group (their cohort, their village). Whereas in the Soviet period political *chastushki* could land one in jail, in the first two post-Soviet decades political *chastushki* functioned as a means of achieving public honor.

Chastushka as Communicative Act

Most *chastushki* sung in the village are about love; only a small percentage express satire about political or economic events or states of affairs. The scholarly literature on *chastushki* emphasizes their improvised quality, but *chastushki* are not usually invented wholesale on the spot. Rather, each singer or group generally has a repertoire of memorized texts that are recycled, recombined, and modified as the expressive "need" arises. The songs were an integral part of village culture before World War II. In the late nineteenth and early twentieth century, rural young women and men sang *chastushki* at village holiday gatherings (Edemskii 1905; Eleonskaia 1910; Knatts 1928). *Chastushki* reached a peak in popularity in the 1920s, and their popularity was further stimulated in the 1930s by officially sponsored public contests (Olympiads, or *smotry*) for collection and performance—on the level of the collective farm, region, city, and province (LaPasha 2001). After World War II, the genre began to lose popularity with young people, and eventually became associated with middle-aged or older people (Kolpakova 1967; Dmitrieva 1972).

For our interlocutors of all three generations, but especially for the second and third generations, *chastushki* functioned socially as a means of communication. They were not just a way to make music and have fun; rather, people took their content seriously. The rural women we talked with were still using *chastushki* to communicate with each other when we visited them in the late twentieth and early twenty-first centuries. For them, *chastushki* function as a speech act.

Chastushki are generally performed in spontaneous group situations: an individual singer or pair sing a *chastushka*, and other singers join in with their own. During a dance, *chastushki* are declaimed in a special way: at a certain point, one of the dancers stops and sings a *chastushka*. The dancers converse in *chastushka* form, not interrupting one another. This process is regulated both by the rhythm of the accordion and by pauses in the dance. By making such a pause, a person signifies that he or she has "taken the floor," that the next line is his or hers. This rule is observed very seriously. Even if a *chastushka* is offensive to one of the dancers, one cannot stop or disrupt the singer, as this would be a violation of the rules; one can only answer in kind, or "sing it off." This manner of performance of *chastushki* suggests a particular communicative convention that defines this genre. In Russian village tradition, the *chastushka* was a legitimate form of public statement. As we know from our informants' stories, any attempt to interrupt the performance of a *chastushka* was taken as a sign of weakness. Conversely, the ability to find an effective answer to a challenge in *chastushka* form was seen as a particularly valuable social skill. Thus, this genre presupposes a defined order of communication.

Celebration of Petrov den' (St. Peter's Day, 29 June), Ivanov Bor, Vologda oblast, 2006. After the official presentation during the village's holiday, local residents decided to sing *chastushki* on stage. (PHOTO BY SVETLANA ADONYEVA)

Those village *chastushka* texts that concerned relations between young men and women were communicated during young people's gatherings. They were always performed in connection with a specific situation, with the present state of affairs on the social scene. For this reason, the *chastushka* was also referred to in one local tradition as an "exemplary song" (*primernaia pesnia*), a song that referred to a concrete social situation.

Several Russian folklore collectors expressed the opinion that *chastushki* functioned in the village like a newspaper. Vasilii Simakov, the well-known folklore collector of the early twentieth century, observed, "I recall a characteristic comparison made by a peasant who compared the *chastushka* to a newspaper: 'You,' he said, 'get all of your city news from newspapers, but we village folk can get the news from *chastushki*'" (Simakov 1913, 13). Dmitrii Zelenin made the same observation regarding the early twentieth-century village *chastushka*: "Increasingly one can find the undistorted, authentic realism of journalism or newspaper accounts in *chastushki* . . . moreover, the *chastushka* always strives to reflect the latest events of local political and social life" (Zelenin 1994, 465). Based upon our analysis of the functions of the *chastushka* among Soviet village youth, we agree with the basic assumption that the *chastushka* was used to report news. But the *chastushka*'s news is not of a factual nature. Rather, it is about people's opinions. In general (although not always) there were two different subject matters for different age groups: while in youth dances the news occurs on the "romantic front," in the *chastushki* performed by older men and women the subject could be any event of local, regional, or national significance, such as a space flight, a party or government decree, a fashion for long or short skirts, opinions on celebrities, the appointment of new local leadership, and so forth.

A few examples follow:

1. A *chastushka* from the 1970s regarding the absence of groceries in stores:

Я купила холодильник
Назвается «Ока»
Мяса нету, масла нету,
Положу говна пока.

[I bought a refrigerator
They call it an Oka,
There's no meat, there's no butter
I'll put some shit in it for now.]

(Woman born in 1929, Panevo, Belozersk region, Vologda oblast, 10 July 1995 [Bel 8-19]. Recorded with euphemisms, but heard in same village in 1988 without euphemisms.)

2. A postwar *chastushka*:

Будь ты проклята, Германия,
И Гитлер—сатана.
Убили ягодиночку—
Осталась я одна.

[A curse on you, O Germany,
And Hitler is a devil.

They killed my darling dearest
And left me all alone.]

3. A *chastushka* from the early 1990s:

С неба звездочка упал
В золотистые поля
С нами Ленина не стало,
С нами Ельцин у руля.

[A star's fallen from the heavens,
Into the golden fields,
Lenin's not with us any longer,
We've got Yeltsin at the wheel.]

(Previous two examples sung by a boy born in 1987, Sredniaia, Belozersk region, Vologda oblast, 7 July 1995 [Bel 8-37])

In these examples the news was not the fact being described but the act of linking the given *chastushka* text—sometimes one those present already knew—with a concrete instance of public performance. The news was a publicly stated point of view and the appraisal of a known fact. Herein lay the performative significance of the *chastushka* (Austin 1962). A publicly performed *chastushka* changed the social space, bringing personal interpretations into the field of public knowledge. The *chastushka* was used to express a personal judgment that aspired to become a collective one. In this process, the speech forms of the convention turned a personal statement into indirect (third-person) speech. The "I" of *chastushka* speech and the *chastushka* performer were not perceived as one and the same person. Switching to the *chastushka* register, like donning a mask, hid the performer's self. Putting on this verbal mask, she or he was freed from the norms of speech behavior that normally applied to her or him as a member of the community. After its first performance, a *chastushka* became, for a time, currency in the process of the community's information exchange. The public circulation of a text and its repetition made the opinion it expressed a general one.

Following Erving Goffman, we argue that *chastushki*, like jokes or theater, function as socially framed discourse. When people enter the *chastushka* sphere, it is as if they agree beforehand to switch to specific rules of social interaction. Within the *chastushka* field, playfulness is institutionalized or stabilized (unlike brief periods of playfulness in the course of normal interaction), and will continue as long as the participants keep singing or reciting *chastushki*. Of course, the *chastushki* sung or declaimed within the frame of performance have an effect on life outside that sphere, as many of our examples show (Goffman

1974, 49–57, 247–49). Participants may limit the degree of their playfulness depending upon who is present, the location, time of day, and so on (and therefore, even within this frame behavior is not always maximally free), but the intention of the genre is to play. In the Soviet period, of course, serious limits on play were placed on *chastushki* singers by the authorities.

The trick of this genre was that the use of *chastushka* speech allowed the public expression of that which the performer did not have the right to express publicly. We can illustrate this with a *chastushka* sung by a woman born in 1927:

У милова у моева
Любопытна матушка:
Спрашивает у людей
Свое ли платьице на ней.

[My darling has a
Most curious mother:
She likes to ask of people,
"Is that your own dress you're wearing?"]

(Sukharevo, Vashkinskii region, Vologda oblast, 24 July 2000 [Vash 8-17])

In the text, a young woman is speaking about her boyfriend's mother. The speaker claims that the older woman suspects her of borrowing clothes for dances—that is to say, she is not wearing her own clothes, or, in other words, she's poor. This statement violated an important behavioral rule of village society. Villagers strictly observed a hierarchy of age: a young woman could not publicly criticize an older woman. Only those of the same age could conflict publicly with one another. Only the older could reproach and judge the younger. Yet in the *chastushka* format, such violations could occur. In fact, we would go so far as to say that violations of the rules of public behavior *were the norm* for the *chastushka*. *Chastushka* speech served as a channel allowing the public transmission to the addressee of a message that could not have been voiced by any other means. To use our notions of the plot and script, the *chastushki* in current use in any community provides a set of plots that participants can adapt, revise, or re-create and apply to their own situations in order to perform their own life scripts.

This form of speech violates not only rules against certain topics of conversation but also communicative taboos. The *chastushka* provides a temporary fissure in the village social hierarchy: younger people can address their elders critically, girls can make romantic approaches to young men, a young woman can speak ill of her in-laws, a rank-and-file kolkhoz worker can speak up against the president.

As a result of such a statement, the line between secret and open is blurred, and once-hidden information is subjected to general discussion. The disclosure of the personal—feelings, opinions, needs, judgments—summons the public to be witnesses. Performers make such speech acts on their own initiative, and the community reacts in its own way, by supporting and approving the *chastushka* (e.g., by singing a similar one) or ignoring it (e.g., by not responding to it, by forgetting it). The community has the right to control the situation, to approve or condemn.

Meanwhile, however, the choice to sing a *chastushka* places the performer in a position of power. The performer in effect forces the public either to share the opinion that she or he has expressed or to answer with another *chastushka* and thereby seize the initiative. The role that the speaker claims for him- or herself by using this form is the role of a bearer of common knowledge or, more precisely, of common opinion.

Chastushka singers make known their intention through a firmly set expressive form: a dancer stops, stomps his foot, and sings, turning to face the addressee. However, the real addressee of the *chastushka* communicative act is the community as a whole (Hymes 1974, 54). It acts as a reviewer to whom is offered the chance to examine and discuss the *chastushka*'s interpretation of a given fact. Thus, within the *chastushka* arena, both the performer and the hearers are in positions of power and agency.

The following account, written by a student collector of folklore, demonstrates how *chastushki* acted on public opinion. This note was contained in an appendix to a 1956 student essay about making field recordings of *chastushki*:

> Min'kina, a kolkhoz worker, told us an interesting story. She said that *chastushki* helped her get her life in order. People say "Min'kina got her husband back with *chastushki*." Min'kina herself gave us the following account. Her husband came back from the war and started to woo another woman. They started fighting, which got people talking around the village. People started singing *chastushki* about her. "I'm not good at speaking," Min'kina recalled, "so I started to come up with *chastushki*."
>
> Min'kina then sang to the collectors:

Тридцать лет песен не пела,
Петь не собиралась.
Меня в песнях позадели,
Я порасчиталась.

[I sang no songs for thirty years,
I wasn't of a mind.
But since they hurt me in song,
I paid them back in kind.]

"Then I came into the club and sang about everything: about what people were saying, about my husband, our whole life, my youth. That did the trick for my husband. Now we live happily." (Podgornaia and Sergeeva 1956, 47–48)

Another example from our interviews, told to us in 2001 in Vologda oblast by a woman born in 1940, emphasizes the bravery of the female protagonist, who publicly excoriated a young man for breaking social rules:

People come up with *chastushki* on the fly. Here's something that happened in our village. So, Tanya Elizarova dressed well, knew how to behave, but was from a really poor family. And she sent [Sasha] Ganichev to Vologda: "Sasha, would you please buy me some stockings?" [Because] this Sasha worked as a loader, so he drove around loading and unloading trucks. . . . He came back, and they asked him, "So, did you get those stockings for Tanyushka Elizarova?" but he says, "What are you talking about? I got curls!" Back then the six-month curl [permanent wave] was in style with the guys. Now, Tanyushka is waiting for her stockings. The truck came back with the products they'd gone to pick up. And while they're unloading, Tanyushka is waiting there. They tell her, "Don't hold your breath, Sashka got a perm, he spent your money." Tan'ka started crying and ran home. So, okay, everyone went to the club. . . . And Sashka danced well, and he'd always come into the club, as soon as the guys opened the door, he'd enter and, no matter who was dancing, he'd do his *prisiadka* [squat and kick]. And here he comes in, and without any warning . . . she stands up in front of him and sings:

Ой, кто это идет,
Посмотрите, девушки!
А Саня Ганичев завился
На чужие денюжки!

[Oh, look, girls,
Look who's coming!
Sania Ganichev got curled
On someone else's money!]

(Chisti, Vashkinskii region, Vologda oblast, 13 July 2001 [Vash 8-25])

The comic effect of *chastushki* is defined by their function: they abrogate social taboos. These could be personal experiences that it was not acceptable to talk about, such as sexual anxiety. They could be political views and judgments that did not correspond to official discourse, or opinions on the behavior of someone known to the listeners. Hidden themes were exposed and thrown into the public communicative space. In addition to taboo themes, *chastushki* allowed speakers to transcend hierarchical taboos. Anyone familiar with the genre could make a statement in this communicative space: old and young, women and men, seniors and subordinates. *Chastushka* speech erased the social hierarchy that other forms of communication formed and supported. We suggest that this was a unique speech register, specially intended for such a function.

Chastushka as Carnival

The laughter that generally accompanied *chastushki* performance was a reaction to the performers' open expression of that which was kept quiet in normal speech. The *chastushka* allowed society to become, for a moment, open, in Bergson's definition of the term ([1935] 1977). Laughter was a psychological reaction to this social transformation. Society opened, abolishing hierarchies and bans on particular topics, and this prompted general merriment. This laughter is "carnival laughter," following Bakhtin's description of this phenomenon in medieval culture. Carnival laughter has three main characteristics, in Bakhtin's formulation: first, it is not individual but done in groups, in a festive atmosphere. Second, everyone both laughs and is laughed at, and this laughter emphasizes the "gay relativity" of the world. Third, this laughter is ambivalent: both joyous and derisive, both affirming and denying (1984, 11–12). In general, the singing of *chastushki* we have described above meets all these criteria, although individual instances of *chastushka*-singing to "get back" at a rival are closer to the "derisive" side of laughter—close to satire itself, which Bakhtin calls "purely negative satire" (12). Yet they are carnivalesque, because they are framed within that metaphorical space in which laughter (including barbed laughter) is part of the rules of the game.

   Bakhtin is famous for his emphasis upon one aspect of carnival laughter: its link with what he calls the "grotesque body." In folk humor, the body is "not a closed, completed unit; it is unfinished, outgrows itself, transgresses its own limits." Carnival humor emphasizes the parts of the body "through which the world enters the body or emerges from it, or through which the body itself goes out to meet the world"—that is, the organs of reproduction, eating, and defecation (16). We see this emphasis in erotic *chastushki*, which are quite popular among our interlocutors. When we sat having tea or after a meal or snack with liquor, middle-aged and older rural women often shared with us *chastushki* of this nature, which they call "*chastushki* with pictures" or *maternye* or *matiuzhnye chastushki*, that is, *chastushki* that incorporate the Russian cursing language called *mat*. The following were recited during such a session by Evdokia Timofeevna Kh. (born in 1932), Zoia Venediktovna K. (born in 1932), and Nina Vasilevna S. (born in 1933), in Pigilinka, Vologda oblast (23 October 2004):

1. А я работала в колхозе
   Заработала пятак
   Пяток закрою жопу
   А пизда осталась так.

2. Белокурая баяночка
   Валялась в борозде
   Я дала бы тебе, милушка,
   Да чирий на пизде.

3. В Америке, в Америку
   Не ходят поезда
   В акурат четыре пуда
   У сударушки пизда

4. Ты играешь, ты и пой
   Да ты откуда хуй такой?
   Из соседнего села
   Шуренька за хуй привела.

5. Из-за леса выезжает
   Конная милиция
   Задирайте, девки, юбки
   Будет репетиция.

[1. I worked in the kolkhoz
   I earned a nickel
   I'll put the nickel on my ass
   But my cunt remains without![1]

2. A blonde accordion
   Was lying in the furrow
   I'd give you some, dear,
   But I've got a pimple on my cunt.

3. To America, to America
   Trains don't go
   My lady's cunt
   Weighs a hundred fifty pounds exactly.[2]

4. "You play; you should sing too
   Where did you come from, such a prick?"

"From the neighboring village
My girlfriend led me here by my dick!"

5. Out of the forest comes riding
   The cavalry militia
   Raise up your skirts, girls
   There'll be a rehearsal!]

Many of these erotic *chastushki* use the humor of nonsense. The third *chastushka* above clearly belong in this category: it makes little sense to report the size of a woman's reproductive organs by weight. Instead, the *chastushka*'s humor is provoked by the unexpected contrast between the first two and the final two lines. Clearly, the purpose of this text is to be nonsensical, irreverent, to mention the reproductive body in a context in which bodies are not normally mentioned, and thereby to provoke mirth in the audience. As Emil Draitser puts it, "the more bizarre the sexual pronouncements are, the *less* likely they are to be taken seriously" (1999, 246). Bakhtin calls similar nonsense the "carnivalization of speech" and emphasizes the essential spirit of freedom conveyed by speech that is not constrained by the demands of logic (1984, 426).

Some of the *chastushki*, such as the second and fourth above, would have a flirtatious quality if sung in a mixed-sex group. Draitser points out that sexual teasing, in which the singer questions a man's masculinity, or sexual seduction, in which the singer speaks of her own sexual attractiveness, are common functions in erotic *chastushki*. Draitser theorizes that women who sing bawdy *chastushki* may be expressing sublimated desire due to a lack of sexual partners (which our interlocutors experienced as a result of World War II) (1999, 245). We do not find it necessary to speculate about whether women's desire was more or less fulfilled than it would be if there were adequate male partners; rather, it is enough to note that the discourse of erotic *chastushki* openly conveys and plays with desire, making desire an accepted, human trait.

Some *chastushki* are not only playful but also satirical. The satiric point may be crystal clear, such as in *chastushki* making fun of girls' loose morals or boys' inability to satisfy girls sexually. In the first *chastushka* above, the point is less obvious, but there is implied criticism of the amount that a kolkhoz worker earns: not even enough to cover two bodily orifices. Here too, nonsense is the principle of construction of the *chastushka*, since using money to cover one's orifices does not make sense, and the contrast of official ("kolkhoz," "earned") and low, unofficial (bodily orifices) speech registers is one of the sources of mirth here.

One notable element of such *chastushki* is their lack of gender restrictions. Women sang them, but these *chastushki* are narrated from both masculine and feminine points of view, as well as sexually indeterminate points of view. For example, it is difficult to determine whether the last one quoted above (about the cavalry militia) expresses men's wish for girls to lift up their skirts, or girls' own desire to offer themselves for the mock "rehearsal." The third one ("To America") clearly has a male point of view, since it refers to "my lady." We noticed many instances of such musical "cross-dressing" (cross-singing, singing songs from the point of view of the opposite gender) for humorous effect.

In general our female interlocutors did not appear to avoid *chastushki* that denigrated women. For example, one might wonder why Russian women are using the word we have translated as "cunt" at all, since the English equivalent is viewed by many American women as one of the most misogynist words in the English language. One explanation is that the *chastushki* sung by Evdokia, Zoia, and Nina did not use the word to refer to a woman (as do many other *chastushki*) but used it exclusively in its anatomical sense. Nonetheless, they did sing other overtly misogynist *chastushki*, such as one, sung by Zoia, that described girls as getting paid for having sex.[3] This received a negative reaction from Evdokia, but the singer defended herself, saying, "What, they give birth to a lot of babies, so . . ." She probably meant that the girls were performing an important social function in the context of Russia's chronically low birth rates (although she was probably being at least partly facetious). Draitser speculates that women may find empowerment through singing misogynist *chastushki*, since they may be tacitly acknowledging their sexual power over men (1999, 245). The notion of women's sexual power is certainly at work in some of the *chastushki*, as in the hyperbolic example we examined in the introduction to this book.

As city dwellers, we often marveled at the ease with which our interlocutors recited such bawdy texts. They would not do so in formal situations, for example when a local official was present, but when we visited their homes, often such texts would emerge in the context of conversation or recitation of *chastushki*. Sometimes our interlocutors would ask if such texts were permissible or a mild one would slip out and they would gauge our reaction; once we gave signs that we liked them, they often poured copious enthusiasm into their recitation. One of the elements of these texts that was surprising for city dwellers was the ease with which matters that were for us deeply private were discussed. A pimple on one's vagina, the size of a sexual organ—for us, it was shocking to hear these things stated in a public text.

One of the intentions of such songs is to shock. To be sure, village living conditions mean that the notion of "privacy" in the village is different than in city culture. Most village homes are composed of a large single room for sleeping and for daytime use, with several beds located in different areas of the room. Parents, children, and grandparents commonly share this single space. Indoor bathroom facilities are rare, and most homes use an outhouse. At night, in order not to have to go outside, the family uses a bucket for urination and defecation, which is then emptied out (often by an adult or elder woman) in the morning. Thus, a notion that Westerners take for granted—that one needs privacy for sex and for "bathroom matters"—is not an accepted assumption in the village. With exposure to city culture, this is changing gradually, but most Russians expect village conditions to be different from those in the city, and are not surprised or shocked at the lack of privacy.

Still, a notion of modesty did and does exist in village culture, as we pointed out in chapter 2. The code of honor remained important to our interlocutors, if not to their daughters and granddaughters (women born in the 1950s and later). In nineteenth- and early twentieth-century tradition, sexual relations between husband and wife were regulated by Church calendar and folk tradition: there were numerous calendar holidays, days of the week, and times in a woman's reproductive cycle when sex was forbidden, and after sexual relations it was considered proper to wash one's body (Baranov 2005e, 623–24). Many of these Church calendar prohibitions were no longer followed to the letter by our interlocutors, but the general notion of sexual relations as unclean and needing to be regulated and kept from public view was followed in practice by the women we interviewed.

Thus, while village erotic *chastushki* may be more shocking to city dwellers than to villagers, they are meant to be transgressive within their native environment. Such transgression has the effect of cultivating social cohesion. As Bakhtin has noted in his treatise on the medieval marketplace, the process of sharing a type of speech that flouts conventions and breaches social norms results in a "special collectivity." Not only do such speech acts create a group that speaks the same language (the language of the unprintable, of profanity) but also a group where preexisting social hierarchies are (temporarily) abolished (1984, 188)—or at least challenged. In its ritual nature, the singing of erotic *chastushki*, like joke-telling and drinking, creates a kind of community cohesion that adds to and goes beyond the everyday sense of community established through the exchange of goods, favors, and invitations (Paxson 2005, 72–78).[4] Herein lies the special function of erotic *chastushki*, then: to generate social leveling and bonding through carnival laughter.

Unfortunately, the authorities did not see *chastushki* as framed speech that created community cohesion, but as a kind of folk speech that was both potentially useful in the right hands (the Party's), and harmful if left to what they viewed as backward, uneducated, and unconscious individuals in the village. As one folklorist put the official view in 1935, during a policy meeting in the Central House of Amateur Art in Moscow, "Not all singers of *chastushki* know their true value. . . . Often *chastushka* listeners don't possess high enough criteria to assess a performance, often their artistic tastes aren't high enough, and then kitsch [*poshlost'*] is taken as art" (Chicherov [1935] 1994, 27).

Chastushka as Satire: The Soviet Context

The above-described set of rules and expectations for *chastushka* speech held sway in the village, but in the twentieth century, as authorities increased their observation of village life and villagers increased their knowledge of issues of national concern, *chastushka* speech began to be seen as satire (i.e., critical speech) rather than harmless or beneficial folk merrymaking. One reason for this change was the increased speed and ease of transmission of *chastushki* from the village to the urban sphere and vice versa. Although *chastushki* were linked with village culture, they spread to cities starting in the early twentieth century; Dmitrii Zelenin wrote in 1922 that urban and village elements were so intertwined in *chastushki* that it was often impossible to tell whether a given text had been created in the city or village (Zelenin 1999, 467). A. Arkhipova and Sergei Nekliudov argue that the catastrophic events of the early twentieth century (wars, revolution, internal migration, hunger) led to a "displacement of peoples" that hastened the exchange of information between people of different social statuses, who heretofore had little chance for contact. This mutual "interference" had its effects upon folklore: "Peasants, for example, whose understanding of reality, as a rule, did not exceed the boundaries of their own village, acquired the possibility—which they had not possessed previously—of relating local events to the happenings taking place on the governmental level and to the actions of the leaders; for this reason, completely traditional folkloric texts started to acquire unprecedented reference to actual political history" (Arkhipova and Nekliudov 2010).

The emergence of various folkloric genres as forums for oppositional political commentary worried the Soviet authorities. In 1927 the Central Committee of the Communist Party issued a decree "on satirical-humoristic magazines," in which it took issue with "negative" criticism of Soviet life; in practice this meant that any use of irony about aspects of Soviet realia could be banned or punished (Arkhipova and Nekliudov 2010). In the early 1930s the Joint State Political Directorate (OGPU) turned its attention to the *chastushka* as one of the main ways that protest against Soviet policies was being carried out; it published a list of villages and names of male and female high school students who had been observed singing political *chastushki* (Berelovich 2005).

The Soviet authorities understood *chastushki* differently than did villagers. For the authorities, the *chastushka* was the personal speech of the performer, not the speech of a mask, speaking for the "spirit" of general opinion. Consequently, those in power reacted like a person attending a village holiday but not knowing the community's communicative code: they took offense and became angry. Being unfamiliar with the conventions of the form, they did not try to come to an understanding but rather resorted to force. In an interview recorded in 1995 an eighty-eight-year-old woman (born in 1908) told us a story of how this happened in her village during the time of collectivization and dekulakization:

> They took everyone away. Whoever was a bit better-off before, they took them all away. One time a young man was walking down the street on a holiday, and he sang this song, which I wouldn't forget in a hundred years:

> У Николки-дурака
> Была белая мука.
> Большевистская-то власть
> До мякины добралась.

[Nikolka the fool
Had white flour.
The Bolsheviks, on the other hand,
Ended up with the chaff.]

They [the authorities] went after him for that. Because of those words. But everyone
knew that they would take him away, so they all stood up for him. They went after
him, but everyone said [the proverb] "you can't toss the words out of a song."
(Danilovo, Belozersk region, Vologda oblast, 11 July 1995 [Bel 8-41])

Those in power perceived the *chastushka* as direct speech, and therefore decided to punish the dissident. Village society stood up for the fellow against the authorities, denying
the possibility of judging the *chastushka* as personal speech. The villagers obeyed the communicative conventions that were active in their community: the folkloric form of speech
removes individual responsibility for a statement.

Women as well as men embraced the *chastushka* as a forum for expression of an ironic
stance toward the policies that affected their lives; both women and men were arrested
for texts deemed anti-Soviet or anti-kolkhoz. For example, in 1936 a twenty-year-old male
tractor-driver from Saratov was sentenced to a year and a half in prison for singing the
following *chastushka* at a village gathering:

Вставай Ленин
Вставай дедка
Нас убила
Пятилетка

[Get up, Lenin
Get up, grandad
The five-year plan
Has killed us]

(Davies 1998, 156)

In another Saratov oblast case, a female kolkhoz worker was convicted for singing a *chastushka* reported as the following:

В колхоз я записался, пишу свою жену
[А] жена меня ругает:
Провались ты с колхозом
В колхоз я не пойду

[I signed up for the kolkhoz and signed my wife up too
My wife curses me:
May you disappear along with the kolkhoz
I won't join the kolkhoz]

(Davies 1998, 157)

The punishment of counterrevolutionary *chastushki* was not just a phenomenon of the height of the purges; it continued after the war. For example, a female kolkhoz worker was tried in 1953 for sending anonymous letters containing *chastushki* about Party and government leaders and kolkhoz life to two local Moscow newspapers, and for singing these *chastushki* in her village (Edelman 1999, 29). This example shows the extent to which women meant these texts as *public* expressions of discontent, aimed at the purveyors of the repressive policies: a sort of answer in a dialogue between the authorities and the "people" (for the metaphor of the dialogue, see Arkhipova and Nekliudov 2010).

In using *chastushki* this way, people were using communicative weapons that the state itself tried to appropriate. Throughout the Soviet period, officials in charge of the ideological reeducation of the population recognized the value of *chastushki* as propaganda. For example, starting in the 1920s, Party leaders called for the use of lively, understandable, and relevant means to conduct antireligious propaganda targeted specifically at rural women, who continued to practice Orthodoxy and to believe in the supernatural. In a time of budgetary scarcity, ethnographers were given funds to study folklore, including *chastushki*, with the condition that they "introduce alterations and additions" in publications for mass consumption in order to help with antireligious propaganda (Andreev 1931, 3; Husband 2004). The ethnographers who publicly embraced this tactic included the eminent folklorist Iurii Sokolov, who spoke about the need to rid Soviet society of prison and bourgeois folklore—while he continued to add to his large collection of precisely this type of folklore.[5] Other authors of such texts included Komsomol members and members of so-called agit-brigades, composed of professional and amateur producers of theatrical and musical propaganda in regional houses of culture, factory clubs, and, more rarely, village clubs. The groups based in regional centers often traveled to villages to present their material. Here they would collect and adapt local *chastushki* for new use, and also present newly composed *chastushki* (Bialosinskaia 1966). The mode used in these poetic texts was a specific type of satire: as one critic described it, praising the satirical caricatures of Boris Efimov, who drew for *Izvestiia*, *Pravda*, and *Krokodil* (the leading satirical magazine): "the healthy humor . . . of an optimist" (Gnedin 1935, 6; Norris 2009). Such humor remained within the limits of mimesis, leaving intact the principal reference points of good and evil, the state and its structures (Ostromoukhova 2009). For example, one set of *chastushki* criticized the leadership of the kolkhoz agronomist in the sowing of millet:

Агроном Колесников
По полю гуляет
Просо поверху лежит
Он не замечает
  Припев:
Хорошо ли сеяли?
Невнимательно.
Куры просо поклюют?
Объязательно.

[Agronomist Kolesnikov
Walks around the field
The millet is lying on the top
And he doesn't notice
  Refrain:
Did they sow it well?
Not attentively.
Will the chickens eat the millet?
Absolutely.]

(Bialosinskaia 1966, 229)

Such texts ended up being used only for a short time: they were "disposable," and became folklorized only with significant changes, or not at all. The difference between this text criticizing the agronomist's direction of the millet-sowing and the genuinely folkloric texts is plain. The spontaneously created folklore makes use of hyperbole ("The five-year plan has killed us"), cursing language ("May you disappear"), and black humor ("Get up, Lenin!"). These *chastushki* are carnivalesque in their evocation of death and rebirth, their reversals of established hierarchies (calling for Lenin to take on Stalin, wife-cursing, and disobeying both husband and Soviet power) (Bakhtin 1984, 80–81). By contrast, the composed texts use mild expressions with simple negation of the desired behavior ("he doesn't notice"; "not attentively"), without disturbing existing values and hierarchies. As Arkhipova and Nekliudov point out, such implanted texts would have to correspond to the world view of the recipients in order to be accepted and transmitted further; in the Soviet Union, they largely did not. Nonetheless, as we show below, they did influence the production of folkloric *chastushki* among rural people.

Other than legal documents and stories of notable *chastushka* performances that landed a fellow villager in jail, we do not possess sources that would tell us who sang political *chastushki* during the Soviet period, and why. Our own collected sources are limited to the post-Soviet period, since before glasnost people did not volunteer political *chastushki* to

ethnographers. One collector, A. D. Volkov (born in 1923), did succeed in collecting copious political and erotic *chastushki* during the Soviet period, but he did so informally, as
a *chastushka* enthusiast, and did not write down whom he collected from, in what situations, and what they thought about their *chastushki*. Nevertheless, Volkov did describe the
difference between collecting during the Soviet period and later. He wrote that with the
advent of Gorbachev's policy of glasnost in 1986, people no longer needed to keep their
chastushki-singing secret: "It was as if it burst out of people [*liudei kak prorvalo*]." Now it
was possible to hear things that earlier people would have been afraid to whisper to each
other (Volkov 1999, 494).

Women's Political *Chastushki* in the Post-Soviet Village

Just after the boom in self-expression initiated by glasnost, folklorists and casual observers
heard many examples of political *chastushki* sung in public. My (LO's) first example took
place in the mid-1990s, in a village in Riazan' oblast. A group of women in their seventies
(born in 1919–24) performed their *chastushki* for a visiting audience consisting of an ethnomusicologist from Moscow, whom they had known for several years, and an unfamiliar
group of Americans, who had come to study their regional musical style. This group regularly
performed *chastushki*, including bawdy and political *chastushki*, at local and government-
sponsored celebrations in the regional center. Nevertheless, before singing the political
chastushki, the leader and author of the texts, Valentina Borisovna B., leaned over and in
a whisper asked the ethnomusicologist for permission to sing them. She recited two of
their most bitter verses as examples. The ethnomusicologist gave her consent, and they
commenced.

In my (LO's) second example, which took place in Vologda oblast in 2004, a woman in
her late seventies (born in 1926), an author of political *chastushki*, said she was not willing
to share her *chastushki* about the kolkhoz (*kolkhoznye chastushki*) with unfamiliar visitors
(myself and a Russian university student), because she feared she would be arrested. Nonetheless, she recited a few that she said were "nothing," and allowed my assistant to film with
my video camera individual pages of her notebook, where she wrote down her *chastushki*.

Despite the encouragement of self-expression under glasnost and the official end of censorship in 1991, in the late twentieth and early twenty-first centuries these elder women
were still afraid of being arrested or punished for their critical *chastushki*. While we assured
them that nothing would happen if their *chastushki* were performed publicly, they had reason to fear reprisals. One reason may have to do with these women's long experience
of repression and of the mechanisms of censorship (which we mean in a broad sense: the
necessity for prior approval for any publication or performance). Such experiences made
a strong impression upon the Soviet population that has continued to this day: even professional journalists still engage in old Soviet habits of self-editing and self-censorship
(Dewhirst 2002, 29–30).

Both of these examples tell us much about the framed nature of *chastushka* discourse. The performance of *chastushki* must be authorized by both performer and audience; such performances both reveal and disrupt power relations (Goffman 1974, 283–92; Preston 1997, 473). Here we can see tensions between women's local social power and their perceived powerlessness before the might of the state. As village elders, these women performed the role of *bol'shukha*. Their position situated them as moral judges of others' conduct. Yet both of the women appeared to emphasize their powerless status by, in the first case, deferring to the Moscow ethnomusicologist for approval, and in the second, playing the role of potential victim, with phrases like "I might be arrested."

The very performance of satirical *chastushki* brought with it cultural capital. The women's reputation for witty *chastushki* led to elevated social status locally, and it also raised their status vis-à-vis their visitors. The author of the *chastushki* in my second example, Tatiana Iakovlevna V., sensed this and played upon it. She told me not to record her *kolkhoznye chastushki* but changed her mind several times during the interview and indeed sang and recited some. Finally she said if I visited again, we could "make a deal" (*dogovorit'sia*). She had already proudly recounted how two notebooks of her *chastushki* were in the regional museum; how, for *chastushka* performances at the village and regional centers, she had won a vase, some fabric for a dress, a chocolate bar, and a third-place medal; and how a television crew came for her seventieth birthday to film a segment about her. Likely a visit by an American would be added to the list of the ways in which her words had been acknowledged. More than that, it was confirmation that her *chastushki*—her life's creative work—were valued. She received social honor, and her voice was heard.

Indeed, it was precisely the hearing of that voice that Tatiana Iakovlevna both feared and desired. *Chastushki* are quintessentially public speech: the genre's raison d'être lies in its ability to make individual speech theatrical. With political *chastushki* we clearly see this tension between the *chastushka*'s public nature on the one hand, and its individual basis on the other. In the Soviet context, *chastushki* commenting upon and invoking Moscow (the center) were only performable due to their symbolic distance from the center. From the individual's point of view, the use of the *chastushka* form effectively put what one sang in quotes so that individual responsibility was shared with the group. The public village forum functioned as a sheltered space in which the sense of being surrounded by "one's own" (*svoi*) held out the promise of safety.

As Margaret Paxson has argued, politically irreverent *chastushki* also performed the function of coalescing villagers' feeling of being a group (a *svoi*-group) in opposition to the center of power (2005, 305). Likely the action of aiming collective and individual barbs at an enemy carried with it certain characteristics of the ancient Greek concept of agon— a scripted, conventional struggle (Adon'eva 2004, 148, 152).[6] Some *chastushki* that Paxson analyzes convey the sense of separateness from central powers, as if the singers were saying "leave us alone" (Paxson 2005, 304–6). But the state did not leave villagers alone: danger was ever-present. While the village space could function symbolically as a safe zone, it could not do so in practice, especially with the implementation of Soviet policies, such as the clubs or houses of culture (*doma kul'tury*), designed to control and civilize villagers.

Thus, those who lived during the Soviet era were all too aware that even if a person's words were socially bracketed, he or she could still land in jail for them. For Tatiana Iakovlevna, the threat of publication or collection of her *chastushki* exposed her to danger (she was particularly worried about our recording devices). Paradoxically, in the glasnost era, the active exposé quality of journalism—a policy intended to increase debate—may have increased the feeling of a threat of exposure for rural women. In this context, oral performance of folk and popular culture—that which is not written down or fixed—may have provided a refuge from governmental control and menace. Mary Magoulick articulates the reasons for women's participation in folk and popular culture: "Women, like any underclass, have a better chance of maintaining control over their own artistic expressions in spontaneous and grassroots situations than they do in forms with high profiles and/or profit potentials" (2006, 2:470).

If that is the case—if Tatiana really fears being arrested, then why does she write down her *chastushki* rather than simply performing them as oral lore? She said she writes them down to remember them, and that her notebook serves her as a kind of diary.[7] As we noted in the previous chapter, rural dwellers all over Russia have their own collections of texts that they use and identify with. These notebooks serve active *chastushka* performers as a kind of "*chastushka* dictionary" that enables them to find the right material to connect to any situation (Adon'eva 2004, 173–74). The writings form a personal body of texts from which their owners can draw when the social need arises. They are a social repertoire, similar to the personal stories that individuals insert into conversations at appropriate situations. We gain social status and help to construct our social identity with such contributions.

For Tatiana Iakovlevna, and likely for other twentieth-century folk performers, authorship is an important constituent of identity. In her notebook of political *chastushki*, she has written on the top of several of its pages the phrase "of my own authorship" (*svoego sochineniia*).[8] For these rural women, the *chastushka* likely functioned as a political voice and an outlet for their intellectual talents. As *bol'shukhi* they had power within their own homes, and local power to judge members of the community; but as women and as agricultural workers, they were doubly marginalized in the Soviet Union. Traditional views of women's roles curtailed women's access to opportunities for advancement in the public sphere (Engel 2004, 172–73). Occupational segregation in the countryside severely reduced opportunities for women to find well-paid and interesting work, leaving many women feeling unfulfilled while the country as a whole grew more educated and skilled (Bridger 1987, 158; Denisova 2003, 179–80, 266–67). In this context, authorship (and particularly written authorship) may have offered a way to ensure one's own voice was heard.[9] Furthermore, folklore was an arena in which rural women were encouraged to create during the Soviet period—the amateur artistic activity movement centered upon it.

Indeed, Tatiana Iakovlevna's *chastushki* appear to be modeled after both the *chastushki* of official propaganda and the grassroots folklore of the village. In other words, her compositions exist on a continuum from the unidirectional, blunted satirical barbs of official texts to the carnivalesque mockery of village humor.

The blunt humor of official texts can be viewed in the type of *chastushki* that Tatiana Iakovlevna called *kolkhoznye chastushki*. One cycle within this group of *chastushki* criticized the way the kolkhoz handled the flax, leaving it in the field to rot and forcing the village's pensioners to go out into the fields with rakes to try to save it:

Лен лежит, лежит ленок
Почернел как уголек
Пришли бабушки с гравлям
Поднимали целым дням
Пенсионеры лен снимали
И трудились целым дням
Но их труд не оправдался,
Замочило все к чертям

[Flax is lying, flax is lying
It's gotten black as coal
The grannies came with rakes
To rake it for several days
The pensioners raked up the flax
They labored for several days
But their labor was all for naught
Everything got wet as hell.]

This set of *chastushki* is similar to the officially composed *chastushka* texts in that it criticizes a specific agricultural misdeed rather than a systemic problem. Like the implanted *chastushki*, it uses official language (*trudilis'* [labored]; *trud ne opravdalsia* [labor was all for naught, was not justified]) rather than the language of the street characteristic of many grassroots *chastushki*. To be sure, it does not constitute "optimistic humor," as did the politely worded *chastushka* about the millet that we used above as an example of official *chastushki* ("Did they sow it well? / Not attentively. / Will the chickens eat the millet? / Absolutely"). Tatiana Iakovlevna's description of the flax as "black as coal" and the *chastushka*'s final line, "Everything got wet as hell," lend a dark tone to the basic story of kolkhoz ineptitude.

This is moral satire: not funny, but sharp and barbed. Tatiana Iakovlevna herself called it *lovko*, clever or adroit, suggesting a kind of satire in which one defeats one's enemy with verbal eloquence. This pair of *chastushki* expresses the author's point of view as a *bol'shukha-starukha* (an elder female head of household), by showing the speaker's alignment with the pensioners who tried to clean up the agricultural misdeed, and her attitude of superiority toward the authorities who committed the mistake. Tatiana Iakovlevna's notebook is full of examples of *chastushki* offering this kind of superior attitude. The following *chastushka* about Gorbachev is a good example. It reconfirms Soviet values, viewing the history of the end of the Soviet Union as a tragedy in which Gorbachev rightly met his political demise. Here the only irony is the use of the nickname "Misha" to refer to Gorbachev, implying the superiority of the speaker over the former president:

В президенты Миша лез
Да его не выбрали
Развалил страну советов
Из Кремля-то выгнали.

[Misha climbed toward the presidency
But they didn't elect him
He ruined the Country of Soviets
And they kicked him out of the Kremlin.]

The appeal of such satire for Tatiana Iakovlevna can be explained by comments that she made during our visit. While she recited *chastushki* critical of the kolkhoz, of Gorbachev, and of many aspects of daily economic life, her neighbor, also a woman in her seventies, voiced dark, negative comments about poverty nowadays: "There's a lot of people who are doing very badly!" Tatiana Iakovlevna reacted strongly to this, shouting: "We have it good, Angelina, don't say things are bad!" Tatiana Iakovlevna's male cousin seconded this thought, linking criticism with lack of patriotism: "Don't slam . . . our Mother Russia so much."[10] For these two, to speak criticism went against a deeply held value.[11] But for Tatiana Iakovlevna, *chastushki* were apparently exempt, even though they expressed essentially the same sentiment. One possible reason is that the kinds of criticisms in Tatiana Iakovlevna's texts were often very specific—reminiscent of the permitted satirical discourse in official satirical publications, such as *Krokodil*, and of the government-authored satirical *chastushki* implanted in villages. To her, they were not transgressive, just judgmental.

Some of her other *chastushki* were more carnivalesque, however. One text was about *blat* (nepotism, bribery): a tractor-driver becomes a good choice of husband if one can get deliveries of needed goods from him. The text is joyfully ambivalent: although sung by a real-life "mother" (*bol'shukha*—Tatiana Iakovlevna herself), the text is spoken from the point of view of a daughter, who argues that tractor-drivers are good catches because of the perquisites they bring to a family. On the other hand, the text criticizes the economic situation in which hay and firewood need to be procured via illegal means:

Полюбила тракториста
Думала что мать убьет
Не ругай меня мамаша
Дров и сена привезет.

[I fell in love with a tractor-driver
I thought my mother would kill me
Don't yell at me, Mom:
He'll deliver firewood and hay.]

In another *chastushka* Tatiana Iakovlevna criticized the quantity and quality of meat in double-voiced fashion. But she inserted this *chastushka* within a story that limited its meaning, suggesting that only *some* meat is poor quality, and attributing the notion that "there is no meat" to a visiting tractor-driver:

> The tractor-driver, the one who comes to me now, came to see me, he was making silage.
> *What was he?*
> Making sileage, for feed, yeah and well, probably they had butchered a skinny chicken, a dry one, see. So he says, they say there's no meat . . . there's no meat, there's nothing, but that's it. And while he's sitting and drinking tea, and I sat with him and we drank tea together. And I made up a *chastushka*:

Корову резали опять,
Трактористам на обед
Погрызем костья ребята,
Даром мяса-то и нет.

[Again they butchered a cow
For the tractor-drivers' lunch
Let's gnaw bones, boys,
Who cares that there's no meat!]

This *chastushka* is double-voiced in its ironic mediation between incongruous positions: the speaker suggests a strong disparity between the expected lunch for the hard-working laborers and the resulting bones, which leads to the ironic conclusion that "who cares" about the lack of meat anyway. Yet Tatiana Iakovlevna's story attempts to limit this *chastushka*'s ambivalence by tying it explicitly to a single personal experience. Her comments make this *chastushka* exempt from the interdiction on cursing Mother Russia, as if she were saying, "it's not subversive speech, it's about my personal experience." But on the other hand, it is subversive speech. The *chastushka* form allows its author to be both active and passive, and emphasizes both personal initiative and group responsibility.

This dual quality of publicly performed *chastushki* makes these utterances tantamount to performatives: in bringing the private to the public, the *chastushka* performance does not simply talk about reality; it also affects reality (Adon'eva 2004, 171, 179). The performance of *chastushki* about personal life affects the local social reality: singing "I got even" with a rival helps one to get even. One might guess that political *chastushki* constitute a different case, that this is one arena where the individual can never affect reality. Of course, a person cannot make meat appear on tables by singing a *chastushka*. But a person can still affect the social reality with her song. She can perform interpretation, as if underlining or putting quotation marks around her words: "I am staking my claim to this utterance. Challenge me if you disagree!" If political *chastushki* are performatives on the social level, that means their intent is not about changing the substandard economic and political reality. Rather, their intent is to raise the social status of the singer by suggesting that she is in a position of power in relation to reality.

The carnival opposition of political *chastushki* comes across most strongly in the musical performances of the Riazan' collective (the first example is from the 1990s).

Эх ты, сыграй-ка, гармонист,
Ты сармача у горюшка.
Не от радости поём,
А поём от горюшка.

Всего много, всего много
Продают в палатках,
А у наших стариков
Все штаны в заплатках.

Очень ловко сообразили
Начальники высшие.
Стала кучка богачей,
А остальные-нищие.

Все старушки деньги клали
[——] на книжку клали
Все правители всё знали,
Сразу всех и обокрали.

Довели нас демократы,
На подворье нет овцы,
Покупателей не стало,
Везде только продавцы.

На деревне каждый двор
Разводил раньше коров,
А теперь правители
Развели одних воров.

Раньше пряли, сами ткали,
Шили штаны модные,
А теперь купили джинсы
Год ходим голодные.

Раньше если обижали,
Мы в райком скорей бежали.
Теперь грабят без стыда,
Жаловаться некуда.

А мы частушки сочиняли
И ногами топали,
А теперь мы вас попросим,
Чтобы вы похлопали.

[Accordionist, play "Sarmacha"
For [our] misery
We're not singing from joy,
We're singing from misery.

So much stuff, so much stuff
Is for sale in the markets
But our old folks' pants
Are in tatters.

Our leaders thought things out
Really cleverly
There's a crowd of rich folks
And the rest are poor.

All the old women put their money
[*garbled speech*] in the bank
All the leaders knew all about it
They immediately robbed everyone.

The democrats cheated us
There are no sheep in the pens
There are no buyers in the markets
There are only sellers everywhere.

In the village every household
Used to raise a cow
But now the leaders
Are raising only robbers.

We used to spin and weave
And sew our own fashionable pants
But now if we buy jeans
We go hungry for a year.

It used to be if we got offended
We'd run to the Regional Commission
But now people steal shamelessly
And there's no place to complain.

We made up our *chastushki*
And stamped our feet
And now we'd like you
To clap for us.]

Taken as a set, the political *chastushki* of Valentina Borisovna and her group take on the point of view of a local, grassroots group with intact common sense and deficient financial means. This group distinguishes itself from "Others"—"bosses," "rulers," and "democrats"—who steal from and manipulate the poor folks. The criticisms are lighthearted due to the *chastushka* form and the manner of performance. For example, the major chord structure, the high whoops imitating the sound of laughter ("i-e-ha-ha!"), the clapping, and the accordion and balalaika accompaniment, which underlines each sung text with a cadence—all contribute to the lighthearted interpretation of the texts. It is as if their performance is saying, "we are harmless, we are fun." The musical presentation emphasizes the clowning nature of the *chastushka*: it is social play.

The texts of these *chastushki* also emphasize incongruity. They use the trope, typical for perestroika and the early post-Soviet era, that everything is the opposite of what it was. Contrasts are made between earlier versus now, good versus bad, Russian versus foreign, Communism versus democracy. Usually this dichotomy is emphasized with a dissimilarity between the meanings of the rhyming words, for example, high/low (*vysshie/nishchie*), putting in/taking away (*klali/obokrali*).[12] The second term of the pair contrasts with the first, while the rhyme, which resolves difference into sameness and usually provides a feeling of reassurance or satisfaction, here underscores the irony of the disparity, and endows each piece with humor (Faber 1988).

This is criticism that appeals to common sense, a sense of moral decency, and a valuing of tradition; it is performative in that it assumes, implies, and acquires the listener's agreement. "Why wouldn't you agree," it seems to say: "we are backed by the wisdom of the collective and of tradition; and anyway, it's all in fun (but serious—wink!)." Like the verbal form ("we") of these *chastushki*, the sung form emphasizes the group aspect of the identity of the speakers: the first line of each couplet is introduced by the solo singer, Valentina Borisovna herself, and after an instrumental interlude, the chorus repeats the line. Without a pause, Valentina Borisovna introduces the first line of the next couplet (solo). This has the effect of a Greek chorus backing up what the speaker has just said. Musically, the pause in between the repetitions of each line has at least three important effects: first, the listener has to wait longer for the rhyme to be resolved in the second line of the couplet (one waits through two repetitions of the first line, plus instrumental interlude), which emphasizes the incongruity; second, it gives the musical feeling that the chorus is introducing, not echoing, the repeated line (since the chorus's line is the introductory melodic phrase of the couplet); and third, it makes it seem as though each *chastushka* grows logically out of the previous one (thus implying that they are a set rather than individual texts). Perhaps the musical solidarity of this collective provides the key to why this group was less afraid than Tatiana Iakovlevna of performing their criticisms in public. Their social play makes their status slippery: they cannot be pinned down, and if "caught" they could simply point to their innocence as poor old folks, who simply wish for a return to the economic and legal protections offered by the Soviet government.

Of course, this raises a question: what kinds of political *chastushki* did these same women sing during the pre-Gorbachev Soviet era? Was there a corresponding place in their lives for such critique, even though their current *chastushki* relate to the Soviet era with nostalgia? Since we collected no political *chastushki* from them that could be unquestionably dated to the pre-perestroika era, we cannot answer this definitively; we can only speculate. The evidence cited earlier, from legal cases (Davies 1998; Edel'man 1999), Volkov (1999), and Paxson (2005), suggests that many women did compose political *chastushki*: the challenge of battling with the mighty giant of the Soviet government was tremendously attractive. This was true despite the equal power of the trope of what Paxson calls the "radiant past"—the time, always in the past, when people lived simply, everyone was equal, and everyone got along. This nostalgia for the past provides inspiration for the future: it is a way of connecting with the group, of feeling the sense of belonging to a *svoi*-community. It also provides a way of judging the present. Thus, to sing one's criticism of how things are now does not negate the nostalgia and the corresponding dream.

Conclusion

That that dream is both tangible and much desired comes across strongly in these political *chastushki*. It is clear that we are looking at the discourse of powerful older women, who are not bound to humility and obedience. They are citizens of a new Russia where they need not (for the time being) fear reprisals for singing political *chastushki*, yet their discourse is informed by texts and moral categories that held sway during the Soviet period. But even if the ideas and ideologies behind those categories are fixed, the playful ambivalence of their humor makes the status of the singers a liminal one: in calling up laughter, these women stand upon ambivalent territory and become mediators. This role is a remarkable one for women: as Cathy Preston writes of women's joke-telling, "when we tell [a] joke, we laugh at cultural attempts to control and thereby erase us" (Preston 1994, 37).

Chastushki comprised a way for women to temporarily challenge established hierarchies, norms, and prohibitions. While this was a framed genre, we have shown that it had effects outside the frame: people were able to raise, establish, or reestablish themselves in the social hierarchy and thus to exercise considerable agency in determining their relationship to the community. Young women used *chastushki* in this manner to gain social status; elder women, who already possessed the highest social status available to them, used this speech genre to gain social glory through their unabashed, wry judgments of those in positions of power.

6

Magical Forces and the
Symbolic Resources of Motherhood

In this section of the book we move from investigation of the discourses of musical texts to the discourses of the spiritual. Women had limited knowledge of and access to the world of spirits until they became mothers. The birth of an infant signaled the first time that a woman would need the magic rituals surrounding care of a new mother, and the birth and care of the infant. The mother's acquisition of this knowledge prepared her to become a *bol'shukha* and to possess corresponding social and moral authority due to her status as an intermediary between the everyday world and the spiritual world.

Motherhood was a key rite of passage for Russian rural women. As we noted in chapter 2, whereas a man's status changed when he married (he became a *muzhik*), a woman's changed both when she married (she became a *molodka*) and again when she gave birth to her first child (she became a *baba*). No parallel nomenclature existed for men who became fathers. The birth of a woman's first child drew her into the role of motherhood and simultaneously into a different relationship with the other world, the world of spirits. With motherhood, a woman was first initiated into the practice of healing magic.

To women of the first two twentieth-century generations, motherhood was understood as a means of acquiring magical skills. Magical skills were necessary for two reasons: first, because giving birth was such an extremely emotional experience that women turned to otherworldly powers to explain what was happening to them. Second, infants were often in need of some kind of assistance (they were ill) or were understood to be in need of assistance—they cried, didn't eat, and so on. In such situations a mother experienced helplessness; Russian traditional culture understood these problems of infant care as situations caused by otherworldly powers and as therefore needing otherworldly means of resolution.

The knowledge—the language and tools—to explain the interactions of the other world and this world with regard to birth or illness was transmitted among women in a vertical direction, from elder to younger. The principle motivating this transmission was the younger woman's fear in relation to the other world. In this situation, as we argue below, the elder woman functioned as a kind of patron who possessed the needed wisdom—the scripts—to both interpret what was happening and to correct anything that was amiss. Different motivations caused the young woman to obey her mother-in-law before and after her first pregnancy. Prior to pregnancy, she listened to her mother-in-law due to the demands of society and tradition. After the first pregnancy, she was motivated by need and sought out the elder woman's wisdom. The former is obedience, while the latter is born out of a fear that is caused by the situation and cultivated by the mother-in-law's own discourse.

That discourse revolves around the mechanisms of the evil eye (*sglaz*) but also the workings of the spiritual world and ways to control it. The evil eye is understood as a harmful supernatural action that a person can wreak on another person. Often the one who inflicts harm does not know he or she is doing so. It happens when a person is jealous of someone else's good fortune. The evil eye is distinct in this sense from *porcha* (spoiling), which is intentionally inflicting a hex or curse. The two terms are not kept reliably distinct in people's everyday discourse: both involve creating harm through thoughts, and both may be caused by jealousy. For this reason, folklorists often ask if the curse is understood to be intentional or not. We treat primarily the evil eye in this chapter, and *porcha*, together with discourse about witches, in the next chapter. The principle behind the evil eye is that of social leveling: through its mechanism, people are encouraged not to show off their social unevenness. Having too much of anything—property, beauty, health, luck— becomes a social liability, so people are encouraged to give generously to their neighbors, lest they invoke the evil eye (Paxson 2005). But if the evil eye occurs, then they turn to elder women in order to remove the curse. Most *bol'shukhi* have positioned themselves as socially strong actors who can carry out the necessary rituals. The symbolic capital of the older woman is the capacity to bring harm through magic (perhaps inadvertently), to control the discourse of magic, and to protect her own family from harm through magic.

Motherhood as Rite of Passage

Childbirth is a practice defined by the biological nature of humankind. This practice is fundamental, tied to the existence of our species. The social institutions that organize it are among the basic mechanisms for the reproduction of culture.

Van Gennep writes: "The life of an individual in any society is a series of passages from one age to another and from one occupation to another. Wherever there are fine distinctions among age or occupational group, progression from one group to the next is accompanied by special acts" (1960, 2–3). One of these progressions is the birth of children, and the means of marking this change is an initiation ritual. This ritual enables people to interpret this event and to master new interpretive, mental, and behavioral strategies. These strategies are necessary so that the participants in this event—mothers, fathers, grand-mothers, grandfathers, and so on—can master their new roles.[1]

Birth, particularly a woman's first birth, symbolizes not only the birth of a child but the birth of a mother as well (Baranov 2005d, 535). Motherhood is a liminal state in which a mother may experience an altered consciousness of herself. That which was once her body separates itself from her. This experience engenders fear. The conscious mind has difficulty coping with the new physical and psychological experience. The baby is still a part of the mother on the level of her psyche, but a part over which she has lost control. After this intense experience, a new mother must learn a manner of behavior that is differ-ent from the roles that she had already actively mastered for successful existence in society. This new behavior will acknowledge the other reality that she discovered as a result of living through this experience.

In the tradition of the Russian village, people understood the new mother's postpar-tum state—whether felt as a liminal state, a postpartum depression, or simply a state of "being other" than she was—as her defenselessness in relation to the world of spirits. The tradition provided for her protection and gave her symbolic ways of understanding her liminality and her changed state. For example, in the late nineteenth and early twentieth centuries, when the institution of the midwife (*babka* or *povitukha*) was still strongly in force, women gave birth in the *bania* (bathhouse) or barn and spent three days there; the new mother and child were kept from public view for forty days after the birth; the mother did not attend church until she "took a prayer" in church at forty days; the mother was given special food; the midwife "fixed" the new mother's body (as well as the baby's body) through manipulation, and so on. Russian ethnographic studies commonly ascribe such practices to the belief that the new mother was "unclean," which we understand to mean not that she was debased because linked with the biblical figure of Eve the Temptress (Atkinson 1977, 14) but that she was in a liminal state and therefore in greater proximity to the other world (Baranov 2005c, 2005d).

Those practices and beliefs began to wane after collectivization, but some of them con-tinued (retention of particular traditions varied by location and even by family). Accord-ing to David Ransel, after World War II traditional practices began to give way to medical assistance. In the 1940s many villages had nurse-midwives or medics (*medichki*) who would travel to help with births; starting in the 1950s, village women commonly gave birth in hospitals in regional cities or on collective farms, although many elected to give birth at home, using the services of a village midwife or medic. It was not until the 1960s that hospitals became commonly accepted as the place for rural women to give birth (Ransel 2000, 125–37).

As a number of scholars have shown, the Soviet handling of childbirth was repressive.[2] Health policies emphasized the message that women were producers of new workers for the state; the state controlled women's bodies, access to doctors, and access to their babies

(Rouhier-Willoughby 2008; Rivkin-Fish 2005). Relatives were not allowed to visit women in hospitals and maternity homes (*roddomy*) (Rouhier-Willoughby 2008, 82–83). Women experienced the maternity homes as alienating, impersonal institutions where they were controlled and humiliated. For this reason, although many accepted the need for medical care, women living both in cities and in villages continued to seek wisdom about care for themselves and their infants from elder female relatives (Rouhier-Willoughby 2008, 112–13). In the village, women also had access to local elder women known for their expertise (*babki*). Soviet policies and campaigns aimed at eradicating the village midwife began in the 1920s and '30s and continued until Stalin's death in 1953; after Stalin, midwives were not persecuted for a time (Ransel 2000). In our experience, in the post-Soviet period each village had one or more elder women who knew how to "wash" infants (an important post-birth ritual), remove hexes from them, or heal colic and other common illnesses. They were not midwives, since home births were rare in the 1990s and later, but they provided assistance to new mothers.

Very common among interlocutors of all generations was the view that during the pregnancy and birth, a woman was in a liminal state and was particularly susceptible to harm via the evil eye (which we discuss in more detail below). If anyone saw her right before the birth, the birth could be very painful for her (Woman born in 1915, Anufrievo, Belozersk region, Vologda oblast, 12 July 1994 [Bel 10-2]). A woman born in 1912 told us that after the birth, "the new mother was never allowed into the *bania* alone [the spirit of the bath might bring harm]. After all, the child was not yet christened." She also said that "a new mother is considered unclean, they still do not allow her near the well even six weeks after the birth" (Mar'ina Gora, Pinega region, Arkhangel'sk oblast, 10 July 1985 [Pin 10-41]). In general, a mother and her child were susceptible to harm during the time before, during, and after the birth, so her isolation from public and her protection by those initiated into the secret of birth (the midwife, her mother, or mother-in-law) were meant to ward off any potential harm.

No matter what practices were actually retained, we argue that the traditional conception of the new mother—as vulnerable in relation to the other world, as needing companionship and care—continued to serve an important purpose for *her*. Traditional magical practices supply the needed language to the mother who lacks the ability to describe her experience; they address her fears of losing control, of her feelings of being other or incomplete. At the very least they give order to the chaos of her feelings. Older women or matriarchs provide the younger women with plots and scripts to communicate and interpret what is happening. As we will show throughout this chapter, this situation provided elder women with a great deal of power.

Tradition not only provided for the treatment and care of the mother herself; it also taught her how to become a mother (and eventually to possess greater power herself), to find her own voice and role in the care of the infant. The young mother was initiated gradually into the magical wisdom meant to defend the child: she became a participant in the magical activities whose purpose was the health of the child. The child's care was equally the job of the mother and the *bol'shukha* (mother-in-law), but the older woman took upon herself the ultimate responsibility for the well-being and health of the family's children.

The Evil Eye: Domination, Control, and Trust in the Female Hierarchy

In the tradition of the first and second generations of our interlocutors, it was through the interaction of the young mother and her older mother-in-law that the skills of taking care of the infant were passed on. Through the teachings of the mother-in-law, the younger woman learned more than she ever had before about the actions of the evil eye, the ways of avoiding its consequences, and of healing them if they did occur. The mother-in-law's contribution was to impart the scripts for this new knowledge through the form of orders, prohibitions, and advice. She taught her daughter-in-law that a child's illnesses were the result of disturbances in the social order: a "wrong" person stood next to you, and that's why your child is upset. She taught her that the supernatural world is responsive to our behavior: do not wear a white scarf after giving birth, instead wear a dark one—or else someone will give you the evil eye; you can't scold your children—the *leshii* (forest spirit) will get them (i.e., you'll lose them); don't fetch water at night—"the water is asleep"; you can't dry swaddling-clothes outside—the child will sleep badly, and so on.

The dynamics of the relationship between mother-in-law and daughter-in-law changed precisely at the stage of motherhood. Whereas before pregnancy, a young wife listened to her mother-in-law because she was obliged to, during her pregnancy and motherhood she began to find her own reasons to listen to her mother-in-law and older women in general. She had need of their experience in interpreting what was happening to her and her child. This is a tactic of the dominated: we follow rules to the letter if we do not know how they work, if we are uncertain about the principles or understandings on which they are founded. The situation changes when we graduate to the level of those in charge, those who possess and construct the understandings that lie at the foundation of social rules.

In this context, the mother-in-law provided a kind of magical patronage for the younger woman. She mediated between the supernatural world and the natural world, between the potentially dangerous social world (which could carry the dangers of the supernatural) and the protected world of the self and the family. The daughter-in-law's need for the mother-in-law's knowledge reinforced the existing vertical hierarchy between generations. In fact, the magical practices connected with motherhood comprised one of the strongest instruments in the creation of the female intergenerational hierarchy in the Russian village: a hierarchy of submission on the one hand, and of the inheritance of traditions on the other.

The traditions that we explain in this section of the chapter primarily have to do with the interactions of the social, supernatural, and natural worlds in the phenomenon known as the evil eye. When our interlocutors speak about a case of the evil eye (*sglaz*) or a spoiling (*porcha*), they are interpreting a situation in the "here and now" as the result of past contact with a person who, they presume, has had negative thoughts, such as "You have something more or something better than others do": "your cows have more milk," "your garden has a richer harvest," "guests come more often" (denoting more connections), "your husband is more affectionate," or "your child is more beautiful." These scripts all revolve around the idea that such thoughts, together with physical proximity, can produce illness. Visitors to the house or people met in the street are all suspect. The following story, told by a woman born in 1940, describes the way the evil eye is transmitted through thoughts, and also shows how she learned about the evil eye and its treatment from an elder woman (even though, as is very common, the narrator initially denies knowing anything):

> They give you the evil eye, so what are you gonna do? Know what you're gonna do. If you don't know anything, then what are you gonna do?[3]
>
> *So probably people knew what to do?*
>
> Me, I don't know anything. It happened to me, my first baby was given the evil eye. An old woman came too, she—they used to rock kids in bassinets, right, there were these cradles and bassinets, woven. The woman came, came up to the bassinet—she [my little daughter] cried and cried, we couldn't do anything. We thought the little girl would cry herself to death. Well, so I had a grandmother there. My auntie. So she passed a bit of water through the door handle [*skobka*; i.e., she passed water between the door and the lever handle], and washed the child with the water. That thing that you open the door with, you see. And she calmed down. The same thing happened with my daughter. My daughter came for her holidays. And there was just the same picture. She brought a friend, they were in school together. She also took my daughter's child in her arms, we thought the girl would cry herself to death. Five of us couldn't do anything. That was how she was jinxed with the evil eye.
>
> [*In response to the question of how they found out who had jinxed her*] . . . find out? If that person was in the house, how would you not find out?
>
> *And if they hadn't come?*
>
> And if they hadn't come over, then it wouldn't have happened. While no one came into the house, it didn't happen. So—how wouldn't you find out? (Ukhtoma, Vashkinskii region, Vologda oblast, 12 July 2000 [Vash 20a-4])

The narrator here first tells the story of her own baby, whose agitation was identified as the result of the evil eye by an older woman (her aunt, who lived with her), and then a similar event that happened to her own daughter when her daughter was a young mother. Events of the physical world (a child's agitation) are explained as events of a mental order: someone had "bad" thoughts. A direct causal connection is established between mental and physical action. The older woman explained what had happened in this way; the younger woman accepted this explanation, and thus accepted and adopted its logic as a tool.

The magical cure she mentions involves sympathetic magic: the child was washed with water that had been passed three times through a door handle. The water has thus been passed through liminal space: the place between a handle and the door, and space between the dwelling part of the house and the entrance hall (vestibule). Such metaphorical connections between the inner world of a person and the world outside a person are called "sympathetic magic," in which "like produces like" or "an effect resembles its cause" (Frazer [1922] 2009, 11–12). Here the handle acquires special significance as part of a threshold. The threshold is the boundary between "one's own" and "the other's" (*svoego i chuzhogo*). It is associated with a host of rules. Young unmarried women cannot step on the threshold, only over it—or they will not marry. But neighboring matriarchs, if they are stopping by without an invitation, will stay on the threshold, and will not enter the other family's space unless invited. In Slavic folklore, the thresholds of the home are commonly viewed as symbolically equivalent to the threshold between this world and the other world and therefore as potentially both potent and dangerous places (Kononenko 2007, 64).

Additionally, in this example as in many from this area of Vologda oblast, the shape of the door handle is significant. In Vologda dialect, the action of the evil eye is called the "glance" (*prikos*). When someone "glances" (*oprikosit*) a child (i.e., throws a "sidelong glance" [*kosoi vzglyad*]), it is necessary to douse all the corners and door handles; that is, it is necessary to cleanse everything "glancing" (*kosoe*), crooked. In the example above, passing the water through the "crooked" or angled door handle (not a knob but a lever) was deemed to heal problems of "crooked" glances.

In another interview, a mother, Valentina Gavrilovna G., born in 1927, and her daughter, Aleksandra Matveevna S., born in 1949, remember how this was done:

AMS: And also, Mama, you washed through a door handle [*skobka*], and you said some words too, right?

VGG: Right, through the door handle was for a curse [*ozyk*]. It was all curses before, people cursed everything, they say. So you washed through a door handle.

AMS: And an *ozyk*—that's what, like when they gave you the evil eye [*sglazili*]?

VGG: Yes, like an evil eye. You washed through a door handle. I don't know how, though.

    And what's that—an evil eye?

VGG: Well, it still exists, the evil eye.

AMS: Well, there's some person . . .

VGG: A bad person.

AMS: He sometimes doesn't know himself that he has such a gaze. He might look at a child, so all the more if the little child is a sweet one, and maybe will say something too: "Oh, how sweet, how pretty!" And the child will become upset. That means the person has that gaze.

And through which door handle?

VGG: So, the door handle.

AMS: Through the handle of the front door.

VGG: You might take the water in your mouth. I had a mother-in-law, so she herself would take some water in her mouth, then go up to the door handle, the water would kind of slide off the door handle, and with that water you'd wash the little child, put it in the bassinet. (Alekanovo, Kaduii region, Vologda oblast, 22 July 2001 [Kad 20-58])

The child's agitation is explained unambiguously as the result of the other person's malevolent action: that person has looked wrong, thought wrong, or insincerely praised (Veselova and Marinicheva 2010). It is important to note that it is always the older women—auntie, mother, mother-in-law—who offer this interpretation, and to whom the younger women, the young mothers, turn for counsel. The older women assume responsibility for the situation, interpret it, and either address it (magically) themselves, or personally summon a wisewoman-specialist. In the dialogue cited above, a connection between three generations of women is present. The mother-in-law of Valentina Gavrilovna belonged to the first generation; she cured the evil eye jinx herself. The mother (Valentina Gavrilovna, second generation) remembers herself as a young wife who did not know how to perform the cure, but she knew about the *ozyk*. That is, she supports the method of interpretation of events that she assimilated from her mother-in-law during the stage of her own motherhood. Her daughter (Aleksandra Matveevna, the third generation) is less sure about this effect: she quizzes her and approaches her as an authority about the *ozyk* and its cure. This is significant: up until the 1970s, the motherhood practices of rural women were built primarily on the foundation of the relationship between the young woman and the *bol'shukha* mother-in-law. But for our interlocutors born after World War II, as we pointed out in chapter 2, the intergenerational conflict meant that women would prefer to appeal to their own mothers for advice with regard to managing a relationship with the other world in order to protect children's health. The content of teachings was basically the same, but the path of transmission had changed.

The word used in the previous example, *ozyk*, and another word for curse, *ogovor*, are dialect words from Vologda oblast that connote the result of the workings of certain speech acts. Their performative sense is revealed by the use of verbs that denote harmful actions—*oboikat'* (lit.: to keep saying 'oi' [in the praising sense]) or *ogovorit'* (from the verb "to speak" [about]), as in the story from this woman, born in 1925:

My first little girl had a curse [*ozyk*], they cursed [*ogovorili*] her. *Ozyk*, like if you curse [*oboikaesh'*] the child, and he gets agitated, cries. So I went to a certain woman. She said some prayers [*sdelala*] on water, and then what—she poured it out over the child's head. And know how they had cursed [*ogovorili*] her? My mother-in-law in the village had a certain friend. Her daughter got married too and had a baby, a boy. My little girl was only a month older. She comes by, I happened to be turning my little girl over then, and she says: "Oh, what a lovely girl, me and Valen'ka have just a thin little man." And then my little girl started to cry, and she cried and she cried and she cried. Well, I noticed that something wasn't right, and so I went there . . . [to the *znakharka* (healer)].

So that neighbor who cursed [ogovorila] *her—did she do it on purpose or by accident?*

No, she did it by accident, just like that, yes. So she was envious, that isn't good. One should never envy someone—it's a sin, a great sin. (Borok, Belozersk region, Vologda oblast, 11 July 2002 [Bel 20a-159])

The young thirty-seven-year-old woman from whom we recorded the following interview in 2002, who already belongs to the fourth generation, retains the same views. Note that she learned them not from her mother-in-law but from her maternal family:

Saying "oi" [*oikat'*]: "oi, oi, oi" [as in praising]. That's considered a bad word. I've heard it from more than one old lady [*babul'ka*] that if you *oi*—"oi, oi, oi, oi!"—it carries some kind of evil—what exactly, they didn't say, they didn't explain . . . For example, I've heard this from a few people. From Aleksandra Alekseevna, my grandmother—although she really loved to *oi*, she always said all the same that it's a bad word. (Woman born in 1965, Belozersk region, Vologda oblast, 30 May 2002 [Be1 20-170])

We offer a linguistic explanation of this phenomenon: women consider the precondition of an unintentional hex to be the convergence of a mental act and a speech act. An uttered compliment becomes a harmful act only in cases when the speaker's joy in the other's child's health and beauty, expressed in the compliment, is not sincere ("You don't know who has what thoughts" was a commonplace in our interviews about the evil eye). In the understanding of our interlocutors, a compliment is not sincere whenever jealousy lies behind it.

In the interpretations of older women, the capacity to inflict harm magically is considered a personal quality that is not necessarily connected with someone's bad intentions. The person himself might acknowledge such a reputation, but in that case, it is considered a natural attribute:

It happened sometimes that I had an evil tongue. Let's say I'm walking, I saw someone at the Feast of the Protection [*Pokrovskoe*]; Let's say I say, "Do such and such"—"All right, fine." If they don't do it, it'll be the worse for them. Something bad's sure to happen. So that they call an "evil tongue." They say it's better not to say anything. (Woman born in 1926, Borok, Belozersk region, Vologda oblast, 8 July 2002 [Bel 24-67])

"Your lot is better than mine" is the kind of mental act ("powerful thought" [*krepkaia duma*]) that can result in giving someone the evil eye. As one woman, born in 1915, told us, one can ward it off with the following words: "Save such and such servant of God [name the potential victim] from evil glances [*prizory*], spells [*otgovory*], powerful thoughts" (Zakolopuno, Vinogradov region, Arkhangel'sk oblast [Adon'eva and Ovchinnikova 1993, no. 220]).

The most common means of warding off the evil eye—preventing its action from taking hold—is a symbolic strengthening of boundaries: attaching a safety pin to clothing; placing "a bad knife or old scissors" into the cradle, as a woman born in 1927 told us in 1986 (Pirenem', Pinega region, Arkhangel'sk oblast [Adon'eva and Ovchinnikova 1993, no. 226]); hanging scissors by the windows and some sharp metal object or horseshoe over the entrance to the house.

Always wear a safety pin in this, in your blouse, a pin should be there. So that nothing sticks to you. And nothing will happen. Or look, when you're walking, if you see someone suspicious, then like this, do this [*makes a "fig" gesture, a fist with thumb inserted between pointer and middle finger*], or in your pocket, or they carry salt in their pockets sometimes. I mean, there are all kinds of people. (Woman born in 1923, Fetinino, Belozersk region, Vologda oblast, 14 July 1994 [Bel 20-106])

With such actions, the mistress of the house marks and safeguards the symbolic borders of her social body, whose dimensions are considerably wider than those of her physical body: within its borders are encompassed the bodies of her grandchildren, daughters-in-law, and sons; the space of the home, and so on.

Another method for warding off the evil eye is to hide everything a woman possesses that is good, that might set her apart from others, for fear of exciting envy. But it is difficult to hide anything in the village: for example, the store and the post office serve as the informational hubs through which personal information is transmitted; there, one can find out everything about everyone—who receives what correspondence when and from whom, who writes to whom and who reads what, the size of pensions and benefits, the quality and quantity of the groceries and goods that each person obtains. The store, where the *bol'shukhi* (without any evident necessity) stood in line for hours on baking days, served as a club, and also as an observation point for the bus stop—yet another informational channel, by which one could learn who came to see whom and with what. Such information allows the *bol'shukhi* to conduct social monitoring through gossip. To avoid being the subject of such talk and susceptible to a hex, people strive not to distinguish themselves in any visible way. As Margaret Paxson writes, "inequality of means can become a social liability" and can set "the dark forces in motion" (2005, 72). A man born in 1926 cites an example of the interpretation of this rule in a general sense:

You know, there's a proverb: Grandma put the evil eye on Liza [*Babushka Lizu sglazila*]. It's even in Pushkin. There was once a granddaughter and grandmother. So, this granddaughter was of unheard-of beauty. And the old woman was always boasting: I have a granddaughter more beautiful than yours. And to another: much more beautiful than yours. Always just like that. So she up and lost an eye. That's it, and the old woman landed in the pond. That's how the proverb went. (Nefedovo, Vashkinskii region, Vologda oblast, 18 July 2002 [Vash 11-17])

Do not boast (do not commit the speech-act of boasting), do not consider anything of yours to be better (do not commit a mental act to the same effect)—this may inspire envy. Since all participants in these relationships consistently employ protections from magical harm, a leveling effect comes about, forcing everyone into a single habitus. The prohibition against the possibility of distinguishing oneself from others, standing out from the common ranks, acts both from without, through a fear that someone will envy and thus put a hex on you; and from within, through a fear of thinking of one's own things as the best, since even a mother's own thoughts about possessing something better can lead to negative consequences:

How can you curse someone [oburochit']?
You have your beautiful child, I came and talked with you, and you had a thought. (Adon'eva and Ovchinnikova 1993, no. 328)

In the incantation: "Get out of my thought, get out of my blood, keep out of my thought! . . ."[4] (Adon'eva and Ovchinnikova 1993, no. 329)

When you bring a child to the *bania*—he could become sick even from your own thought—you repeat in the bath:

С гоголя вода,
с гоголюшки вода,
с раба Божья младёнышка
вся худоба.

[Like water from the [back of the] goldeneye duck
Like water from the little goldeneye's [back]
So from this little one, this slave of God,
[Let] all that is harmful [fall].]

(Woman born in 1928, Shardonem', Pinega region, Arkhangel'sk oblast, 6 July 1984
[Pin 20-26])

Thus, a culture of fear existed, and exists to this day in Russian rural culture (as in other cultures worldwide), in which each action and thought is examined carefully by mothers and matriarchs—the women in charge of making sure that infants and children survived. But when illness did occur, what did women do? Our next section details how knowledge of healing magic was transmitted from elder to younger women.

The Making of a Mother: Learning Magical Practices for Protection and Healing of Children

Much of the healing magic used in villages involves incantations (charms, spells) and their accompanying ritual actions. Incantations are performative speech acts in which language influences reality (Austin 1962): recited texts are designed to affect a situation via magic. Using poetic language and the laws of sympathetic magic, usually a charm describes the current situation, names the patient, and evokes a desired future resolution of the problem (Veldhuis 1991, 58). The performative aspect of healing magic requires and establishes a certain competence, even mastery in the person who uses it.

For example, this story from a woman born in 1916 in Kalitino, Vashkinskii region, Vologda oblast, emphasizes the potency of a charm for fixing dislocations (not just for children but for anyone) that her mother-in-law "gave" her. She conveys not only the power of the words but also her own healing power as, now, a *starukha*:

For dislocations, yes, they come to me. So many people came, and I saved them. The leg or the arm—dislocated. I'd fix it, stroke it, fix it and it'd go away. Well, my mother-in-law knew how to cure it, and I always watched how she did it . . . And then she had to give me these words. So here are the words, for aching, so that it wouldn't ache . . . Here . . .

Колотье,
щемота,
иди в темные леса,
в темное болото,
в темный лес,
на зеленый мох,

на белую березу,

на гнилую колоду,

там боли и шшеми,

а у такой-то не боли.

[Stitch,

ache,

go into the dark forests,

into the dark swamp,

into the dark forest,

to the green moss,

to the white birch,

to the dank trough,

there you can ache and hurt,

but in this one [name of patient]—don't hurt.]

That was it. No more, they don't say anything more—just that. Then I cross it
and the redness and ache go away and then the leg gets better. (8 July 1998
[Vash 20a-85])

Incantations affect reality in that they metaphorically name qualities and confer those
qualities upon a real-life object (Adon'eva 2004, 128). In this case, the words personify
the pain of a dislocation and order that pain to move out, becoming like a wild creature
that belongs in parts of nature not inhabited by people (the terrain of the *leshii* and other
spirits). The metaphorical quality of moving out is conferred upon the real-life object, the
pain. It is the *act* of uttering the charm (which is always accompanied by the healer's magical actions—in this case, "fixing" the dislocation, stroking the arm or leg, and crossing
it) that creates this connection between the real world and the supernatural world, and
thus performs the magical power. We can see this performative power of an elder woman
most clearly in incantations with lines such as "I bite the [umbilical] hernia and I see"
(*Kusaiu ia gryzhu i vizhu*): here, the female speaker literally claims and performs her magical "vision" by metaphorically "biting" the bulging hernia.[5] In trying to relieve the hernia
through her words, the speaker visualizes the destruction of that object via her own magical power. Although the words are important to the healer and are carefully guarded, the
meaning of the words is only of fleeting importance in the healing ritual. What guarantees
the effect is the act itself, the appropriate context, and the authority of the person by whom
it is uttered (Szafran 2009).

In observing and participating in healing rituals, a daughter-in-law learned a dynamic
way of relating to the spiritual world through deeds and words. New addressees were
constructed for her: illness, the dawn, spirits of the home and forest, and so on. These

addressees are the spirits and "masters" (*khoziaeva*) of the surrounding terrain that are an essential part of Russian folk belief (Ivanits 1989; Warner 2002a, 81–82). The younger woman is not just learning the handy skill of healing magic but she is also learning laws for categorizing the world. Certainly she learned some of these laws as a child and young woman—for instance, she undoubtedly knew that the *leshii* controlled the forest and that he could make a person get lost there—but now she had to cultivate a relationship with these spirits. With time, a woman became educated in this manner of establishing existential connections between the other world and this world, between external manifestations (illness) and inner psychological space (the jealousy that causes evil eye). It becomes a way of thinking—of establishing causal and semiotic relationships. And it also becomes a way of acting—controlling one's world by means of semiotic acts.

Often when healing magic was transmitted in the Russian village, no direct teaching or explanation was involved. Instead, the transmission occurred through the simple inclusion of the mother in the technology of healing. Many of the incantations we recorded from village women were used by a pair of women, involving the mother herself. In this way, the mother both participated in the healing of her child and also learned to use the techniques herself.

For example, a woman born in 1926 in Gulikovschina, Vinogradov region, Arkhangel'sk oblast, told us in 1990 that in the event of a child's sickness, two people participated in a magical cure—the child's mother and grandmother (mother-in-law). The mother-in-law stays in one place in the home and speaks for the mother, while the mother with the child in her arms "walks around with him inside the house from window to window at dawn. 'First dawn Marya [the mother-in-law pronounces when the mother approaches the first window], second dawn Darya [at the second], third dawn Peladya [at the third], do not laugh, do not mock at my child. Laugh and mock on the bottom of the river instead . . .'" (Adon'eva and Ovchinnikova 1993, no. 333).[6] With the mother's active participation and in her name, the older woman leads the magical speech, thus gradually providing the younger woman with the right to a voice in the communicative network of "matriarchs" and "forces."

Another woman, born in 1908 in Shardonesh', Pinega region, Arkhangel'sk oblast, showed us how an elder woman's use of an incantation to ward off a baby's fit or restlessness teaches the younger woman (the mother), at the same time, how she should address a sickness. The elder woman, in the presence of the mother, pronounced the following text:

Сама мати носила,
сама мати родила,
сама родимцу говорила,
родимцу скорбному,
сердцевому, жиловому,

исподняжному, исподжильному,
спесивому, сопливому,
дресливому, слезливому,
костовому, ломовому,
трясущему.
Подите прочь, родимцы,
от рабы Божьей Татьяны
в чистое поле,
во синее море,
под гнилую колоду,
там вам вода, земля и место.

[Mama herself carried,
mama herself bore,
said herself to the colic,
to the mournful colic,
to the heart-deep, vein-deep,
to the belly-achy, vein-achy,
to the arrogant, snotty,
to the poopy and teary,
the bone-achy,
the shaky.
Get away, oh colic,
from God's slave Tatiana [child's name],
to the open field,
to the dark-blue sea,
under the rotten hollow log,
there is your water, your earth, your place.]

(6 July 1984 [Pin 20-32])

Both of these cases are similar to the way bridal laments were conducted: the bride echoed an elder woman, who lamented in her (the bride's) name. In the bridal situation the young woman came to comprehend a new life script by mastering its special speech register (Adon'eva 1999). Here, the same principle of learning a script operates at the next stage of life: the powerful intonation of the charm inserts the one chanting—the older woman—into the yet-silent lips of the *mati*, who carried and bore the child—that is, of the young mother.

A young mother was taught symbolic techniques of childcare, care of the cattle, her own health, and the health of others by her mother-in-law. This was true even when the young mother herself was a *bol'shukha*—that is, even if the younger family split off and lived separately from the husband's parents. The mother-in-law herself delivered the babies or, if she herself was still young ("fruitful"), she called in a knowledgeable older woman. In the story below, recorded from a woman born in 1923 (whose births occurred in the postwar period), the physical and symbolic techniques of birth were passed along simultaneously:

> But I had the second one at home.
> *And how was that?*
> I had a cow that was also set to calve. I went to my mother-in-law's and I say, "My cow is fidgeting from foot to foot today, and it's driving me crazy." She says, "Well, go home, I'll come." My mother-in-law lived right nearby. Well then, Lord. She says, "Sit down." I sat. "Squeeze your fanny" [*she laughs and says, "God forgive me"*], "squeeze your fanny"—says—"puff up." Like this I . . . gave birth. The child came out, she picked it up. I say, "So, he has to be wrapped up clean." She wrapped him up in a dirty rag, and what's more laid him by the threshold so the child would be calm.
> *By the threshold? Why?*
> So he'd be calm. I say: "In a clean cloth you have to wrap him, I have enough laid by." All the same she wrapped the little man up in that, what's it called, foot rag, so that he would, he'd be calm and clever. And she laid him by the threshold too. Held him, then pulled him out and put him on the bed. (Ostrov, Vashkinskii region, Vologda oblast, 14 July 2003 [Vash 10-66])

The mother-in-law performs two symbolic acts. First, she lays the child by the threshold. She does not explain the principle of the symbolism; she simply says he will be calm that way. The sympathetic magic of boundaries applies here: the power of magic is strengthened at physical thresholds. The baby is a liminal being: he has just pierced through a physical boundary as he entered into the world. Once again he pierces a boundary but now it is that of his own home.

In this example, for the swaddling the mother-in-law does not choose new fabric but a "foot rag" (a length of cloth used to wrap up the foot as a sock) belonging to the child's father. This is another act of symbolic joining. Bringing the infant in contact with the clothing of his own family symbolically makes him a part of that family. Furthermore, this action is one of several to "gender" the child: the father's clothes are used for a boy, while the mother's would be used for a girl (another example in earlier Russian tradition is the use of a spindle to cut a girl baby's umbilical cord, but an ax or other tool associated with men's occupations to cut the boy's [Baranov 2005b, 406]). The mother-in-law does not explain the interpretive logic, just as we, wanting to know how to work some gadget or another, do not try to understand how it is constructed. It is enough for us to know how the object is used. It is the skill, the instrument, that is passed along, not necessarily the principles of its creation.

The following story shows how important the mother-in-law was in this process of transmission, even during the Soviet period when the state was fulfilling some of the traditional medical roles through the use of trained personnel. A woman born in 1931 whose births occurred after the war learns magical practices from her mother-in-law even though a Soviet-trained *medichka* (medic) has been summoned to the birth. She first recounts the "words" one has to say when washing the child, then tells how her mother-in-law immediately washed the child after the birth:

> *And so, so that the child would be quiet?*
> He was quiet, so he had to be washed. They wash him the first day they bring him home from the hospital—they wash him right away in the bath. They wash him and say this, Anna Iakovlevna [the mother-in-law] taught it to me too: "I wash you as granny Soloman'ia washed Jesus Christ, servant of God [for example] Nelin'ka [child's name], for sleep, for rest, for growing tall, for good health, *tfu* [*she spits*], amen, for ever and ever."[7] You have to say it three times. I wash them, and when I've washed them well, I roll them over three times and recite this, for all my children. I had quiet children.
> *You did this yourself? No one helped you?*
> Myself, Anna Iakovlevna taught me.
> *And did you wash for anyone else?*
> Well, I did go . . .
> *So they turned to you?*
> Mmm-hmm. I studied these words, I memorized them, so I know them all.
> *And when one gives birth at home, for instance you gave birth to one . . .*
> It was just Volod'ia I gave birth to at home.
> *And who delivered him?*
> We had a *medichka*.
> *And so the little one was born, and then what?*
> He was washed at once, my mother-in-law washed him at once.
> *And what do you wrap him in?*
> In those days I raised boys, so I didn't have those pretty little white swaddling-clothes; my mother-in-law washed up some of her old skirts. (Mosseevo, Vashkinskii region, Vologda oblast, 10 July 2002 [Vash 10-22])

Such stories recount the power possessed by the mother-in-law through her healing magic, and the corresponding competence acquired by the younger generation. As this

woman points out, she too "washed" babies for other families. The Soviet medical establishment existed in parallel with this traditional practice, which has remained in active use
for some families to this day.

Of course, some married women did not become mothers, usually because they or their
husbands suffered from infertility. In the case of infertility, Russian traditional culture
taught that childlessness was a sign of the family's misfortune, and a possible hex (*porcha*)
or inherited familial curse. There were healer-specialists who would take on such cases.
An infant's death was experienced as a sorrow but not a tragedy. Peasant conceptions
of motherhood and children did not broach the idea of the special value or "holiness" of
motherhood and the special value of children that was introduced into Soviet official discourse in the 1930s (Iushkova 1937, 28). A child's death was preferable to his suffering,
and infants who failed to thrive were said to have been not strong enough to survive
(Ransel 2000, 183–95). The first of the charms recorded below was recounted by a woman
born in 1908; the second, by a woman born in 1936. Their readiness to accept a child's
death in the face of his suffering and readiness to facilitate death's approach are qualities
that grew out of their understanding of the life cycle as determined by forces beyond
human control:

They'll sprinkle a little one who is sick with dirt from the graveyard, they'll say:

Мати моя,
мать сырая земля,
здоровья давай
иль себе забирай.

[Mother mine,
Mother Moist Earth,
give health
or off with you.]

(Woman born in 1908, Shardonem', Pinega region, Arkhangel'sk oblast, 19 July
1984 [Pin 20-29])

If the child was sick, howling, they put him on the table and tore a piece of linen in
two parts over him: they made a vow [*obet*]. "If you live, I'll hang this shroud on the
cross, and if you die, then I'll cover you [with it]."[8] (Woman born in 1936, Krotovo,
Pinega region, Arkhangel'sk oblast, 18 July 1986 [Pin 20-47])

The "shroud," the fabric, is a gift of thanksgiving that, in Arkhangel'sk oblast, relates to
the so-called vowing [*obetnye*] crosses. Many villages have places where people commonly
place such crosses, at the edge of a village or in the forest. They are placed "by vow" to this

day. In a critical situation, a person makes a promise that if things turn out well, she will erect a cross as a sign of gratitude. Other residents of the village then come to these crosses as well, to make promises and express gratitude. This practice suggests the religious context: the question of life or death was decided by forces not of this world, which could include God. As David Ransel notes, ailing children "were consciously placed in a reserve space closer to God" (2000, 193). In both of these cases it is not stated explicitly, but it is likely that elder women helped the mother make the judgment about how to handle a child whose health was failing. These practices, like others for the child's health, were not needed by a woman before she became a mother.

Role of the Mother-in-Law

As we have shown, a woman mastered everything connected with the experience of "adult" female competence within her husband's family. From the beginning this amounted to mastering a new social role, and a level of personal development connected with it. It manifested itself through an external social action: the necessity for submission. As we pointed out in chapters 2 and 3, traditions of the Russian peasant wedding obligated the young wife to accept a new law—unconditional submission to her husband and his parents. Her own mother admonished the newlywed daughter with the following lament (recorded in 1997 from a woman born in 1928):

Вышла в чужую-то семеюшку,
Да угаживай,
Да головушку ниже пояса держи,
Чтобы ласкова и свекровушке,
И золовушке, и мужу-то,
И послушна.

[You went out into another family,
So abase yourself.
So hold your head below your belt,
So that you are affectionate to your mother-in-law,
And your sister-in-law, and your husband,
And obedient.]

(Zubovo, Belozersk region, Vologda oblast, 19 July 1997 [Bel 2-48])

The wedding instilled in the bride new norms connected with her new role. As daughter she practiced submission to her mother and father; now the young woman was obliged to submit to the elders in her husband's family, and to her husband. In these cases, ritual texts are meant to *create* a format for social relationships: they construct the reality they describe. In this case, the reality described and created is that of submission and obedience on the part of the young *molodka*.

In the first stage of their relationship, the format for the relationship between a mother-in-law and a bride was unquestioning submission, as is shown in the following conservation about customs of family life that took place in 2006 in the Siamzha region of Vologda oblast. Participating in the discussion are folklorists and two village women (neighbors), one born in 1935 (Lia Ivanovna G.), and the other in 1925 (Elizaveta Pavlovna T.):

LIG: Yes, the one who's getting married, she's [not] allowed to dress herself up . . .

EPT: She can't go to feasts anymore. It isn't like now: now you turn up your tail, run off, leave your husband. But then you couldn't run away . . .

What is it you "turn up?"

EPT: Your tail! Look, you wouldn't go, you'd still ask the parents, the mother and father, there were his parents . . .

The mother-in-law?

EPT: Yes, the mother-in-law.

And how would you ask?

EPT: Mama, may I go there?—Go ahead.

LIG: If your mama lets you—[go], and if she doesn't let you, then you don't go out. And [even if] you wanted to go to your own parents, you'd ask: "Will they [the parents-in-law] let you?"

Did you have to ask your mother-in-law in order to visit your parents?

LIG: Of course . . .

EPT: You have to ask about everything—submit . . .

LIG: If your relatives let you, you can go to your hometown, but if they don't let you, you stay at home.

And what, did it really happen that the mother-in-law didn't let you see your parents?

EPT: Well, there was so much work, a stable full of cattle, and you had to feed them, to carry water, to do everything—there was plenty of work in the village.

And so when could you go to your parents? . . .

LIG: You could go to your parents more on Sundays and holidays, just on holidays—on an ordinary day you couldn't run away.

EPT: My [own] mama even lived in the same village, but I still didn't go every day. Come Sunday—she'd come, pick us up [Elizaveta Pavlovna and her children], and take us: some by the hand, some in her arms.

LIG: It's nowadays that you run off wherever you feel like, don't tell anyone, go off . . .

EPT: Then there weren't many divorces, [there wasn't] that kind of life, and you couldn't just go back to your parents—it was shameful.

LIG: Yes, they'd given you up—even if they were boiling you in a cauldron, you
    wouldn't go back home. Your father would say, your dad . . .
    So even if things were completely terrible? . . .
LIG: You wouldn't go, all the same you lived [with the husband's family] . . .
    (Siamzha, Vologda oblast, 14 July 2006)

In the woman's submission to the will of her husband's parents, these women see the basis
for stability in marriage. They compare the standards of behavior when they were young
with the looser standards today. Their parents too shared their belief in the necessity for
such submission.

Countering and balancing this picture are the numerous wedding songs and proverbs
that attempt to represent a young wife's point of view, depicting mothers-in-law unkindly.
In reality, as we have seen from copious interviews with elder women, such relationships
could develop in different ways: the mothers-in-law often became mentors for the younger
mothers. Nevertheless, a daughter-in-law's rebellion must be acknowledged as one of the
themes of folk songs. For example, a cheerful dancing song collected by a Russian folklorist
at the end of the nineteenth century depicted the intergenerational conflict in a fantasy of
magical retribution:

. . . Меня свекоръ-отъ грозилъ,
Онъ и тѣмъ да инымъ,
Да все сыномъ-то своимъ,
Господиномъ-то своимъ.
Еще свекрова гроза—
Не великая бѣда:
Завяжу я въ узелокъ,
Брошу на печь въ уголокъ.
Гдѣ узелъ-отъ лежитъ,
Тамъ и уголъ-отъ дрожитъ,
Потолокъ дребезжитъ.

[. . . My father-in-law threatened me,
With one thing and with another,
And with his son,
With the "lord and master."
And my mother-in-law's threats too—
Not a terrible problem:
Me, I tie them in a little knot,
Throw them in the corner of the stove,

Where that ol' knot takes,
There the ol' coal shakes,
And the ceiling quakes!]

(Sobolevskii 1896, 455–56)

Since folkloric discourse ritually postulated the first stage of the relationship between mother-in-law and daughter-in-law as submission, the only alternative available was transgression or rebellion. This song, which was sung during spring and summer outdoor round dances by unmarried girls, fantasizes the private rebellion of secretly "burning up" the mother-in-law's threats. Of course, the song itself is sung in a quasi-public atmosphere, outdoors. Russian folk culture allowed for such expressions of transgression in the context of holiday merriment, as we showed in the introduction and chapter 5 (*chastushki* were a later variation of such licensed transgressive self-expression).

With the appearance of a child, the relationships of submission and resistance transform into relationships of a different type. The young mother seeks out the company of her mother-in-law, feels a need for her experience, and intentionally learns the techniques of the mother-in-law. Max Weber defined politics as the ability to command compliance from other people, regardless of what this compliance is founded upon. According to Weber, there are three internal justifications for the recognition of domination, in other words, foundations for the legitimacy of domination. First is the authority of the "age-old": the authority of traditions, sanctified by their significance and the habitual tendency to observe them. Second is authority based on recognition of a person's special qualities: the person's charisma and leadership qualities inspire complete personal devotion and trust. And third is domination based upon legality, founded on rationally conceived laws (Weber 1978, 215–55.). If at the beginning stage of married life the authority of traditions guarantees the younger woman's submission, then at the new stage (the stage of motherhood), she acknowledges the special gift of "wisdom" in her mother-in-law and older women, and submits to their authority. She then uses their wisdom—the wisdom of those who are knowledgeable about how the "rules" work—to interpret events.

Fear and Control

In this relationship of patronage between older and younger woman, the wisdom of the elder woman consisted of a new means of interpreting experience. The elder woman taught the younger to see and understand the "social" organization of the forces of the other world, and also gradually taught her control over those forces. By teaching her about the powers of other world, the older woman taught fear; and inevitably, the daughter-in-law acquired a certain fear and respect for the authority of the older woman. That authority was, in its origins, a supernatural one. The older woman guaranteed contact with the world of "forces" (spirits); she formulated the rules, because reaching agreement with these otherworldly forces was her area of expertise. Such power does not permit resistance: the younger woman can only obey the older and turn to her for help, and trust that in time, the "force" will be passed to her. Until this happens (essentially, until authority [*bol'shina*] is attained) the young woman always remains under the patronage of the older. Two relationships of patronage were constructed: the older woman had a metaphysical patron, while the younger moved into patronage with the older.

The older woman taught fear of the unknown, of the powerful forces that populate the other world in Russian folk belief, and fear of a mother's tremendous burden of responsibility (for her children). To address this fear, she provided novel magical means of control and power. For example, a woman recounts how her *babka* (mother-in-law) taught her fear and control: "*Babka* said: wherever you go, if night catches you, every little bush will let you spend the night, but you have to ask permission. Everything has its master" (Woman born in 1936, Krotovo, Pinega region, Arkhangel'sk oblast, 18 July 1986 [Pin 20-205]). That the farmstead and surrounding countryside were controlled by various spirits or "masters" (*khoziaeva*) was a belief that ethnographers commonly ascribed to Russian rural dwellers. We emphasize that the knowledge of how to deal with these masters was passed down from mother-in-law to daughter-in-law.

In the following interview, fear necessitates the ritual of bringing the household spirit (*domovoi*, here *dobrokhodushka*), a protective spirit, into the new home when one moves. The speaker, a woman born in 1932, tells how her grandmother, her mother's mother-in-law, taught her mother how to properly deal with this household spirit when her mother was frightened at night:

> *They say that it's necessary to bring the* dobrokhodushka *with you when you move into a new home?*
> Yes, they used to say that. You would go out into that—into the courtyard . . .
> *In the old house?*
> Into this one—when you'd moved there, like into that one, in this house, yes, you went, and asked the *dobrokhodushka* to make room for you.
> *And how do you say that?*
> "Father-*dobrokhodushka*, mother-*dobrokhodnitsa*, receive us into your place in the new home." If there is livestock in the courtyard, you lead in the animals as well, like: "Father-*dobrokhodushka*, mother-*dobrokhodnitsa*, receive my little animal, give her space, so it isn't cramped, give her drink and feed her full, pet her smoothly, bed her softly"—that's for livestock, not for us, for the livestock that is. And for oneself it's just—you ask to have a good life in the new home, and that's it. . . .
> *And a bride, when she comes into the other home, did you have to petition too?*

Yes, you also had to ask . . . My mama—I was born in Sidorova, she was a
Sidorova native, Goluzinskii village soviet—so she . . . she told me about
everything: . . . [as a child] I was sleeping by her, on her breast, on the bed. "And
look," she says, "someone lay down next to me and tries to pull you over me. And
that hand," she says, "is heavy. I," she says, "got scared, jumped, started to cry. Well,
so, your father's mother, my mother-in-law, well, she heard me crying . . . and I
said," she says, "'Mama'—you used to say 'Mama' before—'Mama,' I say. And
she [the mother-in-law] asks: 'What are you crying for?'" And she said: "'Mama,
someone lay down by me, and his hand," she says, "over me—heavy, heavy hand—
tugging at Raiska," that's me. So look. She says: "And you," she [the mother-in-law]
said, "the little girl, she came, so did you settle [*vodvorila*] her in? You didn't settle
her." And so she came on the morning of the second day to settle me in.

That is, they had to for you too—a child?

Yes, yes, yes, she came to settle me in too. And when she'd settled me in, then
no one [no spirits] came. So, obviously, it was necessary to settle me. I was born in
Sidorova, you see, they brought me from there and didn't settle me, apparently.

And he [the spirit] didn't like it, right?

And he, apparently, didn't like it, that I wasn't settled. So you see, obviously
there is some force [*sila*], of some kind. Well, I heard about that from my mama
more than once.

[. . .]

And you settled your own children as well?

I settled them, how wouldn't I settle them? Before, as it happened, it was like
that . . .

*That is, it was necessary to go into the cowshed [khlev] or barn [sarai] with your
child?*

No, what for? You could go without your child.

Did you have to go out to the barn, or the shed?

To the barn.

And say: father-dobrokhodushka, receive?

Yes, like that. (Monastyrskaia, Siamzha region, Vologda oblast, 11 July 2006
[Siam 20-151])

Thus, older women possess symbolic capital: on the one hand, the capacity to cause harm
magically (unintentional harm, by way of "thoughts," and also intentional harm, as we
discuss in the next chapter), and on the other hand the capacity to magically protect her
family. Only the woman who is prepared for open action, she who openly positions herself
as a participant in battles for supernatural power, can carry out the performative speech
acts associated with sorcery and healing—cursing, blessing, charming.

That fear is a great motivator for women in learning how to deal with the world of spirits was brought home to me (SA) when, in 1984, on a folklore expedition to Pinega, my interviewees (a mother and daughter) found out in the course of the conversation that I was married. Up until the discussion of this aspect of my life, there was not a single word about magic. But as soon as they found out this fact of my biography, they sent my male student colleague "to rest" and related to me a great quantity of wisdom connected with the magical defense and healing of babies. So that the child is not hexed, "when you go out, you must put scissors under his pillow and lean up some little thing, so it's against the door"; "do not hang up swaddling-clothes outside—as they flop in the wind, so the child will mope" (*kak oni maiuts'ia vetrom, tak i dite budet maiat'sia*); "throw a silver coin into the stream, draw up some water there and rub the hurt place so that it doesn't hurt"; and so on. They explained their desire to teach me by saying that I should be ready to become a mother, and they advised me never to pass on this wisdom to anyone else. The wisdom was presented for me personally, with the instruction not to "pass it on" anywhere. I disobeyed: in the evening, I transcribed my recording and, feeling somewhat uneasy about breaking my promise, put the texts into the common pile of materials the group had recorded. In the evening I felt unwell, but the next day, as usual, we left for the neighboring village for the next interview. Our interviewee from yesterday (the daughter) turned up to meet us, and instead of greeting me, she asked: "Well? Get sick yesterday?" Such was my experience of being included in the female hierarchy of power: the position of the dominated one is guaranteed by fear.

This knowledge is kept secret, is strictly controlled and not publicly broadcast. To receive the information is a privilege, as this woman born in 1940 told us:

> Well, for example, my grandmother would read prayers over boils. And then I said,
> "Grandma, tell me, I'm the youngest child, and this secret gets handed down to the
> youngest child." She goes, "You're an empty-headed fool!" She goes, "I won't tell
> you, you'd tell everyone anyway, there wouldn't be any point." Like that. So it died.
> So she never told me: "You're empty-headed. And this," she goes, "you have to
> keep it a secret." So she never told me. (Mianda, Vashkinskii region, Vologda
> oblast, 13 July 2002 [Vash 20-123])

Because of the symbolic resources that the elder mothers possessed, it was they who morally judged the younger. They handed down knowledge as they desired, avoiding those deemed unworthy. Through gossip, these mothers provided a network of judgment and surveillance for the community. *Starukhi*, old women (mothers of mothers, relieved of their "authority"), sitting on the *zavalinkas* (a protrusion around the base of a peasant house that forms a bench), keep an eye on the situation in the village and report to the mothers, and they punish their children (usually through curtailment of freedom) or demand that neighboring matriarchs punish theirs. If the question of a *muzhik*'s, or married man's, incorrect behavior arises, the matriarchs turn to his father or to the older male community through its head patriarch.

This kind of social-matriarchal control mechanism remains up to the present day in villages. Soviet generations retain traditional forms of relationship in their daily life: older women have the right and ability to teach and admonish any children and youth (not only their own grandchildren). Attempts by younger women to contest the judgment of the elders are dangerous because of the supernatural authority, described above, that older women possessed.

7

Magic, Control, and Social Roles

The magical healing and medical practices associated with birth and child-rearing discussed in the previous chapter were located specifically within the provenance of women. In prerevolutionary times women also predominated in other healing practices, such as bone-setting, bloodletting, toothache treatments, and herbal medicine. The different types of specialized practitioners used various means to facilitate healing, but all used magical rituals such as incantations. These *znakharki* or *babki* were older women, often widows, who sought a livelihood through their chosen profession. They consciously learned and passed on their skills, and although they did not earn much, they could subsist on the in-kind payments (food, materials) that people offered them for their services (Glickman 1991, 154–55, 157). In the Soviet period, authorities attempted to stop people from using the services of these *babki*, but the institution was not eradicated.

Another type of magic in Russia was historically associated not only with women but with men as well. This is the type of magic called in Russian ethnographic literature *porcha* (spoiling) and noted in anthropological literature most often under the terms witchcraft and sorcery. Anthropologists working in areas such as Africa and New Guinea distinguish these two concepts (Stewart and Strathern 2004, 6; Turner 1967, 119); however, in Russia the two terms are conflated (Ryan 1999, 69). In Russia both witches and sorcerers use supernatural power directly upon others to kill or harm them; it is often said that they do this to augment themselves or because they "need to." They may also exercise their power indirectly, using spells, substances, or rites to inflict their harmful magic. Witches and sorcerers are said to fly or change the shape of their bodies. Whether the power is deemed voluntary or involuntary depends upon local tradition and/or the particular case. Because the English terms are equally applicable in the Russian case, we will use them interchangeably in this chapter.

In Russian ethnographic and native sources from the seventeenth century to the present, the term most often used for a harmful magician is *koldun* (pl. *kolduny*); the feminine is *koldun'ia* (pl. *koldun'i*). There is overlap between harmful and helpful magic: in reports some *kolduny* are depicted as selling professional services such as casting love spells, finding lost livestock, and reversing other spells (i.e., healing)—sometimes in these cases the practitioners are called *znakhari* or *znakharki* rather than *kolduny*. Others, suspected witches, are said to keep their harmful identity secret, and are feared (Ryan 1999, 78). Such a person may not know she is called a witch behind her back; or a suspected witch may draw upon his or her reputation and offer services.

Reports on the predominant gender of witches diverge considerably; all seem to agree, however, that in Russia, as distinct from the West, both men and women were believed to perform harmful magic.[1] Based upon cases brought to court in Russia in the sixteenth to early eighteenth centuries, Valerie Kivelson argues that gender was not as important a factor as was social status: although 75 percent of the accused were men, it was their liminal status—as wanderers, foreigners, and defiant people—that was a more likely reason for their being suspected of sorcery (2003, 617–20). According to nineteenth- and early twentieth-century sources cited by Rose Glickman, there were more male than female professional sorcerers, while the suspected witches were split more or less evenly between men and women (1991, 151). According to records from Russia and Ukraine examined by Christine Worobec, during the period 1861–1917 over 70 percent of those charged with sorcery were women; women, too, were more likely to be the victims of witchcraft (1995, 168). Olga Khristoforova divides the tradition geographically: in the Russian North, males were said to be the main holders of sorcerers' knowledge; while in the South, the ability was ascribed more often to women (2010, 125). William Ryan notes that Church sources tended to depict women as practitioners of magic due to the association of women with the devil in Christian writings and artifacts; the idea that it was generally females who were witches was probably also due to influences from Poland and Germany (1999, 79, 91). Ryan points out that one often sees in Russian culture a "confusion of witches as real-life practitioners in magic with malevolent female demons of mythology and folklore" such as Baba Yaga (79).

In contemporary Russian culture, the discourse of witchcraft and sorcery has become feminized due to cultural and historical changes. It is likely that Western notions have to an extent influenced belief: our informants told stories about male and female sorcerers alike but mentioned more women practitioners than men. The healers mentioned by our informants were largely female, as well.[2] We attribute this to historical changes in the twentieth century—the decrease in the male population in the village, the increasing association of women with tradition-keeping, the Soviet campaigns against craftspeople, and the campaigns to eradicate superstition that were unevenly applied to men and women.

While the practitioners may be mixed in gender, it is clear that talk about sorcery is a women's discourse. While men do occasionally tell stories about illness caused by harmful magic, for women the magic causes of illnesses and the community figures who bring about or heal illness comprise major topics of gossip. Khristoforova ascribes this to the fact that men have other socially accepted ways of expressing relations of aggression (2010, 128). We link it with women's close association with the supernatural world and their ultimate responsibility for the health of the family.

Furthermore, elder women's interest in the discourse of sorcery is connected with the essential role that control of the supernatural plays in the establishment and maintenance of familial and social power. As we argue in this chapter, the relations that are illustrated and produced through the discourse of sorcery are interactions of conflict, caused by perceived situations of social inequality or transgression of norms. It is a discourse of social control. The discourse—by which we mean not only magic words but also gossip about harm caused magically—not only describes these relations but also produces them: it is a performative speech act. Not all in the community use this means of symbolizing power, but for those who use it, the discourse of harmful magic is a principal means of expressing core values, including the notions of social equality and social homogeny.

The first part of this chapter is largely based upon the lore of one village, which we will call Krasnoe, in Riazan' oblast. Olson had several years of experience here that allowed her to focus upon community social interactions. We will also examine field reports from Vologda and Arkhangel'sk oblasts from 1986 to 2009, located in the folklore archive of Saint Petersburg State University.[3]

In general, belief in sorcery and witchcraft is widespread in post-Soviet Russia, both in cities and villages.[4] Belief in witchcraft is linked to a resurgence of interest in the occult in general. In the post-Soviet period, many people rejected Soviet values and sought new sources of morality and spirituality, which led to the flourishing of a number of religious sects and lifestyle orientations (such as yoga and Hare Krishna), and the resurgence and public acceptance of faith healers (Ramet 1993; Borenstein 1999; Knox 2005). The Ministry of Health even set up a process for licensure of faith healers, witches, and psychics (Knox 2005, 89). However, for our rural informants this flourishing of witchcraft only meant easier access to it. Magic was practiced throughout the Soviet period, despite antireligious propaganda that attempted to eradicate superstition from the population. Nineteenth-century materials do not differ significantly from late twentieth- to early twentieth-first-century materials in terms of the beliefs recounted. It is likely that the secrecy of the discourse, as well as its intrinsic relation to core beliefs and social structure, accounted for its continuation.

Due to the official Soviet position that superstition had been or would soon be eradicated in the countryside, sorcerers' incantations collected during the Soviet period were not published before approximately 1991. Only since this time has scholarly work involving Soviet-era field research on incantations been published.[5] However, historically many of the published analyses in Russian and English have been based upon short folk narratives (memorates and fabulates) about witchcraft or incantations, and either focus upon describing the beliefs or analyzing the poetics of the incantations. By contrast, we are interested in witchcraft as a social phenomenon. Our analyses are based upon extensive conversations with people whose lives have been shaped by sorcery or the belief in sorcery and people who have the reputation of being sorcerers. With this methodology we aim to glimpse the ways in which the discourse of sorcery shapes the contours of community relations.

Power, Knowledge, and Transgression

In the previous chapter, we talked of the evil eye as a revelation of fear vis-à-vis the unknown and also as a discourse legitimizing the authority of elder women as mediators between the human and the other world. The evil eye is attributed to jealousy: those who see themselves as having less while others have more, or those who see themselves as having more while others have less, are believed to cause this phenomenon. The discourse surrounding *porcha* also speaks of fear (i.e., for those without power) and legitimacy (of those who claim such power—healers, *kolduny*, and gossipers), and it also may speak of jealousy. However, explanations of *porcha* tend to be unmotivated in general—jealousy is optional. Rather, they imagine and give symbolic expression to a notion of the pure power of control over other people.[6] This control can be exercised not only due to the suspected sorcerer's jealous feelings but also as punishment for a person's transgressive, nonnormative behavior. And in this arena, power is held not only by the suspected sorcerer but also by those who suspect and spread gossip about it. Gossip itself can be a weapon that offers power—not power as control, but power as influence. All of these roles—healer, sorcerer, gossip—are most often played by elder women.

In Russian, the words used to describe sorcery imply this power of control. People identify witches and sorcerers as those who "know." "To know" is not normally used without a stated or implied concrete direct object; when used in this way, it implies sorcery, an unnamed knowledge (in the sense of an ability). The knowledge can be transferred from person to person and is kept secret as a sign of its potency and transgressiveness. That this knowledge violates others is also communicated linguistically in the phrase "they did you really well" (i.e., they 'got you good,' they hurt you badly through magic). Here the speaker uses a transitive version of the verb "to do" with a person as the direct object (usually, in English and in Russian "to do" is used with inanimate objects and is only used with persons in a limited range of colloquial expressions). Dialect expressions, such as *prisazhivat' kilu* (to set a *kila*, an invisible bodily injury), denote violation of a person's body, causing almost any illness thought to be caused by sorcery: disorders of the internal organs, skin infections, and infections of the respiratory system (with the exception of trauma). Thus, linguistically, we determine that the expressions used to speak about witches suggest they possess both power of control that violates the wills and bodies of others, and also power as ability (in this case, a special, supernatural competency).

That the knowledge is said to be passed as an inheritance underlines its nature as pure and not concretely motivated. Our main informant in Krasnoe, Valentina Sergeevna G. (born in 1925), said: "Her mother—Nastya—was a *koldun'ia*—that means she [the daughter] knows; and Pet'ka, who brings the manure, his wife Tom'ka, she knows. Two sisters, both *koldun'i*. Young."[7] The very fact of having relatives who are suspected of being *kolduny* is offered as proof that one is a *koldun*. The conventional plot of sorcery involves transfer of the magical power through community and kinship networks.

People can also intentionally put themselves in the position to acquire the knowledge from a known, unrelated sorcerer. In such cases the knowledge is desired and sought. In the following example, Valentina Sergeevna tells from whom the *koldun'ia* (Tatiana, whom we meet later in the chapter) got her knowledge: the *koldun* Kurepyi chose to give his knowledge to Tatiana, who was unrelated to him. Valentina views Tatiana as especially powerful because she received knowledge from so many sources: "She took it from her mother. She took it from her aunt, too. From her mother's sister. She knows, and he [Kurepyi] knows and that's why he called her [when he was sick]: 'Only admit Tatiana to me.' And she also took from Kurepyi. Do you know how much? She knows everything in the world" (3 December 2004). Later in the conversation, Valentina paraphrased the same story and added her own reaction: "Her mother and aunt and Kurepyi taught her. And I'm afraid of her." Ivanits and other scholars note that willing, "taught" sorcerers were seen as more powerful than ones who are "born" (1989, 95; Khristoforova 2008, 366–70).

Alternatively, the ability to cast spells can be passed down by the sorcerer to unsuspecting people. In this case, the knowledge is not desired, and it will make the receiver sick if he or she does not know how to or desires not to use it:[8]

> *How do they pass on their knowledge?*
> How do they pass it on? They'll ask you, they'll say, "Give me something to drink." You give her a mug, she drinks and gives it back to you. She just passed you her sorcery.
> *And how can I control my knowledge?*
> You'll control it. They'll teach you. And if you don't, you'll get sick. (3 December 2004)

In this cultural plot, knowledge is power: this special competency offers power of control over others. Not only is sorcery said to be a secret transgressive knowledge, but those who have other kinds of special knowledge are often suspected of sorcery. In nineteenth-century sources, villagers with particular trades (such as millers or shepherds) were often reputed to be sorcerers because they had specific knowledge that others did not possess. Olga Khristoforova writes: "We can reconstruct the logical chain in the following way: 'A specialist's responsibility + experience → particular skills = power over objects = magical power = power over spirits = power over forces of nature = power over animals → power over people'" (2008, 373). Later in this chapter we discuss a few examples of female villagers—suspected sorcerers—who had special knowledge. One knew Church doctrine; another was a woman who managed male tractor drivers; a third was a healer and a beggar.

Suspected sorcerers can have higher or lower status than the norm: either they have more than others and thus may have feelings of competitiveness; or they have less, and thus may have feelings of jealousy. They often have the status of outsiders (who presumably are jealous of those in the ingroup). Since suspicion of sorcery can be harmful to a person's reputation locally (others will avoid that person), gossip about sorcery has the function of creating conformity. Everyone in the community will scrutinize her own behavior to make sure that what she does, how she appears to others, is not suspicious (Adon'eva 2004, 98).

Theorists of economic relationships within peasant communities have offered likely explanations for the origin of this state of affairs (Khristoforova 2010). According to James Scott, peasants living at subsistence level traditionally sought to maximize their economic security even at the cost of productivity. The moral arrangement chosen by the community to maximize security was the principle of egalitarianism: all had to pull together and not leave individuals behind, even if that meant less autonomy and opportunity for advancement (1976, 5). The underlying notion was that of limited good: people believed that if one individual had more, others would have less (Foster 1965). Villagers were conscious that if one inhabitant were abandoned, it would be worse for the group: the envy of the one who was "cut off" would be much more harmful to the group than the "piece of the pie" that they would acquire from his absence (Khristoforova 2010, 119). Gossip and envy—and the belief in sorcery—thus functioned as "redistributive mechanisms" that provided a "minimal subsistence insurance for villagers" (Scott 1976, 5; Khristoforova 2010, 119).

We wish to add to this economic explanation. After all, twentieth-century farmers no longer lived in a system of subsistence farming, and yet the discourse remained actual for them. While the belief in sorcery may once have been economically based, in its current form configurations of "have" and "have not" do not adequately describe the mechanisms by which suspicions of sorcery work. Instead, we would characterize the language of sorcery as one of several discursive means of expressing and affecting power relations in the community.

Bodily and Spatial Metaphors of Suspicion

Much of the talk about sorcery comprises stories of suspicion. The formula for suspicion is as follows: something is not right in a person's life, and he or she attributes this less than perfect state of being to a social conflict. The discourse reads scientifically explainable connections between events (my stomach hurts, therefore I must have eaten some bad food) as changes in connections between people (my stomach hurts, therefore someone must have placed a spell on me). The social sphere is out of balance. This is symbolized through metaphors of body or space.

Sorcery crosses socially determined boundaries of personal space and personal inviolability. Valentina spoke of *kolduny* placing spells on soap, for example. Soap is something that comes into contact with your body in an intimate way. The *koldun* takes advantage of the innocence, necessity, and intimacy of the object. A sorcerer will reverse the effect of the item: it becomes harmful instead of helpful, putting on instead of taking off something bad.

In another example, the sorcery is placed on a drink, something one takes into one's body. Through her competency, the sorcerer removes the competency of others (in this case sexual). Note here the cure is the same as the cause:

I got married. We set the table, invited all our relatives, not mine, but theirs. And we sat. And one woman [*tetushka*] took a bottle and went out. What did she whisper there? What did she know? She brought back a glass for everyone. And said, "Drink up, drink at least a little, just drink." We did drink. And we went to bed, and—it's shameful to say it—we went to bed, [and] his—won't stand up, and my stomach hurts. It hurts, it's sharp, sharp, like 'Help me Lord!' And his won't stand up at all. It was time to do it, and he couldn't do anything.

That is, they put a spell on you?

They put a spell on us.

Who put the spell on?

The old woman—that woman [*babushka—tetushka*].

Why?

Well, if someone knows, they can't hold themselves back, you see. What made her do it? And we tortured ourselves like that. It's shameful to say it, but whom will I tell [besides you].

So how can one get healed?

I went to a healer [*babushka*].

And what did she do?

She also said something over wine. (Woman born in 1912, Zubovo, Belozersk region, Vologda oblast, 19 July 1997 [Bel 20a-3])

Food, drink, clothing, and towels are all used similarly as media that can carry harmful magic. They are items found inside the home, and they fall into the category of personal care. The sorcerer transgresses those boundaries, invades an area she should not according to the community's rules governing private space.

As we pointed out in the previous chapter, complex rules govern who can enter a Russian home, and what rituals must be accomplished before entry. Neighbors who stop by a home without having been invited do not come farther than the threshold of the living space of the home. Only the invitation to enter—repeated several times by the homeowners—makes it possible to cross the boundary of the home to the interior. Even the boundaries of a yard (marked by a fence with a gate) will not be crossed by a neighbor who is not part of the *svoi* group of the household. We have often seen conversations across such boundaries. Women use special signs to indicate that they are closed for visits. A stick, called a *storozhka* or *batozhka*, will be left propped against the door to show that the owner is out. Sometimes women leave such a stick even when they are at home. People explained to us that older women "love to close themselves up"—they symbolically regulate their openness or closedness to communication with this stick outside the door.

Any unexpected changes in a *khoziaika*'s territory—in the yard, cattle shed, or house—will be interpreted as something unsanctioned and therefore dangerous. Thus, one resident of Roksoma in Vologda oblast told us that when her leg started hurting, she began to look inside her home for something amiss. She found a chip of wood stuck between the logs of her home, which allowed her to come to the definite conclusion that someone had placed a spell on her. Another woman, born in 1956 (thus, the fourth generation), told us: "They brought me a pound of charmed salt. I found it under the porch in my house. Under the walkway. There were five crosses buried there [too]. I found it all under the walkway. The Lord gave me the hint. 'Look for it!' he told me, 'Look for it.' I found it all. All the church stones were brought there" (woman born in 1956, Ukhtoma, Vologda oblast, 9 July 2000).

This *khoziaika* found numerous suspicious items under her porch. All of these items suggested the presence of an organization, an order that she did not make. Changes in any part of a *khoziaika*'s own space are seen as the result of someone's unauthorized entry and, in effect, someone performing the role of "master" (*khoziain*) there (Adon'eva 2004, 87).

We had that happen to us, too, at our home in Megra, our daddy received nine cows in an exchange, and all of them wouldn't milk. They wouldn't milk, they kicked. Then we started to take apart the whole household, and we found some metal fasteners that were inserted in the wall. That was preventing it. So then, there was a man in the village who kept horses, and his whole herd was getting sick, and he [also] kept cows, and all their cattle was getting sick. And then they told him, that um, you clean out everything in the yard, everything down to the ashes, take out all the manure. He started to take out all the manure, every bone, everything that was in the yard. He cleaned out everything in the yard, all the bones, he put it in a pit, and then he brought his animals back and the animals weren't sick.

And where were the fasteners?

The fasteners were somehow in the yard, . . . they were inserted on top of the
cattle shed. They were hidden. Who did that? There were all sorts of people.
(Woman born in 1925, Ust'e, Belozersk region, Vologda oblast, 15 July 1995
[Bel 20a-62])

To have fasteners inserted into a wall is normal for log construction, but the speaker
here found ones that appeared to have been inserted differently or in a different place.
As often happens, she transitions from her own story to the story of someone else; in
this speech practice, the fact that both stories share a common cultural plot confirms her
conclusion that "there were all sorts of people." The discourse requires no further motivation for the aggression.

In a similarly invasive fashion, the *koldun* can place spells by touching a person (usually
on his or her back or shoulder): again, breaking through the acceptable boundaries of
personal space. The following example from Valentina Sergeevna G. shows how she considers it an invasion for the *koldun'ia* to touch her: in order to defend herself, she touches
the *koldun'ia* in return. Even though she lacks the power of a sorcerer, her return touch
puts the ill intent back onto the sender. In this story fragment, local women (*baby*) act as
witnesses, censuring and chastising the *koldun'ia* for her invasive behavior.

I go to the store, they had just brought in apples, whole boxes of them, I went past,
and she [the *koldun'ia*] came toward me as if she was going to Tanya's house, that
one, Popalnaia. Panya. I went in, and she immediately returned and touched me on
the back. Aha. And I—I feel it—so standing near her, I also poke her. She pokes me
back, and I poke her back. I went quickly to the counter, and there were five women
[*baby*] there, [one of them says to her,] "You," she says, "What are you doing
running after her?" "Oi—she has to die." (30 April 2005)

Here the would-be victim defends herself from invasion, and has the sympathy of the
crowd of *bol'shukhi*. As we will see later on, Valentina's stories of her pursuit and victimization by sorcerers become a source of social power for her.

Social Dramas of Healing

In the discourse of some Russian villagers, negative events such as illnesses and bad luck
are understood as expressions of social conflict; similarly the ways of fixing them also
belong to the social sphere rather than to physical means. The stories of sorcery often have
two parts: they depict witches as controlling people's well-being through the symbolic
expression of conflict, and also depict the resolution of the conflict. One of two methods
can be chosen for the resolution: the afflicted person can appeal "up the ranks" and seek
an authority—a specialist who is (hopefully) equal in power to the suspected sorcerer.

Sometimes this is a relative, an older woman who is a specialist in magic. In other cases the only one who can remove the hex is the one who originally placed it, as this woman, born in 1928, tells us:

> Others had *kily* [ulcers, bumps] put on them.
>
> *How could you put a* kila *on?*
>
> How can you know how they were put on? A lot of people would ask me that. I say: I don't know such things, how they put them on. Many were put on. People put them on, they put on many.
>
> *But how would a person find out that they'd put* kily *on him?*
>
> What do you mean, how? He would break out in boils. Boils. A *kila* in the shoulders or the legs—kind of lumps.
>
> *And how would they put a* kila *on inside someone?*
>
> Our Lusya now, they killed her. They set her full of *kily* inside. She lived in Kisnem'. She left her husband, went off with another, and the husband up and hung them on her, set her full of deadly *kily*, a young girl too, she died. And the little one—she was pregnant, it was a little girl. She died suddenly, it was the ulcers inside.
>
> *And there wasn't any way to help?*
>
> How would you help? She went once with Galya, her sister, to Novokemskii. A certain [*znakharka*] told them to bring photographs. They brought them—she locked herself up in a room and put the photographs in water, both of them, and said: Galya, nothing will happen to you, but your Lusya will die in December—the photo went black. But yours, she said, was light. And so the girl died. A young girl—thirty years old.
>
> *And there is no remedy, if they've put on* kily?
>
> Well, the one who put them on, that one has to take them off. So, how do you find out? You have to find the one who put them on, so that he takes them off. (Chertezh, Vashkinskii region, Vologda oblast, 7 July 2001 [Vash 20a-70])

The illness makes explicit hidden social conflicts (between Lusya and her husband) and transgressions (Lusya's infidelity). Meanwhile, on the order of spoken communication, the partners are engaged in a social game. In the common wisdom, only the one who "hung on" the *kila* can take it off. One of the consequences of this belief is that it forces the participants in the conflict to solve it face to face (this possibility was not exploited in the case given above). The afflicted person's own power, her psychological and social capital, was required to carry out such a direct action. The fact that she did not make use of this force is evident from the (ineffective) path that she did choose. The victim of the curse (we should note well that, as is consistent with many examples, she was a young woman) did not directly follow the recommended path—to reopen relations with the person with whom one is in conflict, to renew direct contact. The victim chose a roundabout path: her gambit used one who was equal in power to the antagonist, and in so doing, she showed her own inequality.

The above example shows us that healing is configured as a social, not a physical, act. A healer must be socially equal in power to the one suspected of the aggressive act. Compare this more successful ritual of diagnosis and healing, in the case of Valentina's hoarseness: "[The healer said,] 'Oi, my dear, you should have come [to me for healing] long ago. Long ago. [They did] you really well. And more than once, and more than one [woman] did you.' . . . So she read [prayers] over water and tea. And told me, 'I'll need to see you again, they did you really well.'"

This example introduces the idea of an economy of magic. In her comments, the healer discloses information that her client must consider important: that the cause of the illness is witchcraft and who may have done it (or at least that more than one person did it). The healer additionally augments her own business by telling her client that she should have come earlier and needs to come again. In this story the healer's behavior demonstrates her own power to diagnose and cure the illness. In return for her healing and protection, the client may give money, objects, or food. This is not necessarily a business, strictly speaking. It may be part of the village economy, in which case the healer would not take money, or only enough to pay his or her expenses (see Paxson 2005, 70). But in many cases clients come from other villages, and they bring money, often at rates set by the healer. Healing can be expensive: Valentina shared that she had paid 1,000 rubles (3 December 2004).

Just as the power of sorcery is said to be passed from generation to generation, so healers can diagnose and heal rifts inherited through generations. Anthropologist Galina Lindquist, who has studied the healing phenomenon in a city context in post-Soviet Russia, points out that the healer offers his or her clients a cultural or personal narrative (what we call a plot): "What is offered to a patient is his or her personal mythology, embracing several generations of kin, and spelled out in shared terms" (Linquist 2006, 72). That is, the healer will often diagnose a curse as originating in earlier generations of one's family. Thus, the offered plot takes into account both the person as an individual and his or her relation to a social network, a community. The mending takes place when the healer is able to offer a new script, to remove the "terms of affliction" from "the patient's horizon of possibilities" (Lindquist 2006, 72). That is, through her narration, the practitioner makes evident, transforms, and lifts the spell.

As our stories in the next section show, the dividing line between healers and sorcerers is not a clean one. Sorcerers can heal, and healers can perform harmful magic (sometimes inadvertently). As the community reorganizes around an incident of misfortune, the balance of power can shift in one direction or another. Rather than moral battles of good versus evil, stories of sorcery are about shifting social hierarchies and alliances.

Scripts, Plots, and Gossip: How Storytelling Reorganizes Communities

Within the network of sorcery, the main powers are attributed to those who put on spells and those who heal. Additionally, there are people who "see and know" who is a witch and those who spread this information and accuse sorcerers. These may be the same person, or the two functions may be separated, but in both cases these persons hold and create their own power. "The church attendant [*psalomshchitsa*], she knows everyone who's a sorcerer. She sees them all" (Tatiana Vasilevna M., born in 1939, Krasnoe, Riazan' oblast, 4 May 2005). In this case, there is a hint that the church attendant has exceptional knowledge because of her special role in the church and/or her ability to use prayers to protect and heal. Even for people who have no unusual knowledge or ability to heal, to know who is a sorcerer is a kind of power, as Valentina phrases it: "We have a lot of *kolduny*, Laura! A lot. But we know them."

How do people learn to "know" who is a sorcerer? As village women explain it, they make judgments based upon the presumption of inheritance and also the recognition of cause and effect. An illness or misfortune occurs, and they suspect the most likely person they saw close to when the illness set in, based upon a common cultural plot. As we saw with the evil eye, this investigation of cause and effect involves application of a script that says in effect: "If a sudden illness occurs, the cause will be a person who fits a certain description, who had contact with you before the illness occurred." We explore the nature of that "certain description" in more detail below; it involves social power, special ability, success or lack thereof, and otherness. This script is taught via the plots offered in rumor and gossip (many of what we are calling gossip stories would be categorized by folklorists as memorates). Katerina Mikhailovna T., born in 1936, who worked as the local postal carrier in Krasnoe for many years, recounted how she learned to apply the script through the comments of a woman. The story concerns a local woman named Prosa, who was rumored to be a witch:

> Once I was bringing the mail. One old woman [Prosa] lived here. And I was walking, and she took me by the hands, said, "Oh! Your hands are so cold" and touched my hands. And a woman coming toward us comes and says [*laughs*], "Why did you give her your hand to hold! She's a *koldun'ia*." I say, yeah right, *koldun'ia*! And what do you know, the next day I got a lump right here. I couldn't do anything, it happened to be hay-mowing time, I couldn't do anything, I just sat. And then she came begging, going from house to house. She came, and I was sitting like this. I couldn't walk, I was sitting. She—"Why are you sitting?" I said, "Why am I sitting? I've got a *tararyk*!" [*Laughs*] That's what we called it. A kind of sore. They had put me here at the doorstep, crammed me with ointment. And she came and said, "Give me some oil." I gave her a cup of oil, she read [prayers] over it, and my lump burst. And I could walk again. (24 April 2005)

As Katerina made clear in her answers to our questions after the story, she allowed Prosa to treat her because she did not initially believe what the other woman told her about her being a sorcerer. Yet to Katerina, the suggestion that Prosa was a witch, plus Prosa's behavior and the fact that the lump both appeared and disappeared suddenly, confirmed the diagnosis. When I asked why Prosa may have wanted to both harm and heal her, Katerina said, "Well, there comes a moment. Maybe she didn't even want to do it." Others explained similar gestures from *kolduny* as relating to their fear of even higher powers: "Maybe she fears God after all" (Tatiana Vasilevna M., born in 1939, Krasnoe, Riazan' oblast, 4 May 2005).

Rumor and gossip not only accuse individuals but they also teach means of interpretation through the repeated nature of their plots and scripts, which people then apply to their own lives. Gossip, which we defined in chapter 4 as unverified stories about the personal affairs and reputations of others, is a subset of rumor, an unsubstantiated message on any topic.[9] Allport and Postman's 1947 study, *Psychology of Rumor*, suggests that exaggeration plays a large role in gossip and rumor. As rumors travel, they grow shorter and details are omitted. The kinds of changes that are made in rumor are not simply lapses in memory but are linked with the emotional significance of the statement to the speaker. Exaggeration best serves these ends: "The point of any rumor is to convey a unified impression of something deemed important. How better to convey this impression than through the rhetorical device of hyperbole? If a man is attacked by a vicious person, why not say that he is attacked by a maniac?" (1947, 75). In this case, Prosa was likely already known as a healer (i.e., she herself chose that profession in order to subsist). But, due to their fears about her ability and the powers it might entail, people exaggerated what they had heard about her and applied to her the label (and by implication, the plot) of a *koldun'ia*. What Katerina heard from the woman she met on the street was a rumor (Prosa is a sorcerer) together with an interpretation and warning (you should not have let her touch your hands), and it formed the basis for Katerina's later gossip (using a common plot) with others (including folklorists) about Prosa and other local *kolduny*.

Does gossip divide communities or unite them? The work of Max Gluckman (1963) argues that gossip facilitates the unity of the group by reinforcing norms, controlling individuals' behavior, and helping to choose leaders. By contrast, Robert Paine (1967) sees gossip as the discourse of individuals seeking to advance their own status. When speakers denigrate others, they forward their own interests. According to Paine, gossip is a mechanism for social change (Stewart and Strathern 2004, 37). In this example and others, we see elements of both theories. Telling a rumor does further an individual's interests in the sense that the speaker positions herself as an authority. Also, although we have no proof of that in this case, in telling rumors or gossiping an individual may do harm to a rival—for example, may discredit or depose an informal social leader—and therefore enable him- or herself to rise in social standing.

Gluckman's point about unity also holds true here: people in a given social group may feel greater cohesion when they create and regularly perform a discourse that excludes others. In this case, the reason for exclusion is clear: Prosa is a beggar, probably a widowed old woman who does not have relatives willing to support her. From the point of view of the members of the mainstream society, she is lowly and Other, and one of the ways that the group excludes her is by calling her a witch behind her back. It is important here to note a difference between what the discourse says and what is does. It speaks of (and may thereby create) a rupture in the fabric of social cohesion, but in doing so, it produces greater cohesion. Here, the story induces social cohesion not only through a verbal act of exclusion ("Why did you give her your hand to hold!"), which binds together those who exclude, but also through a rapprochement with the liminal figure herself (when Prosa heals the lump). As we mentioned above, asking the very person who put on the spell to take it off is seen as a powerful means of solving physical ailments, and it also heals social rifts in the process. When the accused witch and the assumed victim engage in a healing ritual (successfully, as here, and below in Valentina's story of the sorcerer Kurepyi), the sorcerer as liminal figure is symbolically/ritually re-incorporated into the community network of exchange.

It is important to note that these healing and harming rituals and the gossip about them are conducted privately. The discourse of rumor and gossip creates an atmosphere of secrecy. In this case the gossipers were not afraid to name names, because Prosa is dead. In the course of our conversation, they were more reluctant to name those who were still alive. Secrecy also creates the feeling of group cohesion, because only the initiated have access to the information. Many of our conversations about sorcery were accompanied by admonitions not to retell the secrets being imparted to us. As we have said, there is also the strong sense that behavior associated with sorcery is coded. One must know how to properly interpret gestures, glances, offers, and utterances in order to protect oneself in an interaction with suspected *kolduny*. In the social sphere, everything is symbolic, potent. Since the private speech of sorcery entails secrecy, lies, and coding, to be included in the conversation for the first time (as, for example, in Katerina's story) involves a kind of initiation, a step toward inclusion in the community of those who know about sorcery. This community has its own internal hierarchy of elders and younger members.

An example of a person who gains authority in the community due to her knowledge of and narration about sorcery is our main informant in Krasnoe, Valentina Sergeevna G. A vibrant woman with a sense of humor, Valentina was loved and respected by many in the community. She was trained and worked for many years as a midwife and nurse practitioner, which meant that she was on call at all hours, making house calls to patients on foot. As Valentina tells it, her life story is structured by relationships of harmful magic.

Widowed in the early 1980s, she neither remarried nor declined in strength and activity but told many stories about her husband that made him seem an ideal spouse: always protective and loyal, always admiring and praising her. In her stories and in the accounts of relatives she, too, was protective and loyal: when he took ill (diagnosed as heart disease, but she says he was killed by a witch), she did not let him lift a finger, even if she herself was not feeling well; and she "ripped the cigarettes out of his mouth." Then, in 2004, her daughter's death of lung cancer dealt Valentina a serious emotional blow. The daughter, Olga, had worked as a surgical nurse in Siberia. According to Valentina, Olga had recently been promoted, and a different nurse was passed over. That nurse put a spell on Olga and she took ill. Olga returned home to her mother and together they consulted a local healer, but treatment was ineffective, and Olga died. Valentina's niece told me that in fact doctors had wanted to operate on Olga, but she had chosen to pursue alternative healing first. When she returned to the doctors later on, they told her it was too late. I (LO) found this story striking because not only Valentina but her daughter, too, a surgical nurse, so strongly believed in folk medicine that she did not seek (or delayed) medical treatment.

While Valentina's stories of her courtship and marriage (examined in chapter 3) were not melodramatic, her stories of family tragedy caused by witchcraft are distinctly in the melodramatic mode: their themes are crises, ruptures, crime, betrayal, and villainy. In these stories Valentina plays the victim; this is the common plot of narratives about witchcraft. As Khristoforova puts it, "stories about sorcery are primarily a victim's discourse, which usually do not interpret harm caused by sorcery in terms of a contest of equal rivals" (2008, 372). Yet Valentina also constructs herself as a powerful player in the world of dangerous magic. "I was still stupid then," she says, referring to her lack of knowledge at the time when her husband died, in 1983. At that time, she did not know all the sorcerers in the village, and did not know from whom to seek healing. She tells a long story about how she intended to seek healing for her husband from one *babka* who was recommended to her but was deterred by having to find the healer's apartment in an unfamiliar village. With its questing form and strange turns of events and obstacles, this narrative sounds a bit like a magic (fairy) tale, with the significant exceptions that it is a heroine, not an animal helper, seeking the waters of life to heal her wounded prince, and she fails to find what she seeks—melodramatic stories, unlike fairy tales, end in tragedy. But that was before. Now, in 2004–5, Valentina could list all the sorcerers, and had visited several healers in the area—in that sense, she too "knew," and had reached a higher level of power in the social hierarchy.

We suspected she was a main source of stories about sorcerers in the village: I (LO) heard her stories from her in multiple versions in the context of one-to-one conversations over the years I visited her (1995, 1999, 2004, 2005), and witnessed her telling such stories to others in her close circle of friends. Her stories were the most vibrant, detailed, compelling, and personal of all the stories about sorcery we heard in Krasnoe. Clearly, the stories and their telling were an important part of Valentina's life-world. Because the stories revolved around social alliances and battles between rivals and groups, they not only narrated but also constructed social arrangements.

As narrator, Valentina performs her own social power, which resides in her knowing who is who and watching their movements carefully, being able to interpret the slightest gesture or physical position as a potential threat. In a sense, her strength partly lies in her distrust. Besides her power as a narrator, Valentina's social capital also resides in the services she is able to offer within the village informal gift economy. As described by Margaret Paxson (2005), in Russian village social networks a principal means of establishing and maintaining social connection is through informal, spontaneous gifting of services and homemade goods. Because Valentina is a nurse practitioner (a *fel'dsher*), she is needed by the sorcerers when they are sick. Further, her ability to tell who is a sorcerer is linked with her profession, since she is near the suspected sorcerers when they die. According to Russian lore, a sorcerer must give up his or her knowledge before he or she can die. Therefore, Valentina claims eyewitness authority when she tells stories about dying sorcerers trying to pass on their ability to her through touch, or times when she witnessed family members hovering near dying sorcerers (presumably to receive their knowledge). And finally, Valentina makes moonshine, *samogon*.[10] Before 1992, domestic alcohol production was illegal but at times was a widespread practice, especially during periods when the authorities tried to limit the purchase of legal alcohol, such as 1985–88, when the following story takes place (Zaigraev 2004, 30–31). During such periods of government-controlled temperance, those who drank regularly had to rely on the liquor produced in the village. In general, in the village economy, services associated with magic (such as healing) can be compensated with liquor. The following story demonstrates Valentina's power with regard to sorcery; it also provides excellent illustration of how sorcery reorganizes social groups in the community.

Valentina Sergeevna recounted how, in 1986, at the wedding of her niece, a local woman who is related to them through her husband told Valentina that she wasn't feeling well. Valentina took the woman to her home, gave her some drops, told her to lie down and rest, and left her to go back to the festivities. And there in the room were hanging Valentina's son's clothes. When the son, Kolya, left to go home—he lived in Siberia—he did not feel well. He subsequently remained ill and lost weight. On his next visit to his mother's home, he asked to go to the hospital in the city. The X-ray showed that there was some darkening in his lungs. "And no doctor can cure that. Except for a *koldun*."

And he became skinny, sickly. Kurepyi came to my house, Deriaba's colleague in sorcery. They do it on clothing, not just by touching you, but if your clothing is hanging, they'll do it on your clothing. He came and said, "Sergeevna, give me 100 grams [of *samogon*]." I said, "You know what? Heal my son." "Why heal him? He's all down, he's not good!" I say, "Heal him," I say, "isn't it enough you [pl.] took my husband, at least leave me my son." OK. He [Kurepyi] is sitting there on the steps. Sitting. "Give me water. In a half-liter bottle." I gave him a half-liter bottle, he read over the water, and said, "Put this somewhere where no one will drink it." OK, good. "And that night, when he goes to sleep, let him drink it." [*Laughs*] We laid the table, and I said, "Kolya, drink this, drink. Drink it," I said, "it's holy water." Otherwise he might not have drunk it.

The next morning, Kolya had to drive to a nearby town, and he couldn't; he was too weak. "It's dark before my eyes, I have no strength. I can't get to Kasimov, can't get anywhere." The family sought a driver from the neighbors, and they set out. On the road, they had to stop the car three times for Kolya to go into the forest. He had bloody diarrhea.[11] He went to the hospital, got his heart checked out, and everything was fine with his heart. He felt better, said he could drive, and drove all the way back.

And the *kolduny* are already sitting, Vrotikha and Sakhanishka [two suspected female sorcerers] are sitting by the Kotovy's storage shed, on the bench, waiting to see who will be driving the car. Yura drove on the way out; who's going to be driving on the way back? When we drove up, they got up to look at the road. And Kolya gets out on the left side, and Yura on the right [i.e., Kolya was driving]. For that they [the female sorcerers] gave Kurepyi a hard time. "You so-and-so, why did you go and—why did you go and heal him?" And he [Kurepyi] had told me, if anyone's cow is sick, or even you, if a person is healed [by a healer], if you see even a little bit of blood, it means the person is better. "Why did you go and heal him! You should have let him die!" Sakhanishka said that. Aha. So they cursed him out, and the next day he comes to me. "Sergeevna, let me do it again. Give me an egg, I'll read over an egg, and then he'll be fine." I gave him an egg, he read. [But] 'and then he'll be fine'—that means he's not well again. He [Kurepyi] came out, and I [threw] that egg way out there in the garden.

Aaaa! [*Laughs*] *Weren't you afraid to touch the egg?*

Well, I didn't eat it. That would be [a problem only] if he drank it. A raw egg. But I threw it out. That's it. They cursed him out. They are like that: if anyone heals someone, they curse him out.

But why did you trust him?

Him? I asked him, asked, [said] please.

But why did you trust him, did you think he would not do anything bad?

He would do good.

Why did you think so?

I don't know why. If you tell me tomorrow, if everything's well will you bring [i.e., give something], I'll bring it. I'll bring it if they say he'll be fine. I'll bring [it]. And he did do good. (3 December 2004)

In this story Valentina's *samogon* functions as an important bargaining chip in the village economy. The sorcerer, Kurepyi, comes to her for *samogon* and she is able to convince him to reverse the spell put on by another sorcerer. Effectively she trades vodka for healing, but there is a hint that in this trade she holds more power since she could withhold liquor. To Valentina's mind, Kurepyi's healing must cause friction in the sorcery community: a script attributed to sorcerers requires that they cooperate and work together—incidentally, just as in the ethic of the community at large. Any sorcerer's work is not to be undone by another. The fact that she subsequently sees two other sorcerers on the street apparently paying attention to who gets out of what side of the car (i.e., whether Kolya is healed) gives Valentina proof for her supposition that Kurepyi will be reprimanded. Following this logic, if Kurepyi is given a hard time by the other sorcerers, then he will try to undo the healing. For this reason, although she trusts him the first time (and trusts his diagnosis that if blood comes out of the body, it means the person is healed), she does not trust him when he offers to continue the healing. She is triumphant when she tells how she threw the egg into the yard. Just as the sorcerers "know," she also knew not to trust Kurepyi the second time.

The story imputes jealousy to the suspected witches who supposedly survey the surrounding social terrain for inequality. For the suspected witches, the health and general well-being of Valentina's son suggests he needs to be put down (made ill). For Valentina, the drama of the story revolves around whether her social power is enough to cultivate Kurepyi's loyalty. Will he side with the female sorcerers, who presumably placed the original spell or approved of and/or ordered its placement, or will he side with Valentina, the local *samogon* producer? Here Kurepyi tries to please both sides, and plays the role of a trickster figure who plays one side off the other. Valentina's social vision is one of competition, self-interest, and social masks.

Gender

Gender also plays a role in Valentina's story. The women sorcerers are powerful forces, with whom one (presumably) cannot trade *samogon* for healing, and in any case women are not known for excessive drinking (Denisova 2010, 119). In our acquaintance with her, Valentina told no stories about approaching women female sorcerers for healing and bargaining with them: more often, she expressed how afraid she was of them. The only women magicians Valentina approaches for healing are *babki*, whom she seeks out specifically for their skill. In the story of Kolya's illness, the female *koldun'i* work together and stand behind the scenes, controlling the players as if they were pawns on a chessboard. In Valentina's life story, the *koldun'i* have been attacking husbands and children, killing them to cause the surviving women pain.[12] She says, "If people live better than them, they try to destroy them."

That is, *porcha*, like the evil eye, performs an action of social leveling. The discourse has moral thrust: by giving us the example of suspected sorcerers, it warns us not to be competitive (not to be like these sorcerers); by giving us the example of victims, it warns us not to deviate from the norm (not to attract the attention of sorcerers).

In this arena a woman's capacity for open conflict—as healer, sorcerer, or gossip—is valued as social capital (authority or *bol'shina*) and guarantees her power. Ideally, it is this quality that a woman should have achieved during her apprenticeship under the patronage of a *bol'shukha*. That is to say, as we pointed out in the previous chapter, ideally a woman learns from her *bol'shukha* mother-in-law to position herself in the social realm as a powerful actor with supernatural patronage—or, as we have described here, with her tongue as her weapon.

The Social Network of Sorcery

Given that the gossip of sorcery revolved around the attribution of misfortune to a social cause, we were interested in exploring these constructed social networks. This turned out to be difficult: we could not get hold of many of the alleged sorcerers (they had died or moved away) and so we could not generalize about them en masse. Nonetheless, we talked to two presumed *koldun'i* who feature prominently in Valentina's stories. In this way, we could investigate relationships and form a picture of the social network involving sorcery. Indeed, one of the ways that social networks are imagined in the culture of Krasnoe village is through the lens of sorcery.

Coincidentally or not, the two suspected sorcerers we interviewed were singers, like Valentina, and like me (LO). Conversations about singing helped break the ice in the field-work situation and formed a basis for common interest. One of the women, Aleksandra Pavlovna A. (born in 1941), nicknamed Vrotikha, sang in the same group as Valentina, and occasionally sang the same special part for which Valentina was famed (the high *podgolo-sok*, which in their village is traditionally sung by only one person). Valentina recounted many stories in which she was purposely made hoarse by Aleksandra or her mother, so that Aleksandra could sing the high part at a special recording session or concert in another village. Clearly, this was a relationship marred by a kind of professional jealousy.

The other woman, Tatiana Vasilevna M. (born in 1939), nicknamed Deriaba, did not feature in any of Valentina's stories about singing, but her own story indicated there may have been an area of jealousy there. When speaking about her participation in a local cho-rus, Tatiana was very self-assured and not at all modest. She said that in her singing "every-thing I did came out well," and that "everything [with regard to the chorus] fell apart" after she left the village in 1981. Like Aleksandra, in the chorus she sang mostly Soviet songs, and was active in performing at neighboring village celebrations. Tatiana had stopped singing after the death of her husband in 1987, so Valentina could not claim any recent situations of rivalry for vocal parts with her. Nonetheless, jealousy over vocal parts and performance opportunities could have been established earlier.

In the fieldwork situation, I (LO) made the judgment that it was not possible to tell Aleksandra and Tatiana that others had accused them of being *koldun'i*. Such an accusation would likely not only have offended the women but also would have endangered Valentina's relationships with them. Valentina herself purposely maintained cordial relationships with them, although she did not want to invite them to her house, for example. She avoided talking openly with them about any matters of sorcery. When she talked about these sorcerers with me, she became very fearful that I would somehow leak to them what she told me. For this reason, the names of the participants in these stories and the name of the village have been changed.

Although I (LO) did not accuse these women of being witches, in my conversations with them I became acquainted with their life stories and raised the topic of sorcery with them. Their life stories were not overtly similar. Aleksandra worked for twenty years as a forewoman of tractors and field hands (*brigadir traktorno-polevodcheskoi brigady*) in the sovkhoz. She had to manage the workers, give them orders, and assess their performance. She had to answer for the fuel used, and so on. There were two people filling such a position in the sovkhoz, and when her counterpart took ill and left the job, she took over as forewoman for the entire huge farming area. Her work days lasted from 7:30 a.m. until 9 p.m. When I commented that it must have been difficult for her as a woman to be a supervisor (of male workers), she said, "I'm not bragging, but I want to say this: they obeyed me. . . . I myself assessed what they did and set their salary. Everything, it was all part of my [responsibility]. They obeyed, they listened." She pointed out that she won several contests for how quickly and well her brigade could fulfill its plan, and had received a few awards. Thus, although in private, post-Soviet contexts Aleksandra is accused of being a powerful sorcerer (who took knowledge from her mother), in the Soviet official context she was an authoritative supervisor who took her authority from the sovkhoz administration. She said she had not had any special training to reach this position—but in fact, she had eleven years of education, which was more than many women of her generation possessed. She attributed her success to her inborn wit or *smekalka*. In addition, she said she had a good head for math and understood tractors well enough to know if the drivers were fooling her when they said their machine was broken.

If Valentina's stories of sorcery are about social relations involving power and skill, Aleksandra's story of her work life likewise involves a discourse of power (control over others), success, and skill. She emphasizes the fact of her control over others, repeating "they listened/obeyed" (*slushalis'*) and its synonym "they submitted/obeyed" (*podchinialis'*) four times during her account. The social or institutional power performed by a person might in part account for the suspicion of sorcery. The logic would be: if he or she performs power in one area of life, might he or she not hold sway in the sphere of ultimate power, the area of connection of this world and the other world? Or, put another way: if I am afraid of this person's ability to affect my life in one context, might/should I not be similarly afraid in another context? As Khristoforova writes: "Attributing to a person the ability to perform sorcery not only marks him or her as 'other' [*chuzhoi*] but also demonstrates the fear and respect with which people view him or her" (2008, 374).

Aleksandra's success might also be a reason for others to attribute sorcery to her. While jealousy is often believed to be a cause of the evil eye and of sorcery, the reverse is true as well: people suspect sorcery of those of whom they are (unconsciously) jealous (Il'ina and Toporkov 2006, 445). The village economy and moral system punish those who stand above the crowd. One must not brag or show off one's wealth; to do so invites catastrophe (Paxson 2005, 72–73). Aleksandra twice emphasizes that she is "not bragging," but she does praise herself, mentioning her power, ability, hard work, dedication, and awards. If she were also to praise herself in conversations with local, older women, might those women not suspect that she must have acquired her good fortune in dishonest, unnatural ways? The situation represents a clash and coexistence of values: older village values emphasize community good (Paxson 2005), while newer values seek to maximize good for the individual. In her modest disclaimer, Aleksandra clearly recognizes and gives voice to the older community-oriented value system, yet she was brought up in the Soviet era and clearly bought into the Soviet hierarchical system that, paradoxically, encouraged personal competition and rewarded individuals (as in the Stakhanov program).

As we pointed out in the introductory paragraphs of this chapter, due to economic relations that were formed over centuries, peasant society evolved a collectivist mentality or "cluster psychology," which was designed to compel adherence to socially dictated norms. Cluster structures are self-regulating, and carefully keep (and sometimes even conceal) their inner workings from interference from above (Prokhorov 2002, 83). One of the goals of the inner workings of peasant society is to maintain homeostasis through control of innovative forms of behavior. Rumors and gossip further this goal by accusing members of the society of possessing and using magical powers.

People in Russian village society may react in two different ways to innovative behavior. One way involves imitation of the individual behavior, while the other involves exclusion of this behavior. In the case of imitation, the initiator is assigned the status of a leader, "one who knows." We can illustrate this with one example. On a hot day, my colleagues and I (SA) went down to a river outside of a village. When we returned half an hour later, we found the formerly empty and quiet village full of activity. In all the gardens the families were digging up onions: they pulled them, cleaned them off, and put them in bunches, took them back to their houses, and so on. I started to ask the owner of the house where we were staying about this anomalously synchronic activity. What was the reason for such a collective explosion of activity? Was it some special day for pulling onions? Why did the whole village, without agreeing beforehand, start to do the same thing at the same time? The explanation was simple. One of the neighbors, whom everyone keeps their eye on, started to harvest his onions. And since he started to do it, he must have some information about it. The script seemed to be as follows: he wouldn't be doing it for no reason at all; it must mean that he *knows* something. And once several families had embraced the action, then the spirit of collectivism brought the rest along. After this and several other similar stories, I came to understand the mechanism by which magic knowledge in agriculture is attributed to a specific person—a phenomenon often described in ethnographic literature. The elders, who knew when to begin sowing, when to harvest, and so on, were people who displayed individual initiative. Such initiative was then interpreted by society as evidence of magic powers. These powers were understood as the result of contact with a spiritual force (as many told us, "those who know, know each other" [*znaiushchie—znaiutsia*]). In this case the society observes an action, and using their observations, does the same: "It used to be the *polevoi khoziain* [spirit of the fields] would truly help, would tell the person who managed that field. He gave him wisdom [*um*], what to do, what to sow. The old people used to know on what days, what months to sow what. There were special days, ones for rye, ones for wheat" (woman born in 1922, Ukhtoma, Vashkinskii region, Vologda oblast, 12 July 2000 [Vash 20a-3]).

Here is another example of the curious events showing how someone's initiative works to change behavior. Once our interlocutor, a man, suddenly announced, looking out the window, that "the mushrooms had sprouted." We tried to find out how he knew—were there natural signs, such as sun, clouds, birds, that helped him to make that judgment? He answered that he had just seen his neighbor walk into the woods with a basket. And he knows. The script, the reputation of "one who knows," is to a large extent formed based upon a person's persistent ability to behave with initiative, that is, to realize one's individual potential, to have one's own opinion and express it, and to carry out one's own plans.

Another way that society can react to a person who shows initiative is to exclude that person, attributing their fear of him to a plot in which he commits *porcha* due to "envy." *Porcha* in this sense may be characterized as a form of social repression. The community represses that which is "different" in any sense whatsoever: difference itself is taken as a kind of transgression. A person who is capable of individual behavior appears unsusceptible to *porcha*, and this is interpreted by society—through rumors and gossip—as proof that he or she possesses magic knowledge and powers. If a person allows him- or herself to do that which others do not do—for example, to keep bees, to keep cows of a rare breed, or to engage in handicrafts by him- or herself, this must mean that he or she is a *koldun* or *koldun'ia*. Many times we noticed that someone who had a reputation as a witch also engaged in some sort of independent activity.

Sorcery and Religion

In the case of Tatiana, one suspected sorcerer we talked to in Krasnoe, the independent activity or thinking might have been related to her Christian religious practice. I (LO) noticed that she performed the role of unofficial religious leader in a curious village situation I observed in spring 2005. I had arrived in the village with the intent of observing and participating in one life-cycle ritual—a memorial at the one-year anniversary of Valentina's daughter's death—and two spring rituals: Easter and a local spring holiday that occurs the week after Easter, which the locals describe as "we go around the village" (*obkhodim derevniu*). As soon as I arrived in the village, I began inquiring about the time when the circumambulation would occur. Women had different theories, which they attributed to two local authorities, one of whom was Tatiana, and the other of whom was Antonina Ivanovna Ch. Both were women in their sixties and seventies who locally perform the function of "reading [prayers] over the dead" (*chitaiut po upokoinikam*). I talked to Antonina and she said that the event would take place on Thursday. Given these plans, I traveled to a neighboring village on Tuesday and returned Wednesday, supposedly in plenty of time to join the procession on Thursday. When I returned my hostess told me that I had just missed the event. I was not able to find out why the event was apparently moved until I visited Tatiana, the reputed witch, who told me that because this year Blagoveshchenie (the Annunciation, a holiday in early April) fell on a Thursday, for the whole year one should not do "hard work" or carry things on Thursdays. Therefore, one could not carry icons around the village on this day, as the circumambulation required. She discounted the other theory I had heard—that it had to be Tuesday or Thursday because Wednesday and Friday are "dry days" or semi-fasting days. She pointed out that, since Easter marks the end of the greatest Russian fast, for the whole week after Easter there are no fasting days. In explaining these issues to me, she was very articulate and self-confident. Indeed, she explained them better than anyone in the village had been able to.

Tatiana's self-assured demeanor and her reputation as a witch can be explained by her biography. Tatiana lived and worked for twenty-four years in the regional center, Kasimov, in a bread factory. She says she remained a village woman at heart, visiting her mother in Krasnoe on weekends and just returning to the city to work. After she retired in 1994, she fulfilled a vow to her late mother—she had died in 1992—and moved back to the village with her second husband, whom she described as a city person. Despite calling herself a village person, Tatiana had become citified. At any rate, her living in the city for twenty-four years probably made local, elder women view her as other, which likely contributed to the suspicion of her being a witch. In fact, had she maintained more distant ties with the village, like many children did—returning only a few times a year, especially in summer, to help with the household farm, she might have avoided suspicion, but her status as someone who came and went—as a mediator between city and village—may have made people feel uncomfortable, as if she was trying to bring her city savvy to bear in the world of the village—and, potentially, her city money to the village economy.[13]

A further dimension of Tatiana's local status is her power—of knowledge and of persuasion—in the spiritual realm. Her convincing performance of detailed knowledge of Church matters could be one reason why she is called a powerful witch, someone who

"knows." To an outsider, this might seem counterintuitive, because one might assume that
an apparently religious person who knew Church matters would be above suspicion for
black magic.[14] Indeed, Tatiana not only reads prayers for funerals but also sings in church,
as did her mother; her mother was the church's head financial auditor. But in fact, the lines
between harmful and helpful magic and between Christian and secular contexts for magic
are blurred in the Russian case, both historically and in the post-Soviet period. As we saw
above, a sorcerer who can cast spells can also take off spells and heal. Furthermore, the
healing often involves prayers to Christian figures. Thus, if people thought that Tatiana
had extraordinary knowledge of the Christian spiritual realm, they might assume that she
could manipulate spirits both for good and for evil. She had distinguished herself and was
"other," and these two circumstances would be enough to cause suspicions of her power.

There has long been scholarly disagreement over whether sorcery is the devil's work or
involves appealing to non-Christian spirits (Ivanits 1989, 94–95). Folk incantations for
healing often invoke Christian spirits, even God; they may appear to take the form of
prayers, but they are not Church-sanctioned texts. Our point of view is that these are apocryphal texts that comprised part of the rich tradition of folk Orthodoxy in Russia (Heretz
2008, 22; Levin 1993). As part of this rich folk tradition, sorcery is indeed associated with
Satan: countless legends in nineteenth-century and later collections recount a sorcerer's
initiation into the art as involving a pact with the devil. While we heard no such stories in
Krasnoe, we did hear *kolduny* referred to as "Satans," as in "She's a perfect Satan!" (*Ona
Satana khoroshaia!*). Whether scholars accept its philosophical depth or not, the discourse
of sorcery does involve Christian terms.

In addition, the means of healing always involve Christian symbols. Valentina describes
how the *babka* reads prayers over water for healing: "She has an iron cross, stones, and a
prayer book, and something else, and she stands there, and the water's there, and she reads
over it, and asks your name." Lindquist too notes that "prayer books, candlesticks and
Russian Orthodox icons were always plentiful in magi's working rooms" (Lindquist 2006,
74). She attributes the post-Soviet healers' need to rely on Church symbols to the post-
communist condition. Serguei Oushakine identifies the common experience of Russians,
after the fall of the Soviet Union, as lacking a symbolic language adequate to express their
subjectivity. In this context people search for signifiers and find them in such cultural fields
as the Russian Orthodox Church (Lindquist 2006, 74–75; Oushakine 2000, 1005, 1010).
Here we must distinguish mainstream city culture from rural culture, and elders from
the young people on whom Oushakine bases his research. In the post-Soviet period, elder
villagers have not been affected by a deficiency of symbolic language in the way Oushakine
and Lindquist describe. To a great extent, their sense of self and their behavior are condi-
tioned by habits and dispositions that took root both before and during the Soviet period,
although their belief system and its manifestations were modified by Soviet atheistic pressure. Thus, we see their subjectivity configured in terms of Soviet categories as well as their

negotiations with such categories. When elder villagers embrace Christianity, it is not an empty signifier, because Christian symbols continued to have important meaning for them and for the community throughout the Soviet period. Nonetheless, in the post-Soviet period village dwellers have experienced both an intensification of the need for a language to express the religious sphere and the freedom to physically access and, hence, to reappropriate such a symbolic world for their personal use.

All of the players in these dramas of local power—women in their sixties, seventies, and eighties at the time—are believers and to varying extents wish to present or imagine themselves as holy, spiritual, and/or knowledgeable about spiritual matters. For some of these women—Valentina, for example—the need to be recognized publicly as spiritual is apparent. If reappropriating the world of symbolic Christianity is important to one's self-concept, then to call someone else a "Satan" is to exclude that person from one's community, to state categorically that this person is not only unholy but anti-holy. This rhetorical action has much to say, then, about the speaker's own identity as a spiritual, Christian person. However, as we will show in chapter 9, the definition of what it means to be Christian and spiritual is not identical with what official Christianity prescribes.

In a further illustration of the apocryphal, folk-Orthodox nature of discourse about sorcery in Russian villages, let us look at a story told by Tatiana that emphasized her powerlessness in the face of sorcerers within the physical church. The conversation began with my (LO's) questions about sorcerers and healers. Tatiana told me healers can experience bad effects from their activity—as if, in cleaning up the evil left by the *kolduny*, they absorb some of that evil. The *kolduny*, by contrast, do not have bad effects.

> *But they can't be happy people.*
> No, they aren't. They do such bad stuff to people, in terms of God that's an unpardonable sin. It's an unpardonable sin.
> *An unpardonable sin.*
> Yes. Two years ago, on Great Thursday—Great Thursday, before Easter, we were in the church. We were in the church, I also help at the choir gallery . . . I sing there . . . And I came up there, to the choir gallery, and Auntie Zoia Kazeeva, who sings there, she took ill, and Praskovia Mikhailovna [the parish clerk] called me over, and "Tatiana," she says, "go," she says, "and kick out that woman." And I say, "Which?" and she says, "That one over there, Lid'ka." I say, "Why?" She said, "Zoia was with her, and now she's sick." I say, "I'm not going to kick her out. Do you know why? She's a witch." I say, "[Since] you know she's a witch, [why don't] you go and ask her to leave God's temple. But who am I? How did you figure that I'd go tell her to leave the church? I can't do that." Aha. And I asked, I say, "Praskovia Mikhailovna, if you are in God's temple, the twelve apostles and a service and all that, and if you spoke about that—". . . And she [touches] me three times on the

shoulder: "Tatiana, she knows, she knows, she knows! Be afraid." She was standing right across from me. But what is this "be afraid," how is it "be afraid"—if something would take over her, I'd just leave . . .

So that was Lida . . .

Yes, Lida Shuvalova, it's—Auntie Zoia who reads prayers on the choir gallery, it's her matchmaker [*svakha*]. Her son married her [Lida's] daughter.

So Praskovia thinks that Lida knows.

Well, she doesn't think, but everyone *knows* that she knows.

Aha.

Everyone knows that she knows.

[. . .]

But why didn't Parakha [Praskovia Mikhailovna] go up to her herself?

Yes, I said, I say, Mikhailovna, you know, you go up to her. She's afraid of getting enemies, she's afraid. What if it should come back on her?

But she should be afraid least of anyone, since she has, sort of, God's force— Mikhailovna? Yes, yes, she does. . . . But she's afraid, maybe she knows prayers, but she [also] heals. But she says if *kolduny* are around, you should say the prayers "God is risen" and "Live help." Or copy them on paper and carry them with you, pin them to your clothes or put them in your wallet. You can also buy these little ribbons, these little belts, that have . . . four prayers . . . (4 May 2005)

This story, told by a suspected witch, describes the speaker's lack of power vis-à-vis another suspected witch. She paints herself as afraid, entirely innocent, and unable to confront the sorcerer. Tatiana instead points the finger at the parish clerk, the prosphora-baker—it is she who should remove the suspected witch from God's temple. Tatiana hints, and I know from my interviews with Praskovia Mikhailovna, that she possesses incantations for protection against evil spirits and for healing. To Tatiana's mind, this should make Praskovia powerful, but in Tatiana's story Praskovia, too, is afraid, lest her involvement should make her ill as well. The discourse of sorcery is a discourse of fear. One of the socially acceptable ways to say that one is afraid in these communities is to speak of sorcery. The fear one speaks of may be a spiritual fear vis-à-vis the unknown, for example: "who knows what evil forces there are in the world, and what harm they might do?"; or it may be a social fear, for example: "I am not sure where I stand with this person. Perhaps their power is greater than the ordinary."

That Praskovia Mikhailovna, too, participates in the discourse of sorcery, and that her discourse evokes both the spiritual and social contexts of fear is not entirely surprising. She is a woman from a village twenty kilometers away who devoted herself to religion from an early age but is not a nun. She passed an exam at the Riazan' Diocese that allows her to work in the church, to sing, lead prayers, and to go behind the church altar, which is forbidden for women. She bakes the small ceremonial breads offered at the divine liturgy, prosphora (*prosfirki*), and lives in a hut adjacent to the church. More than other women of her generation we interviewed, Praskovia Mikhailovna spoke of her fears and suffering during her life. Nonetheless, she mentioned some skills and strengths. She wrote poetry during bouts of insomnia and shared several of her religious poems. She spoke of teaching other women to read prayers in Church Slavonic, and criticized those who thought they could read such prayers publicly without a prior blessing. Her fears centered around the gossip mill: there were many rumors about her. She shared that she was devastated by a rumor that she had been sleeping with the priest. She did live with him when she first came to the village but did not sleep with him. She was so outraged at the accusation by the woman who sells the candles at the church that she left the village, until Church representatives came and apologized to her.

Praskovia Mikhailovna was conscious of her vulnerability. Separately, I (LO) heard rumors that she was a hermaphrodite and/or a nun. That she, as a woman, could go behind the altar was mentioned by many local women as a sign that she was not truly a woman. In short, Praskovia Mikhailovna was seen as an outsider to the community and as someone who had special privileges and powers. As far as I knew no one accused her of being a sorcerer, but it was widely assumed or known that she could heal. Perhaps because of her history, she herself made sure she was well-protected. She had a handwritten notebook of what she called "prayers" including "Against Insomnia," "Against the Evil Eye," "For Leg Pain," and "Against Sorcerers." The last reads as follows:

Святой угодниче божий,
Священномученник Киприяне
Скорый помощниче в молитвинниче
О всех к тебе прибегающе.
Прими от нас, недостойных, хваленья наша,
И спроси нам у Господу Бога немоща укрепления
В болезнях исцеленья,
Вещай утешения всем и вся полезная в жизни нашей.
Вознеси ко Господу благодатную Богу мощую твою Марию ту
Да отградит нас от падения греховных
Да научит нас истинному покаянию
Да избавит нас от опленения дьявольского,
От всякого действа, духа нечистых.
Избавит нас от обидящих нас
Будь нам крепки поборник,
На враги видимая и невидимая.
В изкушении подашь нам терпения

В час кончини нашея яви нам заступления от истязателей,

Воздушных мытарствах наших

Да водима тобой за [——] с горней усадима

Из-под ног небес царствия

Со всеми святыми славить воспевати

Пресвятого Отца и Сына и Святого Духа

Во веки веков. Аминь.

[God's holy saint, Holy martyr Cyprianus,

Quick helper and intercessor for everyone who comes for protection

Accept from us, unworthy ones, our praise

And ask the Lord God for us

To give strength to our weakness

To heal our sickness

To bring consolation to all

And everything useful to our life.

Exalt to the Lord God your blessed powerful Mary

[And ask God to] protect us from sinful downfalls

To teach us true repentance

To deliver us from the devil's captivity

From every action of the unclean spirits.

To deliver us from those who insult us,

To be our strong advocate

Against visible and invisible enemies.

To give us patience when we are tempted,

In the time of our death to give us intercession from tormentors,

Our heavenly ordeals

[garbled text]

From underneath the heavenly kingdom

With all the saints we sing the glory

Of the most Holy Father and Son and Holy Ghost

For ever and ever. Amen.]

This "prayer" is somewhat different than ordinary incantations in that it contains no folk language or imagery but is entirely composed of religious imagery. It has some Church Slavonic, but parts of it sound more like Russian than Slavonic (perhaps it has been Russianized through oral transmission). It is like a prayer. Nonetheless, it functions as an incantation, and is clearly intended to undo the magic of sorcery. The church's new, young priest helped me obtain Praskovia's notebook—she had lent it to a local female doctor when I visited the village and told them I was seeking folklore. The priest was interested in the "prayers" and asked to hear the one "Against Sorcerers" quoted above, saying he had not heard that one before. After hearing it, the priest lectured Praskovia:

> Auntie, those people believe that they will receive help [from this incantation], and if the help is not from God . . . They [do it] blindly—they blindly believe that they will receive help. And "According to your faith be it done to you." [Matthew 9:29] Whatever you believe in, that's what you will receive. They'll be healed in body, but spiritually their soul will languish. And why? If it was from God, the soul would not languish so. But if you take communion, your soul will take it joyfully, and you'll be peaceful in your soul. But if they whisper over you [i.e., use magic incantations for healing], you might be joyful that everything has gotten better, that your legs feel better, but your soul will languish and not know what to do. (Father Vladimir, Kitovo, 5 December 2004)

In the presence of the priest, when I (LO) questioned whether these were incantations, Praskovia Mikhailovna denied belief in them. But since they were in her handwritten notebook and this notebook was in active use (it had been loaned to someone else), clearly, they were treasured, owned, and likely used by her and others. My guess is that for those who used them, these texts were not just a matter of making their legs feel better. The user's emotional being, too, probably was enhanced by the protection offered by the "prayers." As Lindquist writes, "people use spells because they resonate with their immediate experiences and agendas, and because they package and congeal their own affects and intentions in evocative and poetically expressive ways. Spells are jewels of social poetics, which both endow human passions with a form perfected over centuries and legitimate these passions by stating that they are integral to core cultural patterns of sociality" (2006, 172).

The above prayer against *kolduny* begins by invoking what Lindquist calls "saints of the Russian Orthodox Church . . . They are Intercessors . . . those who defend people, represent their interests before the higher powers, supplicate for them to the mighty, and mediate between these slaves of God and God Himself in case of His wrath" (2006, 189). The position of the supplicant is the opposite: he or she is lowly, weak, sick, vulnerable. The strength of the incantation thus derives from the position of these higher beings "in the cosmological hierarchy of powers" (189). While the priest denies parts of this cosmological hierarchy, the women who are his parishioners embrace it wholeheartedly. When I told Valentina about my encounter with Praskovia Mikhailovna and the priest, she reacted in the following way:

The priest says it's absolutely forbidden [to use such "prayers"].

Forbidden! And what if people do bad things to me, how can it be forbidden? We go [to healers] so that they will help us.

Valentina relies on her own moral sense and is willing to thwart the teachings of a representative of the Church. Transgression against the letter of the religious law is not an issue for her when her safety is in question. Indeed, Valentina tells several other stories in which she saved herself via prayer; we discuss one such story in chapter 8 (she used the prayer "Live Help" to "prevent" the driver of a car from killing her with a wrench for her cash). In her case, what does it mean to be a Christian? Many scholars would classify this example as a case of "dual belief" (*dvoeverie*), a term that researchers have used to describe the Russian folk combination of pagan and Christian elements. Christian sources coined the term in the Middle Ages to criticize the shallowness of Russian peasant Christian worship. This model of a conflict between two religions—in which neither is "properly" observed—is overly simplified. It conflates all types of non-Christian belief, and rests upon unreliable sources (Levin 1993, 36, 37). In fact, in many contexts, including in Russia, Church officials have cultivated or permitted a magical mentality in their parishioners (supporting such phenomena as patron saints, wonderworking springs, images, protective amulets, invocations of agricultural and human fertility, lay and Church-related faith healers), because they realize that belief in the supernatural is an aid to religious fervor (39). For instance, in Russia examples of priests and nuns using magic to heal or conducting exorcisms abound (Glickman 1991, 152; Ryan 1999, 79). A better, more nuanced model is folk religion: all rites and practices give people a sense of the ordering of the world, an explanation of unknown, and a sense of identity (Levin 1993, 40).

Power and Ritual

Sorcery is a discourse of the emotions. To listen to it is to learn much about the emotional state of the speaker and listener, and the collective emotional condition of the group. We have suggested here several reasons why, in Krasnoe and other Russian villages, individuals and groups may have experienced significant fears about survival and status, and have used talk about sorcery as a means of responding to such fears. In some cases, the interactions between sorcerers and ordinary people mirror social dynamics of exclusion and inclusion ("us" versus "them"). In other cases, the interactions (verbal and behavioral) between sorcerers and others, and among ordinary people themselves, are more closely related to an economy of give and take: people exchange healing, power, and/or status. Sorcery is a plot that can be used to give structure to the story of one's own life and the life of the community. And finally, sorcery is a ritual symbolizing conflict, in which individuals restructure their communities in alliances of power.

In traditional narratives about sorcery, many incidences of witchcraft occur during life-cycle and calendar rituals (see, for example, Ivanits 1989, 190–94). Several of the stories we heard took place at weddings or an engagement; others took place at funerals; Tatiana's took place at Great Thursday (before Easter). The stories of ruptures in community cohesion were pegged to other landmarks in personal and community memory. Sorcery is one way to configure the rifts and social reorganizations that occur during life-cycle and calendar rituals, times when, according to Victor Turner, the community comes together in a state of communitas, emphasizing a shared humanity (1969, 174). Such acts of restructuring remind us that rituals are processes in which communitas exists in tension with social distinctions (gender, age status, social hierarchy). Rituals do not resolve social tensions once and for all; communitas may comprise a fleeting moment, and its emotional intensity can provoke different reactions in different people (1969, 128–29). Further, as David Kertzer reminds us, ritual may both redirect hostilities into symbolic form and keep other tensions alive, such as in ritualized fighting, which uses controlled, symbolic violence to provoke or sustain intergroup hostility (1988, 130). Thus, the ritual cycle of sorcery, illness, and healing is a rite of community rift and subsequent aggregation: one might call it a rite of aggression.[15]

Epilogue

Russian ethnography has often been far too invested in showing a "united front" of folk belief that is presumably the same for all inhabitants in a village. By contrast, we argue that diverse archetypal narratives (plots and scripts), based upon various cultural imperatives, exist simultaneously within the community. Even within one village or one generation, not everyone sees his or her life in terms of battles with sorcerers. Some women that we talked to explain all the illnesses, deaths, and misfortunes in their family this way, but others do not. For example, Ksenia Borisovna M. (born in 1931) explained the drowning death of her grandson from bad *samogon* and prescription drugs without attributing it to witchcraft. She also asserted that she is teaching her grandchildren to work on their marriages, because "you can blame whomever you want for your problems but if you find the right way to treat your husband everything will be OK" (Krasnoe, 7 December 2004), which suggests that she does not attribute a bad marriage to spoiling.

One final example serves as an excellent illustration of this principle. While most of the presumed witches we interviewed likely have nothing to do with magic and may not know of or give credence to their reputations, other women, knowing and acknowledging their reputations, turn themselves into tricksters who use their reputation to attain a more powerful position.[16] The female librarian of a village (born in 1950, Arkhangel'sk oblast, recorded July 2010), who told a series of stories about *porcha*, mentioned this possibility to us. The storyteller maintained that people she thought had brought *porcha* upon someone else always warned beforehand of their intention to do harm. All her stories were based upon the same motif: someone, most often a younger person, insulted an older woman somehow—for example, did not let her into a line in a store, did not give her a ride, did not help—and the older woman said, "You will remember me!" The troubles that happened after this were interpreted by the victims and witnesses of the conflict as *porcha* brought on by an offended "woman who knows" (*znaiushchaia*). Clearly, a person could take advantage of her reputation or just the belief in witchcraft in order to make others treat her well.

Khristoforova studied cases involving pretensions to witchcraft, and calls those who engage in such behavioral tactics "braggarts" (*bakhvaly*): "It is possible to create the impression of a 'knowing one' [*znatkogo*] by imitating some of the traits of appearance, behavior, and speech that are characteristic of the folkloric model. . . . Boasting of one's witchcraft is one factor that contributes to forming the reputation of a 'knowing one'" (Khristoforova 2010, 141).

Examining concrete examples, Khristoforova notes that it is impossible to fully pass for a witch using only self-advertising; rather, self-advertising functions as a strategy for defense and affirmation, likely for a person who feels him- or herself to be weak or in need of protection. What in fact reinforces the self-advertising witch's reputation is serendipity: if significant negative or positive events occur after the verbal threat, then the community might interpret those as resulting from the witch's curse.

We too have encountered cases that involve pretensions to the status of a witch. An elderly woman (born in 1914, Vashkinskii region, Vologda oblast) spontaneously approached a team of folklorists at their home for a talk. Striking up a friendship with one of the female students, she shared malevolent spells with her. For example, a tactic for acquiring power over other people:

> You have to shove them.
> *How's that?*
> Well, say we're going up the stairs, going to them [into the home of a husband's relatives], so I shoved [the wall] with my elbow, [to show] that "I'm the master of this house. So I'm taking over [*zastupaiu*] . . . I take over my husband's tongue, I take over Alexander's tongue, and my father-in-law's and my mother-in-law's. I'm taking over." You have to do that.
> *That's when you enter your groom's home?*
> Uh-huh. You're going in . . . and I say to myself, "I'm taking over the tongue of my husband, of my father-in-law, of my mother-in-law, of everyone." There's lots of neighbors who would do harm. Neighbor devours neighbor there. So this here is good too. As you're entering the house, you have to strike the wall with your heel like this, just here [*she knocks her heel on the lintel*], "I'm the master of the house"—

and strike. With your heel there: "You're my sheep, I'm your wolf. I'm going to shear you. You will bleat, and I will eat you up."

In addition to this magic for a young bride to take power, she also taught her young interlocutor magic against thieves. From the story we cite below, it became clear that the technique of magical struggle with thieves is based not on discovery of the thieves but on malevolent magic directed against the person the storyteller thinks is the thief. She inflicts magical harm upon the one suspected of theft, using for the purpose a piece of his clothing:

> If you smear [a piece of clothing with the clay in the stove], like this, from the ones who steal, if you smear it, they say, they'll die.
> *What do you have to smear?*
> So you tie up some clay [in a bundle], and you tear a little rag off the person's coat, smear it [in clay] so that she'll be tortured-tormented, rolled up into a tub, and then you stick it into the mouth of the stove, stick it into the soot there. It's well stuck. You've stuck it in the stove, so that there's smoke coming out there. If they steal something, then—many people have taken money, or things, from someone, from some people—you [i.e., they] will give it back! [The thief] will go out of his mind if he doesn't return it. He'll go out of his mind [if you do and say this]. [If you say:] "Turn the house away from the wind, the wind away from the tracks, this deed against Russian flesh," that helps.

She recounted her skill at bringing back men who have abandoned a woman, inflicting sadness upon them:

> I used to ask the dawn: "Morning-light—summer lightning, lovely maiden . . ."
> A woman came to me: "Heal me . . . My husband has left me, he lives in Moscow."
> I wrote down the words for her: "Morning-light—summer lightning, lovely maiden, take from God's handmaiden . . . this sadness, inflict it on [Igor], so that he doesn't pass an hour, doesn't pass a minute, eats no eating, drinks no drinking, smokes no smoking, [only] grieves and yearns for God's handmaiden [Tamara]."
> I came home, and she comes to me: "Grandmother, my husband—he came back to me from Moscow!" (Woman born in 1914, Pokrovskoe, Vashkinskii region, Vologda oblast, 7 July 2007 [Vash 20a-79])

As a sign of their trusting relationship, she presented the student with her girlhood braid, a gift that astounded the folklorists. Hair arranged into a braid is a very important attribute of a woman's honor, will, magical power, and so on; it figured prominently in wedding rituals. Some older women showed us their girlhood braids, which they had cut off at different ages, but which all of them kept in the same place as their laying-out clothes, so that the braid would be placed in their graves. In the context of these customs, this gift seemed extremely strange.

The archaism of her magic, the oddity of her behavior—all this made us begin to feel a certain artificiality in the situation. I (SA) asked the mistress of the home where we were staying about this woman and was surprised by the answer. She said that Maria Osipovna did not know a thing; she just pretended, and ran around the village. A proper *bol'shukha* does not invite herself to someone's house; rather, people come to her of their own accord, when the need arises. She mentioned another woman, whom our colleagues had already visited, as a "woman who knows" who gave help to the whole village. I was reminded then of the mythological pair of "cultural hero and trickster." Magical behavior was represented in the village through two different types of behavior. In the case of "heroes" (or rather, heroines), rumors and fame of their ability to give help spread through the village. They generally did not discuss their skills themselves, only at our insistent request. "Tricksters," on the other hand, hurried to tell visiting folklorists about their supernatural abilities.

This example serves as a reminder that the discourse of sorcery is a framed and contested site, in which players may accept or discount each other's narratives. To have one's narrative of sorcery discounted locally means that one is laughed at, one is not sought out for healing (for the issuing of counterspells). But in the case recounted above, we do not know who to believe: the mistress of the house, or Maria Osipovna. Did everyone in the village laugh at Maria Osipovna, or only some people? Were there rival witches in the village, or was there really only one whom people accepted in that role?

When strangers (folklorists) enter the village, the rules change. The discourse of sorcery is a game in which folklorists may not possess the skills to properly assess who is playing by the rules and who is not (who is simply imitating). In addition, the folklorists operate by different rules than locals: while the collectors want to collect only "authentic" texts (texts that are or were really used), the locals may not care about this kind of authenticity. Instead, locals would like to know whose spells actually work. But when they deal with folklorists, they may have other motivations. Many villagers, like Maria Osipovna, may talk to folklorists because they are flattered by the attention. They may be interested in garnering the spotlight, in making a friend, in having someone listen to their stories. What right does a folklorist have to discount any of these stories? How can one judge which motivations are acceptable, and which not? Clearly, Maria Osipovna's stories and spells were not entirely "made up," nor, likely, was her braid fake. These verbal and material pieces constituted her contribution to "tradition." Yet due to the fact that they were offered forcefully and self-consciously, we are inclined to discount them as folklore. It is difficult for us as folklorists to refuse the role we have been given through our academic training, to be the "gatekeepers" for tradition.

8

Constructing Identity in Stories of the Other World

The previous two chapters examined the discourse of magic as a reflection of a woman's position in society: her social power. Here we take a step back to pose a different question: how is knowledge about the other world framed discursively and transmitted, and when and why do people speak about their interactions with spiritual forces? Here (as we did in chapter 3) we focus our attention on the storytelling itself, in addition to the content of the stories. In what ways do such narratives show others and ourselves who we are?

The idea for this chapter came early in the birth of this book. It seemed essential to us to address the question of *how* we heard all these stories and *why* the stories themselves— not just the "information" they "report"—should be of interest to those who want to understand Russian village women. In essence, the chapter was born because we saw that scholars were taking women's stories of the supernatural and extracting little more than "belief" from them. By contrast, the stories gave us important insight into the ways that narrative itself can shape how people view the world and their place in it. When people told us stories about a spirit living in the home (*domovoi*), or the dead coming back to interact with the living (revenants), we saw that they were telling us how they related to their families, to the *rod*, and to us. They were performing a relational identity.

Scholars classify narratives people tell about their experiences with the supernatural as memorates. This genre is known in Russian as *bylichka* (pl. *bylichki*) or mythological story (*mifologicheskii rasskaz*).[1] Russian collectors distinguished the *bylichka* from the myriad of other life-narratives that people tell because these mythological tales recount encounters with the supernatural world, and the collectors saw this as evidence of ancient belief systems. Eighteenth-century scholars, who set great store by the importance of ancient Greek mythology for world culture, tried to create an analogous mythological system within Slavic culture (Zinov'ev 1987, 382). Although *bylichki* were not yet named as such by scholars, in the early nineteenth century they served as sources of information about the otherworldly characters of Russian folk belief. Generally, nineteenth-century collectors wrote down not the texts but only the information that people told them—for example, when one could see a forest nymph or how one could identify a witch. Some collectors utilized retold (not verbatim) *bylichki* as illustrations of villagers' beliefs (Kolchin 1899, 1–59). Many scholars used these superstitious tales as evidence of the backwardness of the people, and expressed hope that their belief in the supernatural would soon die out under the influence of progressive ideas (Zinov'ev 1987, 383).

The first to mention the word *bylichka*—which is a folk term meaning a story about something that really happened—were the brothers Sokolov, in their *Skazki i pesni Belozerskogo kraia* of 1915 ([1915] 1999, 78). Together with N. E. Onchukov, who in his 1909 study *Severnye skazki* mentioned a related genre, the *byval'shchina* (a fabulate with an involved plot, told for entertainment purposes) (1909, 37), these scholars viewed *bylichki* as supplementing the genre of the fairy tale, and that view predominated in the early twentieth century even as scholars began to identify some of the characteristics of the genre. Still, *bylichki* continued to be viewed primarily as informational rather than artistic texts, until the work of E. V. Pomerantseva, who in a 1968 article asserted that the *bylichka* had an aesthetic function as well as the predominating informational function (1968, 275). A later collector, V. P. Zinov'ev, further emphasized the aesthetic characteristics and function of the *bylichka* during the 1980s. Both he and Pomerantseva proclaimed that the aesthetic function was overtaking the informational one, since, they asserted, people no longer believed in the *bylichka* they told (Zinov'ev 1987, 382; Pomerantseva 1968, 287). Zinov'ev wrote that if the narrator claimed belief in the recounted events, he or she did so to intensify the aesthetic effect of the story on the listener: it was one of the rules of the genre (1987, 386, 394). It was politically important for Soviet folklorists to claim that people told such stories mainly to entertain, because to assert the opposite would have implied that the rural population was still backward and that the Soviet education system had failed to change their world view.

By contrast, Western scholars have viewed the teller's belief in the observed events as an important element of the genre. The terms memorate and fabulate were coined in 1934 by Carl Wilhelm von Sydow; the former refers to a story of supernatural experience narrated in the first person, while the latter takes a third-person perspective. Sydow argued that these "purely personal" belief narratives lacked the poetic and traditional formulations of the legend proper (Sydow 1948, 73–74; see also Honko 1964). However, Linda Dégh and Andrew Vázsonyi suggest that this formulation perpetuated a "vicious circle": because "the memorate was not approached as artistic folk poesy, it was carelessly recorded and, consequently, these fragmentary notations do not exhibit artistic skills" (1974, 234). In fact every legend implies a memorate, since legends gain credence only when tellers refer to first-hand experiences—their own or others. Legends are about belief, and the bedrock of belief is personal experience. Further, Dégh and Vázsonyi argue, the line separating memorates (first-hand stories of the supernatural), fabulates (third-person stories), and legends (impersonal stories) is so thin as to be meaningless (1974, 239). Even memorates can be considered traditional in that "the concretely manifested form of expression is already a social product"; the person who observed the event "must have acquired the whole vision, or at least its elements, from common social sources by way of tradition" (237). As we will suggest below, fabulates and memorates not only incorporate conventional themes and aesthetic features but they can also be narratively linked in productive ways.

The Contexts of Storytelling

We begin our study of memorates and fabulates with a description of the contexts in which they are told. We may speak of two contexts: the static context, which does not change throughout the conversation; and the dynamic context, in which social roles are constructed or negated and a metaphorical space of understanding between the parties emerges. This section explains the contextual givens: space, status, and time; in the following section, we give an example of the shifting dynamics of a conversation.

Bylichki are usually told in private contexts, where privacy is defined by the quantity of people, by their social characteristics, and by the physical space itself (often in the home or just outside it). Such conversations are rarely possible during a first meeting. They usually occur face to face, in a small group of no more than five or six people. When we observed local people initiating conversations about the supernatural, usually the participants were age peers and there was a context to support or spark the subject matter: a holiday during which spirits are said to walk the earth, following a funeral or memorial, or during the sharing of life stories over tea. Of course, we do not have access to what would happen if we were not present. Even at times when we "eavesdropped" on conversations, we cannot be sure that the participants in the conversation were not influenced by our presence, even if they seemed not to notice us. When folklorists initiate the conversation by asking questions, those asking and those answering will usually be from different generations.

Both in interviews initiated by fieldworkers and in observed group conversations, tales about personal experiences in rural Russia are usually either transmitted by those higher on the social hierarchy to those of lower status, or they circulate among those of equal social position (usually of the same gender). Conversations of female outsiders with local men are practically impossible if they are age peers, since the participants might be seen as sexual partners. Exceptions include situations of a professional nature, for example when we spoke with a local male historian. Conversations in confidence are also possible between older women and younger men, whose relationship is seen as equivalent to that of "older sister-younger brother" or "aunt-nephew." Though the collecting team at Saint

Petersburg University was mostly female, some male students were able to conduct and transcribe interviews with male informants, and this data has been helpful in observing the gendered nature of encounters with informants. In our experience, ethnographers who wish to hear personal experience narratives must present themselves as same-age peers or as peers of the consultant's children or grandchildren. To avoid establishing an unhelpful power relationship, we also avoided presenting ourselves as collectors of information; the latter role tends to elicit help or compliance but very few narratives. Only in rare contexts—such as an Orthodox Church confession—would a villager tell personal stories to an older person, a person in charge.[2] When the relationship between ethnographer and informant is horizontal (age-peer), stories help build a field of common knowledge by reconfirming or deepening mutual understanding; when the relationship is a vertical one, stories transmit social skills (this transmission is always initiated by the younger/lower person, who needs the knowledge). In our fieldwork, we often presented ourselves as inexperienced new brides who needed to be taught everything.

We emphasize that relations between communicative contexts and narrative are reciprocal: that is, while personal belief is normally shared in a private setting, a private setting is also created in part by discussing these topics. A certain degree of privacy is generated when participants open up about fears, values, or experiences. Thus interviewers must be ready to say honestly, "I am afraid when I sit in the dark," or "I believe in God's existence," or "I am divorced/alone/raising children alone." Such openness reaps openness in return.

Time of day is less important in these narrative contexts than space and status, but female tellers have noted that one does not generally talk of "the unclean" or of the deceased toward nighttime (although many also broke those rules with us). In a sense, speaking of such subjects at night treads upon the liminal territory of the dead, and the action could call unwanted attention to the teller. There is an important difference in this regard between the telling of *bylichki* and folktales (*skazki*). Folktales are usually shared with children before they go to bed in the evening; this is acceptable because while folktales might involve the supernatural, no one believes they are true. *Bylichki*, on the other hand, involve talking about real people's encounters with the supernatural and thus involve more potential risk.

In sum, in rural Russia stories about experience with the supernatural are told by older people to younger people, and by peers to each other, in private daytime conversations. This is the "static" context for the telling of *bylichki* (see also Levkievskaia 2007, 486–88). In the next section, we show how the social positioning of the interlocutors profoundly affects how the conversations themselves unfold.

Telling as Teaching: A Pre-Script-ion

Our next example provides an excellent illustration of the principle of the experienced teller and the ignorant questioner, as well as showing the complex and shifting dynamic context of many of these conversations. In this 2005 interview, two female Saint Peters-burg University students (Daria Tuminas and Iulia Marinicheva), approximately twenty years old, try to elicit a legend regarding the local understanding of the house spirit from an elderly village woman, born in 1926 in Pigilinka village, Vologda oblast. As our com-mentary below reveals, the woman apparently partially understands what the students are seeking, but she has her own agenda, which includes a very important aspect that is often left out of memorate recordings and analysis: she wishes to educate the younger women in the proper way to approach the supernatural world. Since for her the appearance of the house spirit and specific events regarding the house spirit are only the "tip of the iceberg," she does not linger upon these but tries to communicate a deeper and more functional understanding of the house spirit. Trying to "seed" the conversation with the name of the supernatural character they are interested in learning about, and attempting to bring the conversation out of the general ("they," third person plural) into a more personal frame ("you," "we"), Iulia Marinicheva asks the interviewee, Vera Ignat'evna:

> You said that it's not a good idea to go out of the house [without] . . . People told us
> that if you move, there's some kind of dobrokhodushka?—[3]
> [Perhaps not following this complexly coordinated speech] What?
> [Loudly] The dobrokhodushka!
> Ah!

After a pause, and having resigned herself to the idea that she must ask a generalized ques-tion, the collector asks,

> Who is it?
> I haven't seen it.

As becomes clear here, Vera Ignat'evna heard the first question, but she denies that she can speak about it from personal experience. Later, one student researcher again asks the general question "And who is it?" The elderly interlocutor explains by referring to practices common on Pokrov (October 14), a day that signaled the beginning of winter. On Pokrov Eve, cattle were brought into the courtyard for the season and given the last-reaped sheaf of hay in order to keep them well fed and healthy throughout the winter. In an example of sympathetic magic, people gave cattle more than they could possibly eat so that there would be enough food for the whole year (Baranova 2002, 437). Vera Ignat'evna continues: "I haven't seen the dobrokhodushka, so I can't say. But it exists, people have seen it, [when] they have overfed [their cattle]. When I had cattle, the dobrokhodushka gave it hay. But I didn't see it. But it's like if we ask an angel [for something], [in the same way] we ask the dobrokhodushka." Here, she confirms the experiences of others ("people have seen") but immediately turns from the example to the rule: "they have overfed" their cattle. Referring to her own experience, she tells about a commonly held belief that the *dobrokhodushka* cares for the cattle, and she references the speech practice in which the *dobrokhodushka* is addressed on Pokrov. This is a normative type of communication only for those who keep cattle. When she begins using the plural first person, however ("But it's like if we ask an angel"), she turns her attention to more broadly accepted communicative practice, perhaps shared by her visiting interlocutors.

> *Is that so?*
> Yes, when people overfeed the cattle on Pokrov, on Pokrov day, during Pokrov week, they ask the *dobrokhodushka* and the *dobrokhodnitsa* [to look after the cattle].
> [...]
> *So, how do you ask?*
> How do people ask?
> "Father Dobrokhodushka
> And Mother Dobrokhodnitsa,
> Go water, feed
> Mother Cattle,
> Calm her, stroke her,
> So we can let her out.
> Don't rely on me, the provider."[4]
> That's it. Bow to all three corners. And then the cattle, if there's none around, now you don't have to overfeed [them], you don't have to do anything.

Implied in Vera Ignat'evna's explanation is the fact that she no longer needs to communicate with a *dobrokhodushka* because she no longer keeps cattle. Rather, she is a *starukha*, an elderly woman, and as such is well positioned to share her own magical skills with younger interlocutors who may need this knowledge.

> *What do they overfeed them with? Do they give them something, some kind of food?*
> Yes, they do. They give them [food], you see, and after that they take a piece of bread, salt it, and say words over it and give a little bit to everyone, and then they give the cattle their feed, you see. And they overfeed them. They give them more feed than they need on this day, so that they are satisfied [over the winter].

Next, the interviewer decides to address the question of the semantics of the name *dobrokhodushka* (*dobro* [good] + *khodit'* [to go, to walk]):

Does the dobrokhodushka *only belong to good people, to good families?*

Well, it doesn't matter, wherever there's cattle, they say, in every home, they say, there's a *dobrokhodushka*, yes. A *domovoi* [house spirit], you could say, a *domovoi*, *domovoi*. [*Understanding what motivated the question, Vera Ignat'evna gives the* dobrokhodushka *a different name, one free of evaluative connotations.*]

A domovoi?

Yes, yes, a *domovoi*. In every home, they say, there is one . . .

Here, the interviewee again appeals to general norms, to the social world: the *domovoi* is a personification of the order in a home, the way in which a home functions properly as a social mechanism. Later in the conversation, a researcher clarifies, "It doesn't belong to a person, but to a home, is that correct?" Apparently, however, the interviewee does not understand this distinction between a person and a home. For her, a home is not a build-ing but a living space together with the people who live in it: "Who knows! No one sees him, he just lives. And if they do see him, in our village, people say, if they caught him, they saw him." Here Vera Ignat'evna uses a rhetorical device very typical for folkloric speech: "no one sees, one person sees."[5] In so doing, she moves from practical matters to situa-tions, and finally delivers the narrative material that the interviewers are seeking:

Did they catch him?

Yes.

How?

Well, they'd meet him, he'd be giving the cattle [feed]. They saw him, but I didn't see, and I'm not going to lie. But he exists, people say they've seen him, he's like the owner of the house. Looks completely like him.

Continuing to negate personal experience, but here in a way that reinforces the truth of the rest of her story, the teller focuses upon others' experience: someone met up with the mystical twin of the homeowner who was taking care of the cattle. The following questions, in which one of the interviewers distinguishes between the *dobrokhodushka*'s appearance and its character, perplex the informant:

In appearance?

Yes, in appearance and everything else. He gives [feed].

In terms of his character?

[*Explaining that the* domovoi *is dressed just as the homeowner*] Yes, it used to be, you see, there were old folks; in the village there didn't used to be cloth made out of . . . that stuff, everything was handwoven, underwear, I mean long white underpants, made out of canvas, and shirts. So they would see him in all white, if they saw him, and he'd look just like the homeowner, and he'd be giving the cattle [feed]. But I don't know, I haven't seen it. But they say it exists, they have seen it.

Immediately after reporting others' words, however, she shifts perspective until she finally finds a subject position that is acceptable to her. At first she spoke about her own relationship with the *domovoi*, and then, prompted by the interviewer's questions, she spoke about others' experience seeing the *domovoi*. In what follows, she returns to what is most important to her: she offers to share her own experience and knowledge with the researchers:

> If you go to visit someone in the city, invite the *dobrokhodushka* with you.
> *How?*
> Like this: "Father Dobrokhodushka, I have set off, now you come with me."
> [...]
> *Even if you're going for a visit?*
> Yes, for a visit. You'll be less unloved [*tebe men'she napostynet*], he'll give you space [*on mesto tebe dast*]. When you leave, call him with you again.

Here, Vera Ignat'evna does not narrate a specific encounter; instead, she begins to explain a deeper understanding of how the *domovoi* functions in the community, thus offering a window into local values and beliefs. In this community, it is important to call the *dobrokhodushka* when moving to a new social space, so that you can find your proper place there. Vera Ignat'evna uses the verb *napostynet*, formed from the adjective *postylyi*: unloved, a person or thing that one can't bear in a psychological sense.[6] For her, it is important to have a relationship with one's mystical alter ego because he secures one's place in the social space of relationships and connections. Vera Ignat'evna tries to teach her young conversational partners to create their own relationship with him.

> *That is, wherever I go, I should always call the* dobrokhodushka *with me?*
> Yes, yes, yes, yes.
> *So it works out that he is with you all the time.*
> Yes.
> [...]
> *Does he protect you somehow?*
> Yes.
> *And is there some kind of* dvorovoi *[yard-spirit]? [Here, the interviewer again does not understand that the interviewee is talking about how one should behave in the world, and not about the objective description of a mystical creature.]*

That's the same one, it's him, it's all the same: *dvorovoi, domovoi,* and *dobrokhodushka.* It's the same thing.
So outside, on the street, is there some kind of master as well?

Vera Ignat'evna, in her role as the patient teacher, tries to translate the concept into language that she thinks would be more comprehensible for her urban interlocutor: "Even on the street, it's still you, and everyone has his own protector, a guardian angel, [unclear] and the angel will go with you. Everyone has one, when a person is born he is given an angel, they say everyone has one. You go, and he goes alongside you, you don't see him" (20 July 2005 [Siam 24-6]).

Vera Ignat'evna's final pronouncement here gets to the heart of the disconnect between the interlocutors: for her the focus is upon the person: "it's still you." That is, any talk about the *dobrokhodushka* is talk about the social world. The mythological being is simply a reflection of the way in which the social world *here* (in this world), and the social world *there* (in the world of spirits), are inextricably linked. The being's name and his looks are clearly of little importance for her. By contrast, for the young folklorists, the being's name and his looks are the most tangible evidence of an exotic culture with incomprehensible beliefs. If one can find a story about a sighting of the being, one will have further "proof" that this outlandish belief still exists. Obviously, the interviewers are striking dual poses here. They apparently see themselves as "collecting information" (a pose of power that they are *not* encouraged by their teachers to hold) at the same time as they play the role of curious, inexperienced youths confronting the culture of an exotic other.

Since Vera Ignat'evna does not know of or share the goals of the interviewers, she looks for and eventually finds a type of relationship that is fitting in this context. She speaks unwillingly about "events" because they do not explain what a *domovoi* is, but she willingly explains the social norms that one must adhere to. She is happy to transmit her knowledge of how to construct social space, to offer her interlocutors a script that they can use to understand their own life events. The imperative that stands behind this script for behavior is one that is very important for our interlocutors: in one's life, one must give the higher powers room to act. One must not only act oneself but also ask higher powers for assistance: as religious rural people often say, "the Lord commands" (*gospod' upravit*). The higher powers must take over in situations in which one cannot control the outcome oneself, such as when one travels, when one leaves young children alone, when one sends cattle out to pasture, and so on. Vera Ignat'evna offers this wisdom to the young women here, by telling them that the *dobrokhodushka* will care for the cattle, and, indeed, for their own lives as well.

One can observe how in such conversations the discursive development of the theme creates relationships between the interlocutors. Linguists describe this as establishing a subject position:

[W]e position ourselves vis-à-vis the others with whom we are developing and elaborating a meaningful discourse. We attend to the others' ideas and feelings and we assess their capacities, their institutional status, their stance toward us. Not only do we modulate and modify our own ideas and feelings, we also place one another in particular (and changing) discursive positions . . . [P]ositioning is accomplished interactively and involves not just the aims of speakers but also the interpretations of, and effects on, other conversational participants. (Eckert and McConnell-Ginet 2003, 157)

In the process of this conversation, the elder woman seeks and finds a subject position that is acceptable to her—the role of a teacher. At the same time, she finds a way of translating her understanding and creates a general rule that could serve as a script: a *domovoi* is a guardian angel in "your city language."

Stories and Gender Identity

Identity, particularly gender and age identity, plays a large role in the choice of subject position in a conversation. In the previous example, the narrator had been in charge of spiritual matters for her family and her community since she became a *bol'shukha*. Now, as a *starukha*, her role is more clearly that of teacher than of mistress. She now lacks the power to command (which she had as a *bol'shukha*), but she has copious wisdom and life experience that others may learn from. Perhaps folklorists have traditionally come to such women precisely because these women position themselves as purveyors of knowledge about how to relate to the spiritual world.

We have collected examples of elder men, *bol'shaki-stariki*, performing similar roles. For instance, in a 2009 interview, a young male student of Saint Petersburg University asks a man born in 1933 (in the Mezen' region of Arkhangel'sk oblast) whether he has heard of horses stopping at a cross (i.e., at a graveyard, church, or chapel) and refusing to move. The man says that he never personally experienced this but has heard of it. He explains that the phenomenon occurs with those who do not believe in God, and the only way to get the horses to move again is to pray. He asks the younger man if he knows how to pray, and proceeds to teach him how to cross himself. He then teaches him that if he is lost in a forest, he should pray to specific types of trees (birch and spruce) to find his way out. He demonstrates how one embraces the tree and says in a singsong voice: "Embrace me! Don't forget me! Bring me out of this trouble, set me on the right path, the right road, and I will never forget you." The elder man emphasizes that his teaching was passed down from earlier generations of old men: "Write it down. Yes. No one else knows it, of the older men, except me. And I learned it from old men. And there were few such old men in the village." Later he names the people who told him: "My parents taught me. A man named Grandpa Vorontsov taught me. He was an Old Believer. He always put you on the right path" ([Mez 27-001]).

Thus, like Vera Ignat'evna, this elder man adopts the subject position of teacher during his interview with a younger person of his own gender. For him, as for her, this position is dictated by his and the interviewee's age and gender roles. The content of their teachings may also be dictated by gender roles. While his teachings have to do with travel, the *starukha's* teachings concern the care of the home and the cow. Each teaches that with which she or he has had experience in life, and that about which she or he is expected to have knowledge.

Most of the interviews we conducted were with women, but a few successful interviews with men were conducted by male ethnographers. We do not have adequate data to make definitive generalizations about the differences between men's and women's stories of the supernatural, but we can offer our observations based upon the interviews to which we had access. One difference that we see in tales of the supernatural told by men and by women is that some male tellers emphasize, more than female tellers, how they know that what they are telling is true. They often list their sources or emphasize that their teachings are based upon their own personal experience; in other cases they approach the telling of the experience objectively, as if it were about a scientific experiment. For them, such an objective stance seems to be important: they do not take for granted that their stories will be believed. For example, in the interview about the prayers to the tree, the male narrator mentions that he knows this by his "own experience" (using these words or synonyms) five times, and mentions his sources three times, praising them as valuable sources. We did not find such locutions in most stories by women.

Other male tellers offer their stories as objective accounts "for what they are worth," without trying to convince the listener overtly: for example, in an extremely detailed account recorded in 2006 in the Siamzha region of Vologda oblast, a man born in 1933 tells a male student how he was healed of a curse that had left him mentally unstable for two years after the death of his wife (a death that was due to the same curse). The story, concerning his healing process via the magical services of a female neighbor, is offered without much reference to his own feelings at the time. The narrator presents enough information for the experience to be repeated by someone else, and he emphasizes this aspect: "If you don't have the powder, she says, it's not absolutely necessary, the powder she prescribed me" (Siam D-Txt 1-54).

By contrast, we observed that the women tellers we interviewed tended to assume the truth of the tales and the mutual belief of the interlocutor. For them, the main points of the stories lie in the feelings experienced by the witnesses in the tales, and the relationships established or reconfirmed via the actions performed in the stories. In her study of elderly English women's memorates and fabulates, Gillian Bennett finds similar results:

[T]hese women have been taught by the society they have grown up in that the ideal member of their sex is an intuitive, gentle, unassertive person, geared to a caring and supportive role rather than to direct action, independent thought or concern with self. . . . Premonitions and telepathy score so highly on their belief-scale because, par excellence, they are intuitions; because they come unsought, not as the result of the active pursuit of knowledge; and because they turn outwards from the self to the immediate circle of family and friends. They are feelings about and for other people—love of others made manifest, defeated by neither time nor distance, and felt in the deep recesses of the heart where none may challenge their authority. (1987, 29–30)

While the self-concept of Russian women of the first and second Soviet generations differs from the depiction of the Englishwomen offered by Bennett, the two groups show similar motivations for telling stories of the supernatural. Women perform love, intuition, and belief through these stories, and in so doing reconfirm and transmit their values, which include establishing and maintaining relationships with living and deceased members of the clan and with good spirits, and (in the Russian case) protecting the family against evil spirits. Women born during the Soviet period do not tend to be self-effacing or unassertive, as the Englishwomen were (in fact, they often praise themselves for their work-related achievements), but they do place value upon connection with others. One may conceive of their lives as having two planes: the plane of the everyday, in which successes, the battle to make something of oneself or to be recognized for something, jealousy of others' successes, and the use of magic to address this inequality are all important. The other plane is a metaphysical one: here aesthetics, eternal symbols, meaning, love, God, and fate play the main roles. The stories of the supernatural belong mainly to this metaphysical plane, although the two planes can intersect in some of the stories.

Women of the first Soviet generation willingly explore this metaphysical plane in their stories of encounters with the deceased. These are some of the most common stories that we collect. In the remaining part of this section we compare several memorates and fabulates that would be classified as folkloric stories about revenants. We emphasize here the important differences in how the stories are told: each woman highlights different aspects of her situation and places emphasis on different social relationships; and the stories serve various purposes to tellers and listeners. Many of these stories were told during discussions with ethnographers about the rules of the funeral ritual. As people told us, on fixed days—memorial days, the ninth, twentieth, and fortieth days from the day of death, and the year anniversary—relatives of the deceased should not lock the doors of the house, since the soul of the deceased comes to visit his or her home. In the following case, Anna Dmitrievna K., born in 1918, told two stories, the first about someone else, and the second about her own experience, to illustrate this rule.

One woman used to tell [about what happened when] her mother died. And I locked everything, she says, the night before the anniversary [of her death]. There

was a knocking and all. I, she says, open the door: "Who is it? Who's there?"—no
one answers. Knocked three times. I come outdoors, she says, and the blizzard, she
says, grabbed me. How it dragged me, spun me! It spun me in the snow all the way
to the barn. Her mother came, but she hadn't unlocked [the doors], so . . . the
blizzard spun her.

    I had a friend who died. Twenty days went by after they buried her, [and her
family] left. I dreamed, or was it real: someone knocks on the door, and it was as if
I came out, and she says, "What, you locked the doors?"—"I locked them," I say.
And how she flung something, it was as if iron rattled on the floor like pebbles! At
her own house no one was home, so she went from house to house, and nobody let
her in, everyone had gone away. [Even] Tamara, [who lives] over there, says a
shadow came out of our house and went away. (Karl Libknekht [village], Belozersk
region, Vologda oblast, 15 July 1997 [Bel 19-2])

In the first case the family of the deceased locked the home; in the second case they went
away after the twentieth day, without waiting for the fortieth. The house that the deceased
needed to visit was locked. But is this what the woman was talking about?

    The first case might be classified as a fabulate: she is retelling someone else's story that
she heard: "one woman told." However, the entire central part of the story is told in the
present tense, and the only way we know that the story is not about the narrator is because
of the phrase "she says," which serves as oral "quotation marks" for a present-tense story
told in the first person. Due to the immediacy of the narration style, we relive this experience together with the narrator. This present-tense, immediate style of narration is common for women's tales of the supernatural: they tend to concentrate on actions, and their
exclamations give the tales an emotional tone. Rather than "proving" the story's validity,
the teller enacts her belief before our eyes, drawing the listener in to her world.

    We only depart from this story and enter the present tense of the storytelling moment
when the narrator inserts a summarizing coda: "Her mother came, but she hadn't unlocked [the doors]." With this evaluative statement, she returns us to the present time and
explicitly brings her own point of view into the narrative, as if to say: pay attention, here is
the meaning of the story. As Jerome Bruner has written, following Labov and Waletzky's
1967 analysis of narrative, the coda "permits the listener 'to tell the dancer from the dance'"
(Bruner 1997, 64; Labov and Waletzky 1967, 32–41). That is, with the coda we return to
the teller and his or her present perspective; the coda personalizes the story and makes explicit the difference—and the connection—between the narrator's "now" and the "then"
of the story. The role of the coda can also be interpreted with the help of autobiography
studies: any narrative about the self constitutes the self as both subject and object. Narrative
is a performative act; in performing autobiographical narrative, a person ("I") tells about
himself as an object ("me") (Tam 2007, 138–39). The coda, by bringing the narrative into

the realm of the storyteller's present, clearly also constitutes the self as a teller ("I") and an object (the "me" that the story is ultimately about).

It is very important to underline that the "me" that is created during the telling is the result of performance: the self as object is constructed as the result of the communicative work that goes on in the process of the conversation. In this story, the personality created through the story (the "me" created within the interaction of the narrator and listener) is the carrier of a moral value. This value lies at the basis of the story, and it helps to create the identity. The underlying principle is that we should not disrupt the connection between ourselves and our deceased loved ones. The story about the door that was closed against the parent's wandering soul is a tale about a sin, a moral transgression. By implication, the teller enjoins the listeners not to commit this same sin. Here again, gender plays a role because it is women who traditionally took on the role of maintaining connections with the deceased. A woman tells younger women this cautionary story about other women, implying that the listeners should embrace this social role.

The second story, a memorate, may be viewed simply as an extension of the first story's coda. This autobiographical sequel, about the fortieth day after the death of the narrator's friend, is organized in a similar way as the first story: the text is in the present tense, with emphasis on physical actions, and the finale also contains a summarizing coda. Both these stories presuppose a belief that is not actually discussed: in this world, death does not mean non-existence. Not only family but also those we were close with may have need of us after their death. It is important to "be there" for one's friends when they come back seeking "home." The unstated cultural imperative here is that living people must maintain contact with and show respect to otherworldly spirits, particularly the spirits of ancestors. Both stories are framed in negative fashion, however: they are about people's rule-breaking behavior. As part of this rule or imperative, the deceased visit their homes on fixed dates. Strange happenings occur when living people ignore the possibility of the deceased's appearance on these dates. They ignore the rule. Clearly, both narratives confirm the rule by exception. Both the fabulate and the memorate show the structure of a stereotypical plot, used by narrators to organize their experience: something strange happened, and that something strange may be attributed to human misbehavior vis-à-vis the ancestors.

The narrator uses the other's story as an analogy to her own story, which helps her to organize and interpret her own—waking or sleeping—experience. Here we see that one of the important functions of fabulates is to inform—and provoke the creation of—memorates. This instance provides further evidence that the difference between memorates and fabulates is not crucial: whether the story is told about someone else or about oneself, people use these stories to convey important information about their own values, beliefs, and identity. As with autobiographical narrative, people constitute themselves as narrating subjects and as objects of discussion—one might even say as examples. Whether the story is about someone else or about oneself, the storyteller offers an evaluation of correct or incorrect behavior. Even when he or she did not experience the original event, the story can be told as if the narrator relives the event, and the narrative can have all the attendant therapeutic qualities of autobiographical narrative.

Both of these stories recount the fear a person feels upon encountering the other world. Together with the narrator, the listeners also experience the fear she underwent at that time. Meanwhile she is now reliving, assimilating, and assuaging that fear by retelling the story. The unexplainable receives an explanation; it is now linked into the system of norms, which means that it can be accepted.

The following story told by Aleksandra Iakovlevna M., born in 1937, has the same subject—the visit of the deceased on the fortieth day—but the pathos of the story is very different. The emotional axis of the story is the common folkloric metaphor, the disappearing trace.

> On the fortieth day people came [to our house], our daughter was there. And at
> twelve o'clock at night she went out to empty the bucket, we were getting ready
> [for sleep]—on that night people stay up till twelve. And she says, "After I went out
> the door creaked and opened. I'm walking with the bucket, and behind me I hear
> steps, the snow creaks underfoot; I turned around, and stand there [and say]:
> "Papa, sit with us, don't go." And, she says, it's as if the light snow covers, and
> covers, and covers the footprints . . ." And then this little blizzard, little blizzard,
> light snow went away. (Karl Libknekht [village], Belozersk region, Vologda oblast,
> 17 July 1997 [Bel 19-6])

Aleksandra Iakovlevna here is speaking about the death of her husband. For her and for her daughter, clearly, what is important is how he leaves: the light snow "covers" the footprints, the trace. This is repeated three times: she uses the device of tripling, which is typical for folkloric speech. The disappearance of footprints or a road is a metaphor for the disappearance of a concrete connection, the possibility of direct contact. Compare the song:

> Go visit your mother while she's alive.
> And when Mother dies, and when Mother dies,
> The road becomes overgrown, becomes overgrown,
> The wide road is overgrown with thick grass,
> Thick grass, thick grass, green woods.[7]

In Aleksandra's story, when the daughter does not see anyone outside the house and feels the presence of her father, she asks him not to go away but instead of an answer sees the snowstorm moving away. This is a story about loss: the metaphor of the disappearing trace serves as the general focal point of the narrative and gives expression to the feeling that both the narrator and the listeners have felt. With this metaphor, the story becomes a story about the experience of a feeling. If the previous two stories are about the transgression of a moral law, this one—while thematically similar—is about obeying that moral law. The daughter called the father back, expressing her willingness to maintain a connection with the dead, while in answer to her the world sketched a hieroglyph of forgetting: the disappearing trace. The ethical point of the story, its cathartic message for the listener and narrator, consists in the necessity of accepting the fact that this world is a world of loss. Loss must be serenely endured. The familiar cultural plot that underlies this story is the lack of answer—the impossibility of receiving an answer—when the living address the dead. While there is no direct teaching in this story, its mention of a culture-wide metaphor and plot allows the specific case to reach the level of general rule, uniting the teller and listeners in knowledge of the temporary nature of human existence.

The following legend, told by Elena Lvovna S., born in 1916, is about the same basic mythological plot. It uncovers the problematic nature of a field of knowledge that is usually not talked about: is there life after death, and what is it like? Here Elena Lvovna tells how she and her husband made an agreement about "news" from the other world: whoever died first would give a sign. After his death the husband gave such a sign, but he did not adhere to the part of the agreement that stipulated one should "not scare" the other person. Elena reminded him of this when she felt his presence:

My "grandpa" [husband] died. We'd argue: "Listen, Grandpa, if you die first, give a sign. And if I die first, I'll give one. But [be careful] you don't scare [me]." Ivan [her son] was on vacation. They [Ivan and someone] went to Glebovo. And up until forty days I hadn't gone anywhere, I was here. I got up on the stove and I sit. I hear the doors open, and someone comes along the passage. I drew aside the curtain [around the stove]. I thought Ivan had come back. We had a barn there. And I hear someone walking on the floor of the barn. But no one comes in. So I lay down a bit, and at twelve o'clock I went outside. I saw there was no one around anywhere. I grabbed a magazine and was leafing through it. All of a sudden there's a knock, he's coming. The door opened wide. Then it was quiet, then it closed again. It was open a crack. I say: "Grandpa, I'm home alone, don't scare me." The doors opened, but no one came in. (Ishtomar, Belozersk region, Vologda oblast, 18 July 1998 [Bel 19-40])

In its epistemological nature, the story is not typical of women's stories of the supernatural. Elena sought proof of life after death. But her story, while offering that proof, focuses more specifically upon the narrator's fear. Although she only mentions fear at the end ("Grandpa, . . . don't scare me"), her recitation of the unexplained happenings evokes her fear at the time, and is directed at evoking fear and wonder in the listener. The message is clear: the narrator paid for her curiosity with her fear. Her story has somewhat of the character of a folktale. The implied moral seems to be that in making the pact with her husband, she neglected to realize that one cannot control the actions of the inhabitants of the spiritual world. To ask him to "not scare her" is the same as asking the wind not to blow. Thus, the story is about the experience of fear in the presence of the supernatural world.[8]

The following story told by Zoia Pavlovna T., born in 1935, focuses on the continuing power of love after death: "We were three sisters. We used to sleep together. We buried mama, and two days later she came. She strokes [our] head[s]. She smells of incense" (Iskrino, Belozersk region, Vologda oblast, 23 July 1998 [Be1 19-43]). In Russian culture, when an elder (a parent, a priest) touches one's head, it is an act of blessing. In appearing to her children after the funeral, the deceased mother did not leave them without a blessing. This is a story about consolation: about the fact that those who love us continue to do so after death. If our first set of stories emphasized what we must do to respect and honor the dead, this story reminds us that the dead can honor us, too, with their presence and gestures. Such a story might become a touchstone for a woman's entire life: it might offer a sense of origins and life-purpose, and a model for one's own behavior as a mother. The spiritual mother figure who offers blessings recalls, of course, the ultimate model of motherhood for Russian Orthodox Christians, the Mother of God, characterized in Orthodox folk Christianity as the "Birth-Giver of God," the "universal mother and mistress of all things" (Bulgakov 1932, 164–65; Hubbs 1988, 101). In this story of the sanctified mother, we see the centrality of this image for the teller and for other women believers. The story's expression of the senses of touch and smell evokes the feeling of what it means to have such a mother. If our first stories above highlighted rule-breaking and the resulting fear of consequences, our last three stories show the importance of feelings of love for women tellers. Thus, in this section we saw the range of feelings that visits from the supernatural world can invoke.

Communicative Context: Conversation

In the vast majority of cases, *bylichki* are part of a communicative context. When ethnographers observe rituals or performances of songs, they are indeed observers, not the addressees of these forms of folkloric speech. We may listen to and observe the telling of folktales, and in this situation we are in fact listeners. By contrast, the folklore genre termed "oral prose," which includes legends and life stories, involves a very different communicative situation. In it the collector is a participant, an interested party, and the nature of his or her interest is often not clear to the teller. These are always conversations with an unexplained presupposition. Our first example demonstrated this: it is unclear to the interviewee exactly what the interviewer wants to know in asking questions about the *dobrokhodushka*. The interviewee negotiates this complex situation, and finds an equivalent concept: guardian angel. In the process of the dialogue, a new conceptual space is created, and new relationships—that of teacher and pupil—are formed.

Several of our examples emphasized the didactic function of legend and the direct transmission of traditional practices from the older generation, who no longer actively needs or practices these, to the younger generation. While our examples involve young outsiders, we may postulate that young insiders would also hear analogous stories told with didactic intent. It is difficult for researchers to create contexts in which they may observe such transmission from insider to insider, from older to younger generation.[9] However, occasionally we do observe exchanges of stories between insiders, when we are participants in conversations. Our presence plays a role, but we may also see ways in which members of the community elicit and react to each other's stories. Here we clearly see the extent to which storytelling may gain the speaker cultural capital in the local social sphere.

The following story occurred during a social visit between three local women, born in 1925, 1936, and 1940, and a visiting American ethnographer (LO). During the evening the women shared many stories about their lives: about murders, abortions, injuries, near-kidnappings, near-robberies, and near-murders, and about the ways that magic can predict, avert, or heal such disasters. The following story was prompted by a chain of associations: the ethnographer was asking about religious songs the women knew, and one of the local guests asked the hostess, Valentina Sergeevna G. (our main informant in chapter 7), the oldest woman present, whether she used a certain prayer. Valentina averred that she did, and the other woman reminded her that she used to tell a story about how this prayer saved her life. Valentina responded that the prayer saved her life three times; she proceeded to tell us about two of them (we examine only one here). Unlike the conversation about the *domovoi*, this conversation yielded stories about particular events experienced by the narrator. These stories were clearly told for entertainment purposes as well as to provide proof of the teller's belief in and knowledge of the spiritual world—in this case, the world of Orthodox Christianity. Both positions—that of storyteller-entertainer and of proficient summoner of powers of the spiritual world—clearly gained the narrator social capital. In particular, Valentina's apparent desire to show skill with the texts of Orthodoxy may have been provoked by the presence, during this conversation, of the other guest, a local woman who played the role within the community of prayer leader/reader for memorial services. The role was self-initiated (the woman taught herself to read Church Slavonic) but involved some degree of outside approval by the Orthodox Church representatives (the priest). Perhaps for this reason, locals viewed her with respect and perhaps even a degree of envy of her special status. This woman does not speak in this portion of the conversation, but her presence is important. The interlocutors in order of appearance are Katerina Mikhailovna T. (born in 1936), Valentina Sergeevna G. (born in 1925), and Laura Olson (born in 1962).

KMT: When you go to bed, do you recite "Live help," Valya?[10]

VSG: I do. I know it entirely, that prayer.

LO: Do you recite "Live help" in chorus too?

VSG: [TO KMT]: Do you know which ones I recite when going to bed? [to LO] No, not necessarily in chorus.

KMT: No, I don't recite it. Do you remember when you told us how you brought piglets with you in a bus. And you said, I recited and recited it the whole way. "Live help."

VSG: Mmm. That one helped me more than once.

KMT: He wanted to, he wanted to hit her with a wrench.

VSG: Oh, how he reaches in, reaches in there, and I'm reciting, reciting, reciting—There goes a car! He jumps up and that's it. It goes past. It's past, he sees no one's there, he reaches back in there for it. I'm about to open [the door]. And then, I had told her, "Oh, I'm going to Kasimov," I see, so that she wouldn't touch me. Aha. So when we got to Gus', he stopped [and] I said, "I'm getting out here." "[But] you wanted to go to Kasimov?" "No, I'm getting out." So he left me alone.

LO: But how, who did you—?

VSG: I had piglets with me.

LO: [Laughs]

KMT: [She] had money with her.

VSG: I was traveling with money. There were piglets too, they're cheap. And I had one piglet left. Some of those [people from our village] sold theirs. And some were left. "Oi," I said, "maybe I'll catch up with them." I didn't catch up with them—they left in a car. Three women. And I'm alone. A car's coming. And I have a pig [left]. A woman says, "Give it to me." While she took it and carried it home, I waited, she sees—a car's coming. Well, they put me in it. That one put me in it. And he's looking at me. I say, "I went to my sister's. [Laughs] I brought her pigs!" He says, "No way in hell, you can't fool me." [Laughs] I say, "I brought pigs to my sister!" Mmmm, he knows that we went [to sell] pigs. [Sharp intake of breath] Like that—we pulled out, and he reaches for that, there under his seat for that, for his wrench, now [he'll hit] me on the head, he poked it out, and all. [Sharp intake of breath] And I move closer, closer to the door, I hang onto that, I think when he swings with that thing I'll . . . fly out there. And I'm reciting, reciting, reciting "Live help," I see—a car is coming back, coming toward us. And he puts it back. And I recited it all the way to Gus', and he didn't get a chance. And then I say, "I'm getting out here." Aha, I open the door. "You wanted to go to Kasimov?" I say, "No, I'm [getting out] here." (Krasnoe, Riazan' oblast, 8 December 2004)

One interesting facet of this story involves its dual framing of the same material. The narrator first tells the story as if to insiders (who have heard it before), and only secondarily, based upon the ethnographer's questions, explains the story in a more detailed fashion, so that it can be understood by outsiders. As researchers in Russian villagers, we have often noted that when people tell memorates or fabulates they give outlines and highlights of the story. It is only when we request more information that it fully "makes sense" to us.

Two facets of storytelling communication may account for this fact: its theatrical nature and its orality. The performance of the *bylichka* is a kind of theatrical performance. In this case, there is no physical stage or staging and little physical acting out of the story, but the teller verbally "takes the spotlight" with her longer utterances, dramatic intonation, pauses and accelerations, emphatic expressions, and so on. Erving Goffman's concept of "frames" suggests that when everyday behavior becomes self-conscious in this way it may be seen to involve a "theatrical frame." The example we are analyzing follows many of the expected rules of the theatrical genre, including the rule by which the audience is intentionally kept "in the dark" about some of the events depicted. As Goffman explains, for characters in a play to fill in all the necessary details would ruin the dramatic illusion; the audience must be told just enough to understand (1974, 136, 142). Whether the storyteller in this case and in every case of *bylichka*-telling is intentionally withholding information is a question we cannot answer for certain. Likely it is a convention of storytelling. Such withholding would have an additional important function: it would remove the necessity of "setting up" the story and allow the storyteller to concentrate on the moment of action, as the narrator does here. She begins the story at its most dramatic moment, when the man is trying to get the opportunity to seize his weapon while her prayer is apparently preventing him and saving her: "Oh, how he reaches in, reaches in there, and I'm reciting, reciting, reciting!"

This beginning at the climax of the story, typical for *bylichki*, speaks to the predominantly oral quality of the culture to which our older informants belong. Walter Ong calls the existence of oral qualities in literate cultures "residual orality." As Ong argues, in literate cultures we think of narrative as "typically designed in a climactic linear plot often diagrammed as the well-known 'Freytag's pyramid' (i.e., an upward slope, followed by a downward slope)." Oral narrative from oral cultures does not have this kind of plot: the epic poet wants to "get immediately to 'where the action is'"; he "will report a situation and only much later explain, often in detail, how it came to be." These plots do not typically have a well-organized beginning, middle, and end (Ong 2002, 139–41). To be sure, our informants of the second and third generations are literate (with an average of seven grades of schooling), but the generation of their mothers—those born before the Revolution—was either not literate or barely so. Thus, many of the cultural habits our informants employ hark back to a preliterate culture.

This story helps us see another subject position that Russian narrators of supernatural stories may adopt. The narrator paints herself as a capable, independent woman who can competently function in public places alone due to her ability to foretell and take action against threats. In particular, both stories she told about the prayer concern potential violence that would have been perpetrated by men. The narrator depicts her vulnerable social position as a woman alone. As a woman alone she relies on her ability to foresee danger: she had the foresight to tell the driver a lie about her reason for attending the market, so that he would not know she was carrying money. But he saw through her ruse. Her second method of defense is the prayer, the text of which asserts that evil will not befall anyone who honors God. Her stories prove that this is true: the potential evil-doer was apparently prevented from acting by the prayer, which seemed to cause cars (and therefore potential witnesses) to appear on the road. As Paxson has argued, Russian village faith involves a process she calls *obrashchenie* or turning toward: an invocation, petition, or appeal to a higher authority. "The underlying sense of obrashcheniia is that they are what one does when one is beyond hope . . . when something transformative must enter the picture" (Paxson 2005, 159). These appeals may be "aimed in the direction of unseen powers" such as God, saints, or unclean or clean forces (dead ancestors, mother earth, *leshii*, *domovoi*, etc.). In this understanding, as Paxson points out, not only does power create religion (in the sense that institutions, classes, and ideologies create the conditions for religion) but religion creates power (in the sense that people can access power through their religious practices) (2005, 160). Stories of belief both call upon a religious understanding of power, and "perform" power for the narrator. In this case, by framing the narrated event as a successful invocation of supernatural power, the narrator claims and creates social power for herself.[11] The cultural plot implied here ("I successfully appealed to the spirit world") is based upon the cultural imperative that an adult person—in particular, a woman who is head of a household, a *bol'shukha*—should know how to use petitions to the spirit world in order to survive, be healthy, and have success in life.

Contrary to the projections of Soviet-era collectors, it seems that many in rural Russia *do* believe what they tell. In fact, belief is so deeply engrained that it is assumed, appearing in narratives most often as the shadow that organizes plots and shapes scripts. Narrators enact belief in the process of telling, constructing meaning in ways that are familiar to cultural insiders. We have emphasized how the interpersonal contexts of the narrative moment—the relationships and roles of participants—influence the words (and details, and categories, and assumptions) that narrators choose to incorporate or underscore.[12]

Rather than attempting to prove the existence of an other world, for instance, many of the stories we collected were intended to teach listeners about relationships with the dead. Plots and scripts follow from and prescribe these interactions. For the tellers of these stories, the relationships that influence their behavior include those with the family clan (*rod*), in particular with deceased family members, with whom one must have specific forms of interaction. Also important are relationships with nonhuman forces, including—for some—with God. The primary importance of these relationships helps explain why questions from interviewers about the appearance of supernatural beings often are met with bewilderment. What is important is not what the beings look like but how one behaves in relation to them.

Finally, we have called attention to the way these stories negotiate relationships and roles in the present moment. In telling both insiders and outsiders stories of their relationships to supernatural beings, Russian villagers use first- and third-person experience narratives to construct a world of meaning and shape the social networks of the living as well as the dead. In their stories they enact and also teach roles that help them construct a multi-faceted, complex, and always shifting relational identity. Our next chapter describes another aspect of this identity: the ways that rural women enact relationships with their ancestors through their practices relating to death and the dead.

9

Death, the Dead, and Memory-Keepers

Death, and one's attitude toward it, is a prime motivator of religious belief (Malinowski 1954). We take that profound and complex connection between death and religion as the subject of this chapter. Religion was very much a part of the worlds of our interlocutors when we visited them: we have characterized it (in chapter 7) as a rich folk Orthodox spirituality. It was difficult to imagine how we would write about their spirituality, until we realized that all of our religious experiences in villages—or many of them—revolved around death or the dead. In a sense, there is no other important context for spirituality, no other experience that brings the need for spirituality into such relief.

Underlying the human need for spirituality is the fear of death. We are inclined to agree with Sigmund Freud and other psychologists, philosophers, and biologists that such a fear is universal (Becker 1973). Freud saw any belief in immortality as a childish denial of death's reality. Carl Jung countered that view, arguing that living in harmony with an unconscious, timeless myth of eternal life can help make the fear of death less stark and overwhelming. Jung wrote: "Only if we know that the thing which truly matters is the infinite can we avoid fixing our interests upon futilities, and upon all kinds of goals which are not of real importance. If we understand and feel that here in this life we already have a link with the infinite, desires and attitudes change" (Jung 1963, 356–57). That is, immortality is not a myth in the sense of a lie but a myth in the folklorist's sense of a sacred narrative. Jung's wisdom is that it is important for living people to connect with the infinite in order to live a healthy, meaningful life. Working with Jung's principle, psychologists Robert Jay Lifton and Eric Olson (1974, 2004) detail the many ways that humans can connect with the infinite. They define "symbolic immortality" as "concepts, imagery, and symbols adequate to give a sense of significance to experience" (2004, 34).

The traditional practices of our informants give them excellent support in facing death, as many of our examples show. More than that, their culture offers multiple means of symbolizing immortality, as defined by Lifton and Olson. Russian rural culture offers an intense sense of biological immortality, the idea that one lives on through one's descendants. As farmers, rural dwellers have a strong connection to the rhythms of nature. A sense of immortality is implied through the ebb and flow of the seasons: we see this in their holiday celebrations connected to the solar calendar that link awareness of nature with the honoring of the ancestors. Additionally, creative craftsmanship, such as tool-making, carpentry, weaving, embroidery, sewing, and knitting, connects a person with craftspeople who lived and worked long ago, and whose patterns still adorn the spaces of the living. Folk religion offers a well-developed mythology of life after death, heaven and hell, and the immortal soul. Finally, rural women's keen daily awareness and practice of spirituality offers multiple contexts in which individuals can experience transcendence, which Lifton and Olson argue is an important means of coming into contact with immortality. They may do so through extraordinary life experiences involving the suspension of the ordinary awareness of time, for example during childbirth, in the context of ritual, or through an intense experience such as personal grief. As many of our interlocutors recounted, life-changing experiences often caused a person to seek a spiritual outlet. A close brush with a spiritual death leads one to search for a sense of the infinite.

Examining women's narratives about their death preparedness, funeral, and memorial practices, and our observations of such rituals, in this chapter we show that memory-keeping is performed exclusively by women in Russian rural communities. Although women typically accept these functions only after reaching a certain age status, this is not an automatic transition but is one formed by a woman's internal experience of loss. We begin by explaining the traditional Russian views of death that inform these practices.

Death as Practice

As is well demonstrated in the ethnographic literature, a view of life as having a predestined length was characteristic of Russian rural culture. Anyone who died a natural death in old age or after a long illness, or a "positive accidental death," was viewed as having lived out his or her allotted time and as having died at the "correct" time. A proverb said that "One does not die when old, but when ripe" (*umiraet ne staryi, a pospelyi*) (Bernshtam 2000, 180). Russian rural people often call these naturally deceased collectively *roditeli* (parents, ancestors). These ancestors, it is believed, must be honored by the living if the living wish to avoid serious consequences, such as emotional upset, visitations by the dead, and illnesses. In the past it was believed that *roditeli* could also cause poor harvests to the community.

By contrast, one who does not live out one's allotted time is said to die a "bad" or "incorrect" death. Zelenin (using a term from Belorussia) calls such deceased *zalozhnye*, the "set aside" dead, in the sense of a body that is placed separately from others (Zelenin 1916; Warner 2000a, 2000b). Such deaths were murder and suicide victims and victims of accidents. These types of deaths were marked by different funeral practices: they were buried outside the boundaries of the cemetery, and the funeral procession took a different route. The villagers from Karl Libnekht village in Vologda oblast told us that two roads lead to the cemetery. One was used by the "correct deceased" and the other by drunkards and suicides. In Ul'ianovsk oblast people told us that during only one time of the year (Rusal'naia/Trinity week or Whitsunday week) could these "set aside" bodies be transferred to the main cemetery.

A correct death comes with a person's readiness to die. The preparation of the funeral bundle, which is still practiced today, is a gradual mental and gestural preparation for death.[1] In many of our interviews there is a strong sense that one is able to choose one's time of death. When a few years ago we studied the statistics of men's and women's mortality in the Belozersk region of Vologda oblast, we noticed that many people older than seventy died in the same month in which they were born. That suggested to us that these people may have "chosen" this time to die. One woman cheerfully told us, "We all die at eighty-six. And I'm eighty. So I'll still live for a while." Another said, "This year I'll live, and next year I'll pass [go on a journey/*uedu*], either in town or at the cemetery" (Roksoma, Vologda oblast, 2001). And she did: when we came to the village the following summer, we found out that she had died in the spring. As depicted by the discourse of death, she had gone on a journey.

The following conversation about the preparations that individuals make for their own deaths shows the difference between the understandings of death of young and older people. One can see that for the eighteen-year-old student folklorist leading the interview, preparedness for death is a new idea: she asks whether her informant is not afraid to think about death. After all, to think about the dress in which one will be buried is to imagine a time when one will have ceased to exist. In the city youth culture to which the interviewer belongs, people avoid thinking about the things that will happen after they are gone.[2] The elder rural dweller in this interview, on the other hand, does not understand what can be scary about preparing a dress for her funeral. She must look respectable in her coffin, and to prepare for that is a normal part of life.

> *You prepare it for yourself?*
> Who else? All of it.
> *And what is that, you feel your death coming?*
> [*Laughs*] How else? I bought a sarafan, too. I dried it. And everything's ready, too.
> *Oh?*
> Yes, everything.
> *Aren't you afraid?*
> No. I bought shoes and all, boots. Pants and a shirt I bought and all, and a scarf, all I need to do is wrap it up, die and that's it. But what, what's scary about it! It's out there in the yard, let it stay there.
> *In the yard?*

Well, yes.

What do you mean, in the yard?

Mmm, in the barn. (Woman born in 1929, Kolmogora, Leshukonskii region, Arkhangel'sk oblast, 13 July 2009 [Lesh 17-22])

To many dwellers of large cities in post-Soviet Russia, death has become more removed from the family, while in the village, it is accepted as part of daily life. While in the city a family will hire a service to take care of the body and host the funeral, in the village everyone is involved in every funeral (Rouhier-Willoughby 2008, 266).[3] Children are not excluded but are taken to the home to say farewell to the deceased—even if the deceased is only a neighbor, not a relative. They see the dead body, and the parents take the children with them to the cemetery for memorials and funerals.[4] Every member of the village community considers it his or her duty to attend a funeral, to see the deceased off on his final journey. This is a duty to the deceased, more than to the living. It lightens the burden and eases the passage of the deceased as he or she travels to a new place.

Russian ethnographers have taken this seeming nonchalance with respect to death to mean that Russian peasants did not fear death or the dead (see, for example, Firsov and Kiseleva 1993). We would qualify that evaluation. According to our observation, the dead are very much mourned, and people value their own lives highly. No one wants to die before his or her time, and no one wishes the death of loved ones. The acceptance of death remarked by ethnographers is reserved only for "correct" or natural deaths. And nonchalance around dead bodies is a practical matter related to beliefs about death and the nature of community. The dead need certain services that can only be provided by community members: neighbors (not the family), *starukhi*, must wash the body and dress it in its death clothes. Every member of the community must say farewell, and must accompany the body on the initial part of its journey. The sense of connection with the members of the community that Russians call *svoi* extends to them after death. The dead—those who die a natural death—are still *svoi*. They do not become alien, unclean, or ghoulish, as is commonly believed of the dead in urban centers.

Because death is a public matter in the community, it matters what one wears when one is publicly displayed after death. But what one wears also matters because life does not end at the moment of death. Death is an experience, not a lack of being. The myth—the certainty—of life after death underlies this practice of preparing a funeral bundle (*smertnyi uzelok*). The clothing for burial is prepared consciously and carefully for the simple reason that life—with all its conveniences and inconveniences, all its desires and lacks—continues after death. The following interview with a forty-five-year-old woman, Rosa Matveevna N., and her eighty-four-year-old mother, Anna Pavlovna Z., shows that those living in the world of the dead experience an embodied existence: one of them needs soap to wash her hands; another is uncomfortable in the shoes she was buried with. All of these needs are conveyed via dreams, which serve as a channel through which the dead communicate with the living. The living then place the needed objects in the coffin with another deceased, so that the items can be transferred "there." In this economy of trade between worlds, there appears to be only one direction of flow: the deceased are dependent upon the living, and cannot procure for themselves the items that they require for life there.

RMN: It even happened that Tanya dreamed of a deceased relative, who said, "I wash my hands and I don't have soap." Just like that. She dreamed of him all the time: [he said,] "Tanya, I have dirty hands!" What's going on? So they went to their grandmother, and she said, "Where did you put the leftover soap [from the washing of the body], or didn't you put it [in the coffin]?" She said, "You know, so that you don't go crazy here, just take some soap, go to church, and if they are singing over [*otpevaiut*] [some deceased], ask if you can put it in their coffin. So that they would pass it on to him." So that was it, he stopped appearing in dreams, saying there was no soap!

She dreamed that her relative, whom she had buried, had nothing to wash his hands with?

RMN: Yes, nothing to wash his hands with. And so she dreamed all the time: "It's not good here, I . . . I have dirty hands, I don't have anything to wash them with!" And they sent it. And then another one, it happened to her too, also with a relative. That woman was young, thirty-five [when she died]. And they thought for a long time what to put her in [in the coffin]. Not in slippers. She was a young woman, after all. So they put her in the shoes she had worn . . . and she keeps appearing in dreams, walking and having trouble walking. They had put her in shoes, and up till forty days [after death] she appeared almost every day [to her relative]. They had to buy slippers.

They had to be without heels?

RMN: Either in slippers, or in some kind of, the kind they sell in ritual stores, or the ones they have now, the indoor ones . . .

And did they bury them?

RMN: They passed them on through another deceased, passed the slippers on. It was probably in 1998.

[. . .]

[to Anna Pavlovna] *And when did you start getting everything ready?*

APZ: You see, you come . . . Nowadays you see, everywhere there's a lot of stuff [in the markets, to buy], right? It used to be they didn't bring in much. It used to be they would bring it in and you'd buy it up right away . . .

[. . .]

What did you prepare for yourself?

APZ: An undershirt, shirt, dress . . .
    What kind of dress? Flowered or a single color?
APZ: No, a single color!
    What color?
APZ: Gray.
RMN: What do you mean, gray! Talking with you is completely comical! At seventy-
    five she said, "I need a burial dress [*umiral'noe plat'e*], Tanya, bring one!" Tanya
    brought, she bought one, yes. [Anna Pavlovna] lived a bit [i.e., time passed], it
    seemed she wore it, [then:] "I can't fit into it anymore, in my burial dress." "Well,
    it has to have long sleeves, don't put me in a short-sleeved one," and so on. She
    lived a bit more, and said, "That one is tight, I won't wear that one." We said,
    what will Matvei think of you there, if you come in such a bad dress . . . More
    time passed, she turned eighty, so we bought her a dress, a wool one. A normal,
    nice dress.
APZ: Nice, but . . .
RMN: So, she said, "This is my burial dress." We get together for her eightieth
    birthday, everyone came, and she says, "I don't know, I don't have a burial dress."
    I say, again? We gave you one for your eightieth. Did you grow again, you got fat
    again! Again, for your eighty-fifth, we're going to get you a new dress, again?
    How many burial dresses can we outfit you with! [*Laughs*] She said, you know,
    the scarf has too few flowers, don't put me in a calico one. (Woman born in 1922
    and woman born in 1961, Kononovskaia, Siamzha region, Vologda oblast, 14
    August 2006 [Siam D-Txt 1-80])

The elder woman here desires to look good, to feel comfortable in the future life. She wants to be in the correct clothes, with the right amount of flowers and in the correct color. As personal style, aesthetics, and respectability are important here on earth, so they are important *there*. Preparation for death is an occupation in her later years, as her daughter complains: her mother has become too involved, almost obsessed with her burial dress. A burial is like a wedding; death is a life-stage, like being married, for which one must prepare. As with a wedding, death requires the proper costume to mark the change in status. Just as it is (or formerly was) taboo for rural Russian married women to show their hair, so married women are buried in a white cap or shroud that covers their hair; either they prepare it for themselves or other women prepare it for them after death.

    Death, then, is not only an experience one passively undergoes; it is also a practice. Through the practice of death-preparation, our informants gain emotional readiness for their passage. They gain a measure of control over their future existence in the new place to which they are going, the land of death or the other world. They give recognition to the belief that they will join the *roditeli*, the honored ancestors. They live and die with the security that their memory will be preserved actively, via numerous community practices designed to keep the deceased peaceful and happy in their new state.

Honoring the Dead

The practice of remembering the deceased at specific times is a duty the living perform for their deceased relatives, to make their existence *there* easier, and even to move them out of a bad place (hell), should they find themselves there. The forms and times of the practice differ somewhat in different areas, but all over Russia the principle is the same: to remember the deceased is a duty of the living. The simplest way, which many of our village interlocutors perform daily, is a remembrance with one's morning tea. In the Orthodox tradition remembrance is included in the morning prayer ritual.

Our interlocutors go to great lengths to properly remember their dead. In the Russian North, the gradual emptying of the village during the twentieth century resulted in cemeteries that are difficult to reach, since the roads to them are overgrown, no longer used by regular traffic. Village dwellers in Vologda oblast told us that, no matter how far their cemeteries were, they visited them at least once a year. When they move through the forest, looking for the road, they address their *roditeli*, the deceased in the clan, the *rod*: "Grandfathers, grandmothers, help us!" The mandatory visits take place on *roditel'skie* weeks and days, which, depending upon local tradition, may include the following (or variations on these): (1) the Saturday before Maslenitsa week, before Lent; (2) the second, third, and fourth Saturdays of Lent; (3) the Saturday before Troitsa, the ninth day after Ascension day; (4) Radonitsa or Radunitsa, the second Tuesday after Easter; (5) Dmitriev Saturday, a kind of Veterans' day, the Saturday that comes on or before the eighth of November; and (6) Veterans' Day, celebrated in Russia on the ninth of May.

In this manner, the memorial communication with the ancestors of the *rod* becomes one of the ways that living people express their relatedness to each other. Relatives come from other villages and cities, and all join in the partaking of a common meal at the gravesite. The act of remembering the dead is one of the main rituals that creates social cohesion in the village community. Social historians call this ritual *memoria*: "Memory and memorializing create commonality; memoria creates community, and is its constitutive element" (Oexle 2007, 263).

Women are the community's memory-keepers: they are the ones who organize and oversee the honoring of the dead. The following interview with a woman born in 1936 in Arkhangel'sk oblast demonstrates the time commitment and commitment to tradition involved in such a practice: the memorials have prescribed intervals that must be observed. One is not free to practice it simply at will or whenever it is convenient, but one can put one's creativity and personality into the way that one commemorates. Her discourse also demonstrates the way in which elder women see the care of the dead as a reflection upon their public identity: a well-kept grave shows that she is as good a memory-keeper as others

Woman cleans the grave of her mother (1928–2000), while talking with a neighbor on Great Thursday before Easter, Riazan' oblast, April 2005. (PHOTO BY LAURA J. OLSON)

in the community. We begin with her answer to our question of when people go to the cemetery:

> Usually already at around nine, everyone sticks to that . . .
> *In the morning, huh?*
> Yes . . . people don't go early, but by about ten for sure. And why? They say one should not disturb the dead, let them lie! And it's not recommended to go too often.
> *Yes?*
> Yes, also, let them lie peacefully. I mean, let's say my husband dies, we'll have a memorial for him at one year, but we'll go [to the cemetery] at nine days [after death], and then at twenty days, and forty days, and half a year. And then the yearly anniversaries [day of death, day of birth, name day]. That's it. And also, let's say, at the holidays [the *roditel'skie* days], but . . . but it's not recommended to go too often! So . . . personally, I know for myself, that . . . when I go to the cemetery, to

my husband or to Mother or to my mother-in-law, when others have a nicely kept grave, but mine is not nicely kept—I don't like that, I need it to be nicely kept! That's the way. So . . . people try to come at around ten, and at eleven, they eat a meal, you see. Eat lunch. They memorialize, let's say, Mom, Dad, Grandpa, Grandma. (Woman born in 1936, Selishche, Leshukonskii region, Arkhangel'sk oblast, 9 July 2009 [Lesh 17-3])

Preparing food so that the dead can be properly fed and remembered is one of the practices closely tying women, in particular *bol'shukhi*, who are in charge of food production in the home, with the ancestors. Because it was women's responsibility to cook, it was therefore their responsibility to cook for the dead. Many times we observed women taking meals to graveyards to be shared by the family on the remembrance days. The meals contained special foods, such as *kisel'* (a sweetened gelatin made of grain and/or fruit), and often vodka or *samogon*. The food would be eaten by the family and any passersby; then part of the meal would be left on the grave, and the vodka poured into the grave, for the dead. Aleksandra Ivanovna D., born in 1929, of Nikulinskaia, Vologda oblast, described what is done at the grave after a burial:

> *Do they memorialize the dead at the grave right after the burial?*
> They do, they take something and some wine, and baked *pirogi*. We used to bake *pirogi* all the time, I mean I baked *pirogi*. The kinds with filling, every, every kind. If your family was big, you'd fill up the oven with pies. And now I don't bake, don't bake.
> *Do you leave food at the grave? What kind?*
> Yes, we do. When you come to memorialize, you sprinkle grain on the grave, and some pour a glass of wine and leave it there, and if some stranger comes there, you also invite them to drink. Some get so drunk, that they fall asleep at the graveyard. [*Laughs*] (11 August 2006 [Siam 1-12])

On calendar memorial days, the mistress of the home would prepare the food to be brought to the graveyard, but at memorials held at home during the first year after death and at the funeral, the *khoziaika* would be too aggrieved to cook, and would engage others to cook for her. Thus, at a year anniversary memorial of the death of the daughter of eighty-year-old Valentina Sergeevna G. in Riazan' oblast in April 2005, women of the *khoziaika's* own generation—other *bol'shukhi-starukhi*—prepared the ritual dishes of pancakes (*bliny*), fruit gelatin (*kisel'*), and cooked grain (*kutiia*). In the symbolism of the funeral ritual, such foods eaten together by the living symbolize the memory of the deceased. At the memorial table, a certain traditional dish may be called *pomin*, the memory. Often these are sweet grain dishes. In Riazan' oblast, it is the *kisel'* that is called thus. The following description is from my (LO's) field diary for this memorial:

On the adjacent table were sweets—candies, cookies, "zefir" [a meringue-based sweet], "zefir"-like sticks, all store-bought, and homemade *kutiia*, rice with raisins, and a bowl of "*syta*": water with honey, which they poured over the *kutiia* and the *kisel'* after the service. They said of the *kisel'*, "this is the *pomin* itself." I had the impression it was not called *kisel'*, it was called "the *pomin* itself." It was clear, cut into cubes. And they kept repeating that phrase, "This is the *pomin* itself." I entered the world where things don't mean what you think they mean. Is the *pomin* the memory of the person? Or the person itself? There's some kind of embodiment going on. And what relation does it have to the name of this ritual, *pominki*? Can *pominki* exist without a *pomin*?

Moscow folklorist Elena Minyonok, who attended this memorial with me, explained that the fruit gelatin, the *kisel'*, was the embodiment of everyone's memory of this person. For that reason, this special food had to be eaten out of a common bowl, with one spoon (there were not individual portions): in this fashion, everyone "partook" of the memory. Eating in this way would support the entrance of the dead person into the other world.

Antonina Ivanovna Ch. (b. 1940) (foreground) reads prayers for one-year memorial of the daughter of Valentina Sergeevna G. (b. 1925), Krasnoe, Riazan' oblast, April 2005. The table in the background holds food for commemoration of the deceased. (PHOTO BY LAURA J. OLSON)

Community norms strongly dictate that the *khoziaika* prepare (or have prepared) traditional foods for memorials, but the choice of foods and how they are prepared is hers. Exactly how to commemorate and how much work to devote to memorializing is a personal choice, and is related to the internal psychological work that a person does in mourning for loved ones. While some of the work that one does for memorializing is social and public, there are also many private, even secret ways in which women conduct their homage to their *roditeli*. We see that private, internal process clearly in the narrative of Raisa Viktorovna, born in 1931 in Vologda oblast.

I (SA) met Raisa Viktorovna in 1994. She came to help some acquaintances with the hay mowing.[5] While conversing, she accidently revealed that she could perform laments. I then asked her to tell me about lamenting. Everything that happened later was very strange. We saw each other practically every day, but she avoided having this conversation. And suddenly one day she came to us herself, wearing a handwoven shirt. She stood at the threshold, and called me outdoors to have a chat. We went out into the front porch, then quietly walked off. We passed the entire village, reaching the end, and came out to the lake. There she sat on a bench by the bathhouse. I had to sit opposite her, on the grass; and only then and there in this secluded place did our conversation finally begin. Raisa Viktorovna was married for the second time. She had divorced, and subsequently her first husband had died. For her ex-husband, his deceased parents, and also the deceased parents of her new husband, she regularly performed a particular bathhouse ritual on the "day of death" (the day that the death occurred) and "day of the angel" (the saint's day corresponding to the name of the deceased). For each of those dead she kept linen (shirts, towels), which she would take to the bathhouse. She would light the fire in the bathhouse, then heat the water. Her family would wash, then she would wash the bench for the deceased to bathe. She would perform a lament in the bathhouse, summoning the dead to come wash:

> Come to me, my dear father,
> Come to me, my dear,
> And wash, and steam yourself.
> And I soften a branch in a clean bucket for him, and say:
> Come, we won't disturb you.

She explained, "After nine o'clock people don't go into the bathhouse on days of remembrance, but the next morning you pour out that water and leave that bucket standing upside down for a whole day, as if he poured it out. You can keep the soap, then buy a new one" (Anufievo, Vologda oblast, 13 July 1994 [Bel 17-48]).

In this fashion, ten times a year, she heated the bathhouse for the dead. The linen that she takes to the bathhouse is kept separately in the house for each of those commemorated, and is not used for any other purpose. She hangs these things on the partition in the bathhouse, and calls the dead with a lament. Then she goes away, leaving them to have a bath. She returns the next morning, and pours out the water "with which they washed themselves." This means two tubs of water—cold and hot. First she fills them up with buckets (which requires time and strength). Then the buckets sit in the bathhouse the entire night, and in the morning she pours them out completely. Scrubbers that have been laid out for the occasion are also never used for other purposes. The performer of the ritual does not count on anyone's approval for what she is doing. She only cares about the gratitude of the deceased. Fulfilling this is entirely her choice. It would seem that public opinion, as important as it is to villagers, does not determine these private activities in which she engages.

The apparent absence of an explicit social incentive for Raisa Viktorovna's obligations shows that relations with *roditeli* and the self-imposed labor of commemoration are to some degree optional. In the village where everything in the private lives of each person is open to everyone, behaviors are rigidly motivated and controlled by society. There is social pressure to commemorate the dead in public ways, at the cemetery and by having guests for memorial dinners, but such pressure cannot be at work in the types of commemoration that occur secretly. Caring for the fate of the afterlives of relatives and the labor related to it are signs of some kind of serious internal psychological work—perhaps the processing of grief, perhaps upholding of the *rod*—that is performed by a person for him- or herself and in relation to the other world.[6]

This example demonstrates well the particular care that a woman takes upon herself to make her deceased relatives comfortable in providing them with the proper implements for them to take a ritual bath. In this as in all of these examples we are struck by the degree to which, in the discourse of memorialization, the deceased are dependent upon the living. They must be provided with clothes, toiletries, and food; someone must accompany them on the beginning of their journey; and the living must spend effort and time remembering them on certain days. Why?

We can suggest dual answers to this question. First, the ancestors have great power. According to one of the most central mythological scripts, if things do not go right with the *rod*, for example if people suffer infertility or bad harvests, one must look for the cause in the relationship between the living and the ancestors. Along the line, someone must not have behaved correctly toward the deceased: for example, as our stories in chapter 8 showed, a family may have left the village to return to the city, ignoring a day of remembrance. Or there may be discord among living family members: in a lament Raisa Viktorovna dictated to us the deceased warn the living, "Now go, live, and don't fight." Other reports confirm that in local belief, conflict among the living is highly unfavorable to the deceased. Such stories again emphasize the continued connection of the ancestors and the living, and the moral imperative, for the living, of correct behavior with regard to all within the family circle.

Second, we may understand the funeral ritual as a rite of passage for the dead. As Van Gennep (1909) has described life-cycle rituals, initiates first undergo a process of separation from the community, then a marginal or liminal period during which the initiate has ambiguous characteristics, and finally they enter the period called aggregation or reincorporation into the community with the new status. In the funeral ritual, as in the wedding, for example, the initiate (the deceased) has not undergone this process previously and needs guidance and help from the community—from elder women as guides and mediators—through the period of separation and liminality. Since the funeral process involves the deceased physically leaving the community, the third period of reincorporation is the goal of many of the memorial rituals.[7] Although the deceased are bodily located in a new place (underground in the cemetery) and spiritually occupy a new space (the other world), they are still part of the extended community of the living. In order to maintain this contact, the living must accommodate the deceased by moving to "their" space (the space of the cemetery), by including them in toasts and feasts, and by speaking to and about them. The ritual of allowing the deceased to bathe in the bathhouse on memorial holidays may be related to the need to reincorporate the deceased into the world of the living. Bathing is a welcoming and purifying ritual performed for all guests in Russian village homes. Epics recount the bathing of heroes when they return from battle; many times we (ethnographers) were unexpectedly invited to bathe upon our arrival in a village. To bathe the ancestors is to welcome them home.

This work is performed only by elder women, by *bol'shukhi*. But not every *bol'shukha* will take on a leading role. After the birth of her first child a woman begins to participate in funeral and memorial ceremonies, and in this capacity may help cook funeral ritual dishes together with other women from the community. But she does not typically take a principal role in organizing such rituals until later, when she experiences the death of someone close to her. In the funeral ritual there is more than one initiate: not only the deceased but also close family members are transitioning to a new state. When she loses a husband, a woman becomes a widow; when she loses even one parent, she gains the new status of an orphan. The role of guide and mediator in funeral rituals can only come after a woman has achieved either of these statuses. She builds up her ability to lead over time, by attending other funerals and beginning to take an active role in them: by lamenting, singing prayers or spiritual songs, or reading liturgy. Eventually she may lead the singing, chanting, or reading. Others in the village depend upon her and call for her when the time comes. Some women at this stage are *starukhi*, and traditionally it was only *starukhi*—women whose life-giving energy was coming to a close—who washed and dressed dead bodies (Prokop'eva 2005, 638). In the late twentieth to early twenty-first century, many of the women we saw leading funeral rituals functioned as *bol'shukhi* (in everyday life). These *bol'shukhi-starukhi* have reached an additional stage of life, for which the only life-stage terms are widow or orphan.

Lamenter as Mediator

Russian theologian and philosopher Pavel Florenskii, in writing about the movement upward of souls in the ancient Greek tradition, described death as a situation that demands particular skill from the deceased: "A person dies only once in life, and since he does not have experience, he dies awkwardly [*neudachno*] . . . But death, as all activity, requires skill. In order to die better, one must know how to die, must acquire the skill of dying, must learn death" (Florenskii 1996, 167–68). The Russian funeral tradition provides guidance for the dead and the mourners as they enter a new life-stage. One of the responsibilities of elder women is to guide the initiates—both those who have died and those who are entering the new status of a widow or orphan—through the rite of passage. Because she has experienced grief at the loss of a loved one, the widow or orphan *bol'shukha* or *starukha* has already "looked over" the land of the dead, "although from afar." She had help from elder women during her first loss, although most of the work she has done is internal. Now she turns to help others, the new initiates.

The ritual of lamenting is one of the traditions that is believed to help both the newly dead and the newly grieving. Grief must be expressed publicly, and the lament allows this to be done in a socially acceptable manner, with the community and in a verbal form. Too much grief, and especially grief expressed privately via crying, is not viewed positively in Russian rural communities, as numerous stories attest. Many of these legends were about widows who cried too much, and were visited by their husbands in his own form, or in the form of a fiery snake—in either case, the devil in disguise.

In our interviews we could see the attitudes toward this public activity of lamenting changing from generation to generation. Rural women of the first Soviet generation (the second generation in our study) were completely competent in lamenting. Of the twenty-five laments the Saint Petersburg Department of Folklore recorded in Belozersk in the 1980s and 1990s, twelve were recorded from women of the first generation (1899–1916), thirteen from women born in 1917–29, and not a single one from younger women. Women of the third generation witnessed laments and described them but had not typically performed them themselves. With lamenting dying out for the generation born in 1930 and later, other funeral- and memory-related practices were taking its place. For example, in Ul'ianovsk oblast there was a well-developed tradition of spiritual songs sung at funeral and memorial rituals. Women collected the songs, trading their texts with other women by passing around handwritten notebooks. Like laments, some of these were applicable specifically for certain situations, such as the death of a parent, a mother, or a child (Gladkova n.d.).

The following interview with a woman born in 1941 in Vologda oblast suggests how the lamenting tradition began to die out during her lifetime, and also shows that her view of those who did perform laments attributes to them a great deal of social power.

Do you know, did people perform laments, did they lament?

Now no one laments, but earlier they lamented, yes, there were laments. Auntie Manya Isaeva used to know a lot of laments, she was the only one who lamented, before she—may she be given the kingdom of heaven—died, she was the one who lamented.

Do you remember the words?

Oi, everyone has her own words. They're right here. They would sing from their own self, they'd lament, so it's very hard to remember.

Maybe a phrase or two?

No, not even one, we were little then, and when we grew up, no one lamented anymore. They used to take special women to lament, they'd hire a person for that. You know, when I was little my father died, and already no one lamented. And when my sister died they didn't lament.

Did it happen that a lamenter would lament on behalf of the family, speaking from their point of view?

Yes, there were lamenters, I was little, and I remember that there were lamenters then. They'd start, and everyone would start crying. It was really like hypnosis, the effect it had, at first one, and sometimes they'd hire two lamenters so that people would cry even more, and then everyone would just start crying. It was like they were hypnotizers. (Woman born in 1941, Kirsnovo, Kirillov region, Vologda oblast, 7 July 2006 [Kir 17a-2])

Lamenters were women with special knowledge, and their activity had particular effects upon others, including those who witnessed the event. Their competency included knowledge about how the afterlife is configured, and also the ability to meditate poetically upon the mystical world of death. With the repeated rhythm of the chant, they entered into a trance-like state so that they could "see" that which cannot be seen: the land of the dead. In the laments they told the initiates, the newly dead, about this world that they were about to enter. For example, in the interview below, Natalia Nikolaevna T., born in 1904, recounted to the folklorist her lament at the funeral of her young nephew. Speaking as a widowed woman and as his guide, she tells him what will happen to him. In this interview the lamenter also comments upon her lamenting, telling the folklorist that she is having trouble reproducing the lament:

Here's how I lamented for my own, my son.

Blow, winds,—Oh, I can't, I can't, no way!
From the midday side.
Come, two angels,
Winged angels,

Bring the soul,—I can't!—angels.
Cleave yourself, mother damp earth,
—One can lament well, but telling comes out badly, and I can't do it. Oi!—
In two, in three halves
And in four quarters. Oi.
Spread wide, white arms—I've already forgotten it somehow—
And open, bright eyes,
And lift yourselves on light feet,
And let us go, my dear sweet one,
To the final release,
To the final farewell.—Like that!

>   *That's how you lamented.*
>   But you see you have to draw it out a long time. But then . . .

You will go, my dear sweet one,
On a long road,
Beyond the forests, the sleeping ones,
Beyond the swamps, the quicksandy ones,
Beyond the lakes, the deep ones,
Beyond the seas, the wide ones.
There are guards
There are loyal ones,
There are sentries, strong ones.
They will not let you go, dear one,
To your native land.

>   You just keep lamenting. You can put whatever else you want in here. I just did a
> little. That's what, girl. Did you understand?
>   *Aha. Like that, huh?* (Ivanovskii, Belozersk region, Vologda oblast, 23 July 1997
> [Bel 17a-36)[8]

In the poetic text of this lament Natalia Nikolaevna pictures herself as a guide who
accompanies her young nephew, up until the middle of the text, at which point the pronoun
changes from "we" to "you": "And let us go, my dear sweet one / To the final release / To the
final farewell. / You will go, my dear sweet one, / On a long road . . ." Although it depicts
a life hereafter, the lament emphasizes that there can be no return home for the deceased.
Russian traditional culture is not in denial about the finality of death.

The woman who sang this lament for the folklorist Natalia Gerasimova in 1997 emphasized afterward that she had these bits of text fresh in her memory since her nephew had
recently died. But, as she said, there is much more that one can "put in" a lament. This

was just a small sample, but she could not deliver a long lament, and kept complaining that she "couldn't," presumably because she was lacking the proper context. The mediator between life and death would spring into action when needed, but a folklorist's wish to hear a lament did not constitute a genuine need.

Another interview speaks to this point. A man, born in 1954, remembers his grandmother's ability to turn on and off her lamenting skill:

> I was a boy, yes. In that house over there, an old man died. And my grandma and he didn't like each other for some reason, but in the village there was no one left to lament. So they came to ask for grandma: "Nadezhda Ivanovna, come, lament a bit. The old man Aleshen'ka Kostrov has died." Grandma got ready to go and was cursing the old man: "Ekh, what kind of so-and-so do I have to lament for!" And I thought: Probably, grandmother is not going to go. No, grandmother went, and sat by the coffin. How she raised her voice! They say that there—raise your voice [*golosit*]. It was genuine, her tears came down like hail. I thought, what do you know, when she was going there she said such unpleasant things. In short, she did her time, and came home. And she had already forgotten about this old man.
> 	*Did they pay her money for that?*
> 	I think they didn't. It was just that she, so to speak, was like a professional lamenter, who was able to express her feelings in such a way that all the relatives simply sobbed. And she sobbed, too. She would go out, and it would all go away, she would return to normal life, and it was as if she forgot it all. It was a theater, you understand, a village theater, but terribly genuine. They would lament like: how great he was. It would come out in such a sob, that everyone around understood— what a person had died! (Man born in 1954, Ekimovo, Vashkinskii region, Vologda oblast, 19 July 2000 [Vash 17a-2])

Again we call upon the theories of Goffman to make sense of this: clearly, the ritual behavior of the lamenter exists within a theatrical frame, in which certain conventions of the stage are followed. The performer typically sits on a chair, her upper body bent forward, partially covering her face with her hands. The lament is sung on a particular melody with a downward contour, using a sobbing vocal quality. Often the singer chooses a high tessitura, such that the voice is thin. In most regional styles the singer cuts off the last syllable of the word at the end of each poetic line, ending each line in a downward glissando (slide). Despite its conventional and performative features, in the above-quoted interview a carrier of the culture calls it "terribly genuine": no one is faking emotion. Instead, the emotion is "required" and produced by the ritual situation.

In performing a lament, a singer is tapping in to her memory of her own emotional experiences. Many interviewees stated that they could not lament, but as they began showing us, they started sobbing and lamenting authentically. The performance brought tears to the eyes of those present as well. The school in which one learned the ways of death was one's own experience of grief, as Natalia Nikolaevna, the lamenter in the previous example, explained:

> *Who taught you to lament?*
> No one taught me, I learned by myself.
> *By yourself. But how? You heard how others lamented?*
> Well, yes, I heard a little from people.
> *Aha.*
> Dear one, when grief arrives, you'll learn yourself. While there's no grief, then
> you won't. (Woman born in 1904, Zubovo, Belozersk region, Vologda oblast,
> 23 July 1997 [Bel 17a-36])

Initiates and the Initiated

The school of grief motivated a host of spiritual activities in the village of Pot'ma in Ul'ianovsk oblast. The example of this village tells us much about women's roles as spiritual mediators in the post-Soviet period, and about how spiritual leadership roles are transmitted within a social group. In this village since the 1930s there has been an active tradition of local elder women placing themselves in charge of spiritual matters for the community. While researchers see this often in the post-Soviet village, the situation in Pot'ma is especially interesting because the women persist in conducting church services (services normally conducted by a priest in a church) in their homes. Their story shows how a combination of internal (emotional) and external (historical, social) forces led the women to take on the roles of spiritual leaders for their community. The local church, formerly a community-wide institution within a formal hierarchical national structure, became a secret, informal, often literally underground organization. Instead of a patriarchal institution, it became entirely gynocratic, although not immediately (initially men, former church employees, also guided activities) and not intentionally so. Rather, knowledge of Church practices and the printed sources necessary to conduct Church rituals were passed from woman to woman because it was women who sought involvement with this spiritual sphere.

In general, during the Soviet period, the main attendants of those churches that remained open were elderly women (Lane 1978, 66). Antireligious campaigns, which had peak periods of intensity during the 1920s and '60s, combined with active atheist education in schools, meant that younger people were taught to ridicule all forms of religious belief and practice, although the extent to which this education was successful has been debated by scholars (Bridger 1987, 186). Consequences were greatest for those who wished to acquire or maintain a career in the Soviet Union: Communist Party members who attended church could be expelled (Berman 1993, 359). But most Party members were men; Susan Bridger has estimated that the proportion of Party members who were rural women was about 8 percent by the late 1970s (1987, 188). On the other hand, authorities often turned a blind eye to elder rural people's religious practices (Rogers 2008, 122).

The tradition of women leading services in Pot'ma began in this fashion: the local church was converted to a *klub* (an official Soviet institution in charge of recreation) in 1930; the physical building was then destroyed in the 1960s.[9] When the local church was closed, the women who used to sing and assist in the church started to meet to conduct services secretly in what locals call *kel'i* (cells), which are either in the basements of houses or separate structures like root cellars: a shallow hole is dug in the ground, a small log frame with a door and sometimes a window is erected, and the whole structure is covered in earth. Vera Ivanovna, born in 1923, who now leads many of the services, said the women who at first conducted the clandestine services were called *starki*, for *starye devy* (old maids). They were also dubbed *monakhini* (nuns) because, as unmarried women

One of the religious books used in services in homes in Pot'ma, Ul'ianovsk oblast, 2005. The book is titled "Triodion, Tripesnets" (Book of the three odes, used during Orthodox Great Lent) and was printed in Lvov, probably in the late nineteenth to early twentieth century. The spots on the page are wax stains. (PHOTO BY LAURA J. OLSON)

associated with the Church, they seemed like nuns. These women kept the church's books in their homes and brought them to services to read prayers from them.

As the *starki* died, services were shifted to the home of Vera Ivanovna's sister Natalia, and the books, icons, and other religious items gradually stayed in Natalia's home. Natalia was illiterate, so other women, like Vera herself and Elizaveta Onufrievna, born in 1915, read the prayers. To read prayers in the Orthodox tradition requires special skill: one must learn how to pronounce Church Slavonic, which is a language related to but different from Russian, and to read fluently the many standard abbreviations in older texts. Most of the women learned by listening to others read and by reading aloud to themselves at home. As Vera, Elizaveta, and the other prayer leaders aged, they brought in younger women who had the desire and were willing to put in time to learn to read. One of these women was Liubov Vladimirovna, born in 1939, the youngest of the women who lead services in Pot'ma. As she recounted, once when she was present at a funeral service, Vera Ivanovna became tired of reading and asked Liubov Vladimirovna to take a turn. Vera Ivanovna liked how the younger woman read and asked her to read the *Psaltyr'* (psalter) from then on.

Although it was after Easter, Vera Ivanovna M. revealed for the camera the Christ's coffin used in Easter services, Pot'ma, Ul'ianovsk oblast, 18 June 2005. It formerly belonged to the local church and was preserved by local women since the 1930s. (PHOTO BY LAURA J. OLSON)

Ironically, then, women's literacy—a gift of Soviet education—contributed to women's ability to learn to read Church Slavonic and to act as lay priests in what would function as a substitute for the defunct Church. What provoked their religious activity, however, was an internal drive as well as the social benefits of acceptance into a moral community and the feeling of self-worth obtained from leadership there.

The internal drive was what women wanted to tell us about. The discourse of grief, loss, and personal suffering was richly developed in Pot'ma. Several of the women who lead services told interviewers about their long or deep experiences with grief: in particular, three had had tragic lives and had lost loved ones in difficult circumstances, causing them to "need" the spiritual activity. One woman had lost her husband, daughter and son-in-law, and son and daughter-in-law in tragic deaths; another woman's two sons had been found guilty of murder. Vera Ivanova told me (LO) the story of her two-year-old daughter's death in a domestic fire accident. She summed it up: "What makes us [lead services]? Grief!"

Liubov Vladimirovna attributed her turn to religious matters to her encouragement by Vera Ivanovna, but most of all to her mother's death in 1997. It was after her mother's death that she bought a *Psaltyr'* to read (at a good deal of trouble and expense, which she recounted in detail). Her mother was a religious woman, the middle child of eleven siblings, who had never had any education and could not sign her name. Liubov Vladimirovna's father had died in World War II and her mother had raised her and her sister by herself, "put her whole soul into us." Like other women of her generation, Liubov had preferred not to live with her mother-in-law and after eight months of marriage brought her husband to live with her mother, a situation she found difficult because she did not know whom to please, her husband or mother. She told the story of her mother's death in great detail, and spoke about the time when one realizes the loss of the support and wisdom that the parent provides:

> You can't know everything! What [exists], how [to do stuff], all that? We can't find out everything. "To live life is not like crossing a field," everyone says.
> *Also, we don't want to receive the knowledge of our parents, at least I don't want to.*
> Especially when they lecture us.
> *Oh, exactly!*
> We don't want to hear it. But, Laura, with time you will understand.
> *Maybe.*
> I . . . My mother used to say something, and I'd say to her, "Oh come on!" . . . But now that I've become old, I've understood.
> *You've understood? Why?*
> I don't know! Here's when I started to understand—when mama was gone!
> *Ah!*

That's when I understood! . . . Why didn't I ever obey her! . . . Mama wants
the best for you and wants to give you advice. Mama is mama. There is no one
greater than mama and more *rodnaia* [close in the sense of family] than mama.
(21 June 2005)

Liubov Vladimirovna's story touches on key points in the discourse of suffering. She refers
to her first experience of profound grief (after her mother's death); this corresponds to the
moment when a person becomes an orphan, although Liubov does not use this word (tech-
nically, she grew up an orphan, although she did not know her father). According to her
story, her mother's death marked the moment when she understood that the beliefs, values,
and traditions her mother passed on to her were valuable not only because they existed or
because of sentimental reasons but also because they had practical value for her in her new
life-stage. She implies that only after her mother's death did she begin to wonder and
worry about the relationship between this world and the other world. In this context, the
proverb Liubov Vladimirovna quotes, "To live life is not like crossing a field," suggests that
one needs knowledge in order to negotiate the mysteries and difficulties of life. Mother
gives that support and knowledge to her child; but the child does not listen to what Mother
has to say until she must negotiate the terrain herself, which ironically only happens when
the parent is gone. For a woman, depending upon her family configuration (the number of
siblings she and her mother have and their age and sex), the death of her mother may make
her the eldest female in the *rod* of her birth family. Even though a married woman adopts
the *rod* of her husband, many women feel the pull toward the *rodina* (homeland, place of
birth) and look after the dead of their birth family as well (Paxson 2005, 204).

These images of life as a road, parents (particularly mothers) as guides, and loss as
impetus to exploration of faith are commonplaces in the personal narratives of religious
belief that we heard in our fieldwork. The mythological, nostalgic language of Liubov
Vladimirovna's narrative is balanced by the story's tacit recognition that the mother-
daughter relationship was fraught with difficulty, and that transmission of wisdom,
although desired, was incomplete.

While observing the religious activities of the women of Pot'ma, we noticed how elder
women, not just mothers, serve as guides for younger initiates and spiritual leaders for
the entire community.[10] During a memorial at forty days after the death of a village man,
the "mother"-guide for the new widow and orphan was an unrelated elder woman. The
forty-day ritual is viewed as a particularly emotionally fraught one, in which guidance is
important. As Liubov Vladimirovna explained to me (LO) later, and as is characteristic of
folk belief all over rural Russia, for the first ten days after death, the deceased's soul stays
near the house; after this, he or she is given a tour of heaven and hell to see what treatments
await him or her in the hereafter, based upon his or her sins during life. On the fortieth day,
the soul of the deceased finally leaves the vicinity of the earth and flies up to heaven, where

it is presented to God by the angels. At this time it is judged based upon its earthly acts and the prayers and charitable acts of the living undertaken in the name of the deceased during those forty days. The special number forty is based upon the story of Jesus Christ's resurrection: on the fortieth day after his resurrection, he ascended to God. The actions of the participants in the ritual of the fortieth day are meant to send him safely on his way, to ease the difficult transition, and to ensure his installment in heaven. During the forty days after death a glass of water (or vodka) stands in the home of the deceased with a spoon in it; people say that the deceased drink from this glass using the spoon. At the fortieth-day ritual, we were told, a family member must say three prayers: *Sviatyi Bozhe, Slava*, and *Otche nash*, bow three times, and pour the leftover water out against the outside front corner of the house, symbolically severing the ties of the deceased with this world.

The ritual we observed handled this moment somewhat differently: aspects of it appeared to be improvised specifically to fit the particular needs of the family and the feelings of the spiritual leader. At the end of this fortieth-day ritual all the participants exited the house, saying "let us see the soul off" (*dushu provozhat'*), and stood facing the street as the local women sang the aforementioned prayers. The widow was too infirm and distraught to complete this act of throwing the water on the house, and her daughter did not know how to perform it, so an unrelated villager, Maria Mikhailovna E. (born in 1933), who had been asked by the family to lead the prayers during the memorial service, completed it for and with the daughter. Standing by the front corner, she said the "Thrice Holy" prayer, "Holy God, Holy [and] Mighty, Holy [and] Immortal, have mercy on us," while the daughter was approaching the corner. The daughter installed herself on her knees in front of the corner while Maria Mikhailovna, who was standing, came closer to the corner. Maria Mikhailovna then ad-libbed a prayer. First she addressed the Lord Jesus, asking for their prayers to reach the Lord and for the Lord to forgive them everything. Then she addressed the deceased apparently from her own point of view as "my sweet one, Syomka" and urged his soul to be on its way, that he should forgive them and have mercy. In several short tosses that made up a cross shape, she poured the water from the glass on the outside corner of the house corresponding to the icon corner in the room inside, while saying twice, "In the name of the Holy Father the Holy Son and the Holy Ghost, Amen" and "Amen, amen, my sweet one," while crossing herself and bowing. Next she addressed the deceased from the point of view of the daughter, with tears in her voice: "Forgive me, my papa, my buried one. [May the] Kingdom of heaven [be yours]." And finally, changing her tone to a more matter-of-fact one, she addressed the daughter: "That's it, my sweet one, that's your papa, that's enough, it's forty days already."

During this short ceremony the daughter expressed nothing and made no gestures except for short bows while Maria Mikhailovna pronounced "Amen." Afterward, her face was blank. Maria Mikhailovna also walked away with the air of one who was finished with a job. The only emotion shown was during the phrases spoken by Maria Mikhailovna for the daughter. As we saw with lamenters, women who take on the roles of spiritual leaders fulfill a role for the family of the deceased, sometimes by standing in for them, expressing their thoughts and grief for them. Maria Mikhailovna herself had long experience both with religious matters and with grief: she was from a family of church choir singers and had experienced the suicide by hanging of her first husband, the loss of her daughter and son-in-law in one traffic accident, and her son and daughter-in-law in another car accident three years later. She was an experienced guide in funeral matters, who had made her involvement in spiritual matters part of her identity. As one of the other local spiritual leaders remarked about her, she always wore black, even when it was not necessary—as if to show (or perhaps, they suggested, show off) her identity as a spiritual leader.

The example of Maria Mikhailovna's actions as a spiritual guide shows that mediating may not always involve teaching. During the ceremony, Maria Mikhailovna did not encourage the daughter's participation. Nonetheless, the daughter went through the ceremony as an initiate and emerged initiated into the new role of orphan. Her passivity during the ceremony suggests that she was fulfilling the role of the lowly novice, who was debased before moving up in status (Turner 1969). In that role she received laconic spiritual guidance from Maria Mikhailovna: "That's it, my sweet one, that's your papa, that's enough, it's forty days already." We take this to be an expression of the sentiment often heard in stories about grieving, that one should not cry too much or too long. In this regard the forty-day mark has a practical, therapeutic purpose for the living, beyond its role in the myth of the deceased's transition to the afterlife. It is the end of the liminal period both for the soul of the deceased and for the living. The living now remove the symbolic ties to the deceased—the food and water for him—from their living space and return to their lives, now changed forever.

Orphans do not change their appearance but enter the status of the orphaned, for whom there are special wedding and funeral laments and songs. Widows change their dress and behavior, in some cases permanently, in other cases for a year or more. The community determines the length of mourning and the behaviors expected, as is shown in the following interview from Arkhangel'sk oblast. The folklorist and an informant were discussing whether they could get together the local "grandmothers" to sing. Nina Osipovna B., born in 1936 in Arkhangel'sk oblast, spoke about one of them:

> Maybe she won't, her son died not long ago, so . . .
> *Oh. . . . She mustn't sing?*
> Yes. It hasn't been a year yet. It hasn't been even half a year.
> *She shouldn't sing?*
> Yes, yes, yes. So she is keeping away from it. She does . . . walk around [go visiting]! But she keeps away from singing.
> *And that . . . is when who dies? When a husband dies, and when . . . a son dies . . . ?*

Yes, yes, I also did, I mourned for a year. I wore a headscarf...

What kind of scarf?

A black one.

So people wear a black scarf?

Yes, yes, yes. And I didn't go anywhere. Anywhere! (Selishche, Leshukonskii region, 8 July 2009 [Lesh 17-2])

The *bol'shukhi* are in charge of setting and maintaining the standards of the community, and they do so through judgments expressed as gossip. Nina Osipovna here implies that this woman is doing the right thing in not singing but that she is doing the wrong thing in "walking around." In 2005, when I (LO) stayed with Valentina Sergeevna G., then eighty, who had lost her daughter a year ago, she still did not "walk around," that is, attend social gatherings. When one of her friends had a birthday party, she sat on a bench outside the gate, so that people could see that she was not attending a celebration. She viewed my attendance of the party as "attending in her stead." She loved to sing but would sing only religious songs, saying she was afraid of community censure if she sang secular tunes. Even when we listened to tapes of non-religious singing I had made in previous years, she asked me to keep the volume low so that the neighbors would not hear. I asked when she would be able to sing again. In our conversation the number five years emerged as a safe number, so she cheerfully invited me back to sing with her in five years, when she would be eighty-five.

What purpose does such regulation of behavior serve? The change in behavior marks the change in status. One cannot have a major life change without a resulting change in one's daily life. To do so would be to remove the traces of the experience, to deny it had happened. Cultural life scripts dictate that the pain of loss not be forgotten; rather, the script of loss will influence the narratives individuals tell about themselves. In this way loss is assimilated and one moves forward into a new status.

Memory-Keepers

Besides guiding the dead and the living through the funeral rite of passage, elder women in Russian villages are in charge of memorializing the dead. Usually this is done by each *bol'shukha-starukha*, who will organize ritual meals on memorial days and also, if she attends church, gather the names of the family's ancestors and have them read in church on certain holidays or memorial days. In Pot'ma, the women go beyond their own families and communally commemorate all the ancestors of each family in the community. Three times yearly, at Maslenitsa, *Oktiabr'skii* (Dmitriev Saturday), and the Saturday before Trinity Sunday, the women gather in a home for a memorial service. Each comes bearing several (ten or more) small notebooks, in which are handwritten the names of all the members of a family who have died, going back several generations.

During these services, after prayers, each woman begins to read out loud all the names in each notebook, starting with her own family and moving on to the families of neighbors and friends who could not be present. When we attended, it did not matter who read the names: visiting ethnographers were also given notebooks to read aloud. Similarly, how one read was not important: it could be loud or soft, fast or slow. The reading was not emotional: no one cried. Everyone read at once, so the result was a steady hum of voices. The names, first names only (in Church Slavonic form), were read in the accusative case, implying that one was beseeching God to "remember" these people. Each group of names was initiated by a prayer that asked God to give them peace, and followed by a prayer for them to be forgiven for all sins, intentional and unintentional, to be saved from eternal torture, and to be given the kingdom of heaven.

According to local tradition, on these three days per year, even drowning and hanging victims (suicides) may be remembered; in general, these are considered "unclean dead," but an exception is made for them on these days. However, babies who died before baptism and adults who die without being baptized (there are many due to Communism's prohibitions) are yet different cases; for babies their parents need to read special prayers, while an adult is responsible for his own baptism and is not allowed to be memorialized in these religious contexts.[11] As Anastasia Valentinovna V. (born in 1942) told us, if a person is not baptized, it means he was not given a name; he did not "exist" in this world.

Anastasia Valentinovna's stories about her own relationship to these practices and prohibitions tell us much about the moral stances of elder rural women. To many of them, as we learned from interviews, observance of Church doctrine is not as important as is the expression of compassion; morality comes not from institutions but from human beings and their sense of relatedness (see also Zigon 2008, 108). Thus, Anastasia Valentinovna chose to transgress against Orthodox law rather than to discount a fellow human being's suffering.

Although under Orthodox canon suicide is an unpardonable sin and it is considered a sin to commemorate someone who has committed suicide, Anastasia Valentinovna herself did this. She had a woman neighbor who had heart problems and diabetes and could not lie down, so she spent the last year of her life sitting up. She had no one to help her, and her family disposed of her like "shit from a shovel." Her older son became alcoholic, while her younger one did not live with his wife. Because she was all alone, Anastasia Valentinovna took care of her in the last year of her life. At one point this woman told Anastasia that she was tired of this life and was going to hang herself after she saw her children next. She was very religious and was aware of her sin, but her last request was to be buried as a normal Christian. Anastasia Valentinovna emphasized that "she had no other choice" but to commit suicide; suffering led her to it. For this reason, Anastasia made sure that her last wish was granted and she was buried in a regular cemetery—an act that goes against official Orthodox regulations, according to which only those who commit suicide due to reasons of insanity can be given a regular Church burial (Stepa-nenko 2006).

Anastasia Valentinovna's dream later confirmed that this was the correct decision: she dreamed she walked by the river and saw this woman washing something happily. When the woman noticed Anastasia Valentinovna, she said to her: "Christ will save you for this." Anastasia Valentinovna was shocked at the dream's message but continued to memorial-ize her at nine and forty days after her death, by giving *potainye milostyni* or *milostynki*—secret charitable gifts (a traditional practice that we discuss below). Thus, despite clear doctrine to the contrary, Anastasia listened both to her own heart (her own pity), which told her that suffering justified suicide, and to a sign from the other world that, to her, clearly validated her actions. In the moral world of Anastasia and others we met, pity and compassion establish grassroots, emotionally based connections among both kin and non-kin. The other world establishes its presence within an individual in dream form, and functions as a higher authority than any worldly institution (including the Church).

Selfless giving is one of the ways in which women's moral authority is constituted in the Russian village community. These acts reflect the general principle in Orthodoxy (and Christianity), according to which wealth should be distributed since all assets are be-stowed by God. Almsgiving has redemptive power since it is understood the poor will pray for the souls of those who give to them (Lasser 2010a, 2010b; see also Bernshtam 2005, 283). A version of this principle is described by Margaret Paxson as central to village morality: *dobrom dobro* is the idea that good things result when one performs good and disinterested deeds (2005, 186). Anastasia did not use this language, but the basic rule is demonstrated by the institution of the secret charitable gifts. That the *milostyni* are secret suggests that they do not contribute to the giver's worldly authority or social power; they are disinterested.[12] These *milostyni* are small bags of goods that are given to members of the community to remember a loved one. Anastasia Valentinovna says that she did it for her mother: she gave nine *milostyni* on the ninth day after her death, twenty on the twen-tieth day, and forty on the fortieth day. Each *milostynka* consisted of a piece of bread, a can-dle, a box of matches, money tied with thread, all tied up in a handkerchief. She would place these *milostynki* at night at the entrances of houses in such a way that the owner would see it in the morning. Anastasia Valentinovna's husband remembered that during and after World War II the women sewed little bags and would put flour or grain in it; later people started to live better and would put more things in their *milostyni*. Nowadays they put small purchased crosses in the *milostynki*, along with an onion or a piece of bread. Those *milostynki* were always made by women but were given both to women and men.

A particular kind of *milostynka* may be used for suicides and other sinners. Anastasia told a story of how the relative of one suicide by hanging said that they had to purchase forty roosters as *milostynki* and only after that would the priest "sing" (*otpoet*) the deceased (chant final prayers over him). The rooster had to have a reddish tint, not white or black, probably because it was associated with hell: it was supposed to sing the deceased out of hell.

We asked why these commemorations had to be secret. Anastasia Valentinovna said she did not know, but she remembered that when her grandmother saw a *milostynka* in front of her door, she picked it up with the words, "Lord, may you bring peace to the soul of the deceased, the servant whose name I do not know." Her grandmother told her that the secret gifts make their way to God faster than open ones. That is, precisely the humble quality of these gifts, the fact that they cannot be used to create worldly social power, guarantees their effectiveness.

One additional chapter of Anastasia's story shows again the link between personal loss and suffering and the practices of commemoration. As in other cases, the transformative loss was that of a mother. For Anastasia Valentinovna, the circumstances of her mother's death had motivated her to perform these charitable acts. Her mother became paralyzed and died alone; her sons and daughters were not able to help her. In her account to us Anastasia moaned, "Mama, we abandoned you in your moment of need, we couldn't help you." Because she had a lot of pity for her mother and grief about her death and cried a lot, Anastasia Valentinovna said, she had several dreams in which her mother appeared to her. One of these was a frightening experience in which, after seeing her mother standing in the room where she was sleeping, Anastasia's tongue swelled up and she felt she was suffocating. After that, she stood in front of the icon and said: "Oh Lord, I don't need any more visions like that one." She stopped crying for her mother as much: "The *starki* say, you should not cry so much." But Anastasia Valentinovna did not forget her mother: she told us with pride that she had commemorated her with a special memorial meal in her home every year for thirty years, except for the year that she was in the hospital for treatment of an ulcer.

Although it is undeniably a social duty, the practice of memorialization is motivated internally, through the individual experience of loss. In Anastasia's narrative we clearly see that the practice of offering secret charitable acts to the community substitutes for the act of crying. Both are secret, private acts. But in this view, crying is self-indulgent, while *milostyni* open the self to others, offering good that emanates and returns as good.

As women's narratives highlight, the memory-keepers of the Russian village are self-appointed. They come to their practices for various reasons: each person has her own story to explain why she does it. The commemoration has traditional form, and may be influenced by social pressure, but the impulse comes from the heart—the emotional center—of each woman. Each woman applies her creativity, her craftsmanship, to the ways that she commemorates. Our enumeration of these women's practices helps us to understand why women have been seen—by scholars and in the popular imagination—as the main bearers of tradition in the Russian village. They are not in fact the main or only bearers of tradition: tradition lives everywhere, in the culture of men, teenagers, and children just as much as in the culture of women. But only elder women are in charge of memory, which is central to the spiritual life of the Russian village community. Memory and the practices of memorialization provide symbolic immortality, an important means of connecting with the unknowable, that which is beyond the narrow confines of the self. By constantly going beyond the self, Russian rural women lead their communities toward spiritual health and wisdom.

Conclusion

Who are Russian village women, and how can one know them? We have tried to know them through their conversations with us and others, and through their rituals and practices as we experienced them. We have tried to tell our readers about these women by retelling, translating, and contextualizing their stories, by explaining the coherence of their worlds (Asad 1986, 150). We have tried to deconstruct fixed notions of who they are, both by suggesting that ethnography has often misread women's contributions to the corpus of Russian folklore and also by offering additional ways of understanding the diversity within the national, geographical, and gendered group designation "Russian village women." We have spoken of generational differences, differences in age status, regional differences, and individual variations. We have analyzed not just the subjects themselves but also the ways our conversations with rural women position *us* as subjects. These multiple techniques for knowledge of a group of people do not capture a complete or "true" picture, however. We acknowledge here Talal Asad's caution that "the ethnographer's translation/representation of a particular culture is inevitably a textual construct" (1986, 163). If an ethnographic report travels back to the location where the fieldwork was originally done, that construct can then influence or "construct" the very "folk memories" about which it purports to inform, since "our" culture privileges writing over oral means of transmission.

Asad and others have emphasized the power relations inherent in ethnographic practice. As researchers, we choose what we want to write about; in interviews, we choose what questions to ask. Our subjects are materially impoverished, far from central loci of power, and often have minimally functional literacy skills. It is easy to assume that anything we would write would be a hegemonic text that purports to speak "for" our marginalized subjects. But, as feminist critics have begun to argue in the past two decades, following Foucault, power is "a decentralized, shifting, and productive force," and it is held by informants when they withhold information and choose what information to give (Ong 1995, 353). We have focused upon the most powerful group of women in Russian villages, the *bol'shukha* or female head of household. These are authoritative, self-assured women who take on the role of "namers" in the community (Thien 2005): they judge, they decide whom to include or exclude, they bestow nicknames and labels. We have tried to show that within interviews and in interactions with us, they have understood our questions as they wished and spoken about that which concerned them, and they have both named and judged us. In some cases their judgments and prohibitions have silenced us bodily, as when Adonyeva felt ill after transcribing the incantations she had transcribed illicitly.

Due to the nature of power, then, there are silences within interviews and within our study. One of those silences is the people we did not write about: those rural "others" who "lurk in [the] shadow" of the empowered women that we concentrated upon (Thien 2005, 79–81). In the rural communities where we worked, we can name a few of these residents who have remained relatively silent in our study: a disabled, unmarried sister that one of our elderly interlocutors cared for in her home but never introduced us to; a woman in her forties who stood inside the church entryway and received handouts of bread or money; an unhappy, irritable elder woman who did not want us to interview her and said she "didn't know how to talk" and "had nothing good in her life"; a city woman who came to the village seasonally and who came across as brash, flirtatious, and pushy; younger women, who were busy with their families or work. These are all people who did not fit into the categories of our study, did not attract our attention, were inconvenient to interview, refused to talk, or appeared too similar to ourselves. Even when we did interview such women, we often were unable to situate them in our narrative. Just as the speech of our interlocutors is shaped by predetermined plots, so our narrative is shaped by notions of that which is permissible in scholarly book-writing (e.g., to write about marginalized women would require a separate chapter, etc.). Like our interlocutors, we follow as well as helping to construct and transmit the "rules of the game."

Silences and gaps are characteristic of any narrative, any text. They are the starting points for future work. Perhaps the greatest gap in this text is about men. While we have seen great value in concentrating on women's worlds, the men's stories are equally interesting. Several Russian scholars and a handful of Western scholars have focused their work on rural men's culture, but studies of rural men's contemporary culture are as yet rare (see, for example, Worobec 2002; Smith 2002; Morozov 2001, 2004, 2007; Kay 2006).

While gaps provide texture in cloth, one pays more attention to the threads that weave a pattern. We wish here to gather the threads that we did weave into our narrative, to reconsider these disparate points from a perspective removed from the immediate context of interview text, in order to make that pattern more distinct. One of the central focuses of our investigation has been tradition, which we defined as a habit of saying, doing, and thinking in a certain way. In each of the sections below, we contemplate tradition and its transmission, facilitated by the use of plots and scripts that construct one's reality and enable one to share it with others.

Women, Men, and Tradition

We return here to one of the main questions that provoked this book: How do Russian rural women relate to tradition? We have suggested that the *bol'shukha* role, itself a traditional role (a plot), predisposes women to see and position themselves as tradition-keepers. It was the *bol'shukha*'s responsibility to maintain the family's health and well-being. A central imperative of the Russian traditional belief system held that a family's well-being cannot be preserved unless ancestors are honored and a reciprocal relationship is maintained with the spirit world. It was in part women's function to do this, and this is why women have intentionally poured copious creative energy into healing and funeral activities. While before collectivization men also participated in the maintenance of a relationship with the spirit world, by and large this relationship centered around particular activities, many of which were essential to the everyday running of the home but also physically peripheral to the home space. For example, male tasks such as beekeeping, livestock care, fishing, hunting, blacksmithing, milling, ceramics, carpentry, home construction, and so on required calling upon the protection of spirits in order to ensure a successful outcome (Kholodnaia 2005a, 377). Those occupations were disassociated from the domestic sphere under collectivization, and/or were no longer essential to sustaining the household economy. In the post-Soviet period, with high unemployment for rural men, we have seen these occupations regaining value. Nevertheless, we have also seen their feminization: women engaging in beekeeping and shepherding, or elder women regarded locally as authorities for magic related to fishing or hunting (incantations to ensure the positive involvement of the spirit world).

While women have been tradition-keepers in Russian villages for as long as history can document, men also participated in tradition-keeping. The importance of their contribution diminished only after collectivization. Overall, collectivization removed men's incentive to keep tradition and made the areas in which men specialized less important to the village economy. Nonetheless, as those areas undergo a renaissance in the post-Soviet period, we have seen evidence that men's knowledge and skill in these activities are highly valued in village households.

The activities that were women's responsibility both prior to the Revolution and in the Soviet period—household garden, food preparation, childcare, health care, care of the ancestors—help to establish a domestic sphere that, for many, seems essential to the construction and maintenance of family members' identities. We have seen that even for women of later generations—the third generation and later—who chose to live outside the village and to work full-time in a non-agricultural occupation, the desire to continue to fulfill these roles remains. These women often sustain a city home and also visit the village on important holidays, maintain the family's gravesite, and offer help (food preparation or other material assistance) to elder relatives still living in the village.[1]

Why do women persist in this role? Is it a personal, desired choice, or is this a responsibility they would like to delegate, share, or escape? We did not directly ask this question as part of our fieldwork (partly because it seems like a leading question that presupposes a liberal feminist point of view), but we paid attention to the ways women express their relationships to their activities. As we have shown with the example of the cow in chapter 2, we observed that village elder women were reluctant to part with these roles and responsibilities. Rather, as we showed in chapters 6 and 9, they used their agency and creativity to find ways that they could fulfill their roles with regard to care of sick children and of the dead ancestors.

To be sure, we did hear complaints about the hard work that women do: arthritis and back pain, for example, were common motifs in the litanies of hard work and suffering that comprised a ritual speech act for our interlocutors (Ries 1997, 86). We noticed that in the households of women of our third generation, if there was a functioning adult male he sometimes performed roles that were traditionally women's—if a woman needed or desired it. For example, the husband might help with the care of cows, in which case husband and wife would joke that the husband was taking on a woman's role, or he would wear a kerchief on his head when he went to milk, saying that the cow would not accept him without this costume change. That is to say, the responsibility had not shifted; it was still hers, but he was helping her. This kind of role-switching had been socially taboo, especially in the Russian North, until relatively recently (Kholodnaia 2005a, 377–78). The greater public acceptance of such code-switching suggests that women see value in this kind of "transgression." It is tempting to say that women's increased self-assertiveness and the social acceptance of egalitarian behavior in the Soviet period contributed to such a change. Nonetheless, such compromises must always have existed; people would not have spoken of a prohibition if there had not been occasional breaking of the rule.

In general, our interlocutors did not view tradition as worth keeping simply because it came from the past (Shils 1981, 13). They viewed as worth repeating practices that were functional for their lives; they repeated habits of thought (e.g., spiritual beliefs) that were assimilated from their upbringing and that helped to explain their experience. The past was important for them only insofar as it was their own past: a song or practice came from one's own mother, or was associated with particular memories. The subjects of our study did not fetishize pastness itself; they were reflective, not restorative nostalgics (Boym 2001).

We see no evidence that the traditions associated with women's roles are "dying," as a common argument with regard to folklore has maintained for at least a century and a half (Rothstein 1994). Rather we have argued that women approach tradition when life experience nudges them in its direction. Thus, the fact that only old people sing certain types of songs (laments or spiritual songs) does not mean that singing is dying but that women come to these spiritual practices only after they experience loss of a loved one. To be sure, tradition is *changing*—for example, in some areas laments are being replaced by spiritual songs, and those may in future be replaced by other practices, perhaps even non-musical. Yet we maintain that the impulse itself—to perform practices that mark these life events and fulfill internal needs—is not likely to change over historical time. Given the symbolic importance, in Russian culture, of the *rod* and the connection to the land where one's ancestors are buried (the *rodina*), practices aimed at their safeguarding are likely to remain within the repertoires of Russian village women.

Power and Transmission

Women's social roles are sources of power for them, and this may be one additional reason why women actively choose and preserve these roles. The actions (for example) of cooking food for the anniversaries of the deceased and organizing family members to visit the grave—and then telling stories about contacts with revenants—construct village women as social leaders, as people in charge of a whole sphere of knowledge and activity. This is the power of agency, of "being one's own person" and of exercising one's competence in order to affect situations (Newton 1981, 6). The same is true of the power to protect children and loved ones from unseen harm by otherworldly forces.

We have argued that transmission of this power occurs willingly and because of a need on the part of the younger woman. Yet social roles are able to be transmitted only when role models exist—when there is a visible script for behavior—and when these role models are socially approved. These conditions did not obtain in the case of young men: they lost their male role models with collectivization and World War II. With women, those events did not have the same effect. We see transmission occurring today. Teenage girls may appear not to ascribe much importance to what their grandmothers do in regard to funerals and babies: teenagers may be more interested in learning English, playing the flute, or wearing the latest fashions. Yet because the role models exist and are not only socially approved but also viewed as necessary to the protection of the *rod*, these roles will continue to have value. Even a young woman who lives separately with her family in the city will see and participate in the activities her grandmother leads during summer and on calendar holidays. That vision of grandmother may then influence the woman later in life, when she comes of age and experiences the need to connect with a protective force or with the spirits of ancestors.

The social power of Russian rural women, in this configuration, is neither necessarily a method of coercion of a younger generation nor a route to independence; rather, it is a force that supports both individuals and social bonds. Elder women support younger women when they need knowledge to face the forces of the other world; coeval women support each other by providing social networks. Such networks of support belong to men as well, both in the past and now; the rigors of Russian rural life demand cooperation, sharing, and generosity (Paxson 2005, 72). Men's and women's networks overlap but are largely separate in the Russian village worlds with which we are familiar, and are divided according to the separate spheres of activity and influence.

Public and Private

We have argued that women's traditions, central to the maintenance of a village household before the Revolution, became more isolated and separated from the sphere of officially sanctioned activity under collectivization. The Soviet period inaugurated a separation of public and private spheres that did not exist in the pre-Soviet village economy, where both men and women worked to serve the needs of their own homestead. Socialist utopian ideas of abolishing the bourgeois distinction between public and private by socializing the domestic tasks that traditionally fell to women never took hold; the nationalist goals of replenishing the population and strengthening male self-worth rose in importance, and the state recruited women for this purpose. The state tried to infiltrate the arena of the personal in particular by shaping women's reproduction and childcare through education, social programs, incentives, and the withdrawal of choices (prohibiting abortion and folk midwifery and not providing alternative birth control) (Gal and Kligman 2000, 45–46, 48–49). This socialization of maternity, we have argued, did not put a stop to the transmission of traditional methods of childcare (the magic of maternity), which took place in a "split-off" private sphere.

In the Soviet era this perceived strengthening of a separate private sphere locked away from all but *svoi*, one's own social network, was a fiction, but an important one, as Susan Gal and Gail Kligman remind us: the private sphere seemed like a haven from state control, but the two spheres were intertwined. Everyday life involved numerous transactions and negotiations that redefined *svoi*; it brought the state into family concerns and vice versa: we saw the example with Valentina Sergeevna G.'s life story in chapter 3, in which she utilized personal family connections to obtain her position as a nurse, and then her supervisor, in order to retain her, falsely told supervisors in a different location that she was soon to be married locally (which then turned out to provoke her boyfriend into making a proposal). Despite the interdependency of public and private in daily life, women continued to be associated with the sphere of the home, even as that sphere was now revalued—from the point of view of the state, the home was the invisible reproducer of labor and enabled underpaid (or in fact as many of our interlocutors reminded us, unpaid, paid-in-kind) farmers to continue working and babies to continue to be conceived. From the point of view of women, the home was their sphere of power and thus positively viewed even while it may have seemed like an overwhelming burden; from the point of view of rural men, the home could be a place of refuge from state control but also a reminder of that control, as women (*bol'shukhi*) became associated with the parental state (Gal and Kligman 2000, 51, 55).

We saw the complex interweaving of public and private with the activity of singing. Starting in the 1930s, folk singing was redefined by the state as a public activity done under state patronage, but women turned songs into private chronicles of their lives, as is shown by the numerous examples of village women who keep personal notebooks of song texts. Lyric songs (we examined romances and *chastushki*) comprise a discourse that speaks about that which people consider personal, not official: the world of feelings. Because of this strong link between lyric songs and personal feelings, the lyric genre offered a means of (implied or explicit) resistance against state authority. In the post-Soviet period, even though that context has changed, there remains some attraction in the transgressive or self-indulgent discourse of lyric song.

With the apparent strong need for expression of the personal, we expect group lyric singing to continue in the foreseeable future. Russian ethnomusicologists have often argued that traditional singing is dying out since local stylistic features are not being preserved—which we see especially in non-official contexts or official groups whose organizer is not knowledgeable about local folklore (Olson 2004). By contrast, we have taken an interpretive stance that de-emphasizes the importance of particular traditional stylistic features. We have argued that even popular music that is learned from radio, television, or other media, when sung, played, or danced to in spontaneous contexts, can function as folklore and can be of interest to cultural critics. Again, we are arguing that tradition has changed and will continue to change but is not likely to disappear altogether.

Singing is one of women's spheres that helps to create meaningful social networks based upon ensemble aesthetic creation, nostalgia, and connection with family history. The activity is maintained by transmission both vertically and horizontally: elders may teach younger women directly by singing with them, or provide role models that are heeded only later in life. Most commonly, peers participate together and teach each other informally, by singing together. Today, we do not often see young people participating in traditional singing unless an elder person, often a professional club organizer salaried by the state, starts a local folk group or singing group (these are fairly common—each region or *raion* may have from one or two to a dozen or more). Nonetheless, we do see middle-aged women joining elder women's informal singing groups, especially when they socialize with these women (e.g., because they are neighbors). Russian ethnomusicologist Andrei Kabanov said that when in the 1970s he and others observed that people tend to begin singing at middle age, the researchers concluded that this type of transmission might be traditional rather than a sign of the aging (and therefore imminent death) of folk music practice. That is, perhaps singing in non-ritual contexts has historically been the provenance of middle-aged and elder people, those whose children are grown (interview with LO, 18 November 1998). Increased leisure time (after child-raising is done) offers women the possibility to engage in practices that fulfill them emotionally and spiritually, and that are part of the public image of aged womanhood in contemporary Russia.[2]

Magic is a deeply private discourse, in part because it was persecuted by Soviet authorities, but in part also because of the danger of talking about it openly, as we showed in our
discussion of witchcraft (chapter 7). We see this as well in our chapter on motherhood
(chapter 6), where the knowledge of the magic of motherhood is only given to women on
an as-needed basis. In these contexts privacy lends power: to openly declare one's incantations robs them of their magical force, and to privately "know" who is a sorcerer allows
one to hold some power over them. Of course we note that, as much as our informants
swore us to secrecy or told us whom not to tell, they did in fact tell us much about these
supposedly private, secret practices. We might liken this kind of telling to the speech genre
of gossip. Participants invariably convey that the "news" or secrets they distribute should
not be spread in order to retain their value. Yet just as the very aim of gossip is to spread
itself in order to provide a social consequence for incorrect behavior, so one of the aims of
the discourse of magic is to be transmitted in order for the force to continue its healing
function (Phillips 2004).

Religion, too, had private aspects prior to the Revolution; the Soviet persecution of religious practice made this already partly private matter even more secret. We have argued
that while caring for one's ancestors is in part regulated by community norms and is publicly displayed, the particular way that a woman shows care for her dead ancestors is in fact
a personal choice that involves the application of her agency to a matter that she deems of
highest importance. While Soviet persecution of religion affected all of our interlocutors,
it did not prevent the performance especially of those practices that are done in secret,
such as bathing the ancestors and *potainye milostyni*, secret charitable gifts.

Transgression and Compromise

Thus, in the Soviet period, transgression took the form of the continued practice of traditions against the explicit or implicit prohibitions of the state and its representatives. But
transgression took other forms as well. Our interlocutors told us of their transgressions
against tradition itself, as when young people preferred *chastushki* and fox-trot to round-
dances and lyric folk songs. They viewed these acts of omission as intentional refusal of
that which tradition offered; one may speculate that they acted in this way purposely in
order to fulfill their own internal needs for self-definition or rebellion. When the life
script of rebellion had been fulfilled, older scripts called them back to tradition, and they
returned to the practices of earlier generations.

A different type of transgression took place when young mothers seized the *bol'shina*
from their mother-in-law. Again, these were transgressions against tradition, but the purpose of these acts was not rebellion against the strictures of tradition itself. Rather, these
women desired the power offered by tradition but were writing new life scripts for the
usurping of such power. We noted that the impetus to seize power was based upon the
advice of peers, not elders or husbands. The peer group as a source of life scripts was not

an entirely new development in the Soviet era, but it gained strength over the Soviet years due to the education that emphasized both the strength and value of the coeval collective and the importance of individual agency, as we argued in chapter 3.

While transgression involved a specific, often intentional rupture with tradition, compromise happened when an individual's particular traits and needs collided with tradition. One could say that compromise occurred in each interaction with tradition. For example, women were called to tradition when they became mothers due to the culture of fear that surrounded pregnancy and the care of the infant. The implied compromise was roughly as follows: if you take care of the infant the way tradition prescribes, then all should be well. Care of the ancestors was also motivated by a complex mixture of emotions: fear, grief, respect, love, pity. Memorial practices required heavy compromise (women structured their lives around the fulfillment of these scripts), but all were chosen by women themselves in order to guarantee the health of the living and of the *rod*, and establish their own spiritual, moral, and social authority. Probably no person was perfectly suited to undergo that which tradition prescribed; no one's life script exactly followed the script defined by the cultural imperative. On the other hand, we have argued that tradition was capacious enough, generous enough, and flexible enough to accommodate variations, creativity, individual agency, compromise, and even transgressions.

Subjectivity

Throughout this work we have endeavored to think and theorize about the subjectivities of our interlocutors. This process began with our exploration in chapter 1 of the ways that rural women's culture has been seen and understood (or not seen and not understood). There we critiqued the understanding of Tradition with a capital "T," the notion that Tradition is a Thing that is passed down from generation to generation, which is either properly preserved (good) or changed/not preserved (bad). Until about the mid-1980s, Russian scholars tended to assume that when women changed tradition, they were harming something valuable to "mankind"; when men changed it, they were expressing their individuality.

In the West, individual subjectivity is often thought to be at odds with tradition, as Edward Shils has pointed out. Proponents of tradition tend to see burgeoning individuality as a process that erodes tradition; proponents of individuality see tradition as a brake on individual self-expression: "There is a belief . . . that within each human being there is an individuality, lying in potentiality, which seeks an occasion for realization but is held in the toils of the rules, beliefs and roles which society imposes" (1981, 11). Herderian Romanticism combines the two views: individual creativity arises precisely from the wellspring of tradition; true genius (a Shakespeare) is inspired by, not hampered by, the tradition that is practiced mindlessly by others (by peasants).

Soviet official policies on folklore were based upon the Herderian view: it was the job of trained writers, composers, artists, and choreographers to "polish the gem" of folk culture and bring this product to the masses, so that rural people would both be cultured and also still appreciate their national culture (Olson 2004, 43–50). Individual performers were accorded the status of composers or writers only in exceptional circumstances and when their performances could be used to further the goals of the regime. Official discourse frowned upon individualism, but paradoxically, the system cultivated individualization through the practices of self-perfection (through hero emulation, etc.), self-policing, and the formation of a split-off private self (Kharkhordin 1999, 357–58).

There is another way to view the interrelationship of subjectivity and tradition. We have argued that women's subjectivity was formed in consonance with both a relational and individual self. Thus, for rural women the formation of selfhood was not necessarily opposed to tradition, and we too are inclined to view tradition in this way. Rather, since tradition comprises the plots, scripts, and practices learned from others, it is an important means through which we construct ourselves in relationship to others. The maintenance of folk-loric tradition is then not a goal in and of itself; instead, by adopting, adapting, or rejecting traditional practices and stories, we claim social roles and create our own biographies.

Glossary

ataman: Leader of a group of men or boys.

baba (pl. *baby*): A married woman.

bania: Bathhouse.

bobyl' (pl. *bobyli*): Unmarried man of middle age or older.

boevaia: "Fighting," feisty girl or woman.

boikaia: Self-assertive girl or woman.

bol'shak (pl. *bol'shaki*): Master of a household.

bol'shina: The role or institution of being in charge of a household.

bol'shukha (pl. *bol'shukhi*): Female head of household; matriarch.

bylichka (pl. *bylichki*): Narratives people tell about their experiences with the supernatural; memorates.

chastushka (pl. *chastushki*): Two- or four-line rhymed lyrics that are often composed by the singer and sung solo in the context of a musical "conversation," with accordion accompaniment.

chest': Honor.

chuzhoi (pl. *chuzhie*): Unfamiliar, strange; characteristic of strangers.

devichnik: A party at the bride's house the evening before the wedding ceremony.

devka (pl. *devki*): Girl, from birth to marriage.

devuskha (pl. *devushki*): Girl, from birth to marriage.

dobrokhodushka: A dialectal name for the house spirit *domovoi*.

dolia: Fate, lot, or share.

domovoi: House spirit, associated with ancestors and with well-being in the home.

fabulate: A story of supernatural experience narrated in the third person.

khorovod: A circle dance in which girls walk, holding hands, while singing a song.

khoziain (pl. *khoziaeva*): Master; master of household or spirit-master of a terrain such as a forest.

khoziaika (pl. *khoziaiki*): Mistress; female head of household; matriarch.

kila (pl. *kily*): Ulcer; bump; invisible bodily injury created through magic.

kisel': A gelatin made of sweetened grain and/or fruit.

klub: State-sponsored cultural center; building where cultural events are held.

kokoshnik: Headdress that shows a girl is entering the courtship period; also, married woman's headdress. Form varies by geographical region; covers head entirely.

koldun (pl. *kolduny*): Harmful magician; sorcerer.

koldun'ia (pl. *koldun'i*): Feminine form of *koldun*.

krasna krásota (*krasota*): Literally, "beautiful beauty"; flowers worn by bride.

kutiia: Cooked sweetened grain used for funerals and memorials.

leshii: Forest spirit or forest demon, sometimes said to be allied with Satan.

Lichnoe Podsobnoe Khoziaistvo (*LPKh*): Literally, "Personal Subsidiary Farm." An official Soviet term for small land plots for family use; included the right to own small numbers of domestic animals.

Maslenitsa: A Russian folk holiday celebrated for a week before the Great Fast (Lent). The Russian equivalent of Mardi Gras.

memorate: A story of a supernatural experience narrated in the first person.

milostynki: Charitable gifts.

moloditsa (pl. *moloditsy*): A young bride who had married the previous season.

molodka (pl. *molodki*): Young bride, from marriage to the birth of her first child or her first daughter.

muzhik (pl. *muzhiki*): A married man, from marriage until he becomes a *khoziain/bol'shak*.

nevesta: A bride or marriage-eligible girl.

obshchina: Village commune.

paren' (pl. *parni*): Boy, from birth to marriage.

plots: Standard formulations of past actions that allow people to speak about past experience in ways that are accepted and conventional.

podgolosok: Upper voice in polyphonic Russian folk singing, often sung by only one person at a time.

pomin: Memory (of a deceased person).

pominki: Memorial ritual including religious service and meal.

porcha: Spoiling; the use of supernatural power directly upon others to kill or harm them.

potainye milostyni: Secret charitable gifts.

poviazka: Headdress that shows a girl is entering the courtship period. A decorated band of fabric tied around the girl's head.

povitukha (pl. *povitukhi*): Midwife, usually a *starukha*.

Psaltyr': Psalter, prayer book.

rod (pl. *rody*): Clan; extended family, going back many generations.

rodina: Homeland; place where one's *rod* lives/lived/is buried.

roditeli: Parents; ancestors.

samogon: Moonshine or hard liquor made illegally at home from sugar, potatoes, or other products.

scripts: Conventional ways of speaking about present or future events.

sglaz: Evil eye; a hex placed (inadvertently) due to the curser's envy (especially while the person is uttering praise, or after the victim's boasting).

skhod: Village assembly; the collective governing organ of the village, consisting of *bol'shaki*.

slava: Glory or reputation.

sprava: The personal possessions of a young man; his symbolic capital.

starik (pl. *stariki*): Old man, from the time that a *khoziain* is too weak to manage the farm until his death.

starukha (pl. *starukhi*): Old woman, from physical infirmity until her death.

svad'ba: Celebratory part of the wedding; reception.

svakha: A female relative of the groom who engages in matchmaking for him.

svatovstvo: Engagement.

svaty: Matchmakers of either gender.

svoi (pl. *svoi*): A group of people who consider themselves closely socially connected.

tetka (pl. *tetki*): "Auntie," a term of address for a married woman unrelated to the speaker.

trudoden': Labor-day in-kind compensation system that operated from 1930 to 1966, according to which kolkhoz workers were paid not in money but in shares of the kolkhoz's production.

vataga (pl. *vatagi*): Group of *parni*, typically from one village.

venchanie: Church service of a wedding.

volia devich'ia: Freedom as a girl.

vybliadok (pl. *vybliadki*): Children of whores, i.e., children born out of wedlock.

zapevala: Singer who starts a song in Russian polyphonic singing.

zastol'e: A group celebration at a table with food and drink.

zavalinka: Ledge surrounding a village house.

zhenikh: Groom or eligible bachelor.

znakhar' (pl. *znakhari*): Male folk healer.

znakharka (pl. *znakharki*): Female folk healer.

Notes

Introduction

1. Mekhnetsov 1981. On the site "Kul'tura Vologodskoi oblasti" (http://www.cultinfo.ru/arts/folk), audio file and transcription of this song are given without the final stanza.

2. An example of the norm is a well-known South Slavic ballad type that features deliberate sibling incest, in which the brother's initiation of the act is punished: the sister curses him and runs away, and he is struck by lightning and killed. See Vidan 2003, 45–50.

3. Vladimir Propp (1995) interprets ritual as a process by which magic power is delivered from those who have it in abundance to those who need it. In this sense, magic's power is directed toward the future, and is productive. Other interpretations include those by Veselovskii (1873) and Chicherov (1957). All these interpretations have in common their search for a myth that would explain the ritual action, while we study the social functions of ritual.

4. As in the United States, in Russia there exists a great quantity of jokes regarding the mother-in-law, most of which convey the son-in-law's wish that she would die; within the corpus of Russian fairy tales, the mother-in-law is often characterized negatively as a witch or Baba Yaga.

5. One Russian erotic folktale contains a similar exaggerated suggestion of a mother-in-law's desire for her daughter's new husband. See Afanas'ev (1865) 1994, 110–18.

6. See, for example, Sobolevskii 1902, 200–201:

Mother-in-law baked pies for son-in-law:
Malt and flour she bought for 4 rubles
Sugar and raisins for 8 rubles more
The pie came together for 12 rubles in all.
The son-in-law sat, ate it all at one sitting
Mother-in-law paced the guest room in a bother
Lightly reprimanded her son-in-law:
"How could you, son-in-law, not explode?"
Son-in-law heard her: "You'd have done better not to offer it!
Oh mother-in-law, mother, come to me Wednesday of Maslenitsa week,
I'll give you such an honor:
A two-handled whip, and make you bend to order!"

7. Fieldworkers who collected the data for this book are author Laura Olson (Laura Olson Osterman, born in 1962, New York) and author Svetlana Adonyeva (Svetlana Adon'eva, born in 1963, Saint Petersburg), as well as students of Saint Petersburg State University (ranging in age from 17 to 23) and colleagues of Saint Petersburg University (ranging in age from 25 to 40). Olson's fieldwork took place in Riazan', Vologda, Ul'ianovsk, Saratov, Voronezh, and Kaluga oblasts during trips in 1995, 1996, 1998–99, and 2004–5; collected materials are in her private archive. Adonyeva's fieldwork took place in Vologda and Arkhangel'sk oblasts yearly between 1983 and 2010. These materials are housed at Saint Petersburg University's Propp Center. The corpus of material includes more than two thousand interviews with men and women born between 1899 and the 1960s. To protect the privacy of our Russian informants, pseudonyms are used throughout this book; some village names are also pseudonyms.

8. References to interviews done by the students and faculty of the Folklore Department of Saint Petersburg State University (Propp Center) are indicated with a number corresponding to the collection, folder, and file in the electronic archive—in this case collection Vash (Vashkinskii region of Vologda oblast), folder 22 (Signs, Prophetic Dreams, Stories about Fortunetelling), file number 96. The names of interviewers are located in the files but are not given here in order to avoid clutter (groups of students often conducted interviews). Interviewers' questions and comments are given in italics. Olson's interviews, located in the personal archive of the author, are arranged by date, place, and pseudonym.

9. On the distinction between narrated event and narrative event, see Bauman 1986, 5–6.

10. Tannen explains, "On the basis of one's experience of the world in a given culture (or combination of cultures), one organizes knowledge about the world and uses this knowledge to predict interpretations and relationships regarding new information, events, and experiences" (1993, 16). The idea that mental structures based upon prior experience are necessary tools in interpreting reality has been discussed at length since the 1970s in scholarly literature in the fields of psychology, artificial intelligence, anthropology, and linguistics (e.g., Rumelhart 1975; Abelson 1975, 1976; Schank and Abelson 1975; for a useful summary, see Tannen 1993). These mental scripts, structures, or schema are frameworks that enable taken-for-granted modes of functioning within cultural contexts, what Searle might call "background" abilities, or Bourdieu the "habitus" (Searle 1995; Bourdieu [1977] 1995).

Chapter 1. Traditions of Patriarchy and the Missing Female Voice in Russian Folklore Scholarship

1. Based upon Laura Olson's review of published studies on folk culture and also notebooks and diaries of collectors housed in the Institute of Russian Literature of the Russian Academy of Sciences (Pushkinskii dom) folklore archive. Many folklore and music collectors in first half of the twentieth century wrote down only the names of the people from whom they collected, and they tended to collect from individuals rather than groups. A few collectors, primarily essayists and journalists, described the lives of their subjects.

2. Bernshtam's work is also indebted to the work of Russian scholars who noted the importance of sex and age in understanding Russian rituals: Petr Bogatyrev, Dmitrii Zelenin (especially his *Russische (Ostslavische) Volkskunde*, 1927), and Vladimir Propp. Our own view is indebted to this lineage, although unlike Bernshtam we use fieldwork sources.

3. Rather than regarding folk texts in isolation, ethnographers tend to view folklore as part of the social and economic life of human beings.

4. A different explanation, but one that does not necessarily contradict ours, is given by Natalie Kononenko. She writes that scholars were not interested in performers "because they assumed that the oral literature originated among the upper classes and that the folk from whom they collected merely remembered the texts created elsewhere and remembered them badly at that" (1994, 29).

5. By productive we mean actively producing new variants, not only a "remembered" text. See Dégh 1995, 34–35.

6. See Brodskii 1904, 8–9; Azadovskii 1932, 1:23; Howell 1992, 161–63, 169, 172–73, 176. Later the theory that tales were told by professionals fell out of favor. See, for example, Howell 1992, 206.

7. Contemporary folklorist Jack Haney repeats some of the same opinions as generally known fact, without citing them, in his *An Introduction to the Russian Folktale* (1999, 18).

8. The Sokolovs themselves make the comparison with women's poetry ([1915] 1999, 1:129).

9. This kind of misinterpretation of tales as vaguely reflective of ethnographic reality is one of the problems with Russian scholarship on folktales, according to twentieth-century ethnographer Tatiana Bernshtam. She argues that scholars do so "without any idea of the role played by the folktale in the traditions and culture of the collective" (1996, 620).

10. Pomerantseva writes: "The teller herself does not sense the generic differences of various types of tales, which explains the fact that she on the one hand easily and naturally brings everyday realistic details into the magical tale and by doing this connects it with contemporary life, and on the other hand fills her everyday tales with elements of folktale rituality" (Pomerantseva 1969, 16, 20–21).

11. Linda Dégh agrees with Azadovskii and Onchukov, and gives evidence from Hungarian tales to show that tales told by women stress "the feminine point of view" due to their different life experiences (1995, 69). In accordance with the different goals of this work, we did not undertake an analogous type of analysis for Russian tales.

12. A caveat: since some collectors noted that female tellers told them "adult" (erotic) tales, we can assume that women did tell such tales for their peers (whether such audiences were single or mixed sex is not known). See, for example, Onchukov's ([1908] 1998) commentary on his teller Natalia Dement'eva, who told him five "pornographic" tales completely without shame. Also see Kadikina n.d.

13. Mastery includes size of repertoire and degree to which the storyteller improvises, as well as the notion of "fairy-tale rituality" (*skazochnaia obriadnost'*). Female and male tellers both excelled in terms of these criteria; to some degree, older tellers excelled more than adolescents. See the descriptions of tellers, for example, in Karnaukhova's work ([1934] 2006, 389, 392, 394, 399–400).

14. For an analysis of non-ritual tales, in Russian dubbed "everyday tales," see Iudin 1988, 402. Iudin does not address the question of who told these tales. Karnaukhova does address this question in describing the tellers she interviewed in the late 1920s ([1934] 2006, 389–446). In her study, men often told witty tales about soldiers, but women were as likely to tell "everyday tales" about priests, clever wives, devils, etc. Members of both sexes told witty tales with an erotic component.

15. Kadikina (n.d.) points out that researchers usually chose to focus on a single genre; she implies that the choice of genre was somewhat arbitrary, often relating to the scholar's agenda. Meanwhile, in their biographies and autobiographies, most women informants stated that their repertoires consisted of far more than one genre.

16. Haney (1999, 18) likewise asserts that in the twentieth century men did not tell animal tales, considering them too naïve, and women did not tell coarse tales. Neither of these assertions holds completely true. In the collections by the Sokolovs and Onchukov, men did tell tales featuring fish, bears, donkeys, and the like. And according to Onchukov ([1908] 2008, 1:230), at least one woman did tell coarse tales, which the collector considered unprintable.

17. We counted all texts in these collections, including tales that might be classified as legends or personal histories; we excluded only animal tales, nonsense tales, and tale prologues. In cases where a man and a wife were involved, we judged which character carried out the major action, or which character had the upper hand in the end. The figures are: Sokolov collection (vol. 1): fourteen female tellers told

twenty-three about men, six about women, four other; thirty-three male tellers told 120 about men, four about women, six other. Onchukov collection ([1908], 2008, vol. 1): thirty female tellers told fifty-four about men, twenty-seven about women, seven other; sixteen male tellers told forty-seven about men, two about women, eleven other. Onegina 1986: fourteen female tellers told twenty-one about women and fourteen about male heroes. The eleven male tellers told seven about heroines and twenty-one about heroes. One final statistic: a twentieth-century anthology (Lutovinova 1993) of eighty-seven tales about stepmothers and stepdaughters contained twelve told by men (14 percent). Dégh's statistics from Hungarian tradition differ radically, suggesting this question could use further cross-cultural research (1995, 67).

18. Natalie Kononenko expresses this idea in even stronger terms: she asserts, citing Roman Jakobson, that only men sang epic—an idea with which it is hard to agree, given the evidence presented here. See Kononenko 1994, 18; Jakobson 1966, 444. Kononenko (1994, 28) attributes women's singing of epics in the nineteenth century to their skill with lament.

19. This is the conclusion reached by Irina Semakova (n.d., n.p.), researching a similar phenomenon among the Karelians living around the White Sea in Russia. She writes: "Almost all the women of White Sea Karelia knew runes in some capacity or other, but told them mostly in the presence of women."

20. About existing taboos, see Bernshtam 1983, 206. Kononenko takes the opposite view of the one we outline here. Following the majority of Russian scholars, she states that women were "allowed" to sing epics only when the tradition started to die out (1994, 28).

21. In a 1938 study Astakhova reversed this pronouncement, and proclaimed that the tradition was living. However, due to scholarly politics, her earlier statements were likely more accurate (1938, 90, 103, 104).

22. Or because, as one collector noted, during the time of collection most of the men were temporarily absent from the village, having gone fishing or hunting (Markov [1909] 2002, 1028).

23. See, for example, Grigor'ev 1904, 187–89, 205–6, 304–20; all three informants named are women.

24. Rybnikov identifies this epic as beloved by women; however, several men also told it (Rybnikov 1909, 82; Gorelov et al. 2001–, 2:454–56, 4:666–70).

25. In one ballad collection, which contains a selection of recorded versions of the song, two of the four versions were listed as sung by women and one by a man; the other did not name the source (Kirdan 2001, 415).

26. That is, by entering his house while he is present, she has de facto rendered herself Dmitrii's bride. In contemporary communities this is called marriage as a *samokhodka*. See chapter 2.

27. "Kniaz' Dmitrii and Domna" is represented by four versions in Kirdan 2001, 157–68; three of the four are by women and one version does not name its informant. "Stavr Godinovich" is represented in Gorelov et al. 2001–, vol. 2 (Pechora river valley), with versions from one female and four male singers (450–52).

28. Examples include "Dobrynia and Alesha," with sixteen female and seven male tellers (Gorelov et al. 2001–, 3:483–99), and "Dobrynia Nikitich and the Dragon," with five women and five male tellers (Gorelov et al. 2001–, 3:466–74). See also Bailey and Ivanova 1998, 81.

29. The tradition of bringing epic singers for performance tours in Moscow and Saint Petersburg began in the 1870s with two male singers; in the 1890s one male singer toured; in 1915 and 1922 Krivopolenova; and in 1927 a male and female singer (Sokolov 1929).

30. As scholars at the time put it, the prerevolutionary scholars had not correctly assessed the skill of these creators. See Sokolov 1939, 9.

31. She uses this as evidence to support her argument that for women, wedding laments were more important than funeral laments.

32. Further, collectors' biases or even the biases of the informants themselves may have led to the collection of more funeral laments about men.

33. Chistov (1988, 227) makes the point that before Barsov's collection of Fedosova's laments, almost nothing was known of laments as a genre.

34. On the image of death in the lament, see Chistov 1997, 474.

35. These methods were used primarily in the 1920s, the Thaw period of 1956–64, and the 1980s, due to cultural politics.

Chapter 2. Age and Gender Status and Identity

1. This view is expressed by Worobec (1991, 159) and by Rancour-Laferriere (1995, 150, 195).

2. In ethnographic literature referring to the nineteenth century, *paren'* is further broken down into *mal'chik*, birth to age seven, and *parnyshka*, age seven to fifteen, in which case *paren'* refers to a young man of marriageable age (sixteen to eighteen). We use the term *paren'* for all these categories since the women we spoke with most often used *paren'* for boys from birth to marriageable age.

3. Card File of the Pskov Oblast Dictionary (*Pskovskii oblastnoi slovar'*). Handwritten cards kept in the Professor B. A. Larin Interdepartmental Dictionary Office, in the Philological Department of Saint Petersburg State University.

4. For an example, see the biography of A. V. Leont'evich of the village of 2nd Malinovka, Seleznevskii sel'sovet: http://selezni.tamb.ru/sov_vlast.htm.

5. The oven (*pech'*) is a main feature in a peasant house. Built of brick and reaching from floor nearly to the ceiling, it usually occupies a large part of the floor space of the main room. The fire is located in one part of the oven for cooking, and people often lie or sleep on another part of the oven, which is built as a platform, and retains a pleasant warmth. In the North, ovens were built large enough for an adult to go inside. After the fire had died down, a person could go inside to wash.

6. For competitive relations between mistresses of households, see Kabakova 2001.

7. See, for example, the following saying when the wedding bells in the church sounded: "хоть об углы бейся—назад не вернешься" (Now go ahead and try beating [your head] in the corner, you can't go back) (woman born in 1923, Pokrovskoe, Vashkinskii region, Vologda oblast, 14 July 1998 [Vash 1-2]). Another woman told us that her grandmother tried going back and was told by her own parents to return to the family of her husband (woman born in 1980, Azapol'e, Mezen' region, Arkhangel'sk oblast, 16 July 2008 [Mez 1-147].

8. Data given below has been borrowed from my field journal (SA).

9. Kolkhoz workers were not paid in money but in terms of shares of the kolkhoz's production (grain, etc.), based on amount of labor contributed. This system operated from 1930 to 1966.

10. To be sure, in cases where the fathers were present and active, sons did view themselves as subordinate to the fathers.

11. To be sure, Valentina's status as the closest family member of the deceased meant that she would not be expected to cook for the memorial feast.

Chapter 3. Subjectivity and the Relational Self in Russian
Village Women's Stories of Courtship and Marriage

1. We make this judgment based upon our observation of women's singing of funeral laments. Other scholars have emphasized the improvisational quality of wedding laments: see, for example, Shmeleva 1980, 31.

2. Various symbols are used to stand for the symbolic beauty/will of the bride: a ribbon, a decorated small tree, or a decorated burdock stem.

3. Her recordings are available on the Pan Records CD *Travushka Muravushka* (Pan 2042).

4. "Он бьет мое тело сколь угодно. / Уж я тут старому покорилась, / В праву ноженьку поклонилась, / Я вперед такова боле не буду, / Целовать тебя, миленькой, буду."

5. See, for example, song no. 301, "Skuchno bylo mne, bednoi," in Sobolevskii's 1899 collection, 231–32.

6. Grades one through four became mandatory starting in 1930–31 (called "universal primary" education). In rural schools one additional grade was phased in each year starting in 1937, such that in principle the mandatory education reached the seventh grade by 1939–40. Fitzpatrick 1996, 224.

Chapter 4. The Pleasure, Power, and Nostalgia of Melodrama

1. Many scholars of mythology have linked these gendered roles with the agricultural cycle: the men's rituals occurred as the earth needed to be plowed and seeded (inseminated), while the women's occurred when the earth gave birth to new life (Bernshtam 1988, 139, 146–47; Rice 1994, 135–36).

2. Exceptions include women who play balalaika or small button accordions. Female accordionists and *rozhok* (horn) players were and are rare. When groups of village women found themselves without an accordionist, they sang a particular form of "mouth music" (called *pod iazyk*) as accompaniment for *chastushki*.

3. Dates when handiwork parties (called *besedy* or *vecherki* or *posidelki*) and traditional weddings ceased to be practiced varied by region and by village. World War II serves as a general marker, but we did hear, for example, of weddings with traditional singing in the 1960s in Vologda villages.

4. Elena Vladimirovna A., born in 1928, Krasnoe, Riazan' oblast, 19 October 1998.

5. On Semeiskie, see Levitt 2001.

6. See Waters 1991; films featuring backward female peasants include *Baby* (*Village Women*) (Vladimir Batalov, 1940); *Svetlyi put'* (*Radiant Path*) (Grigorii Aleksandrov, 1940); and *Svinarka i pastukh* (Swineherd and Shepherd) (Ivan Pyrev, 1941).

7. LO, field diaries, Krasnoe, Riazan' oblast, and Rezhe, Vologda oblast, 2004 and 2005.

8. Interview with LO, Pigilinka, Siamzha region, Vologda oblast, 19 October 2004. This group had another *chastushka* about rehearsals and fighting women: "Не пойду на кино / Пойду на репетицию / У подруги перебью (кавалера) / Пусть идет в милицию!" (I won't go to the movies / I'll go to rehearsal / I'll steal my girlfriend's [man], / Let her go to the police!).

9. The situation in other Slavic countries was even less accepting of women's public performance: see Hofman 2011, 97–100.

10. "Kakim ty byl" is from *Kubanskie Kazaki* (Kuban Cossacks) (Ivan Pyr'ev, 1949), with music by Isaak Dunaevskii and lyrics by M. Isakovskii and M. Vol'pin. "Ognei tak mnogo zolotykh" is from *Delo bylo v Pen'kove* (It Happened in Penkovo) (Stanislav Rostotskii, 1957), with words by N. Dorizo and music by Kirill Molchanov. "Napilas' ia p'ianoi" was popularized in the 1990s by Nadezhda Kadysheva and her group "Golden Ring," but its origins are earlier. I (LO) was not able to find its composer. Due to its implied message (the speaker gets drunk because of an unfaithful husband) it was not published during the Soviet period but has been widely published in songbooks since then. Other songs named as popular by our village informants include "Moskva zlatoglavaia" ("Moscow the Golden-Domed"), a city-style romance about Moscow in winter; and "Chernyi voron" ("Black Raven"), with words by N. Verevkin, about a soldier who dies in battle.

11. It is difficult to obtain reliable data on motivations for singing, since asking questions about why a person sings a song may either influence the interviewee's answer or result in a non sequitur. My (LO's) collection methods included asking the singers to explicate the meaning of the song, which was a natural stance for me as a non-native speaker. I received reliable and valuable insights from observing conversations that led to and resulted from song performances. Dégh describes a similar methodology in researching fairy tales (1995, 14) and legends (2001).

12. Epics in which the unfaithful wife is punished with death include: "Churila i nevernaia zhena" ("Churila and his unfaithful wife"), Astakhova 1961, 59–61; and "Ivan Godinovich," Gorelov et al. 2001–, 4:347–50. A ballad with a similar theme is "Oklevetannaia zhena," *Russkii fol'klor*, http://rusfolklor .ru/archives/109.

13. Older lyric songs also featured tropes of deep feelings: *retivoe serdtse* (ardent heart) and *kruchina* (woe) were staples of epics and lyric folk songs. However, these feelings were consonant with expected behavior. They described a young woman's love and longing for a particular young man or her loneliness in married life, not (as here) her lapsed morals. In "Am I Guilty," neither the above clichés nor their synonyms are mentioned; instead, the subtlety of the sign (the wavering voice) hints at the depth of the emotion. Cf. "Batiushku ia govarivala," Sobolevskii 1897, 8–9; "Kalinku s malinkoi voda poniala," Rozov 1988, 144–45.

14. Women's drinking was not considered inappropriate at holidays, but drunkenness was frowned upon and could affect a family's reputation (Denisova and Mukhina 2010, 111–19).

15. Classified by folklorists as "family lyric songs." Compare, for example, "Katia, Katen'ka, Katerinushka," which is the monologue of a young wife: getting drunk with her lover is justified, because of her disrespect for her husband, a "bitter drunkard" (Sobolevskii 1896, 341–42).

16. Compare the traditional peasant lyric: "Кабы знала я, ведала, / Молоденька чаяла / Свою горьку долю, / Несчастье замужества, / Замуж не ходила бы, / Доли не теряла бы!" (If only I'd known, foreseen, / Felt as a young wife / My bitter lot, / The unhappiness of marriage, / I wouldn't have married, / Wouldn't have lost my lot!). Shein 1898, no. 1197.

17. Compare traditional lyric songs from the point of view of young married women, which often imaginatively describe the bride's return to the parental home or to the mother's grave to complain about married life. See Rozov 1988, 146–48, 150.

18. Dégh (2001, 2, 418) states the same about legend. Our thanks to Jeanmarie Rouhier-Willoughby for this insight.

19. Our definition differs somewhat from but is partly indebted to the one offered by Rosnow and Fine 1976, 131.

Chapter 5. Transgression as Communicative Act

1. When asked what this song was about, the singer of this *chastushka* explained that the singer "needed one more nickel." One would put a nickel on one's anus to prevent passing gas.

2. When we asked what the last two lines of this song meant (since it didn't appear to make sense to weigh an organ that delineated an opening in the body), the singer, Nina Vasilevna S., said, "I don't know, that's how the song goes!" (and laughed).

3. The *chastushka* was: "Ой девушки-голубушки, / Народ мастеровой / Зарабатывают деньги / На соломе яровой." (Oh, you dear girls, / You masterful people, / They earn money / On springplanted straw.).

4. *Chastushka*-singing may be likened to Victor Turner's category of rituals of status reversal, in which individuals experience social cohesion and leveling (communitas), emphasizing equality and the essential human bond (1969, 109–10, 177).

5. As Arkhipova and Nekliudov (2010, n. 96) explain this phenomenon, folklorists such as Sokolov hoped to acquaint the public with a type of folklore they loved, while publicly proclaiming these texts to be a throwback to Tsarist times and inappropriate for current use.

6. In her 2004 book, Adon'eva speaks of battles taking place in the "forum" of *chastushka*-singing within the community, whereas here we are emphasizing battles of insiders versus outsiders.

7. Tatiana's words were: "Не пою, да забуду, я каждый день пела, бывать да постынут . . . Она [тетрадь] у меня никуда не девается. Это она у меня как дневник." (If I don't sing, I'll forget; I used to sing every day, it happens that [the words] wane . . . It [my notebook] is always nearby. It's like my diary.).

8. Whether she is in fact author can of course be questioned. In other words, Tatiana Iakovlevna may not be entirely aware of the degree of "folk" authorship of her *chastushki*. She may be recycling well-known material, either parts or whole *chastushki*. Our thanks to Mark Leiderman for this insight.

9. In the same vein, the rural female (born in 1915) author of an autobiography said she wrote in order not to disappear like a grain of sand (Kozlova and Sandomirskaia 1996).

10. "Нет, много . . . и таких! Что очень плохо." "У нас добра, Ангелина. . . . ты не говори што худо!" "Много-то не хульте. . . . нашу-то Россию-Матушку." Unidentified neighbor, Tatiana Iakovlevna, and Pavel Kozlov, interview with author (LO), 27 October 2004.

11. The conversation could well have been influenced by my presence, and/or by the presence of her cousin.

12. For a similar example, see Volkov 1999, 245, no. 1504.

Chapter 6. Magical Forces and the Symbolic Resources of Motherhood

1. The notion that births comprise a ceremony of transition, in any type of culture, is a fact that today no longer demands proof. See, for example, anthropological works devoted to modern institutions of maternity care: Davis-Floyd 1992, 1994.

2. See Belousova 1998; Belousova 2003, 339–70; Belousova 2007; Belousova and Nekliudov 2001, 275–302; Shchepanskaia 1994, 15–27; Shchepanskaia 1999, 389–423; Shchepanskaia 2001, 236–65; Rouhier-Willoughby 2008, 63–118.

3. "Сглазят, так чё будешь делать-то? Знай, чё будешь делать-то. Если ничего не знаешь, дак чего будешь делать."

4. "От своей думы, от своей крови, чур мою думу."

5. "Кусаю я грыжу и вижу. / Аминь. Аминь. Аминь. / Сидит кошка на окошке / С железными зубами, / С железными когтями. / Аминь. Аминь. Аминь. / Она грыжу переедает и перекусывает, / И переуранывает. / Аминь. Аминь. Аминь." (I bite the hernia and see. / Amen. Amen. Amen. / A cat sits on the windowsill. / With iron teeth, / With iron claws. / Amen. Amen. Amen. / She eats the hernia and takes a bite, / And drops it. / Amen. Amen. Amen.). Woman born in 1921, Bekrenevo, Belozersk region, Vologda oblast, 1988 (Adon'eva and Ovchinnikova 1993, 100).

6. "Первая заря Марья, вторая заря Дарья, третья заря Пеладья, не смейся, не галься над моим дитем. А смейся и галься на дне речном . . ."

7. "Я тебя мою как бабушка Соломанья Исуса Христа, рабу божью, например, Нелиньку, на сон, на покой, на рост, на доброё здоровьё, тфу, аминь, во веки веков." Granny or Mother Soloman'ia is a saintly figure often appealed to in incantations regarding the health of newborns: in the Apocrypha she was supposedly summoned by Joseph as a midwife when Mary gave birth to Jesus. See Adon'eva and Ovchinnikova 1993, 167–68; Iudin 2011.

8. "Как будешь жить, пелену повешу на крест, а умрешь, дак закрою."

Chapter 7. Magic, Control, and Social Roles

1. In the West approximately 80 percent of accused witches were female (Kivelson 1991, 74).

2. Of course, there are male healers as well. Margaret Paxson has written an in-depth study of the practice of one male healer in Vologda oblast (2005).

3. These have been published in part in Adon'eva and Ovchinnikova 1993.

4. See, for example, Kozlova and Stepakhina n.d.; Il'ina and Toporkov 2006; and Kostyrko 2003.

5. A fairly complete description of the published material is offered in Kliaus's 1997 study.

6. On women's powers of control, influence, and ability, see Newton 1981.

7. Throughout this chapter, when an informant is not named, it is Valentina Sergeevna G.

8. On passing on sorcery, see Ivanits 1989, 95–96.

9. Our differentiation differs somewhat from, but is partly indebted to, the one offered by Rosnow and Fine (1976, 131).

10. Women, particularly widows, were among the traditional purveyors of illicit homemade liquor in the village (Denisova and Mukhina 2010, 111).

11. Note the folkloric form of the story: the healing is revealed in the purging of the effects of sorcery from the body, three times. Other stories had the victim throwing up three times. The forest is also a significant, symbolic location for the purging in this case.

12. To be sure, it is not just the women *koldun'i* who threaten the male population: Valentina and her friend also said one male *koldun* "took out [the men at] one whole end of the village."

13. As part of the *trudoden'* system in 1930–66, village workers were paid in grain or other produce. On money in the contemporary Russian village economy, see Paxson 2005, 69.

14. Ryan asserts that *kolduny* were commonly supposed not to go to church; he cites no source (1999, 77).

15. Following Van Gennep's model of ritual (in Turner's 1969 modification) and Kertzer's (1988) definition of ritual (as repetitive, standardized symbolic action).

16. Such tricksters are attested in documents from Prerevolutionary Russia as well. See Worobec 1995, 166.

Chapter 8. Constructing Identity in Stories of the Other World

1. The term *bylichka* can mean either memorate or fabulate. *Bylichki* can be told from the first or third person. But in general they are closer to the memorate than the fabulate, as they imply a certain immediacy of experience.

2. During confession, supplicants reassess their experience using the form offered by the church. The priest tells confessors that they are standing before God, and narrators adopt the standpoint of someone standing before a figure of ultimate power as they recount and reflect upon their pasts. In the case of *bylichki*, however, the reliving and reshaping of personal experience is a self-sufficient, sovereign act.

3. *Dobrokhodushka* is a local word (northeast Vologda oblast) for the house spirit *domovoi*. As we were told by some informants, the name *dobrokhodushka*, with the root *khodit'* (to walk), emphasizes the local belief that the spirit can move with a person. It was also explained with a different root, *khotet'* (to want), suggesting that the spirit desires good for his human partner.

4. "Батюшка-доброходушка / и матушка доброходница, / ходите, пойте, /кормите матушку-скотинку, / ладьте, гладьте, / чтобы выпустить./ На меня на кормленщицу не надейтесь."

5. See this motif in the animal tale "The Bear with the Linden Leg" (listed in Barag 1979, type 161A; and Aarne and Thompson 1961, type AT 163B), in which the bear sings: "In the villages all are sleeping, /

In the hamlets all are sleeping, / One old woman isn't sleeping, / She's sitting on my skin ..." (Maria Vladimirovna S. [born in 1931], Koltyrikha, Siamzha region, Vologda oblast, 17 July 2006).

6. V. I. Dal' (1973) has the following definition: "*Postylet'*, to make oneself or to become *postylyi*, unloved, reviled, hated."

7. "Ходи к матушке в гости, пока матушка жива. / А как матушка умрет, а как матушка умрет— / Дороженька зарастет. Зарастет дороженька, / Зарастет широкыя травою-муравою. /Травою-муравою, травой-муравою, / Рощею зеленою" (Glinkina 1969, 70).

8. Tatiana Shchepanskaia explores the nature of fear with relation to men's experiences with the supernatural. For male practitioners of magic, control over one's own and others' fear is tantamount to controlling the supernatural. By contrast, for female practitioners of magic, the most important conception is that of "blood," associated with the protection of the deceased members of the clan (2001, 80).

9. Timothy Rice describes such a situation in the context of learning to play the Bulgarian bagpipe (1994, 65–67). In the Russian rural context, O. Davydovskaia (n.d.) attempts to piece together transmission of mores, beliefs, and stories, using interviews with teenagers.

10. "Live help," *Zhivye pomoshchi*, is the folk name for the folk version of Psalm 90 in the Orthodox Bible (in Western Christianity, Psalm 91). The folk text is in a corrupted version of Church Slavonic. The uncorrected text of the prayer in Valentina's notebook is as follows: "Живый в помощи вышняго, в крови Бога небесного водворитья, речят Господеви: заступник мой еси и прибежище мое, Бог мой, и уповаю на него, яко той избавит тя от сети ловчи и от словеси мятежня; плещмя своима осенит тя, и под криле Его надеешься, оружием обыдет тя истина Его. Не убоишися от страха нощного, от стрелы, летящия во дни, от вещи во тьме преходящия, от стяща и беся полудённого. Падет от страны твоея тысяща и тьма одесную тебе, к тебе же не приближится; обаче очима твоима смотриши и воздаяние грешников узриши. Яко ты, Господи, упавание мое; Вышняго положил еси прибежище твое. Не придет к тебе зло и рана не приближится телеси твоему. Яко Ангелом стоим заповесть о тебе, сохранити тя во всех путях твоих. На руках возмут тя, да не когда преткнеши о камень ногу твою, на аспида и Василиска наступиши, и попереши льва и змия. Яко на мя упова, и избавию и покрою и яко позна имя мое, Воззовет ко мне и услышу его, с ним есть в скорби, изму его и прославлю егоь долготою дней исполню его и явлю ему спасение мое." (He who dwells in the shelter of the Most High will rest in the shadow of the Almighty. / I will say of the LORD, "He is my refuge and my fortress, my God, in whom I trust." / Surely he will save you from the fowler's snare and from the deadly pestilence. / He will cover you with his feathers, and under his wings you will find refuge; his faithfulness will be your shield and rampart. / You will not fear the terror of night, nor the arrow that flies by day, nor the pestilence that stalks in the darkness, nor the plague that destroys at midday. / A thousand may fall at your side, ten thousand at your right hand, but it will not come near you. / You will only observe with your eyes and see the punishment of the wicked. / If you make the Most High your dwelling—even the LORD, who is my refuge— / then no harm will befall you, no disaster will come near your tent. / For he will command his angels concerning you to guard you in all your ways; / they will lift you up in their hands, so that you will not strike your foot against a stone. / You will tread upon the lion and the cobra; you will trample the great lion and the serpent. / "Because he loves me," says the LORD, "I will rescue him; I will protect him, for he acknowledges my name. / He will call upon me, and I will answer him; I will be with him in trouble, I will deliver him and honor him. / With long life will I satisfy him and show him my salvation.") (New International Version, 1984).

11. Both the narrated event and the narrative events are performatives in the perlocutionary sense in that they attest "to the generation of a force which causes something to be accomplished" (Gill 1977,

154; see also Austin 1962); in particular, the narrative event is not merely illocutionary (expressive) but perlocutionary since the story of the successful prayer speech act aims to convince the addressees that the narrator is a competent user of that speech genre.

12. Cf. scholarship on participant relations and participant structures: Hymes 1972, 58–59; and a useful summary by Shugar and Kmita 1990, 275–77.

Chapter 9. Death, the Dead, and Memory-Keepers

1. Warner (2000b) notes (based on interviews with two informants born in 1915 and 1927) that this practice has fallen out of use in Pskov province among the Orthodox, while Old Believers still practice it. However, we encountered it in all our areas of research.

2. Rouhier-Willoughby (2008) has shown that city dwellers do practice many of the same customs as do rural dwellers, including funeral practices.

3. Many city families, approximating village practice, have the deceased brought home on the night before the burial, so that people can visit the deceased one last time (Rouhier-Willoughby 2008, 266).

4. Nursing mothers and pregnant women (from the time that the pregnancy was noticeable) were an exception: they were kept away from the body (man born in 1929, woman born in 1926, Anufrievo, Belozersk region, Vologda oblast, 25 July 1994 [Bel 10-22]).

5. I later learned that such assistance presupposes receiving a portion of the final product of the hay: a helper will later receive a piece of meat from an animal slaughtered in autumn as a token of gratitude.

6. On the funeral ritual as enabling the processing of grief, see Rouhier-Willoughby 2008, 185, 196.

7. For alternate interpretations of the applicability of Van Gennep's structure to the Russian case, see Warner 2000b and Loginov 1993.

8. "Вот я причитала по своему дак, сыну. 'Ай, завейте-ка, ветерочеки,'—ой, не могу, я не могу никак. / 'Завейте, ветерочики, / С полудённой, со сторонушки. / Да прилетите-ка два ангела, / Ангелочеки крылатые, / Да принесите . . . принесите,'—не могу—'душу, ангелы. Вот / Расколись-ка, ты мать-земля,' / —Причитать-то хорошо можно, а рассказывать-то плохо, да я и не могу. Ой.— / 'Расколись-ка, мать-сыра земля, / На две, на три половиночки /Да на четыре четвертиночки. Да. Ой. / Размахнись-ка белым рученькам.'—Как-то уже что же и забыла уж— / 'Да открой-ка очи ясные, / Да поднимись на резвы ноженьки, / Да пойдём-ка, мила ладушка /На последнее простиньице, / На последнее прощаньице.' / —Вот так."

Вот так причитали.

"Да вот причитать-то тянуть надо долго. Но потом . . . 'Ты пойдешь, да мила ладушка, / В дальнюю дороженьку, / За леса да за дремучие, / За болота за зыбучие, / За озёра да глубокие, / За моря да за широкие. / А там ести . . . / Сторожа да ести верные, / Караулы ести крепкие. / Да не отпустят тебя, ладушка, / Да на родимую сторонушку.'"

"Только причитается. Тут укласть ещё много чего можно. Я только тут маленько. Вот, девушка. Поняла?"

Угу. Вот так, да?

9. One of the sources for information in this account was M. P. Cherednikova's 2006 article on this village's traditions. Information on Pot'ma was generously shared by folklorists Maina Pavlovna Cherednikova and Mikhail Grigorievich Matlin of Ul'ianovsk State Pedagogical University, who invited me (LO) to accompany them on an expedition there for Troitsa (Whitsunday) in May 2005.

10. Indeed, members of our research team who practiced Russian Orthodoxy commented that everything that was read and practiced in Pot'ma differed from that which is typically done in a church or by a priest.

11. This was a local tradition; in Arkhangel'sk and Vologda oblasts, for example, everyone was memorialized because all were considered to have been baptized. During the Soviet period, grandmothers "baptized" the infants when they performed the special washing ritual.

12. A New Testament passage, Matthew 6:1–4, emphasizes the necessity to give alms secretly in order to be humble and not hypocritical (i.e., self-serving). This passage was not cited by our interviewees.

Conclusion

1. Of course, migrants to the city who have chosen not to perform these functions do exist. We did not meet them in the village but occasionally heard about them: children who do not visit.

2. See, for example, the fame of the group "Buranovo Babushkas," who appeared on Russia's *Who Wants to Be a Millionaire?* television show in 2011 (Greene 2011) and took second place representing Russia at the Eurovision 2012 contest in Baku, Azerbaijan.

References

Aarne, Antti, and Stith Thompson. 1961. *The Types of the Folktale: A Classification and Bibliography.* Folklore Fellows Communications, vol. 75, no. 184. Helsinki: Academia Scientarum Fennica.

Abelson, R. P. 1975. "Concepts for Representing Mundane Reality in Plans." In *Representation and Understanding: Studies in Cognitive Science,* edited by D. G. Bobrow, 273–309. New York: Academic Press.

———. 1976. "Script Processing in Attitude Formation and Decision Making." In *Cognition and Social Behavior,* edited by J. S. Carroll and J. W. Payne, 33–46. Hillsdale, NJ: L. Erlbaum.

Abu-Lughod, Lila. 1993. *Writing Women's Worlds: Bedouin Stories.* Berkeley: University of California Press.

———. 2006. "Writing Against Culture." In *Feminist Anthropology: A Reader,* edited by Ellen Lewin, 153–69. Malden, MA: Blackwell Publishing.

Adon'eva, S. B. 1998a. "Belozerskaia svad'ba." In *Belozer'e: Kraevedcheskii al'manakh,* edited by Iu. S. Vasil'ev, 2:231–49. Vologda: Legiia.

———. 1998b. "Etnografia severnorusskikh prichitanii." In *Biulleten' foneticheskogo fonda russkogo iazyka, Prilozhenie 7, Obriadovaia poezia russkovo severa: Plachi,* 63–85. St. Petersburg: Bokhum.

———. 1998c. "O ritual'noi funktsii zhenshchiny v russkoi traditsii." *Zhivaia starina* 1:26–28.

———. 1999. "'Ia' i 'Ty' v ritual'nom tekste: Situatsiia granitsy." In *Pogranichnoe soznanie: Pogranichnaia kul'tura; Al'manakh "Kanun,"* edited by V. E. Bagno and T. A. Novichkova, 5:47–74. St. Petersburg: Kanun.

———. 2001. "Kategoriia nenastoiashchego vremeni: Kul'turnye siuzhety i zhiznennye stsenarii." In *Kategoriia nenastoiashchego vremeni: Antropologicheskie ocherki,* 101–12. St. Petersburg: Peterburgskoe vostokovedenie.

———. 2002. "Lamentation dans le Nord de la Russie: Texte et ritual." In *Les études régionales en Russie (1890–1990): Origines, crise, renaissance,* Cahiers slaves 6, 431–43. Paris: Université de Paris-Sorbonne.

———. 2004. *Pragmatika fol'klora.* St. Petersburg: Amfora.

———. 2007. "Bol'shaki i bol'shukhi." *Personal-miks,* nos. 2–3. http://lit.phil.pu.ru/article.php?id=15.

———. 2009. *Dukh naroda i drugie dukhi.* St. Petersburg: Amfora.

———. 2010. "Bol'shaki i bol'shukhi." *Russkii fol'klor v sovremennykh zapisiakh* (website of the Propp Center, St. Petersburg State University). http://folk.ru/Research/adonyeva_bolshak.php.

Adon'eva, S. B., and E. Bazhkova. 1998. "Funktsional'nye razlichiia v povedenii i roli zhenshchiny na raznykh etapakh ee zhizni." In *Belozer'e: Kraevedcheskii al'manakh*, 2:204–12. Vologda: Legiia. http://www.booksite.ru/fulltext/2be/loz/erye/17.htm.

Adon'eva, S. B., and N. M. Gerasimova. 1996. *Sovremennaia ballada i zhestokii romans*. St. Petersburg: Izd-vo Ivana Limbakha.

Adon'eva, S. B., and O. A. Ovchinnikova. 1993. *Traditsionnaia russkaia magiia v zapisiakh kontsa XX veka*. St. Petersburg: Friendlikh-Taf.

Afanas'ev, A. (1865) 1994. *Poeticheskie vozzreniia slavian na prirodu*. Vol. 1. Moscow: Indrik.

Agapkina, T. A. 2002. *Mifopoeticheskie osnovy slavianskogo narodnogo kalendaria: Vesenne-letnii tsikl*. Moscow: Indrik.

Alekseev, Gleb, and Viktorin Popov. 1937. "Zhivaia letopis." *Novyi sever* 3:84–88.

Allport, Gordon, and Joseph Postman. 1947. *Psychology of Rumor*. New York: Russell and Russell.

Andreev, N. P. 1931. "Fol'klor i antireligioznaia rabota." *Voinstvuiushchii ateizm* 12 (December): 3.

Apte, Mahadev L. 1985. *Humor and Laughter: An Anthropological Approach*. Ithaca, NY: Cornell University Press.

———. 1992. "Humor." In Bauman 1992, 69–70.

Arkhipova, A. S., and S. Iu. Nekliudov. 2010. "Fol'klor i vlast' v zakrytom obshchestve." *Novoe literaturnoe obozrenie* 101. http://magazines.russ.ru/nlo/2010/101/ar6.html (accessed 27 November 2010).

Asad, Talal. 1986. "The Concept of Cultural Translation in British Social Anthropology." In *Writing Culture: The Poetics and Politics of Ethnography*, edited by James Clifford and George E. Marcus, 141–64. Berkeley: University of California Press.

Astakhova, A. M. 1927. "Bylina v Zaonezh'i." In *Krest'ianskoe iskusstvo SSSR*, vol. 1, *Iskusstvo severa: Zaonezh'e*, 77–103. Leningrad: Academia.

———. 1938. *Byliny severa*. Vol. 1, *Mezen i Pechora*. Moscow: Izdatel'stvo Akademii nauk SSSR.

———. 1939. "Belomorskaia skazitel'nitsa M. S. Kriukova." *Sovetskii fol'klor* 6:176–77.

———. 1951. *Byliny severa*. Vol. 2, *Prionezh'e, Pinega i Pomor'e*. Moscow: Izdatel'stvo Akademii nauk SSSR.

———. 1961. *Byliny Pechory i Zimnego Berega: Novye zapisi*. Leningrad: Izdatel'stvo Akademii nauk SSSR.

Atkinson, Dorothy. 1977. "Society and the Sexes in the Russian Past." In *Women in Russia*, edited by Dorothy Atkinson, Alexander Dallin, and Gail Warshofsky Lapidus, 3–38. Stanford: Stanford University Press.

———. 1983. *The End of the Russian Land Commune, 1905–1930*. Stanford: Stanford University Press.

Austin, J. L. 1962. *How to Do Things with Words*. Cambridge, MA: Harvard University Press.

Azadovskii, Mark K. 1932. "Russkie skazochniki." In *Russkaia skazka: Izbrannye mastera*, edited by M. K. Azadovskii, 1:9–90. Moscow: Academia.

Azov, V. 1932. "Satira pod spudom." *Poslednie novosti*, 14 May, 2.

Bagizbaeva, M. M. 1979. *Fol'klor semirechenskikh kazakov*. Part 2. Alma-Ata: Bektep.

Baiburin, A. K. 1993. *Ritual v traditsionnoi kul'ture: Strukturno-semanticheskii analiz vostochnoslavianskikh obriadov*. St. Petersburg: Nauka.

Bailey, James, and Tatiana Ivanova. 1998. *An Anthology of Russian Folk Epics*. Armonk, NY: M. E. Sharpe.

Bakhtin, Mikhail. 1981. *The Dialogic Imagination: Four Essays*. Translated by Michael Holquist. Austin: University of Texas Press.

———. 1984. *Rabelais and his World*. Translated by Helene Iswolsky. Bloomington: Indiana University Press.

———. 1993. *Toward a Philosophy of the Act.* Translated by Vadim Liapunov. Edited by Michael Holquist and Vadim Liapunov. Austin: University of Texas Press.

Balashov, D. M., and Iu. I. Marchenko. 1985. *Russkaia svad'ba: Svadebnyi obriad na Verkhnei i Srednei Kokshen'ge i na Uftiuge.* Moscow: Sovremmenik.

Balashov, D. M., and T. A. Novichkova. 2001. "Russkii bylinnyi epos." In *Byliny v 25 tomakh,* vol. 1, *Byliny Pechory,* edited by A. A. Gorelov et al., 21–78. St. Petersburg: Nauka.

Barag, L. G., et al. 1979. *Sravnitel'nyi ukazatel' siuzhetov: Vostochnoslavianskaia skazka.* Leningrad: Nauka.

Baranov, D. 2005a. "Brak." In Shchepanskaia and Shangina 2005a, 75–77.

———. 2005b. "Novorozhdennyi." In Shchepanskaia and Shangina 2005a, 406–12.

———. 2005c. "Rodil'nyi obriad." In Shchepanskaia and Shangina 2005a, 525–27.

———. 2005d. "Rozhenitsa." In Shchepanskaia and Shangina 2005a, 533–36.

———. 2005e. "Soitie." In Shchepanskaia and Shangina 2005a, 623–25.

Baranova, Ol'ga. 2002. "Pokrov Bogoroditsy." In *Russkii prazdnik: Prazdniki i obriady narodnogo zemel-edel'cheskogo kalendaria,* edited by I. Shangina, 433–38. St. Petersburg: Iskusstvo.

Barsov, E. V. 1997a. "O zapisiakh i izdaniiakh 'Prichitanii severnogo kraia,' o lichnom tvorchestve Iriny Fedosovoi i khore ee podgolosnits." In Barsov 1997b, 262–77.

———. 1997b. *Prichitan'ia severnogo kraia.* Edited by K. V. Chistov and B. E Chistova. St. Petersburg: Nauka.

———. 1997c. "Svedeniia o voplenitsakh, ot kotorykh zapisany prichitan'ia." In Barsov 1997b, 253–61. St. Petersburg: Nauka.

Bauman, Richard. 1986. *Story, Performance, and Event: Contextual Studies of Oral Narrative.* New York: Cambridge University Press.

———. 1992. *Folklore, Cultural Performances, and Popular Entertainments: A Communications-Centered Handbook.* New York: Oxford University Press.

Bazanov, V. G, and A. P. Razumova. 1962. "Prichitaniia russkogo severa v zapisiakh 1942–45 godov. Vsuplenie." In *Russkaia narodno-bytovaia lirika: Prichitaniia Severa v zapisiakh V. G. Bazanova i A. P. Razumovoi,* 3–44. Leningrad: Akademii Nauk SSSR.

Becker, Ernest. 1973. *The Denial of Death.* New York: Free Press.

Belousova, E. A. 1998. "Rodovaia bol' v antropologicheskoi perspektive." *Arbor mundi: Mezhdunarodnyi zhurnal po teorii i istorii mirovoi kul'tury* 6:48–57.

———. 2003. "Sovremennyi rodil'nyi obriad." In *Sovremennyi gorodskoi fol'klor,* edited by A. F. Belousov, I. S. Veselova, and S. Iu. Nekliudov, 339–70. Moscow: RGGU.

———. 2007. "Fol'klor v sovremennom rodil'nom obriade: Primety i sovety." *Natural Birth.* http://naturalbirth.ru/public/ebel.php (accessed 21 June 2010).

Belousova, E. A., and S. Iu. Nekliudov. 2001. *Rodiny, deti, povitukhi v traditsiiakh narodnoi kul'tury.* Moscow: RGGU.

Bennett, Gillian. 1987. *Traditions of Belief: Women and the Supernatural.* New York: Penguin.

Berelovich, A., et al. 2005. "Spetsspravka PP OGPU SKK o nastroeniiakh i antisovetskikh proiavleniiakh sredi sel'skoi molodezhi russkikh raionov kraia." In *Sovetskaia derevnia glazami VChK-OGPU-NKVD, 1918–1939: Dokumenty i materialy,* edited by A. Berelovich and V. Danilov, 3:2:95–97. Moscow: ROSSPEN.

Bergson, Henri. (1935) 1977. *The Two Sources of Morality and Religion.* Notre Dame, IN: University of Notre Dame Press.

Berman, Harold J. 1993. *Faith and Order: The Reconciliation of Law and Religion.* Atlanta: Scholars Press.

Bernshtam, T. A. 1983. *Russkaia narodnaia kul'tura Pomor'ia v XIX–nachale XX v.: Etnograficheskie ocherki.* Leningrad: Nauka.

———. 1988. *Molodezh' v obriadovoi zhizni russkoi obshchiny XIX–nachala XX veka: Polovozrastnoi aspekt traditsionnoi kul'tury.* Leningrad: Nauka.

———. 1991. "Sovershennoletie devushki v metaforakh igrovogo fol'klora (traditsionnyi aspekt russkoi kul'tury)." In *Etnicheskie stereotipy muzhskogo i zhenskogo povedeniia,* edited by A. K. Baiburin and I. S. Kon, 234–57. St. Petersburg: Nauka.

———. 1996. "Le conte dans la vie et dans la culture de la paysannerie slave orientale." *Ethnologie française* 26:619–27.

———. 2000. *Molodost' v simvolizme perekhodnykh obriadov vostochnykh slavian: Uchenie i opyt tserkvi v narodnom khristianstve.* St. Petersburg: Peterburgskoe Vostokovedenie.

———. 2005. *Prikhodskaia zhizn' russkoi derevni: Ocherki po tserkovnoi etnografii.* St. Petersburg: Peterburgskoe Vostokovedenie.

Beumers, Birgit. 2011. "New Russia's Legendary Heroes: The Animated Blockbuster." Paper presented at the Annual Meeting of the Association for Slavic, East European, and Eurasian Studies, Washington, DC, November 17.

Bialosinskaia, N. S. 1966. "Fol'klor i agitbrigada." In *Sovremennyi russkii fol'klor,* edited by E. V. Pomerantseva, 225–46. Moscow: Nauka.

Bikmetova, N. V. 2009. "Semantika svadebnogo obriada russkikh poselenii poberezh'ia reki Samary." *Izvestiia Samarskogo Nauchnogo Tsentra Rossiiskoi Akademii Nauk* 11 (4–6): 1626–30. http://www .ssc.smr.ru/media/journals/izvestia/2009/2009_4_1626_1630.pdf (accessed 15 March 2011).

Bogdanov, K. A., and A. A. Panchenko. 2001. "Gender kak gender: Vmesto predisloviia." In *Mifologiia i povsednevnost': Gendernyi podkhod v antropologicheskikh distsiplinakh; Materialy nauchnoi konferentsii,* 5–10. St. Petersburg: Aleteiia.

Borenstein, Eliot. 1999. "Suspending Belief: 'Cults' and Postmodernism in Post-Soviet Russia." In *Consuming Russia: Popular Culture, Sex, and Society since Gorbachev,* edited by Adele Marie Barker, 437–62. Durham, NC: Duke University Press.

Borisova, Anna. 2011. "Rasskazy o 'porchennykh devkakh' kak instrument sotsial'nogo kontrol'ia." Course paper, St. Petersburg State University, Department of Folklore and Theory of Literature.

Bourdieu, Pierre. (1977) 1995. *Outline of a Theory of Practice.* Cambridge: Cambridge University Press.

———. 1990. *The Logic of Practice.* Stanford: Stanford University Press.

Boym, Svetlana. 2001. *The Future of Nostalgia.* New York: Basic Books.

Bragina, A. S. 2008. "Maslenitsa byla, prazdnik." In *Pesni i prichitaniia Vologodskoi oblasti. Sukhona: Iz sobraniia Fonogramarkhiva Instituta russkoi literatury.* Sound recording. Pushkinskii dom, RAN.

Bridger, Susan. 1987. *Women in the Soviet Countryside: Women's Roles in Rural Development in the Soviet Union.* New York: Cambridge University Press.

Brodskii, N. L. 1904. "Sledy professional'nykh skazochnikov v russkikh skazkakh." *Etnologicheskoe obozrenie* 2:1–18.

Brooks, Jeffrey. 2001. *Thank You, Comrade Stalin! Soviet Public Culture from Revolution to Cold War.* Princeton, NJ: Princeton University Press.

Brooks, Peter. 1995. *The Melodramatic Imagination: Balzac, Henry James, Melodrama, and the Mode of Excess.* New Haven, CT: Yale University Press.

Brown, R., and A. Gilman. 1960. "The Pronouns of Power and Solidarity." In *Style in Language,* edited by Thomas Sebeok, 253–76. Cambridge, MA: MIT Press.

Bruner, J. 1997. "Labov and Waletzky, Thirty Years On." *Journal of Narrative and Life History* 7 (1–4): 61–68.

Buber, Martin. 1970. *I and Thou*. Translated by Walter Arnold Kaufman. New York: Touchstone.

Bulgakov, Sergei. 1932. *L'Orthodoxie*. Paris: Alcan.

Chatterjee, Choi. 2002. *Celebrating Women: Gender, Festival Culture, and Bolshevik Ideology, 1910–1939*. Pittsburgh: University of Pittsburgh Press.

Cherednikova, M. P. 2006. "Prazdnik v sovremennom sele: Polovozrastnaia i etnicheskaia stratifikatsiia." In *Morfologiia prazdnika*, 266–76. St. Petersburg: Izd-vo S.-Petersburgskogo universiteta.

Chernenko, K. U., M. S. Smirtiukov, and Kommunisticheskaia partiia Sovetskogo Soiuza. 1967. *Resheniia partii i pravitel'stva po khoziaistvennym voprosam: Sbornik dokumentov*. Moskva: Izd-vo polit. lit-ry.

Chicherov, V. I. (1935) 1994. "Melodii chastushek i printsipy otbora ikh." In *Fol'klor Rossii v dokumentakh sovetskogo perioda, 1933–1941 gg.: Sbornik dokumentov*, edited by E. D. Grin'ko and L. E. Efanova, 26–35. Moscow: Gosudarstvennyi respublikanskii tsentr russkogo fol'klora.

———. 1957. *Zimnii period russkogo narodnogo zemledel'cheskogo kalendaria XVI–XIX vekov: Ocherki po istorii narodnykh verovanii*. Moscow: Akademiia Nauk.

Chistov, K. V. 1988. *Irina Andreevna Fedosova: Istoriko-kul'turnyi ocherk*. Petrozavodsk: Karelia.

———. 1997. "'Prichitan'ia Severnogo kraia, sobrannye E. V. Barsovym,' v istorii russkoi kul'tury." In Barsov 1997a, 400–495.

Chistov, K. V. 1960. "Russkaia prichet'." In *Prichitaniia*, edited by K. V. Chistov and B. E. Chistova, 5–46. Leningrad: Sovetskii pisatel'.

Churkin, V. F. 2006. "Samoidentifikatsiia krest'ianstva na perelomnom etape svoei istorii." *Istoriia gosudarstva i prava*, no. 7: 27–31.

Cixous, Hélène, and Catherine Clément. (1975) 1986. *The Newly Born Woman*. Translated by Betsy Wing. Minneapolis: University of Minnesota Press.

Clifford, James. 1986. "Introduction: Partial Truths." In *Writing Culture: The Poetics and Politics of Ethnography*, edited by James Clifford and George E. Marcus, 1–26. Berkeley: University of California Press.

Dal', V. I. 1973. *Tolkovyi slovar' zhivogo velikorusskogo iazyka*. 4 vols. Lichtenstein: Kraus Reprint.

Danilov, V., R. Manning, and L. Viola, eds. 1999. *Tragediia sovetskoi derevni: Kollektivizatsiia i raskulachivanie: Dokumenty i materialy, 1929–1939*. Vol. 1, *May 1927–November 1929*. Moscow: ROSSPEN.

Davies, Sarah. 1998. "The Crime of 'Anti-Soviet Agitation' in the Soviet Union in the 1930s." *Cahiers du Monde Russe: Russie, Empire Russe, Union Soviétique, États Indépendants* 39 (1–2): 149–67.

Davis-Floyd, Robbie. 1992. *Birth as an American Rite of Passage*. Berkeley: University of California Press.

———. 1994. "The Rituals of Hospital Birth in America." In *Conformity and Conflict: Readings in Cultural Anthropology*, edited by James P. Spradley and David W. McCurdy, 323–40. New York: Harper-Collins.

Davydovskaia, O. n.d. "Utrom veriu, vecherom ne veriu: Aktual'nye znaniia derevenskikh molodykh liudei." *Russkii fol'klor v sovremennykh zapisiakh* (website of the Propp Center, St. Petersburg State University). http://www.folk.ru/Survey/2001-2008/davidova.php (accessed 12 August 2009).

de Certeau, Michel. 1984. *The Practice of Everyday Life*. Translated by Steven Rendall. Berkeley: University of California Press.

de Lauretis, Teresa. 1987. *Technologies of Gender: Essays on Theory, Film, and Fiction*. Bloomington: Indiana University Press.

Deigh, Linda. 1995. *Narratives in Society: A Performer-Centered Study of Narration*. Helsinki: Suomalainen Tiedeakatemia, Academia Scientiarum Fennica.

———. 2001. *Legend and Belief: Dialectics of a Folklore Genre*. Bloomington: Indiana University Press.

Dégh, L., and A. Vázsonyi. 1974. "The Memorate and the Proto-Memorate." *Journal of American Folklore* 87:225–39.

Denisova, L. N. 2003. *Zhenshchiny russkikh selenii: Trudovye budni.* Moscow: Mir istorii.

Denisova, L. N., and Irina Mukhina. 2010. *Rural Women in the Soviet Union and Post-Soviet Russia.* New York: Routledge.

Dewhirst, Martin. 2002. "Censorship in Russia, 1991 and 2001." *Journal of Communist Studies and Transition Politics* 18 (1): 21–34.

Dinnerstein, Dorothy. 1976. *The Mermaid and the Minotaur: Sexual Arrangements and Human Malaise.* New York: Harper & Row.

Dmitrieva, S. I. 1972. "Sovremennoe sostoianie traditsionnogo fol'klora." In *Traditsionnyi fol'klor Vladimirskoi derevni (v zapisiakh 1963–1969 gg.),* edited by E. V. Pomerantseva, 44–68. Moscow: Nauka.

Dobrenko, Evgeny. 1997. *The Making of the State Reader: Social and Aesthetic Contexts of the Reception of Soviet Literature.* Stanford: Stanford University Press.

Draitser, Emil. 1999. *Making War, Not Love: Gender and Sexuality in Russian Humor.* New York: Palgrave Macmillan.

Dundes, Alan. 1965. "What Is Folklore." In *The Study of Folklore,* 1–3. Englewood Cliffs, NJ: Prentice-Hall.
———. 1989. *Folklore Matters.* Knoxville: University of Tennessee Press.

Dunham, Vera Sandomirsky. 1990. *In Stalin's Time: Middleclass Values in Soviet Fiction.* Durham, NC: Duke University Press.

Dunn, Stephen P., and Ethel Dunn. 1974. "The Intellectual Tradition of Soviet Ethnography." In *Introduction to Soviet Ethnography.* Berkeley: Highgate Road Social Science Research Station.

Eckert, Penelope, and Sally McConnell-Ginet. 2003. *Language and Gender.* New York: Cambridge University Press.

Edel'man, O. V. 1999. "Nadzornye proizvodstva prokuratury 58.10." In *58[10]: Nadzornye proizvodstva prokuratury SSSR po delam ob antisovetskoi agitatsii i propaganda; Annotirovannyi Catalog, Mart 1953–1991,* edited by V. A. Kozlov, S. V. Mironenko, O. V. Edel'man, et al., 5–10. Moscow: Demokratiia.

Edemskii, M. B. 1905. "Vecherovan'ie i gorodki (khorovody) v Kokshen'ge Totemskogo uezda." *Zhivaia starina* 3–4:459–512.

Efendiev, A. G., and I. A. Bolotina. 2002. "Sovremennoe rossiiskoe selo: Na perelome epokh i reform. Opyt institutsional'nogo analiza." *Mir Rossii* 11 (4): 34.

Eleonskaia, E. 1910. "Stradan'ia, prigudki, pripevki, chastushki." *Etnograficheskoe obozrenie* 86–87 (3–4): 92–99.

Engel, Barbara A. 1990. "Peasant Morality and Pre-Marital Relations in Late Nineteenth-Century Russia." *Journal of Social History* 23 (4): 695–714.
———. 1993. "Russian Peasant Views of City Life, 1861–1914." *Slavic Review* 52 (3): 446–59.
———. 2004. *Women in Russia, 1700–2000.* New York: Cambridge University Press.

Engels, Friedrich. 1942. *The Origin of the Family, Private Property, and the State.* Translated by Alick West. New York: International Publishers. http://www.marxists.org/archive/marx/works/1884/origin-family/index.htm (accessed 6 August 2008).

Erikson, Erik H. 1959. *Identity and the Life Cycle.* New York: International Universities Press.

"Eshche raz o narodnykh instrumentakh." 1965. *Sovetskaia muzyka* 10:107–8.

Eval'd, Z. 1928. "Pesni svadebnogo obriada na Pinege." In *Krest'ianskoe iskusstvo SSSR,* vol. 2, *Iskusstvo severa,* 177–87. Leningrad: Academia.

Faber, M. D. 1988. "The Pleasures of Rhyme: A Psychoanalytic Note." *International Review of Psycho-Analysis* 15:375–80.

Farnsworth, Beatrice. 1992. "Village Women Experience the Revolution." In *Russian Peasant Women*, edited by Beatrice Farnsworth and Lynne Viola, 145–66. New York: Oxford University Press.

Firsov, B. M., and I. G. Kiseleva, eds. 1993. *Byt velikorusskikh krest'ian-zemlepashtsev: Opisanie materialov etnograficheskogo biuro kniazia V. N. Tenisheva*. St. Petersburg: Izdatel'stvo Evropeiskogo Doma.

Fitzpatrick, Sheila. 1996. *Stalin's Peasants: Resistance and Survival in the Russian Village after Collectivization*. New York: Oxford University Press.

Florenskii, P. A. 1996. "Ne voskhishchenie nepshcheva." In *Sochineniia*, 2:142–87. Moscow: Mysl'.

Foster, George M. 1965. "Peasant Society and the Image of Limited Good." *American Anthropologist* 67 (2): 293–315.

Foucault, Michel. 1978. "Politics and the Study of Discourse." *Ideology and Consciousness* 3:7–26.

———. 1979. *Discipline and Punish: The Birth of the Prison*. New York: Vintage Books.

———. 1980. *Power/Knowledge: Selected Interviews and Other Writings, 1972–1977*. Translated and edited by Colin Gordon. New York: Pantheon Books.

Fox, Jennifer. 1987. "The Creator Gods: Romantic Nationalism and the En-Genderment of Women in Folklore." *Journal of American Folklore* 100:563–72.

Frank, Gelya. 1979. "Finding the Common Denominator: A Phenomenological Critique of Life History Method." *Ethos* 7 (1): 68–94.

Frank, Stephen. 1992. "'Simple Folk, Savage Customs?' Youth, Sociability, and the Dynamics of Culture in Rural Russia, 1856–1914." *Journal of Social History* 25 (4): 711–36.

Franz, Marie-Louise von. 1995. *Shadow and Evil in Fairy Tales*. Rev. ed. Boston: Shambhala Publications.

Frazer, Elizabeth, and Nicola Lacey. 1993. *The Politics of Community: A Feminist Critique of the Liberal-Communitarian Debate*. Toronto: University of Toronto Press.

Frazer, Sir James George. (1922) 2009. *The Golden Bough: A Study in Magic and Religion*. New York: Cosimo Classics.

Friedman, Susan S. 1998. "Women's Autobiographical Selves: Theory and Practice." In *Women, Autobiography, Theory: A Reader*, edited by Sidonie Smith and Julia Watson, 72–82. Madison: University of Wisconsin Press.

Frierson, Cathy A. 1993a. *Peasant Icons: Representations of Rural People in Late Nineteenth-Century Russia*. New York: Oxford University Press.

———. 1993b. Preface to *Aleksandr Nikolaevich Engelgardt's Letters from the Country, 1872–1887*, xvii–ix. Edited and translated by Cathy A. Frierson. New York: Oxford University Press.

Gaditskaia, M. A., and A. P. Skorik. 2009. *Zhenshchiny-kolkhoznitsy iuga Rossii v 1930-e gody: Gendernyi potentsial i mentalitet*. Rostov-on-Don: Severo-Kavkazski nauchnyi tsentr.

Gal, Susan, and Gail Kligman. 2000. *The Politics of Gender after Socialism: A Comparative-Historical Essay*. Princeton, NJ: Princeton University Press.

Garfinkel, Harold. 1967. *Studies in Ethnomethodology*. Englewood Cliffs, NJ: Prentice-Hall.

Giddens, Anthony, and Christopher Pierson. 1998. *Conversations with Anthony Giddens: Making Sense of Modernity*. Stanford: Stanford University Press.

Gil'ferding, A. F. 1873. *Onezhskie byliny, zapisannye letom 1871 goda*. St. Petersburg: Tip. Imp. akademii nauk.

Gill, Sam D. 1977. "Prayer as Person: The Performative Force in Navajo Prayer Acts." *History of Religions* 17 (2): 143–57.

Gilligan, Carol. 1982. *In a Different Voice: Psychological Theory and Women's Development*. Cambridge, MA: Harvard University Press.

Gladkova, O. n.d. "Tipologiia sovremennogo dukhovnogo stikha, funktsioniruiushchego v pokhoronno-pominal'noi obriadnosti." *Russkii fol'klor Ul'ianovskoi oblasti*. http://ulfolk.ru/Statji/003.pdf (accessed 18 September 2010).

Gledhill, Christine. 1987. "The Melodramatic Field: An Investigation." In *Home Is Where the Heart Is: Studies in Melodrama and the Woman's Film*, 5–39. London: British Film Institute.

Glickman, Rose. 1991. "Peasant Woman as Healer." In *Russia's Women: Accommodation, Resistance, Transformation*, edited by Barbara Evans Clements, Barbara Alpern Engel, and Christine D. Worobec, 148–62. Berkeley: University of California Press.

Glinkina, A. I. 1969. *Narodnye pesni Smolenskoi oblasti, napetye A. I. Glinkinoi*. Edited by G. B. Pavlova and A. M. Rudneva. Moscow: Sovetskii kompozitor.

———. 2007. *Nevol'noe detstvo: Vospominaniia*. Moscow: Luch.

Gluckman, M. 1963. "Gossip and Scandal." *Current Anthropology* 4 (3): 307–15.

Gnedin, E. 1935. "Boris Efimov." Foreword to *Politicheskie karikatury, 1924–1934*, by Boris Efimov, 5–19. Moscow: Sovetskii pisatel'.

Goffman, Erving. 1959. *The Presentation of Self in Everyday Life*. New York: Anchor Books.

———. 1967. "Interaction Ritual." In *Interaction Ritual: Essays in Face-to-Face Behavior*, 113–36. Chicago: Aldine Publishing.

———. 1974. *Frame Analysis: An Essay on the Organization of Experience*. New York: Harper & Row.

Golembo, S. Ia., and Vsesoiuznyi institut iuridicheskikh nauk. 1949. *Ocherki po istorii organov sovetskoi gosudarstvennoi vlasti: Materialy k izucheniiu istorii sovetskogo gosudarstva i prava*. Moscow: Gos. izd-vo iurid. lit-ry.

Gorelov, A. A., et al., eds. 2001–. *Byliny v 25 tomakh*. St. Petersburg: Nauka.

Gor'kii, A. M. 1953a. "Na vystavke." In *Sobranie sochinenii v tridtsati tomakh*, 23:188–92. Moscow: Gos. izd-vo khudozh. lit-ry.

———. 1953b. "S Vserossiiskoi vystavki (Vpechatleniia, nabliudeniia, nabroski, stseny i t. d.): Voplenitsa." In *Sobranie sochinenii v tridtsati tomakh*, 23:230–34. Moscow: Gos. izd-vo khudozh. lit-ry.

Green, Rayna. (1977) 1990. "Magnolias Grow in Dirt: The Bawdy Lore of Southern Women." In *Calling Home: Working-Class Women's Writings; An Anthology*, edited by Janet Zandy, 189–97. Rutgers, NJ: Rutgers University Press.

Greene, David. 2011. "Russian Women Prove It's Hip to Be a Babushka." *National Public Radio*, 27 June. http://www.npr.org/2011/06/27/137368820/russian-women-prove-its-hip-to-be-a-babushka (accessed 27 June 2011).

Grigor'ev, A. D. 1904. *Arkhangel'skie byliny i istoricheskie pesni, sobrannye A. D. Grigor'evym v 1899–1901 gg. S napevami, zapissannymi posredstvom fonografa*. Vol. 1, part 1: *Pomor'e*; part 2, *Pinega*. Moscow: Imp. akademii nauk.

———. 1910. *Arkhangel'skie byliny i istoricheskie pesni*. Vol. 3, *Mezen'*. St. Petersburg: Imp. akademii nauk.

———. 1939. *Arkhangel'skie byliny i istoricheskie pesni*. Vol. 2, *Kuloi*. Prague.

———. (1904, 1910, 1939) 2002–3. *Arkhangel'skie byliny i istoricheskie pesni, sobrannye A. D. Grigor'evym v 1899–1901 gg.: S napevami, zapisannymi posredstvom fonografa*. 3 Vols. St. Petersburg: Tropa Troianova.

Grinkova, N. P. 1936. "Rodovye perezhitki, sviazannye s razdeleniem po polu i vozrastu (Po materialam russkoi odezhdy)." *Sovetskaia etnografiia* 2:23–24.

Gromyko, M. M. 1986. *Traditsionnye normy povedeniia i formy obshcheniia russkikh krest'ian XIX v.* Moscow: Nauka.

Gusdorf, Georges. 1980. "Conditions and Limits of Autobiography." In *Autobiography: Essays Theoretical and Critical*, edited by James Olney, 28–48. Princeton, NJ: Princeton University Press.

Haney, Jack. 1999. *An Introduction to the Russian Folktale*. Armonk, NY: M. E. Sharpe.

Heretz, Leonid. 2008. *Russia on the Eve of Modernity: Popular Religion and Traditional Culture under the Last Tsars*. New York: Cambridge University Press.

Hindus, Maurice G. 1988. *Red Bread: Collectivization in a Russian Village*. Bloomington: Indiana University Press.

Hoffmann, David L. 2003. *Stalinist Values: The Cultural Norms of Soviet Modernity, 1917–1941*. Ithaca, NY: Cornell University Press.

Hofman, Ana. 2011. *Staging Socialist Femininity: Gender Politics and Folklore Performance in Serbia*. Leiden: Brill.

Holbek, Bengt. 1989. "The Language of Fairy Tales." In *Nordic Folklore: Recent Studies*, edited by Reimund Kvideland, Henning K. Sehmsdorf, and Elizabeth Simpson, 40–65. Bloomington: Indiana University Press.

Holmgren, Beth. 2002. "The Importance of Being Unhappy, or, Why She Died." In *Imitations of Life: Two Centuries of Melodrama in Russia*, edited by Louise McReynolds and Joan Neuberger, 79–98. Durham, NC: Duke University Press.

Honko, Lauri. 1964. *Memorates and the Study of Folk Beliefs*. Finland: Suomen uskontotieteellinen seura.

Howell, Dana Prescott. 1992. *The Development of Soviet Folkloristics*. New York: Garland.

Hubbs, Joanna. 1988. *Mother Russia: The Feminine Myth in Russian Culture*. Bloomington: Indiana University Press.

Humphrey, Caroline, and James Laidlaw. 1994. *The Archetypal Actions of Ritual: A Theory of Ritual Illustrated by the Jain Rite of Worship*. New York: Clarendon Press.

Husband, William B. 2004. "Mythical Communities and the New Soviet Woman: Bolshevik Antireligious Chastushki, 1917–32." *Russian Review* 63 (1): 89–106.

Hymes, Dell H. 1972. "On Communicative Competence." In *Sociolinguistics: Selected Readings*, edited by J. B. Pride and Janet Holmes, 269–93. Harmondsworth: Penguin.

———. 1974. *Foundations in Sociolinguistics: An Ethnographic Approach*. Philadelphia: University of Pennsylvania Press.

Il'in, E. P. 2010. *Pol i gender*. St. Petersburg: Izd-vo Piter.

Il'ina, Tatiana and Andrei Toporkov. 2006. "Kruglyi stol: Koldovstvo i narodnaia religiia v Rossii i Zapadnoii Evrope." *Antropologicheskii Forum* 6:439–45. http://anthropologie.kunstkamera.ru/files/pdf/006/06_11_ilina-toporkov_k.pdf (accessed 20 July 2010).

Ioffe, Grigory Viktorovich, Tatiana Grigor'evna Nefedova, and Ilya Zaslavsky. 2006. *The End of Peasantry? The Disintegration of Rural Russia*. Pittsburgh: University of Pittsburgh Press.

Istomin, F. M., and G. O. Diutsh. 1894. *Pesni russkogo naroda: Sobrany v guberniiakh Arkhangel'skoi i Olonetskoi v 1886 godu*. St. Petersburg: Imp. russkor geograficheskoe obshchestvo.

Istomin, F. M., and S. M. Liapunov. 1899. *Pesni russkogo naroda: Sobrany v guberniiakh Vologodskoi, Viatskoi, i Kostromskoi v 1893 godu*. St. Petersburg: Imp. russkoe geograficheskoe obshchestvo.

Iudin, A. V. 2011. "Babushka Solomoniia v vostochnoslavianskikh zagovorakh i istochniki ee obraza." *Slavianskii i balkanskii fol'klor: Vinograd'e*, edited by A. Gura, 11:215–24. St. Petersburg: Indrik.

Iudin, Iu. I. 1988. *Russkaia narodnaia bytovaia skazka*. Moscow: Academia.

Iushkova, V. A. 1937. *Sovetskaia zhenshchina—schastlivaia mat'*. Moscow.

Ivanits, Linda. 1989. *Russian Folk Belief*. Armonk, NY: M. E. Sharpe.

Ivanov, V. V. 1990. "Materialy O. E. Ozarovskoi v arkhive Gos. Muzeia Etnografii SSSR." In *Iz istorii russkoi fol'kloristiki*, edited by T. G. Ivanov and A. A. Gorelov, 3:61–67. Leningrad: Nauka.

Ivnitskii, N. A. 1972. *Klassovaia bor'ba v derevne i likvidatsiia kulachestva kak klassa (1929–1932 gg.)*. Moscow: Nauka.

Jakobson, Roman. 1966. "Slavic Epic Verse: Studies in Comparative Metrics." In *Selected Writings*, 4:414–65. The Hague: Mouton.

Jung, C. G. 1963. *Memories, Dreams, Reflections*. New York: Pantheon Books.

Kabakova, G. I. 2001. *Antropologiia zhenskogo tela v slavianskoi traditsii*. Moscow: Ladomir.

Kadikina, Ol'ga. n.d. "O skazochnitsakh." *Fol'klor i postfol'klor: Struktura, tipologiia, semiotika; Letniaia shkola po tipologii fol'klora*. http://www.ruthenia.ru/folklore/kadikina1.htm (accessed 31 May 2007).

Kalashnikova, R. B. 1999. *Besedy i besednye pesni Zaonezh'ia vtoroi poloviny XIX veka*. Petrozavodsk: Izd-vo Petrozavodskogo gos. universiteta.

Kaplan, E. Ann. 1992. *Motherhood and Representation: The Mother in Popular Culture and Melodrama*. London: Routledge.

Karatygin, V. G. 1927. *Zhizn', deiatel'nost', stat'i i materialy*. Leningrad: Academia.

Karnaukhova, Irina V. (1934) 2006. *Skazki i predaniia severnogo kraia*. St. Petersburg: Tropa Troianova.

Kay, Rebecca. 2006. *Men in Contemporary Russia: The Fallen Heroes of Post-Soviet Change?* Burlington, VT: Ashgate.

Kelly, Mary B. 1996. "The Ritual Fabrics of Russian Rural Women." In *Russia—Women—Culture*, edited by Helena Goscilo and Beth Holmgren, 152–76. Bloomington: Indiana University Press.

Kertzer, David I. 1988. *Ritual, Politics, and Power*. New Haven, CT: Yale University Press.

Kharkhordin, Oleg. 1999. *The Collective and the Individual in Russia: A Study of Practices*. Berkeley: University of California Press.

Kholodnaia, Vera. 2005a. "Muzhik." In Shchepanskaia and Shangina 2005a, 371–79.

———. 2005b. "Paren'." In Shchepanskaia and Shangina 2005a, 425–30.

———. 2005c. "Parnishka." In Shchepanskaia and Shangina 2005a, 431–38.

———. 2005d. "Rebiata." In Shchepanskaia and Shangina 2005a, 520–25.

Khristoforova, O. B. 2008. "'Znat' i 'delat' v narodnoi kul'ture." In *Kirpichiki: Fol'kloristika i kul'turnaia antropologiia segodnia*, edited by S. Iu. Nekliudov, A. S. Arkhipova, et al., 364–81. Moscow: Russian State University for the Humanities.

———. 2010. *Kolduny i zhertvy: Antropologiia koldovstva v sovremennoi Rossii*. Moscow: Ob"edinennoe gumanitar'noe izdatel'stvo.

Kierkegaard, Søren. 1971. *EitherOr*. Vol. 2. Translated by Walter Lowrie. Princeton, NJ: Princeton University Press.

Kirdan, B. P. 2001. *Ballady*. Moscow: Russkaia kniga.

Kivelson, Valerie A. 1991. "Through the Prism of Witchcraft: Gender and Social Change in Seventeenth-Century Muscovy." In *Russia's Women: Accommodation, Resistance, Transformation*, edited by Barbara Evans Clements, Barbara Alpern Engel, and Christine D. Worobec, 74–94. Berkeley: University of California Press.

———. 2003. "Male Witches and Gendered Categories in Seventeenth-Century Russia." *Comparative Studies in Society and History* 45 (3): 606–31.

Kliaus, V. L. 1997. *Ukazatel' siuzhetov i siuzhetnykh situatsii zagovornykh tekstov vostochnykh i iuzhnykh Slavian*. Moscow: Nasledie.

Knatts, E. E. 1928. "'Metishche'—Prazdnichnoe gulian'e v Pinezhskom raione." In *Krest'ianskoe iskusstvo SSSR*, vol. 2, *Iskusstvo Severa*, 188–200. Leningrad: Academia.

Knox, Zoe Katrina. 2005. *Russian Society and the Orthodox Church: Religion in Russia after Communism.* New York: RoutledgeCurzon.

Kolchin, A. 1899. "Verovaniia krest'ian Kur'skoi gubernii." *Etnograficheskoe obozrenie* 11 (3): 1–60.

Kolpakova, N. 1928. "Svadebnyi obriad na r. Pinege." In *Krest'ianskoe iskusstvo SSSR*, vol. 2, *Iskusstvo severa*, 117–76. Leningrad: Academia.

———. 1967. "Pesennyi fol'klor Mezeni." In *Pesennyi fol'klor Mezeni*, 9–32. Leningrad: Nauka.

Kon, I. S. 2002. "Maskulinnost' kak istoriia." In *Gendernyi kaleidoskop*, edited by M. M. Malysheva, 209–29. Moscow: Academia.

Kononenko, Natalie. 1994. "Women as Performers of Oral Literature: A Re-examination of Epic and Lament." In *Women Writers in Russian Literature*, edited by Toby Clyman and Diana Greene, 17–34. Westport, CT: Greenwood Press.

———. 2007. *Slavic Folklore: A Handbook.* Westport, CT: Greenwood Press.

Korzhikhina, T. P. 1986. *Istoriia gosudarstvennykh uchrezhdenii SSSR.* Moscow: Vysshaia shkola.

Kostyrko, Vasilii. 2003. "Koldovstvo v Rossii: klassiki i sovremenniki." Review of *Otrechennoe chtenie v Rossii XVII–XVIII vekov*, edited by A. L. Toporkov and A. A. Turilov. *Otechestvennye Zapiski* 4 (12). http://www.strana-oz.ru/2003/4/koldovstvo-v-rossii-klassiki-i-sovremenniki (accessed 20 July 2010).

Kozlova, N. N., and I. I. Sandomirskaia. 1996. "Predislovie: Istoriia liubvi; Referent: Poriadok mira." *"Ia tak khochu nazvat' kino," "Naivnoe pis'mo": Opyt lingvo-sotsiologicheskogo chteniia*, 7–16, 58–87. Moscow: Gnozis. http://www.a-z.ru/women/texts/kis_235r.htm (accessed 22 August 2010).

Kozlova, N. K., and A. S. Stepakhina. n.d. "Siuzhety vostochnoslavianskikh mifologicheskikh rasskazov o koldovstve na svad'be." *Fol'klor i postfol'klor: Struktura, tipologiia, semiotika.* http://www.ruthenia.ru/folklore/kozlova5.htm (accessed 20 July 2010).

Kremleva. I. A. 2004. "Pokhoronno-pominal'nye obychai i obriady." In *Russkii sever: Etnicheskaia istoriia i narodnaia kul'tura XII–XX veka*, edited by I. V. Vlasova, 661–705. Moscow: Nauka.

Kristeva, Julia. 1980. "Woman Can Never Be Defined." Translated by Marilyn A. August. In *New French Feminisms: An Anthology*, edited by Elaine Marks and Isabelle de Courtivron, 138–41. Amherst: University of Massachusetts Press.

Kruglov, Iu. G. 1979. *Fol'klornaia praktika.* Moscow: Prosveshchenie.

Krylova, Anna. 2010. *Soviet Women in Combat: A History of Violence on the Eastern Front.* Cambridge: Cambridge University Press.

Kulagina, A. 2001. "Balladnye pesni." In Kirdan 2001, 5–26.

Labov, W., and J. Waletzky. 1967. "Narrative Analysis: Oral Versions of Personal Experiences." In *Essays on the Verbal and Visual Arts*, edited by June Helm, 12–44. Seattle: University of Washington Press.

Lane, Christel. 1978. *Christian Religion in the Soviet Union: A Sociological Study.* Albany: State University of New York Press.

LaPasha, L. Robin C. 2001. "From *Chastushki* to Tchaikovsky: Amateur Activity and the Production of Popular Culture in the Soviet 1930s." PhD diss., Duke University.

Lapidus, Gail Warshofsky. 1978. *Women in Soviet Society: Equality, Development, and Social Change.* Berkeley: University of California Press.

Lasser, Justin M. 2010a. "Charity." In *The Encyclopedia of Eastern Orthodox Christianity*, edited by John Anthony McGuckin, 109–10. Hoboken, NJ: Wiley.

———. 2010b. "Wealth." In *The Encyclopedia of Eastern Orthodox Christianity*, edited by John Anthony McGuckin, 628–30. Hoboken, NJ: Wiley.

Lazutin, C. G. 1965. *Russkie narodnye pesni.* Moscow: Prosveshchenie.

Ledeneva, Alena. 1998. *Russia's Economy of Favours: Blat, Networking, and Informal Exchange.* Cambridge, UK: Cambridge University Press.

Ledkovsky-Astman, Marina, Charlotte Rosenthal, and Mary Fleming Zirin, eds. 1994. *Dictionary of Russian Women Writers.* Westport, CT: Greenwood Press.

Levin, Eve. 1993. "*Dvoeverie* and Popular Religion." In *Seeking God: The Recovery of Religious Identity in Orthodox Russia, Ukraine, and Georgia,* edited by Stephen K. Batalden, 31–52. DeKalb: Northern Illinois University Press.

Levinton, G. A. 1977. "Iz slavianskikh kommentariev slavianskomu obriadovomu tekstu." In *Slavianskoe i balkanskoe iazykoznanie: Antichnaia balkanistika i sravnit. grammatika,* edited by L. A. Gindin and G. P. Klepikova, 325–48. Moscow: Nauka.

Levitt, Marcus. 2001. "Notes on a Joint Russian-American Expedition to the Semeiskii Old Believers of Transbaikal." *Journal of the Slavic and East European Folklore Association* 6 (2): 11–27.

Levkievskaia, E. E. 1999. "Dolia 2." In *Slavianskie drevnosti: Etnolingvisticheskii slovar',* edited by N. I. Tolstoi, 2:114–16. Moscow: Mezhdunarodnye otnosheniia.

———. 2001. "Magicheskie funktsii khoziaina v vostochnoslavianskoi traditsionnoi kul'ture." In Morozov 2001, 106–14.

———. 2007. "Vostochnoslavianskii mifologicheskii tekst: Semantika, dialektologiia, pragmatika." Diss., Institute of Slavistics, Russian Academy of Sciences.

Lifton, Robert J., and Eric Olson. 1974. *Living and Dying.* New York: Praeger.

———. 2004. "Symbolic Immortality." In *Death, Mourning, and Burial: A Cross-Cultural Reader,* edited by Antonius C. G. M. Robben, 32–39. Malden, MA: Blackwell.

Likhachev, D. S. 1987. *Poetika drevnerusskoi literatury.* Vol. 1 of *Izbrannye raboty v trekh tomakh.* Leningrad: Khudozhestvennaia literatura.

Lindner, P., and A. Nikulin. 2004. "'Everything Around Here Belongs to the Kolkhoz, Everything Around Here Belongs to Me': Collectivism and Egalitarianism; A Red Thread through Russian History?" *Europa Regional* 12 (1): 32–41.

Lindquist, Galina. 2006. *Conjuring Hope: Magic and Healing in Contemporary Russia.* New York: Berghahn Books.

Lineva, E., and F. E. Korsh. 1904–9. *Velikorusskie pesni v narodnoi garmonizatsii.* 2 vols. St. Petersburg: M. M. Glazunova.

Lipets, R. 1939. "Vvedenie." In *Byliny M. S. Kriukovoi,* edited by E. Borodina and R. Lipets. Moscow: Gos. lit. muzei.

Loginov, K. K. 1993. *Semeinye obriady i verovaniia russkikh zaonezh'ia.* Petrozavodsk: Karel'skii nauchnyi tsentr RAN.

Lutovinova, E. I. 1993. *Russkie narodnye skazki o machekhe i padcheritse.* Novosibirsk: Nauka.

Madlevskaia, E. L. 2005. "Baba." In Shchepanskaia and Shangina 2005a, 21–30.

———. n.d. "Podbliudnye gadaniia." Russian Ethnographic Museum website. http://www.ethnomuseum.ru/section62/2092/2088/3983.htm (accessed 27 December 2010).

Magoulick, Mary. 2006. "Women in Popular Culture." In *Encyclopedia of Women's Folklore and Folklife.* http://www.faculty.de.gcsu.edu/~mmagouli/popculture.htm (accessed 19 April 2009).

Malinowski, Bronisław. (1944) 2002. *A Scientific Theory of Culture and Other Essays.* New York: Routledge.

———. *Magic, Science and Religion, and Other Essays.* Garden City, NY: Doubleday.

Mamaeva, E. S. 2010. "Zhiznennyi stsenarii sovetskoi zhenshcheny—'Boikaia'." Master's thesis, St. Petersburg University.

Manning, Frank. 1992. "Spectacle." In Bauman 1992, 291–99.

Markov, A. V. (1909) 2002. "Predislovie ko vtoroi chasti 'Materialov sobrannykh v Arkhangel'skoi gub. letom 1901 g.'" In *Belomorskie stariny i dukhovnye stikhi: Sobranie A. V. Markova*, 1018–29. St. Petersburg: Dmitrii Bulanin.

Maslow, Abraham. 1970. *Motivation and Personality*. 2nd ed. New York: Harper & Row.

Matich, Olga. 1983. "Typology of Fallen Women in Nineteenth Century Russian Literature." In *American Contributions to the Ninth International Congress of Slavists*, vol. 2, *Literature, Politics, History*, edited by P. Debreczeny, 325–43. Columbus, OH: Slavica.

Matossian, Mary. 1968. "The Peasant Way of Life." In *The Peasant in Nineteenth-Century Russia*, edited by Wayne Vucinich, 1–40. Stanford: Stanford University Press.

McReynolds, Louise, and Joan Neuberger, eds. 2002. Introduction to *Imitations of Life: Two Centuries of Melodrama in Russia*, 1–24. Durham, NC: Duke University Press.

Mekhnetsov, A. M., comp. 1981. *Poiut narodnye ispolniteli Vologodskoi oblasti (Narodnye pesni Vologodskoi Oblasti. Pesni srednei Sukhony)*. Sound recording. Leningrad.

Mercer, John, and Martin Shingler. 2004. *Melodrama: Genre, Style, Sensibility*. Short Cuts 22. London: Wallflower.

Merriam-Webster. 2003. *Merriam-Webster's Collegiate Dictionary*. 11th ed. http://www.merriam-web ster.com/dictionary/world (accessed 14 May 2010).

Metayer, Leon. 1996. "What the Heroine Taught, 1830–1870." In *Melodrama: The Cultural Emergence of a Genre*, edited by Michael Hays and Anastasia Nikolopoulou, 235–45. New York: St. Martin's Press.

Meyer, Alfred G. 1991. "The Impact of World War I on Russian Women's Lives." In *Russia's Women: Accommodation, Resistance, Transformation*, edited by Barbara Evans Clements, Barbara Alpern Engel, and Christine D. Worobec, 208–24. Berkeley: University of California Press.

Mironov, B. 1985. "The Russian Peasant Commune after the Reforms of the 1860s." *Slavic Review* 44 (3): 438–67.

Modleski, Tania. 1982. *Loving with a Vengeance: Mass Produced Fantasies for Women*. New York: Methuen.

Morozov, I. A. 2006. "Prazdnik: 'Vnutrennee' i 'vneshnee'." In *Morfologiia prazdnika*, 85–102. St. Petersburg: Izd-vo S.-Peterburgskogo universiteta.

———, ed. 2001. *Muzhchina v traditsionnoi kul'ture*. Vol. 1 of *Muzhskoi sbornik*. Moscow: Labirint.

———, ed. 2004. *"Muzhskoe" v traditsionnom i sovremennom obshchestve*. Vol. 2 of *Muzhskoi sbornik*. Moscow: Labirint.

———, ed. 2007. *Muzhschina v ekstremal'noi situatsii*. Vol. 3 of *Muzhskoi sbornik*. St. Petersburg: Indrik.

Morozov, I. A., and I. S. Sleptsova. 2004. *Krug igry: Prazdnik igra v zhizni severnorusskogo krest'ianina, XIX–XX vv*. Moscow: Indrik.

Morozov, I. A., et al. 1997. *Dukhovnaia kul'tura severnogo Belozer'ia: Etnodialektnyi slovar'*. Moscow: RAN.

Newton, Judith Lowder. 1981. *Women, Power, and Subversion: Social Strategies in British Fiction, 1778–1860*. Athens: University of Georgia Press.

Nikolaev, Oleg R. n.d. "Pochemu my ne poem 'russkie narodnye' pesni do kontsa." *Fol'klor i postfol'klor: Struktura, tipologiia, semiotika*. http://www.ruthenia.ru/folklore/nikolaev1.htm (accessed 24 February 2003).

Norris, Stephen. 2009. "'Laughter is a Sharp Weapon and a Powerful Medicine': Boris Efimov and Soviet Visual Humor." Paper presented at the Totalitarian Laughter Conference, Princeton University, 15 May.

Novichkova, T. A. 2000. "V puti za zhivym slovom." *Piatirechie: Babushkiny stariny, piatirechie, epicheskaia poeziia*, edited by O. E. Ozarovskaia, 3–26. St. Petersburg: Tropa Troianova.

Oexle, Otto Gerhard. 2007. "Memoria i memorial'naia traditsiia v ranee srednevekov'e." In *Deistvitel'nost' i znanie: Ocherki sotsial'noi istorii srednevekov'ia*. Moscow: Novoe Literaturnoe Obozrenie.

Olson, Laura J. 2004. *Performing Russia: Folk Revival and Russian Identity*. New York: RoutledgeCurzon.

Onchukov, N. E. (1908) 1998. *Severnye skazki: Sbornik N. E. Onchukova*. St. Petersburg: Tropa Troianova.

———. 1909. *Severnye skazki*. St. Petersburg: Tip. A. S. Suvorina.

Onegina, N. F., ed. 1986. *Skazki Zaonezh'ia*. Petrozavodsk: Karelia.

Ong, A. 1995. "Women out of China: Traveling Tales and Traveling Theories in Post-Colonial Feminism." In *Women Writing Culture*, edited by Ruth Behar and Deborah A. Gordon, 350–72. Berkeley: University of California Press.

Ong, Walter J. 2002. *Orality and Literacy: The Technologizing of the Word*. New York: Routledge.

Ortner, Sherry B. 2006. *Anthropology and Social Theory: Culture, Power, and the Acting Subject*. Durham, NC: Duke University Press.

Ostromoukhova, B. V. 2004. "KVN: 'Molodezhnaia kul'tura shestidesiatykh'?" *Neprikosnovennyi zapas* 36 (4): http://magazines.russ.ru/nz/2004/4/ost5.html (accessed 5 October 2010).

———. 2009. "Production of Comic Theater by Soviet Students, 1953–1970." Paper presented at the Totalitarian Laughter Conference, Princeton University, 16 May.

Oushakine, Serguei A. 2000. "The Quality of Style: Imaginary Consumption in the New Russia." *Theory, Culture, and Society* 17 (5): 97–120.

Paine, R. 1967. "What Is Gossip About? An Alternative Hypothesis." *Man* 2:278–85.

Partlett, William. 2004. "Breaching Cultural Worlds with the Village School: Educational Visions, Local Initiative, and Rural Experience at S. T. Shatskii's Kaluga School System, 1919–1932." *Slavonic and East European Review* 82 (4): 847–85.

Pashina, O. A., ed. 2003. *Kalendarnye obriady i pesni*. Vol. 1 of *Smolenskii muzykal'no-etnograficheskii sbornik*. Moscow: Indrik.

Paxson, Margaret. 2005. *Solovyovo: The Story of Memory in a Russian Village*. Bloomington: Indiana University Press.

Pesikin, F. A., G. I. Bravo-Zhivotovskaia, Russian S.F.S.R. Glavnoe arkhivnoe upravlenie, and Gosudarstvennyi arkhiv Gorkovskoi oblasti. 1982. *Organy sovetskoi gosudarstvennoi vlasti na territorii nizhegorodskoi gubernii, 1917–1929: Kratkii spravochnik*. Gorkii: Volgo-Viatskoe knizhnoe izd-vo.

Phillips, Sarah. 2004. "Waxing Like the Moon: Women Folk Healers in Rural Western Ukraine." *Folklorica* 9 (1): 13–45.

Podgornaia, A., and K. Sergeeva. 1956. "Pesni i chastushki Vologodskoi oblasti (Vytegorskogo, Andomskogo, i Kovzhinskogo raionov)." Course paper, St. Petersburg State University, Department of Folklore and Theory of Literature.

Polanyi, Livia. 1985. *Telling the American Story: A Structural and Cultural Analysis of Conversational Storytelling*. New York: Ablex Publishers.

Pomerantseva, E. V. 1968. "Zhanrovye osobennosti russkikh bylichek." In *Istoriia, kul'tura, fol'klor i etnografiia slavianskikh narodov: VI mezhdunarodnyi s"ezd slavistov*, 274–93. Moscow: Nauka.

———. 1969. "Skazochnitsa A. N. Korol'kova." In *Russkie narodnye skazki*. Moscow: Nauka.

Pomerantseva, E. V., and S. I. Mints. 1959. *Russkoe narodnoe poeticheskoe tvorchestvo*. Moscow: Gos. uchebno-pedagog. izd-vo.

Preston, Cathy. 1994. "Cinderella as a Dirty Joke." *Western Folklore* 53:27–49.

———. 1997. "Joke." In *Folklore: An Encyclopedia of Beliefs, Customs, Tales, Music, and Art*, edited by Thomas A. Green, 471–75. Santa Barbara, CA: ABC-CLIO.

Prokhorov, A. P. 2002. *Russkaia model' upravleniia*. Moscow: Zhurnal Ekspert.

Prokop'eva, N. 2005. "Starukha." In Shchepanskaia and Shangina 2005a, 635–39.

Propp, V. Ia. (1961) 1993. "The Russian Folk Lyric." In *Russian Folk Lyrics*, edited by Rebecca Reeder, 1–56. Bloomington: Indiana University Press.

———. 1995. *Russkie agrarnye prazdniki*. St. Petersburg: Azbuka.

Pskovskii oblastnoi slovar'. 1950–70. Filologicheskii Fakul'tet, Sankt Peterburgskii Gosudarstvennyi Universitet.

Pushkareva, L. A., and M. N. Shmeleva. 1974. "The Contemporary Russian Peasant Wedding." In *Introduction to Soviet Ethnography*, edited by Stephen P. Dunn and Ethel Dunn, 1:349–360. Berkeley: Highgate Road Social Science Research Station.

Pushkareva, N. L., and Eve Levin. 1997. *Women in Russian History: From the Tenth to the Twentieth Century*. Armonk, NY: M. E. Sharpe.

Pypin, A. 1856. "O russkikh narodnykh skazkakh." *Otechestvennye zapiski* 4:41–68.

Ramet, Sabrina P. 1993. "Religious Policy in the Era of Gorbachev." In *Religious Policy in the Soviet Union*, 31–54. Cambridge: Cambridge University Press.

Rancour-Laferriere, Daniel. 1995. *The Slave Soul of Russia: Moral Masochism and the Cult of Suffering*. New York: New York University Press.

Ransel, David L. 2000. *Village Mothers: Three Generations of Change in Russia and Tataria*. Bloomington: Indiana University Press.

Riasanovsky, Nicholas. 1993. *A History of Russia*. 5th ed. New York: Oxford University Press.

Rice, Timothy. 1994. *May It Fill Your Soul: Experiencing Bulgarian Music*. Chicago: University of Chicago Press.

Ries, Nancy. 1997. *Russian Talk: Culture and Conversation during Perestroika*. Ithaca, NY: Cornell University Press.

Rivkin-Fish, Michele R. 2005. *Women's Health in Post-Soviet Russia: The Politics of Intervention*. Bloomington: Indiana University Press.

Rogers, Douglas. 2008. "Old Belief between 'Society' and 'Culture': Remaking Moral Communities and Inequalities on a Former State Farm." In *Religion, Morality, and Community in Post-Soviet Societies*, edited by Mark D. Steinberg and Catherine Wanner, 115–48. Bloomington: Indiana University Press.

Rosnow, Ralph L., and Gary A. Fine. 1976. *Rumor and Gossip: The Social Psychology of Hearsay*. New York: Elsevier.

Rosslyn, Wendy, ed. 2003. *Women and Gender in Eighteenth-Century Russia*. Burlington, VT: Ashgate.

Rothstein, Robert A. 1994. "Death of the Folk Song?" In *Cultures in Flux: Lower-Class Values, Practices, and Resisatance in Late Imperial Russia*, edited by Stephen P. Frank and Mark D. Steinberg, 108–20. Princeton, NJ: Princeton University Press.

Rouhier-Willoughby, Jeanmarie. 2008. *Village Values: Negotiating Identity, Gender, and Resistance in Urban Russian Life-Cycle Rituals*. Bloomington, IN: Slavica Publishers.

Rowbotham, Sheila. 1973. *Woman's Consciousness, Man's World*. London: Penguin.

Rozanov, I. P. 1940. "Bor'ba s 'domostroem' v narodnoi lirike (po pesennikam Chulkova, Pracha, Shnora i dr.)." In *Problemy realizma v russkoi literature XVIII veka: Sbornik statei*, edited by N. K. Gudzii, 183–225. Moscow: Akademiia nauk SSSR.

Rozov, A. N. 1988. *Russkie narodnye pesni*. Leningrad: Sovetskii pisatel'.

Rubtsov, F. 1958. "Ot sostavitelia." In *Narodnye pesni Leningradskoi oblasti*, 3–7. Moscow: Sovetskii kompozitor.

Rudneva, A. 1994. "Russkoe narodnoe khorovoe ispolnitel'stvo." In *Russkoe narodnoe muzykal'noe tvorchestvo: Ocherki po teorii fol'klora*, edited by A. V. Rudneva, L. F. Kostiukovets, and N. N. Giliarova, 190–213. Moscow: Kompozitor.

Rumelhart, David. 1975. "Notes on a Schema for Stories." In *Representation and Understanding: Studies in Cognitive Science*, edited by Daniel G. Bobrow and Allan Collins, 185–210. New York: Academic Press.

Ryan, William F. 1999. *The Bathhouse at Midnight: An Historical Survey of Magic and Divination in Russia*. University Park: Pennsylvania State University Press.

Ryan-Hayes, Karen L. 1995. *Contemporary Russian Satire: A Genre Study*. New York: Cambridge University Press.

Rybnikov, P. N. 1861–67. *Pesni sobrannye P. N. Rybnikovym*. 4 vols. Moscow: A. Semen.

———. 1909. "Zametka sobiratelia." In *Pesni sobrannye P. N. Rybnikovym*, vol. 1, 60–102. 2nd ed. Moscow: Sotrudnik shkol.

———. (1910) 1991. *Pesni sobrannye P. N. Rybnikovym*. 3 vols. Petrozavodsk: Karelia.

Saf'ianova, A.V. 1989. "Vnutrennii stroi russkoi sel'skoi sem'i altaiskogo kraia vo vtoroi polovine XIX–nachale XX v." In *Russkie: Semeinyi i obshchestvennyi byt*, edited by M. M. Gromyko and T. A. Listova, 91–110. Moscow: Nauka.

Sapir, E. 1929. "The Status of Linguistics as a Science." *Language* 5 (4): 207–14.

Savchenko, S. V. 1914. *Russkaia narodnaia skazka: Istoriia sobiraniia i izucheniia*. Kiev: Tip. Imp. universiteta.

Schank, Roger C., and Robert P. Abelson. 1975. *Scripts, Plans, and Knowledge*. New Haven, CT: Yale University Press.

Schulman, Collette. 1977. "Individual and Collective." In *Women in Russia*, edited by Dorothy Atkinson, Alexander Dallin, and Gail Warshofsky Lapidus, 375–84. Stanford: Stanford University Press.

Schütz, Alfred. 1962. *Collected Papers*. Vol 1, *The Problem of Social Reality*. Edited by Maurice Natanson. The Hague: Martinus Nijhoff.

———. 1967. *The Phenomenology of the Social World*. Evanston, IL: Northwestern University Press.

Scott, James C. 1976. *The Moral Economy of the Peasant: Rebellion and Subsistence in Southeast Asia*. New Haven, CT: Yale University Press.

Searle, John R. 1995. *The Construction of Social Reality*. New York: Free Press.

Semakova, Irina. n.d. "Kak Belomorskie Karely nauchilis' pet' pesni." *Astrakhanskaia pesnia: Gosudarstvennyi fol'klornyi tsentr*. http://www.astrasong.ru/c/science/article/601 (accessed 22 July 2009).

Shangina, I. 2005. "Devushka." In Shchepanskaia and Shangina 2005a, 177–83.

Shchepanskaia, T. B. 1994. "Mir i mif materinstva (ocherki zhenskikh traditsii i fol'klora)." *Etnograficheskoe obozrenie* 5:17–25.

———. 1999. "Pronimal'naia simvolika." In *Zhenshchina i veshchestvennyi mir kul'tury u narodov Rossii i Evropy*, edited by L. S. Lavrent'eva and T. A. Bernshtam, 149–90. St. Petersburg: Peterburgskoe vostokovedenie.

———. 2001. "Sila (Kommunikativnye i reproduktivnye aspekty muzhskoi magii)." In Morozov 2001, 71–94.

———. 2005. "Babii kut." In Shchepanskaia and Shangina 2005a, 30–35.

Shchepanskaia, T. B., and I. I. Shangina. 2005a. *Muzhiki i baby: Muzhskoe i zhenskoe v russkoi traditsionnoi kul'ture*. St. Petersburg: Iskusstvo.

Shchepanskaia, T. B., and I. I. Shangina. 2005b. "Pol i narodnaia kul'tura." In Shchepanskaia and Shangina 2005a, 5–16.

Shchurov, Viacheslav. 2007. "Predislovie: Agrafena Ivanovna Glinkina i ee zhizneopisanie." In Glinkina 2007, 3–9.

Sheehy, Gail. 1976. *Passages: Predictable Crises of Adult Life*. New York: E. P. Dutton.

Shein, P. V. 1898. *Velikoruss v svoikh pesniakh, obriadakh, obychaiakh, verovaniiakh, skazkakh, legendakh, i t. p.* Vol. 1. St. Petersburg: Izd. Imp. Akademiia nauk.

Shils, Edward. 1981. *Tradition*. Chicago: University of Chicago Press.

Shmeleva, T. 1980. "Svadebnyi obriad i poeziia: Vstupitel'naia stat'ia." In *Obriadovaia poeziia Pinezh'ia: Materialy fol'klornykh ekspeditsii MGU*, edited by N. I. Savushkina, 29–31. Moscow: Iz-vo. Moskovskogo universiteta.

Showalter, Elaine. 1977. *A Literature of Their Own: British Women Novelists from Brontë to Lessing.* Princeton, NJ: Princeton University Press.

Shugar, G. W., and G. Kmita. 1990. "The Pragmatics of Collaboration: Participant Structure and the Structure of Participation." In *Children's Language*, vol. 7, edited by Gina Conti-Ramsden and Catherine Snow, 273–304. Hillsdale, NJ: L. Erbaum.

Simakov, V. I., comp. 1913. *Sbornik derevenskikh chastushek.* Iaroslavl': Tip. K. F. Nekrasova.

Smirnov, D. V. 1996. "Pervye etnograficheskie kontserty v Moskve." *Zhivaia starina* 2:20–24.

Smith, Steve. 2002. "Masculinity in Transition: Peasant Migrants to Late-Imperial St. Petersburg." In *Russian Masculinities in History and Culture*, edited by Barbara Evans Clements, Rebecca Friedman, and Dan Healey, 94–112. Houndmills: Palgrave.

Sobolevskii, A. I. 1896. *Velikorusskie narodnye pesni.* Vol. 2. St. Petersburg: Gosudarstvennaia tipografiia.

———. 1897. *Velikorusskie narodnye pesni.* Vol. 3. St. Petersburg: Gosudarstvennaia tipografiia.

———. 1899. *Velikorusskie narodnye pesni.* Vol. 5. St. Petersburg: Gosudarstvennaia tipografiia.

———. 1902. *Velikorusskie narodnye pesni.* Vol. 7. St. Petersburg: Gosudarstvennaia tipografiia.

Sokolov, B. 1929. "Byliny." In *Literaturnaia entsiklopediia*, edited by P. I. Lebedev-Polianskii et al., 1:38. St. Petersburg: Izd-vo Kommunisticheskoi akademii.

Sokolov, B., and Iu. Sokolov. (1915) 1999. *Skazki i pesni Belozerskogo kraia.* 2 vols. St. Petersburg: Tropa Troianova.

Sokolov, Iurii. 1939. "Predislovie." In *Byliny M. S. Kriukovoi*, edited by E. Borodina and R. Lipets. Moscow: Gos. lit. muzei.

Sorokovikov, E. I., L. E. Eliasov, and M. K. Azadovskii. 1940. *Skazki Magaia.* Leningrad: Khudozhestvennaia literatura.

Spender, D. 1980. "Confessions and Autobiography." In *Autobiography: Essays Theoretical and Critical*, edited by James Olney, 115–22. Princeton, NJ: Princeton University Press.

Stepanenko, Maksim. 2006. "Samoubiistvo: Otnoshenie Pravoslavnoi tserkvi, ego dukhovnye prichiny, uchast' samoubiits posle ikh strashnoii smerti." *Ufimskie eparkhial'nye vedomosti*, nos. 2–3, 8–9. Reprinted in *K istine*. http://www.k-istine.ru/suicide/suicide_help.htm (accessed 12 January 2010).

Stewart, Pamela J., and Andrew Strathern. 2004. *Witchcraft, Sorcery, Rumors, and Gossip.* New York: Cambridge University Press.

Sugarman, Jane C. 1997. *Engendering Song: Singing and Subjectivity at Prespa Albanian Weddings.* Chicago: University of Chicago Press.

Sweet Wong, Hertha D. 1998. "First-Person Plural: Subjectivity and Community in Native American Women's Autobiography." In *Women, Autobiography, Theory: A Reader*, edited by Sidonie Smith and Julia Watson, 168–82. Madison: University of Wisconsin Press.

Sydow, Carl W. von. 1948. *Selected Papers in Folklore.* Copenhagen: Rosenkilde and Bagger.

Szafran, Denice. 2009. "If You Cannot Whisper: The Performative Language of Magical Spells." *Northeastern Anthropological Association Newsletter* 32 (1): 1, 11–13.

Tam, Kwok-Kan. 2007. "The Self as Hybrid Contestation: Three Autobiographical Stories from Singapore and Malaysia." In *Oral and Written Narratives and Cultural Identity: Interdisciplinary Approaches*, edited by Francisco Cota Fagundes and Irene Maria Blayer, 138–52. New York: Peter Lang.

Tannen, Deborah. 1993. *Framing in Discourse*. New York: Oxford University Press.

Thien, Deborah. 2005. "Recasting the Pattern: Critical Relations in Gender and Rurality." In *Critical Studies in Rural Gender Issues*, edited by Jo Little and Carol Morris, 75–89. Burlington, VT: Ashgate.

Tilly, Charles. 2002. *Stories, Identities, and Political Change*. New York: Rowman & Littlefield.

Tirado, Isabel. 1996. "The Komsomol and the Krest'ianka: The Political Mobilization of Young Women in the Russian Village, 1921–1927." *Russian History* 23 (1–4): 345–66.

Turner, Victor. 1967. *The Forest of Symbols: Aspects of Ndembu Ritual*. Ithaca, NY: Cornell University Press.

———. 1969. *The Ritual Process: Structure and Anti-Structure*. Chicago: Aldine Publishing.

Ul'ianov, I. I. 1914. "Voin i russkaia zhenshchina v obriadovykh prichitaniiakh nashikh severnykh gubernii." *Zhivaia starina* 23 (3–4): 233–70.

Uspenskii, E., and E. N. Filina. 2001. *V nashu gavan' zakhodili korabli*. Vol. 5. Moscow: Strekoza.

Van Gennep, Arnold van. 1909. *Les Rites de Passage*. Paris: Émile Nourry.

———. 1960. *The Rites of Passage*. Translated by Monika B. Vizedom and Gabrielle L. Caffee, et al. London: Routledge & Kegan Paul.

Veldhuis, Niek. 1991. *A Cow of Sîn*. Library of Oriental Texts 2. Groningen: Styx/Brill.

Veselova, Inna S. 2006. "Krasnye devushki i kumach: Tsvetovye atributy prazdnika." In *Morfologiia prazdnika*, 103–20. St. Petersburg: Izd-vo S.-Peterburgskogo universiteta.

Veselova I. S., and Iu. Iu. Marinicheva. 2010. "'Zhaba tebe v rot' ili 'figa v karmane.'" In *Prostranstvo koldovstva*, edited by O. B. Khristoforova, 156–71. Moscow: Rossisskii gos. gumanitarnyi universitet.

Veselovskii, A. N. 1873. "Sravnitel'naia mifologiia i ee metod." *Vestnik Evropy* 10:637–80.

Vidan, Aida. 2003. *Embroidered with Gold, Strung with Pearls: The Traditional Ballads of Bosnian Women*. Cambridge, MA: Milman Parry Collection of Oral Literature.

Vinogradova, Liudmila. 1986. "Mifologicheskii aspekt polesskoi 'rusal'noi' traditsii." In *Slavianskii i balkanskii fol'klor: Dukhovnaia kul'tura Poles'ia na obshcheslavianskom fone*, edited by N. I. Tolstoi, 88–133. Moscow: Nauka.

Viola, Lynne. 1987. *The Best Sons of the Fatherland: Workers in the Vanguard of Soviet Collectivization*. New York: Oxford University Press.

———. 1996. *Peasant Rebels under Stalin: Collectivization and the Culture of Peasant Resistance*. New York: Oxford University Press.

———, ed. 2005. *The War Against the Peasantry, 1927–1930*. Annals of Communism: The Tragedy of the Soviet Countryside, 1927–1939. New Haven, CT: Yale University Press.

Vishnevsky, A. G. 1998. *Population of Russia in 1998*. Annual Demographic Report. Moscow: Center of Demography and Human Ecology.

Volkov, A. D. 1999. *Zavetnye chastushki iz sobraniia A. D. Volkova*. Vol. 2, *Politicheskie chastushki*. Edited by A. V. Kulagina. Moscow: Ladomir.

Volkov, V. V. 1998. "Sledovanie pravilu kak sotsiologicheskaia problema." *Sotsiologicheskii zhurnal* 3 (4): 156–70.

Vowles, Judith. 2002. "The Inexperienced Muse: Russian Women and Poetry in the First Half of the Nineteenth Century." In *A History of Women's Writing in Russia*, edited by Adele Marie Barker and Jehanne M. Gheith, 62–84. Cambridge: Cambridge University Press.

Walker, Nancy A. 1988. *A Very Serious Thing: Women's Humor and American Culture*. Minneapolis: University of Minnesota Press.

Warner, Elizabeth A. 2002a. "Russian Peasant Beliefs and Practices concerning Death and the Supernatural Collected in Novosokol'niki Region, Pskov Province, Russia, 1995. Part I: The Restless Dead, Wizards and Spirit Beings." *Folklore* 111 (1): 67–90.

―――. 2002b. "Russian Peasant Beliefs and Practices concerning Death and the Supernatural Collected in Novosokol'niki Region, Pskov Province, Russia, 1995. Part II: Death in Natural Circumstances." *Folklore* 111 (2): 255–81.

Waters, Elizabeth. 1991. "The Female Form in Soviet Political Iconography, 1917–32." In *Russia's Women: Accommodation, Resistance, Transformation*, edited by Barbara Evans Clements, Barbara Alpern Engel, and Christine D. Worobec, 225–42. Berkeley: University of California Press.

Weber, Max. 1978. *Economy and Society: An Outline of Interpretive Sociology*. Vol. 2, edited by Guenther Roth and Claus Wittich. Berkeley: University of California Press.

Williams, Linda. 1998. "Melodrama Revisited." In *Refiguring American Film Genres: History and Theory*, edited by Nick Browne, 42–88. Berkeley: University of California Press.

Wittgenstein, Ludwig. (1953) 2009. *Philosophical Investigations*. Edited by Gertrude E. M. Anscombe, Peter M. S. Hacker, and Joachim Schulte. Chichester: Wiley-Blackwell.

Worobec, Christine. 1991. *Peasant Russia: Family and Community in the Post-Emanciption Period*. Princeton, NJ: Princeton University Press.

―――. 1995. "Witchcraft Beliefs and Practices in Prerevolutionary Russian and Ukrainian Villages." *Russian Review* 54 (April): 165–87.

―――. 2002. "Masculinity in Late Imperial Russian Peasant Society." In *Russian Masculinities in History and Culture*, edited by Barbara Evans Clements, Rebecca Friedman, and Dan Healy, 76–93. Houndmills: Palgrave.

Zaigraev, Grigory. 2004. "The Russian Model of Noncommercial Alcohol Consumption." In *Moonshine Markets: Issues in Unrecorded Alcohol Beverage Production*, edited by Alan Haworth and Ronald Simpson, 29–38. New York: Brunner/Routledge.

Zelenin, D. K. (1914) 1997. *Velikorusskie skazki Permskoi gubernii*. Moscow: Dmitrii Bulanin.

―――. 1916. *Ocherki Russkoi mifologii*. Petrograd: A. V. Orlov.

―――. 1991. *Vostochnoslavianskaia etnografiia*. Translated from the German by K. D. Tsivina. Moscow: Nauka.

―――. 1994. *Izbrannye trudy: Stat'i po dukhovnoi kul'ture, 1901–1913*. Moscow: Indrik.

―――. 1999. "Sovremennaia russkaia chastushka." In *Zavetnye chastushki*, vol. 2, *Politicheskie chastushki*, edited by A. D. Volkov and A. V. Kulagina, 459–83. Moscow: Ladomir.

Zemtsovskii, I. I. 1964. *Russkaia narodnaia pesnia: Nauchno-populiarnyi ocherk*. Moscow: Muzyka.

―――. 1965. "Sel'skaia khorovaia samodeiatel'nost' i fol'klor." In *Problemy muzykal'noi samodeiatel'nosti*, 70–89. Moscow: Muzyka.

Zigon, Jarrett. 2008. "Aleksandra Vladimirovna: Moral Narratives of a Russian Orthodox Woman." In *Religion, Morality, and Community in Post-Soviet Societies*, edited by Mark D. Steinberg and Catherine Wanner, 85–114. Bloomington: Indiana University Press.

Zinov'ev, V. P. 1987. "Bylichka kak zhanr fol'klora i ee sovremennye sud'by." In *Mifologicheskie rasskazy Russkogo naseleniia vostochnoi Sibiri*, 381–400. Novosibirsk: Nauka.

Zorin, N. V. 2004. *Russkii svadebnyi ritual*. Moscow: Nauka.

Zubova, N. P. 1984. "Pesni literaturnogo tipa v ustnoi narodnoi traditsii (na materiale zapisei ekspeditsii 1970-kh–nachala 1980-kh godov." Diss., Moscow State University.

Index